Monetary Theory

The International Library of Critical Writings in Economics

Series Editor: Mark Blaug

Professor Emeritus, University of London
Consultant Professor, University of Buckingham
Visiting Professor, University of Exeter

Monetary Theory

Edited by

Thomas Mayer

Professor of Economics
University of California, Davis

An Elgar Reference Collection

Published by
Edward Elgar Publishing Limited
Gower House
Croft Road
Aldershot
Hants GU11 3HR
England

Edward Elgar Publishing Company
Old Post Road
Brookfield
Vermont 05036
USA

H G
221
.M 8154
1990
15 3653
Sept. 1991

British Library Cataloguing in Publication Data
is available.

ISBN 1 85278 180 7

Printed in Great Britain by Galliard (Printers) Ltd, Great Yarmouth

Contents

Acknowledgements

The editor and publishers wish to thank the following who have kindly given permission for the use of copyright material.

American Economic Association for articles: H. Minsky (1964), 'Longer Waves in Financial Relations: Financial Factors in the More Severe Depressions', *American Economic Review*, **54,** May, 324–35; M. Levi and J. Makin (1978), 'Anticipated Inflation and Interest Rates: Further Interpretation of Findings on the Fisher Equation', *American Economic Review*, **68** (5), 801–12; R. King and C. Plosser (1984), 'Money, Credit and Prices in a Real Business Cycle', *American Economic Review*, **74** (3), 363–80; B. Friedman (1988), 'Lessons on Monetary Policy from the 1980s', *Journal of Economic Perspectives*, **2** (3), summer, 57–64 (excerpt).

Basil Blackwell Ltd for article: J. Hicks (1935), 'A Suggestion for Simplifying the Theory of Money', *Economica*, NS **2,** February, 1–19.

Committee for Economic Development, New York for excerpt: J. Tobin 'An Essay on the Principles of Debt Management', Commission on Money and Credit, *Fiscal and Debt Management Policies*, 149–67 (excerpt).

Elsevier Science Publishers B.V. for articles: E. Fama (1980), 'Banking in the Theory of Finance', *Journal of Monetary Economics*, **6,** January, 39–57; K. Brunner, A. Cukierman and A. Meltzer (1983), 'Money and Economic Activity, Inventories and Business Cycles', *Journal of Monetary Economics*, **11,** May, 281–319; G. Akerlof and R. Milbourne (1978), 'New Calculations of Income and Interest Elasticities in Tobin's Model of the Transactions Demand for Money', *Review of Economics and Statistics*, **60** (4), November, 541–6; and for excerpt: R. Dornbusch 'Comments on Brunner and Meltzer' from *Monetarism*, J. Stein, 104–25.

John Wiley and Sons, Inc. for articles: W. Baumol (1952), 'The Transactions Demand for Cash: An Inventory Theoretic Approach', *Quarterly Journal of Economics*, November, 545–56; M. Miller and D. Orr (1966), 'A Model of the Demand for Money by Firms', *Quarterly Journal of Economics*, August, 413–35.

Ohio State University Press for articles: D. Patinkin (1969), 'The Chicago Tradition, The Quantity Theory and Friedman', *Journal of Money, Credit and Banking*, **1,** February, 46–71; J. Tobin (1969), 'A General Equilibrium Approach to Monetary Theory', *Journal of Money, Credit and Banking*, **1,** February, 15–29; J. Peek and

J. Wilcox (1987), 'Monetary Policy Regimes and the Reduced Form for Interest Rates', *Journal of Money, Credit and Banking*, **19** (3), August, 273–91.

Philip Allan Publishers Ltd for excerpt: D. Laidler (1982), 'On the Demand for Money and the Real Balance Effect' from *Monetarist Perspectives*, D. Laidler, 37–65.

Sprenkle, C. for his article: 'The Uselessness of the Transaction Demand Models' from *Journal of Finance*, **24** (5), December 1969, 835–47.

University of Chicago Press for article: M. Friedman (1988), 'Money and the Stock Market', *Journal of Political Economy*, **96** (2), 221–45: and for excerpt; M. Friedman (1956), 'The Quantity Theory of Money: A Restatement' from *Studies in the Quantity Theory of Money*, M. Friedman (ed.), 3–21.

Every effort has been made to trace all the copyright holders but if any have been inadvertently overlooked the publishers will be pleased to make the necessary arrangement at the first opportunity.

In addition the publishers wish to thank the Library of the London School of Economics and Political Science for their assistance in obtaining these articles.

Introduction

When I decided to select about 20 papers for a 'Readings' book on monetary theory the task looked easy. But soon two problems appeared. First there are many more papers than could be included. Second, there is very little agreement about which articles are 'must' reading. Edward Tower (1985) has compiled readings lists from courses in monetary and macroeconomics in a number of American universities. These lists show remarkably little agreement. Surprisingly few articles are listed on more than one reading list, and only a trivial number are required reading in more than two of the courses. This probably results less from disputes about how the economy functions than from disagreements about the delineation of monetary theory, and about what questions are central to this subject. The latter disagreement, in turn, reflects a disagreement about the desirable degree of abstraction.

There are two feasible responses. One is to compromise and select one or two articles that correspond to each of the conflicting views about what the central issues are. The second is to make one's own choices, and disregard other economists' tastes. While the first alternative demonstrated due modesty it provides a too superficial tour of a complex landscape. Moreover, it ignores a principle dear to economists, the division of labour. The market is large enough to allow several types of Readings books to coexist. A recent book edited by Ross Starr (1988) caters to those who are interested in the highly abstract issue of how money fits into a general equilibrium model. An earlier book by Robert Clower (1969) deals with considerably less abstract topics. This book is still less abstract. It takes as its central core the question of how changes in the supply or demand for money and for other financial assets affect prices, output and interest rates. It thus deals with the applied theory of money. But it excludes one important aspect of applied monetary theory, the money supply theory because that topic is closely related to monetary policy.

Much of the work on applied monetary theory consists of the empirical testing of theories. While this is not ignored here it is only sparsely represented. As time passes papers presenting empirical details become outdated by other papers with additional data. Theoretical papers have a longer half-life.

The book concentrates on articles that deal with money as conventionally defined, that is a medium of exchange, standard of value and liquid store of wealth. It therefore excludes the extensive 'overlapping generations' literature in which money is treated as the only form of wealth, thus losing the distinctive characteristics of money.

Even with these limitations there remains a vast number of excellent papers to choose from. One criterion is to select one article written by each of the recognized leaders in the field. Another is to choose papers that launched many other papers. A third is to collect papers that are the pedagogical most valuable because they demonstrate a fruitful line of research, or present a complex issue in a simple way. I have compromised among all these criteria. Another compromise, required by the space constraint, is the omission of very long items. This explains the omission of Don Patinkin on the real balance effect, and Friedman and Schwartz on 'Money and Business Cycles' (1963).

The Microeconomics of Money Demand

The initial set of papers explains the demand for money by individual households and firms. The first one, widely considered a classic, is William Baumol's application of inventory theory to the transactions demand for money. Money is held as an inventory of liquid purchasing power, and hence the demand for transactions balances should depend on the same factors as the demand for inventories of any good, that is on the costs of reordering compared with the carrying cost of the inventory. This leads Baumol to present a remarkably simple and elegant solution for the optimal transactions balance. However, its simplicity has a price. Baumol's model suffers from an 'integer problem'; it may tell you to replenish your money holdings, say 3.7 times during the year, an obvious impossibility. In a subsequent paper Tobin (1956) takes the integer constrain into account, to reach essentially similar results in a substantially more complicated model.

Baumol's paper is often misinterpreted. He first presents a simple case in which transactions cost (i.e. reorder costs) are fixed, and in which agents start out with holdings of bonds instead of money, an unrealistic condition since wages are paid in money. For this case he derives the remarkable solution that both the income and interest elasticities of the demand for money are (in absolute values) 0.5. What has attracted much less attention is Baumol's second, more realistic model in which transactions costs depend in part on the amount transacted, and in which agents are paid in money rather than in bonds. In this case the interest and income elasticities do not obey the square root rule.

The second paper, by Merton Miller and Daniel Orr, presents a more complex model of cash management. They deal with a firm that has continuous stochastic inflows and outflows of money. The optimal money holdings of such a firm depend, not on the level of income, but on the variance of income. The optimal cash balance is then a much more complex expression than in the Baumol model. In deriving it Miller and Orr have to make what seem to be quite strong assumptions. But in a subsequent paper (Miller and Orr 1968) they show that their overall results hold also under much weaker assumptions. Their model is explicitly one of cash management by firms. However it can also be applied to households; probably many, if not most, households manage their cash by allowing it to drift between upper and lower limits as Miller and Orr's firms do.

Both the Baumol model and the Miller–Orr models are normative since they analyse what money balances agents *should* hold. Do households and firms actually hold such optimal balances? For households one cannot be certain because we cannot measure the 'time and bother' components of the brokerage costs and the implicit yield on deposits. But for firms Case Sprenkel has plugged reasonable estimates of all the parameters into transactions-demand models. As he shows in the third paper American firms hold vastly more money than these models predict. The data include precautionary and speculative balances as well as transactions balances. But since firms have ready access to near-money assets it is hard to imagine that their precautionary and speculative balances amount to the large multiple of transactions balances, that would be needed to reconcile Sprenkel's data with the transactions-demand models. Perhaps the existence of compensating balances provides the answer.[1] This does not mean that the transactions models are useless; they may explain well those money balances that are held in excess of compensatory balances. One of the services that American banks offer to attract business customers is to provide them with models to calculate optimal transactions balances. They would not do so if these models were not useful.

In the final paper in this section George Akerlof and Ross Milbourne deal with a motive for money holdings that has been largely ignored since the Keynesian revolution, though it was prominent before then. In their model households save some of their income in the form of money until they have accumulated sufficient funds to make investment worthwhile. Their model combines a Baumol–Tobin transactions story (specifically they use Tobin's model) with an asset demand for money that arises from saving. Using plausible figures for the various coefficients they find that, if the asset demand is ignored, the interest elasticity of demand for money is under usual conditions very low, but that the inclusion of the asset demand for money raises the interest elasticity.

The Portfolio Approach

In a general way nearly all economists use a portfolio approach to the demand for money in the sense of explaining the demand for money by such variables as wealth and relative rates of return. But some economists emphasize portfolio adjustments more than others. The classic work of applying portfolio theory to the demand for money is that of Sir John Hicks in what is perhaps the most influential paper ever in monetary economics. When it appeared in 1935, most economists were thinking of the demand for money in a mechanistic way divorced from maximizing behaviour. Hicks opens the door to integrating monetary analysis and general economic theory. The modern reader must keep in mind conditions at the time it was written, the Great Depression, with Britain having suffered a decade of massive unemployment. It is therefore not surprising that it stressed the instability of capitalism. It starts with a discussion of Keynes's *Treatise on Money*, published five years earlier, that had shaken up monetary economics.[2] It foreshadows subsequent developments in macro-economics in an amazing way, see for example the importance attributed to understanding how expectations are formed.

James Tobin has carried the portfolio approach further than most economists by focusing on the substitutability between money and a wider-than-usual variety of assets. In his 'A General Equilibrium Approach to Monetary Theory' Tobin eschews both the *General Theory's* simplification of lumping capital and bonds into a single asset juxtaposed to money, and the quantity theory's simplification of juxtaposing money to all other assets including consumer goods.[3] Indeed, in Tobin's model money is just one type of government debt, distinguished from other debt by not paying interest.[4] To Tobin money is important, not because it is a medium of exchange, but because its yield is fixed. With the yield on money being fixed, when the quantity of money changes, it is the yield on other assets that must adjust.

The most important of these yields is the yield that portfolio managers require to purchase claims to capital, and hence to set the investment process into motion if the price of capital exceeds its reproduction cost. Various theories focus on different aspects of homo economicus. Traditional Keynesian theory tells a story in which the main actor is a firm considering physical investment by comparing the marginal efficiency of investment with the marginal cost of funds. In the quantity theory the focus is on agents who decide on their real money balances, and on central banks that determine the nominal money supply. Tobin focuses on the portfolio holder who decides what claims and physical assets to hold.

The third paper in this section is an excerpt from a much longer discussion of debt management, a much debated issue at the time this paper was written. Tobin's main task in this commissioned paper was to recommend whether the federal government should try to stabilize aggregate demand by shifting counter-cyclically between issuing long and short debt.[5] To do so Tobin had to discuss the substitutability of debt, money and capital. This is one of the most recalcitrant issues in monetary theory. Some models, like Tobin's, assume that debt is a closer substitute for money than for capital, while others assume the opposite. Often, the results of a model depend critically on this assumption. Despite this many economists make either one or other assumption about the money – debt – capital substitutability, without offering much, if any, justification (but see Frankel, 1985). Tobin, however, sets out the case for his choice – a case one may or may not agree with, but should consider carefully.

Although Tobin is one of the leading Keynesian economists, the portfolio approach is not the property of Keynesians. Two stellar monetarists, Karl Brunner and Allan Meltzer, have also developed a portfolio model. They reject the standard IS-LM paradigm because it ignores the effects of changes in assets, and does not incorporate price theory. In its place they offer a model in which, as in Tobin's model, bonds are a closer substitute for money than for capital. In their model the budget constraint plays an important role. Both fiscal and monetary policy matter. The potentially powerful role that their model allows for fiscal policy has led some economists to question whether their model is not really Keynesian rather than monetarist. They reply that their theoretical model provides roles for both fiscal and monetary policies, and lets the data decide which is more important.[6] Their exposition of their model is hard to follow. Fortunately, in the fourth paper in this section Rudiger Dornbusch has provided a simple diagrammatic exposition.

Brunner and Meltzer's criticisms of the IS-LM model do not induce them to reject it entirely. In the last paper of this section they, along with Alex Cukierman, use an IS-LM model that is augmented by differentiating shocks into permanent and transitory components, with agents using information on past shocks to estimate the relative size of permanent and transitory components. As a result, transitory shocks can have effects that linger for a longer time.[7]

The Demand for Money, the Quantity Theory and Nominal Income

The papers in this section deal with the quantity theory and the demand function for money. The first one, surely one of the most influential papers in macroeconomics, is Milton Friedman's classic restatement of the quantity theory. It is the introductory essay in a book presenting empirical applications and tests of the quantity theory by his students. At the time it appeared the quantity theory was widely considered to be an old, exploded fallacy, generally known only by the crude and rigid version presented in textbooks. Friedman is therefore concerned first with showing that the quantity theory is a subtle and flexible theory that opens the door to numerous worthwhile research projects, something of great importance in getting economists to change their minds and take a theory seriously. Substantively Friedman makes three main contributions. First, he presents the quantity theory as a theory that explains nominal income, and not just the price level. Second, he applies the quantity theory to the short run, as well as the long run. Third, he does not assume that velocity is a constant. Instead, by using a portfolio approach to money, he treats the demand for money like the demand for any capital good, so that it depends on wealth and on the yields of money and of other assets.

In the following paper Don Patinkin argues that Friedman's theory differs sharply from the quantity theory that was taught at Chicago in the 1930s, and is more accurately described as a development of Keynesian monetary theory. Specifically, Patinkin argues, Chicago economists did not have a theory to explain velocity and, in contrast to Friedman's stock approach used a flow approach. Friedman (1972) responded to Patinkin by reaffirming his belief that he was presenting what was taught at Chicago, though Friedman (1964) does agree that his reformulation of the quantity theory was much influenced by Keynes's liquidity preference theory. Since the Chicago tradition in monetary economics is largely an oral tradition, and since both Friedman and Patinkin were students at Chicago around the same time, it is hard for outsiders to say who is right. But the answer probably depends upon whether one classifies a theory by its empirical assumptions and conclusions or by its mechanism, such as its use of stock or flow analysis. Friedman's theory is clearly a Chicago quantity theory with respect to his empirical assumptions and conclusions.

Friedman formulated the quantity theory as a theory that explains the demand for money. Hence it is not surprising that, following the publication of his essay, much of the work of monetary economists consisted of fitting money demand functions. The third paper presents Friedman's most recent work on this topic. It seems intuitively obvious that a change in stock prices could affect the demand for money, but exactly how it does so is far from obvious. Friedman provides a thorough discussion of the complex channels by which stock prices affect the demand for money, and tests his hypothesis. To do so he uses long-run money demand functions that he and Anna

Schwartz had previously employed to explain money demand in the US and Britain for a period of almost a hundred years (Friedman and Schwartz 1982).

One problem with money demand functions is that the available data are observations of money supply rather than of money demand. This has usually been brushed aside with the response that the money market clears rapidly, so that the observed supply of money is an accurate proxy for the demand for money. But it turned out that for the short-run money demand function the inclusion of last period's money balances improves the fit substantially. Hence these balances are usually included with the justification that this models the adjustment lags one could reasonably expect in a demand function. David Laidler's paper challenges both the identification of money supply with money demand and the justification for lagged balances. He points out that if we take the supply of nominal money as exogenous, then for the money market to clear rapidly it is the arguments in the money demand function that must adjust rapidly for the observed money supply to represent points on the demand curve. And further, if it is the arguments in the money demand function that adjust to an exogenous supply of nominal money, then we cannot explain the use of lagged money balances by referring to a plausible slow adjustment of money holders. Laidler raises a disturbing question: what, if anything, do the short-run money demand functions signify?[8]

The fundamental questions raised by Laidler are not the only problems that beset money demand functions and hence the quantity theory. While a weak version of the quantity theory merely asserts that *ceteris paribus* changes in the money supply generate proportional changes in nominal income, a stronger version asserts that velocity is predictable, so that, never mind *ceteris paribus*, one can explain and predict changes in nominal income if one knows the changes in the nominal money supply.[9] During much of the postwar period this stronger version seemed valid, at least in the US; money demand functions gave good fits. But in the early 1970s money demand functions started to substantially overpredict money holdings, probably as a result of financial innovations (see Judd and Scadding 1982). A standard response was to abandon money demand functions and to rely instead on the remarkably stable trend of velocity. But reliance on unexplained regularities is often dangerous, and so it was in this case. Around early 1982 the stable trend of M-1 velocity came to an abrupt end. Now neither most M-1 demand functions nor an M-1 velocity trend predict well.[10] It is too early to know exactly what happened, but the culprit is probably the payment of explicit interest on the checkable deposits of households. Benjamin Friedman, in the final paper in this section, documents the devastating effect that the changing behaviour of velocity has for the quantity theory's predictions of nominal income.

Money and Interest Rates

A basic question in monetary economics is whether and how changes in the monetary growth rate affect nominal and real interest rates. This is important, not only because of its significance for monetary policy, but also for its relevance to the theory of income determination. Suppose that a rise in the growth rate of money lowers interest rates. Velocity will then be lower, and income will rise by less than the quantity theory predicts. The proportionality between changes in money and in nominal income therefore requires either that changes in the money supply do not affect interest rates, or else that velocity, while in principle a function of the interest rate, is highly interest-inelastic.

The modern discussion of the effect of monetary growth on the interest rate was initiated by Milton Friedman (1968) who discussed three effects. First, there is a temporary 'liquidity effect'. This causes the interest rate to fall as the quantity of money increases. But the increase in the money supply generates a temporary rise in output, and permanently higher prices. As a result, real balances fall back to their previous level, so that the interest rate, and hence velocity, also return to their previous levels. And once the public becomes aware that the central bank is following more inflationary policies the nominal interest rate rises above its previous level due the 'Fisher effect'.

Subsequent discussions showed that changes in the monetary growth rate can affect real interest rates in several ways. Thus a higher monetary growth rate, and hence a higher inflation rate, lowers the real value of wealth, thus stimulating saving which, in turn, lowers interest rates, the 'Mundell effect'. It also temporarily raises saving as income rises, and the economy moves along the short-run Phillips curve. In addition, recipients of interest income pay higher taxes as inflation raises nominal interest rates, and they pass this tax burden on in the form of higher before-tax interest rates, the 'Darby effect'. Levi and Makin, in the first paper of this section, discuss these effects in the context of a small general equilibrium model, a model that focuses on the movement along the Phillips curve.

Economic theory tells us that nominal changes should have first order effects only on nominal variables, so that, if the Mundell effect is minor, the equilibrium real after-tax interest rate should not be a function of the growth rate of money. Many economists have tried to verify this proposition. In most of these papers the expected result did not appear. However, Joe Peek and James Wilcox, in the final paper of this section, confirm the expectation that the real after-tax rate is unaffected by the growth of money. Their paper contains an important innovation. Previous investigations treated the monetary growth rate as though it were exogenous, thus ignoring the well-established fact that the Federal Reserve smoothes interest rates by adjusting the monetary growth rate. Peek and Wilcox, however, include a variable that measures the extent to which the Federal Reserve has adjusted the monetary growth rate in response to interest-rate changes. It is a rare example of a paper that takes changes in policy regimes into account.

Real Theories

The data show unequivocally that fluctuations in the monetary growth rate and in the growth rate of income are correlated. What is more equivocal is whether causation runs primarily from money to income or from income to money.[11] Real theories of the business cycle have been developed in which fluctuations in income and employment are due to fluctuations in the productive potential of the economy and not to changes in the ratio of actual to potential output. But if fluctuations are due to real factors what explains the correlation between them and the growth rate of money?

Robert King and Charles Plosser present a neoclassical model of output, money demand and money supply. The demand for real money is explained by the maximizing behaviour of firms and households, that is, by variables, such as the value of time, while the output of inside money is explained by the profit-maximizing behaviour of the banking industry. In this model it is real shocks, not shocks to aggregate demand that cause income to fluctuate, but these income fluctuations are accompanied by fluctuations of inside money, and depending on central bank policy, perhaps of outside money. They find that the broad implications of their model are consistent with the data.

In the next paper Eugene Fama discusses the nature of banks, and since banks create the greater part of our money supply, also the nature of money. He deals with both an unregulated banking system in a world without a medium of exchange, as well as with regulated banks coexisting with a medium of exchange. In doing so he exploits both Tobin's insight of treating banks like other profit-maximizing firms, and the implications of the Modigliani–Miller theorem for banks. He shows that, in principle, the central bank need not control the quantity of 'money' to control the price level. Since deposits and currency are imperfect substitutes, control over *either* currency or bank deposits suffices to make the price level determinate. In principle, fiat money is not needed for economic efficiency – banks could provide a medium of exchange without it.[12]

The final paper represents a paradigm that also stresses real factors, but is antithetical to neoclassical theory, the Post-Keynesian paradigm. The quantity theory explains cyclical turning-points by exogenous shocks to the supply of money, such as bank failures. By contrast, Hyman Minsky makes bank failures and financial crises endogenous in a model that combines insights from both Keynes and Irving Fisher. The issue raised by Minsky is not a, more or less, arbitrary decision whether to make a variable endogenous by expanding the model, but is a fundamental issue, the stability of a capitalist system. According to Minsky, unless there are stringent government controls, bank failures are part of our financial system, and hence not something that should be treated as exogenous.

Thomas Mayer
March 1990

Notes

1. American banks often require borrowers to keep a proportion of the loan, called 'compensating balances' as demand deposits in the bank.
2. The heart of the *Treatise* are Keynes's 'fundamental equations' for the price level. Hicks gives the one for consumer prices. The symbols he uses have the following meaning: P is the price level of consumer goods, E the earnings of the factors of production, O total output, I' investment, S saving, and R the output of consumer goods.
3. In his Nobel Prize lecture Tobin presented a dynamic version of this model (see Tobin 1981).
4. When Tobin formulated this model US banks could not pay interest on checkable deposits. But since the interest rate that banks now pay on these deposits is inflexible, Tobin's analysis is still applicable.
5. Tobin's paper was commissioned by a private study group, the Commission on Money and Credit, set up to investigate problems of the US financial and monetary system. At that time, late 1950s, many economists believed that debt management, by shifting the composition of the debt counter-cyclically between long- and short-term securities could be used as a stabilization tool.
6. For an excellent discussion of how the Brunner–Meltzer model fits into monetarism, and for the nature of monetarism in general, see Brunner and Meltzer (1976).
7. More recently Meltzer (1986) has used Kalman filters to distinguish between various types of shocks, with important results for such issues as the stability of the private sector, the appropriate exchange rate system, and the causal role of money.
8. For a more empirically documented questioning of short-run money demand functions see Gordon (1984).
9. This strong version of the quantity theory requires also that either the demand for money is highly inelastic with respect to interest rates, or else that the interest rate can be predicted accurately. In addition, the income elasticity of the demand for money must be close to unity, or else one must be able to predict the breakdown of changes in nominal income between changes in real income or in prices.
10. Demand functions for M-2 have performed much better. But since they include a hard-to-predict variable, the interest rate on time deposits, their use in forecasting and in making monetary policy is limited.
11. A number of papers have used Granger tests to evaluate the monetarist hypothesis that money is the causal variable. These tests run into the problem that monetarists do not deny that, due to central bank policy, income does cause money, as well as money causing income. What they claim is not mono-causality, but that prior to cyclical downturns some exogenous shocks, e.g. a restrictive monetary policy, cause a fall of the monetary growth rate.
12. For an insightful discussion of Fama's paper see Kevin Hoover (1988).

References

Brunner, Karl and Allan Meltzer (1976), 'Reply – Monetarism: the Principle Issues, Areas of Agreement and Work Remaining', in Jerome Stein (ed.), *Monetarism*, Amsterdam, North-Holland, 1976, 150–82.

Clower, Robert (1969), *Monetary Theory*, London, Penguin Books.

Frankel, Jeffrey (1985), 'Portfolio Crowding-Out Empirically Estimated', *Quarterly Journal of Economics*, **100,** Supplement, 1041–63.

Friedman, Milton (1964), 'Trends in Monetary Theory and Policy', *National Banking Review*, **2** (1), 1–11.

Friedman, Milton (1968), 'The Role of Monetary Policy', *American Economic Review*, **58,** March, 1–17.

Friedman, Milton (1972), 'Comments on the Critics', *Journal of Political Economy*, **80,** September/October, 906–50.

Friedman, Milton and Anna Schwartz (1963), 'Money and Business Cycles', *Review of Economics and Statistics*, **45,** February, Supplement, 32–64.

Friedman, Milton and Anna Schwartz (1982), *Monetary Trends in the United States and the United Kingdom*, Chicago, University of Chicago Press.

Gordon, Robert (1984), 'The Short-Run Demand for Money: A Reconsideration', *Journal of Money, Credit and Banking*, **16,** November, Pt 1, 403–34.

Hoover, Kevin (1988), *The New Classical Macroeconomics*, Oxford, Blackwell.

Judd, John and John Scadding (1982), 'The Search for a Stable Money Demand Function', *Journal of Economic Literature*, **20,** September, 993–1023.

Meltzer, Allan (1986), 'Size, Persistence and Interrelation of Nominal and Real Shocks: Some Evidence from Four Countries', *Journal of Monetary Economics*, **17,** January, 161–94.

Miller, Merton and Daniel Orr (1968), 'The Demand for Money by Firms: Extensions of Analytic Results', *Journal of Finance*, **23,** December, 735–60.

Starr, Ross (1988), *General Equilibrium Models of Monetary Economies*, San Diego, Calif., Academic Publishers.

Tobin, James (1956), 'The Interest Elasticity of the Transactions Demand for Cash', *Review of Economics and Statistics*, **38,** August, 241–7.

Tobin, James (1981), 'Money and Finance in the Macro-Economic Process', *Journal of Political Economy*.

Tower, Edward (1985), *Macro and Monetary Economics Reading Lists*, Durham, NC, Eno River Press.

Part I
The Microeconomics of Money

[1]

THE TRANSACTIONS DEMAND FOR CASH: AN INVENTORY THEORETIC APPROACH

By William J. Baumol

A stock of cash is its holder's inventory of the medium of exchange, and like an inventory of a commodity, cash is held because it can be given up at the appropriate moment, serving then as its possessor's part of the bargain in an exchange. We might consequently expect that inventory theory and monetary theory can learn from one another. This note attempts to apply one well-known result in inventory control analysis to the theory of money.[1]

I. A Simple Model

We are now interested in analyzing the transactions demand for cash dictated by rational behavior, which for our purposes means the holding of those cash balances that can do the job at minimum cost. To abstract from precautionary and speculative demands let us consider a state in which transactions are perfectly foreseen and occur *in a steady stream.*

Suppose that in the course of a given period an individual will pay out T dollars in a steady stream. He obtains cash either by borrowing it, or by withdrawing it from an investment, and in either case his interest cost (or interest opportunity cost) is i dollars per dollar per period. Suppose finally that he withdraws cash in lots of C dollars spaced evenly throughout the year, and that each time he makes such a withdrawal he must pay a fixed "broker's fee" of b

---

1. T. M. Whitin informs me that the result in question goes back to the middle of the 1920's when it seems to have been arrived at independently by some half dozen writers. See, e.g., George F. Mellen, "Practical Lot Quantity Formula," *Management and Administration,* Vol. 10, September 1925. Its significant implications for the economic theory of inventory, particularly for business cycle theory, seem to have gone unrecognized until recently when Dr. Whitin analyzed them in his forthcoming *Inventory Control and Economic Theory* (Princeton University Press) which, incidentally, first suggested the subject of this note to me. See also, Dr. Whitin's "Inventory Control in Theory and Practice" (elsewhere in this issue, *supra,* p. 502), and Kenneth J. Arrow, Theodore Harris, and Jacob Marschak, "Optimal Inventory Policy," *Econometrica,* Vol. 19, July 1951, especially pp. 252–255. In addition to Dr. Whitin, I am heavily indebted to Professors Chandler, Coale, Gurley, Lutz, Mr. Turvey, and Professor Viner, and to the members of the graduate seminar at Harvard University, where much of this paper was first presented.

dollars.[2] Here T, the value of transactions, is predetermined, and i and b are assumed to be constant.

In this situation any value of C less than or equal to T will enable him to meet his payments equally well provided he withdraws the money often enough. For example, if T is \$100, he can meet his payments by withdrawing \$50 every six months or \$25 quarterly, etc.[3] Thus he will make $\frac{T}{C}$ withdrawals over the course of the year, at a total cost in "brokers' fees" given by $\frac{bT}{C}$.

In this case, since each time he withdraws C dollars he spends it in a steady stream and draws out a similar amount the moment it is gone, his average cash holding will be $\frac{C}{2}$ dollars. His annual interest cost of holding cash will then be $\frac{iC}{2}$.

The total amount the individual in question must pay for the use of the cash needed to meet his transaction when he borrows C dollars at intervals evenly spaced throughout the year will then be the sum of interest cost and "brokers' fees" and so will be given by

$$(1) \qquad\qquad \frac{bT}{C} + \frac{iC}{2}.$$

2. The term "broker's fee" is not meant to be taken literally. It covers all non-interest costs of borrowing or making a cash withdrawal. These include opportunity losses which result from having to dispose of assets just at the moment the cash is needed, losses involved in the poor resale price which results from an asset becoming "secondhand" when purchased by a nonprofessional dealer, administrative costs, and psychic costs (the trouble involved in making a withdrawal) as well as payment to a middleman. So conceived it seems likely that the "broker's fee" will, in fact, vary considerably with the magnitude of the funds involved, contrary to assumption. However, *some* parts of this cost will not vary with the amount involved — e.g., postage cost, bookkeeping expense, and, possibly, the withdrawer's effort. It seems plausible that the "broker's fee" will be better approximated by a function like $b + kC$ (where b and k are constants), which indicates that there is a part of the "broker's fee" increasing in proportion with the amount withdrawn. As shown in a subsequent footnote, however, our formal result is completely unaffected by this amendment.

We must also extend the meaning of the interest rate to include the value of protection against loss by fire, theft, etc., which we obtain when someone borrows our cash. On the other hand, a premium for the risk of default on repayment must be deducted. This protection obtained by lending seems to be mentioned less frequently by theorists than the risk, yet how can we explain the existence of interest free demand deposits without the former?

3. In particular, if cash were perfectly divisible and no elapse of time were required from withdrawal through payment he could make his withdrawals in a steady stream. In this case he would never require any cash balances to meet his payments and C would be zero. However, as may be surmised, this would be prohibitive with any b greater than zero.

THE TRANSACTIONS DEMAND FOR CASH 547

Since the manner in which he meets his payments is indifferent to him, his purpose only being to pay for his transactions, rationality requires that he do so at minimum cost, i.e., that he choose the most economical value of C. Setting the derivative of (1) with respect to C equal to zero we obtain[4]

$$-\frac{bT}{C^2} + \frac{i}{2} = 0,$$

i.e.,

$$(2) \qquad C = \sqrt{\frac{2bT}{i}}.$$

Thus, in the simple situation here considered, the rational individual will, given the price level,[5] demand cash in proportion to the square root of the value of his transactions.

Before examining the implications of this crude model we may note that, as it stands, it applies to two sorts of cases: that of the individual (or firm) obtaining cash from his invested capital and that of the individual (or firm) spending out of borrowing in anticipation of future receipts. Since our problem depends on non-coincidence of cash receipts and disbursements, and we have assumed that cash disbursements occur in a steady stream, one other case seems possible, that where receipts precede expenditures. This differs from the first case just mentioned (living off one's capital) in that the individual now has the option of withholding some or all of his receipts from investment and simply keeping the cash until it is needed. Once this withheld cash is used up the third case merges into the first: the individual must obtain cash from his invested capital until his next cash receipt occurs.

We can deal with this third case as follows. First, note that any receipts exceeding anticipated disbursements will be invested, since, eventually, interest earnings must exceed ("brokerage") cost of investment. Hence we need only deal with that part of the cash influx which is to be used in making payments during the period

4. This result is unchanged if there is a part of the "broker's fee" which varies in proportion with the quantity of cash handled. For in this case the "broker's fee" for each loan is given by $b + kC$. Total cost in "broker's fees" will then be

$$\frac{T}{C}(b + kC) = \frac{T}{C}b + kT.$$

Thus (1) will have the constant term, kT, added to it, which drops out in differentiation.

5. A doubling of *all* prices (including the "broker's fee") is like a change in the monetary unit, and may be expected to double the demand for cash balances.

between receipts. Let this amount, as before, be T dollars. Of this let I dollars be invested, and the remainder, R dollars, be withheld, where either of these sums may be zero. Again let i be the interest rate, and let the "broker's fee" for withdrawing cash be given by the linear expression $b_w + k_w C$, where C is the amount withdrawn. Finally, let there be a "broker's fee" for investing (depositing) cash given by $b_d + k_d I$ where the b's and the k's are constants.

Since the disbursements are continuous, the $R = T - I$ dollars withheld from investment will serve to meet payments for a fraction of the period between consecutive receipts given by $\dfrac{T - I}{T}$. Moreover, since the average cash holding for that time will be $\dfrac{T - I}{2}$, the interest cost of withholding that money will be $\dfrac{T - I}{T} i \dfrac{T - I}{2}$. Thus the total cost of withholding the R dollars and investing the I dollars will be

$$\frac{T - I}{2} i \frac{T - I}{T} + b_d + k_d I.$$

Analogously, the total cost of obtaining cash for the remainder of the period will be

$$\frac{C}{2} i \frac{I}{T} + (b_w + k_w C) \frac{I}{C}.$$

Thus the total cost of cash operations for the period will be given by the sum of the last two expressions, which when differentiated partially with respect to C and set equal to zero once again yields our square root formula, (2), with $b = b_w$.

Thus, in this case, the optimum cash balance after the initial cash holding is used up will again vary with the square root of the volume of transactions, as is to be expected by analogy with the "living off one's capital" case.

There remains the task of investigating $R/2$, the (optimum) average cash balance before drawing on invested receipts begins. We again differentiate our total cost of holding cash, this time partially with respect to I, and set it equal to zero, obtaining

$$-\frac{T - I}{T} i + k_d + \frac{Ci}{2T} + \frac{b_w}{C} + k_w = 0,$$

i.e.,

$$R = T - I = \frac{C}{2} + \frac{b_w T}{Ci} + \frac{T(k_d + k_w)}{i},$$

THE TRANSACTIONS DEMAND FOR CASH 549

or since from the preceding result, $C^2 = 2Tb_w/i$, so that the second term on the right hand side equals $C^2/2C$,

$$R = C + T\left(\frac{k_w + k_d}{i}\right).$$

The first term in this result is to be expected, since if *everything* were deposited at once, C dollars would have to be withdrawn at that same moment to meet current expenses. On this amount two sets of "broker's fees" would have to be paid and no interest would be earned — a most unprofitable operation.[6]

Since C varies as the square root of T and the other term varies in proportion with T, R will increase less than in proportion with T, though more nearly in proportion than does C. The general nature of our results is thus unaffected.[7]

Note finally that the entire analysis applies at once to the case of continuous receipts and discontinuous payments, taking the period to be that between two payments, where the relevant decision is the frequency of investment rather than the frequency of withdrawal. Similarly, it applies to continuous receipts and payments where the two are not equal.

II. Some Consequences of the Analysis

I shall not labor the obvious implications for financial budgeting by the firm. Rather I shall discuss several arguments which have been presented by monetary theorists, to which our result is relevant.

The first is the view put forth by several economists,[8] that in a

6. Here the assumption of constant "brokerage fees" with $k_d = k_w = 0$ gets us into trouble. The amount withheld from investment then is never greater than C dollars only because a strictly constant "broker's fee" with no provision for a discontinuity at zero implies the payment of the fee even if nothing is withdrawn or deposited. In this case it becomes an overhead and it pays to invest for any interest earning greater than zero.

For a firm, *part* of the "broker's fee" may, in fact, be an overhead in this way. For example, failure to make an anticipated deposit will sometimes involve little or no reduction in the bookkeeping costs incurred in keeping track of such operations.

7. If we replace the linear functions representing the "broker's fees" with more general functions $f_w(C)$ and $f_d(I)$ which are only required to be differentiable, the expression obtained for R is changed merely by replacement of k_w, and k_d by the corresponding derivatives $f_w'(C)$ and $f_d'(I)$.

8. See, e.g., Frank H. Knight, *Risk, Uncertainty and Profit* (Preface to the Re-issue), No. 16 in the series of Reprints of Scarce Tracts in Economic and Political Science (London: The London School of Economics and Political Science, 1933), p. xxii; F. Divisia, *Économique Rationelle* (Paris: G. Doin, 1927), chap. XIX and the Appendix; and Don Patinkin, "Relative Prices, Say's Law and the Demand for Money," *Econometrica*, Vol. 16, April 1948, pp. 140–145. See also, P. N. Rosenstein-Rodan, "The Coordination of the General Theories of Money and Price," *Economica*, N. S., Vol. III, August 1936, Part II.

stationary state there will be no demand for cash balances since it
will then be profitable to invest all earnings in assets with a positive
yield in such a way that the required amount will be realized at the
moment any payment is to be made. According to this view no one
will want any cash in such a stationary world, and the value of money
must fall to zero so that there can really be no such thing as a truly
static monetary economy. Clearly this argument neglects the
transactions costs involved in making and collecting such loans (the
"broker's fee").[9] Our model is clearly compatible with a static world
and (2) shows that it will generally pay to keep some cash. The
analysis of a stationary monetary economy in which there is a meaningful (finite) price level does make sense.

Another view which can be reëxamined in light of our analysis
is that the transactions demand for cash will vary approximately in
proportion with the money value of transactions.[1] This may perhaps
even be considered the tenor of quantity theory though there is no
necessary connection, as Fisher's position indicates. If such a
demand for cash balances is considered to result from rational behavior, then (2) suggests that the conclusion cannot have general
validity. On the contrary, the square root formula implies that

9. It also neglects the fact that the transfer of cash takes time so that in
reality we would have to hold cash at least for the short period between receiving
it and passing it on again.

It is conceivable, it is true, that with perfect foresight the difference between
money and securities might disappear since a perfectly safe loan could become
universally acceptable. There would, however, remain the distinction between
"real assets" and the "money-securities." Moreover, there would be a finite price
for, and non-zero yield on the former, the yield arising because they (as opposed
to certificates of their ownership) are not generally acceptable, and hence not
perfectly liquid, since there is trouble and expense involved in carrying them.

1. Marshall's rather vague statements may perhaps be interpreted to support this view. See, e.g., Book I, chap. IV in *Money, Credit and Commerce* (London, 1923). Keynes clearly accepts this position. See *The General Theory of
Employment, Interest and Money* (New York, 1936), p. 201. It is also accepted
by Pigou: "As real income becomes larger, there is, prima facie, reason for thinking
that, just as, up to a point, people like to invest a larger proportion of their real
income, so also they like to hold real balances in the form of money equivalent to
a larger proportion of it. On the other hand, as Professor Robertson has pointed
out to me, the richer people are, the cleverer they are likely to become in finding a
way to *economize* in real balances. On the whole then we may, I think, safely
disregard this consideration . . . for a close approximation. . . ." *Employment
and Equilibrium*, 1st ed. (London, 1941), pp. 59–60. Fisher, however, argues:
"It seems to be a fact that, at a given price level, the greater a man's expenditures
the more rapid his turnover; that is, the rich have a higher rate of turnover than
the poor. They spend money faster, not only absolutely but relatively to the
money they keep on hand. . . . We may therefore infer that, if a nation grows
richer per capita, the velocity of circulation of money will increase. This proposition, of course, has no reference to *nominal* increase of expenditure." *The Purchasing Power of Money* (New York, 1922), p. 167.

THE TRANSACTIONS DEMAND FOR CASH 551

demand for cash rises less than in proportion with the volume of transactions, so that there are, in effect, economies of large scale in the use of cash.

The magnitude of this difference should not be exaggerated, however. The phrase "varying as the square" may suggest larger effects than are actually involved. Equation (2) requires that the average transactions velocity of circulation vary exactly in proportion with the quantity of cash, so that, for example, a doubling of the stock of cash will *ceteris paribus*, just double velocity.[2]

A third consequence of the square root formula is closely connected with the second. The effect on real income of an injection of cash into the system may have been underestimated. For suppose that (2) is a valid expression for the general demand for cash, that there is widespread unemployment, and that for this or other reasons prices do not rise with an injection of cash. Suppose, moreover, that the rate of interest is unaffected, i.e., that none of the new cash is used to buy securities. Then so long as transactions do not rise so as to maintain the same proportion with the square of the quantity of money, people will want to get rid of cash. They will use it to demand more goods and services, thereby forcing the volume of transactions to rise still further. For let ΔC be the quantity of cash injected. If a proportionality (constant velocity) assumption involves transactions rising by $k \Delta C$, it is easily shown that (2) involves transactions rising by more than twice as much, the magnitude of the excess increasing with the ratio of the injection to the initial stock of cash. More precisely, the rise in transactions would then be given by[3]

$$2\,k\,\Delta\,C + \frac{k}{C}\Delta\,C^2.$$

Of course, the rate of interest would really tend to fall in such circumstances, and this would to some extent offset the effect of the influx of cash, as is readily seen when we rewrite (2) as

(3) $$T = C^2\,i/2b.$$

Moreover, prices will rise to some extent,[4] and, of course, (3) at best

2. Since velocity equals $\dfrac{T}{C} = \dfrac{i}{2b}\,C$ by (2).

3. This is obtained by setting $k = C\,i/2b$ in (3), below, and computing $\Delta\,T$ by substituting $C + \Delta\,C$ for C.

4. Even if (2) holds, the demand for cash may rise only in proportion with the money value of transactions when all prices rise exactly in proportion, the rate of interest and transactions remaining unchanged. For then a doubling of all prices and cash balances leaves the situation unchanged, and the received argument holds. The point is that b is then one of the prices which has risen.

is only an approximation. Nevertheless, it remains true that the effect of an injection of cash on, say, the level of employment, may often have been underestimated.[5] For whatever may be working to counteract it, the force making for increased employment is greater than if transactions tend, *ceteris paribus*, toward their original proportion to the quantity of cash.

Finally the square root formula lends support to the argument that wage cuts can help increase employment, since it follows that the Pigou effect and the related effects are stronger than they would be with a constant transactions velocity. Briefly the phenomenon which has come to be called the Pigou effect[6] may be summarized thus: General unemployment will result in reduction in the price level which must increase the purchasing power of the stock of cash provided the latter does not itself fall more than in proportion with prices.[7] This increased purchasing power will augment demand for commodities[8] or investment goods (either directly, or because it is used to buy securities and so forces down the rate of interest). In any case, this works for a reduction in unemployment.

Now the increase in the purchasing power of the stock of cash which results from fallen prices is equivalent to an injection of cash with constant prices. There is therefore exactly the same reason for suspecting the magnitude of the effect of the former on the volume of transactions has been underestimated, as in the case of the latter. Perhaps this can be of some little help in explaining why there has not been more chronic unemployment or runaway inflation in our economy.

III. THE SIMPLE MODEL AND REALITY

It is appropriate to comment on the validity of the jump from equation (2) to conclusions about the operation of the economy. At

5. But see the discussions of Potter and Law as summarized by Jacob Viner, *Studies in the Theory of International Trade* (New York, 1937), pp. 37–39.

6. See A. C. Pigou, "The Classical Stationary State," *Economic Journal*, Vol. LIII, December 1943.

7. Presumably the "broker's fee" will be one of the prices which falls, driven down by the existence of unemployed brokers. There is no analogous reason for the rate of interest to fall, though it will tend to respond thus to the increase in the "real stock of cash."

8. The term "Pigou effect" is usually confined to the effects on consumption demand while the effect on investment demand, and (in particular) on the rate of interest is ordinarily ascribed to Keynes. However, the entire argument appears to antedate Pigou's discussion (which, after all, was meant to be a reformulation of the classical position) and is closely related to what Mr. Becker and I have called the Say's Equation form of the Say's Law argument. See our article "The Classical Monetary Theory; the Outcome of the Discussion," *Economica*, November 1952.

best, (2) is only a suggestive oversimplification, if for no other reason, because of the rationality assumption employed in its derivation. In addition the model is static. It takes the distribution of the firm's disbursements over time to be fixed, though it is to a large extent in the hands of the entrepreneur how he will time his expenditures. It assumes that there is one constant relevant rate of interest and that the "broker's fee" is constant or varies linearly with the magnitude of the sum involved. It posits a steady stream of payments and the absence of cash receipts during the relevant period. It deals only with the cash demand of a single economic unit and neglects inter-actions of the various demands for cash in the economy.[9] It neglects the precautionary and speculative demands for cash.

These are serious lacunae, and without a thorough investigation we have no assurance that our results amount to much more than an analytical curiosum. Nevertheless I offer only a few comments in lieu of analysis, and hope that others will find the subject worth further examination.

1. It is no doubt true that a majority of the public will find it impractical and perhaps pointless to effect every possible economy in the use of cash. Indeed the possibility may never occur to most people. Nevertheless, we may employ the standard argument that the largest cash users may more plausibly be expected to learn when it is profitable to reduce cash balances relative to transactions. The demand for cash by the community as a whole may then be affected similarly and by a significant amount. Moreover, it is possible that even small cash holders will sometimes institute some cash economies instinctively or by a process of trial and error not explicitly planned or analyzed.

2. With variable b and i the validity of our two basic results — the non-zero rational transactions demand for cash, and the less than proportionate rise in the rational demand for cash with the real volume of transactions, clearly depends on the nature of the respon-siveness of the "brokerage fee" and the interest rate to the quantity of cash involved. The first conclusion will hold generally provided the "broker's fee" never falls below some preassigned level, e.g., it never falls below one mill per transaction, and provided the interest rate, its rate of change with C and the rate of change of the "broker's fee" all (similarly) have some upper bound, however large, at least when C is small.

9. I refer here particularly to considerations analogous to those emphasized by Duesenberry in his discussion of the relation between the consumption func-tions of the individual and the economy as a whole in his *Income, Saving and the Theory of Consumer Behavior* (Cambridge, Mass., 1950).

The second conclusion will not be violated persistently unless the "brokerage fee" tends to vary almost exactly in proportion with C (and it pays to hold zero cash balances) except for what may roughly be described as a limited range of values of C. Of course, it is always possible that this "exceptional range" will be the one relevant in practice. Variations in the interest rate will tend to strengthen our conclusion provided the interest rate never decreases with the quantity of cash borrowed or invested.[1]

It would perhaps not be surprising if these sufficient conditions for the more general validity of our results were usually satisfied in practice.

3. If payments are lumpy but foreseen, cash may perhaps be employed even more economically. For then it may well pay to obtain cash just before large payments fall due with little or no added cost in "brokers' fees" and considerable savings in interest payments. The extreme case would be that of a single payment during the year

---

1. For people to want to hold a positive amount of cash, the cost of cash holding must be decreasing after $C = 0$. Let b in (1) be a differentiable function of C for $C > 0$ (it will generally be discontinuous and equal to zero at $C = 0$). Then we require that the limit of the derivative of (1) be negative as C approaches zero from above, where this derivative is given by

$$\text{(i)} \quad -b\frac{T}{C^2} + \frac{T}{C}b' + \frac{i + i'C}{2}.$$

Clearly this will become negative as C approaches zero provided b is bounded from below and b', i, and i' are all bounded from above.

The second conclusion, the less than proportionate rise in minimum cost cash holdings with the volume of transactions, can be shown, with only b not constant, to hold if and only if $b - b'C + b''C^2$ is positive. This result is obtained by solving the first order minimum condition (obtained by setting (i), with the i' term omitted, equal to zero) for $\frac{T}{C}$ and noting that our conclusion is equivalent to the derivative of this ratio with respect to C being positive.

Now successive differentiation of (i) with the i' term omitted yields as our second order minimum condition $2(b - b'C) + b''C^2 > 0$ (note the resemblance to the preceding condition). Thus if our result is to be violated we must have

$$\text{(ii)} \quad b - Cb' \leqq -b''C^2 < 2(b - Cb'),$$

which at once yields $b'' \leqq 0$. Thus if b' is not to become negative (a decreasing *total* payment as the size of the withdrawal increases!) b'' must usually lie within a small neighborhood of zero, i.e., b must be approximately linear. However we know that in this case the square root formula will be (approximately) valid except in the case $b = kC$ when it will always (by (i)) pay to hold zero cash balances. Note incidentally that (ii) also yields $b - Cb' \geq 0$ which means that our result must hold if ever the "brokerage fee" increases more than in proportion with C.

Note, finally, that if i varies with C the first order condition becomes a cubic and, provided $\infty > i' > 0$, our conclusion is strengthened, since T now tends to increase as C^2.

THE TRANSACTIONS DEMAND FOR CASH 555

which would call for a zero cash balance provided the cash could be loaned out profitably at all. Cash receipts during the relevant period may have similar effects, since they can be used to make payments which happen to be due at the moment the receipts arrive. Here the extreme case involves receipts and payments always coinciding in time and amounts in which case, again, zero cash balances would be called for. Thus lumpy payments and receipts of cash, with sufficient foresight, can make for economies in the use of cash, i.e., higher velocity. This may not affect the rate of increase in transactions velocity with the level of transactions, but may nevertheless serve further to increase the effect of an injection of cash and of a cut in wages and prices. With imperfect foresight, however, the expectation that payments may be lumpy may increase the precautionary demand for cash. Moreover, the existence of a "broker's fee" which must be paid on lending or investing cash received during the period is an added inducement to keep receipts until payments fall due rather than investing, and so may further increase the demand for cash.

4. The economy in a single person's use of cash resulting from an increase in the volume of his transactions may or may not have its analogue for the economy as a whole. "External economies" may well be present if one businessman learns cash-economizing techniques from the experiences of another when both increase their transactions. On the diseconomies side it is barely conceivable that an infectious liquidity fetishism will permit a few individuals reluctant to take advantage of cash saving opportunities to block these savings for the bulk of the community. Nevertheless, at least two such possible offsets come to mind: (a) The rise in the demand for brokerage services resulting from a general increase in transactions may bring about a rise in the "brokerage fee" and thus work for an increase in average cash balances (a decreased number of visits to brokers). If cash supplies are sticky this will tend to be offset by rises in the rate of interest resulting from a rising total demand for cash, which serve to make cash more expensive to hold. (b) Widespread cash economizing might require an increase in precautionary cash holdings because in an emergency one could rely less on the ability of friends to help or creditors to be patient. This could weaken but not offset the relative reduction in cash holdings entirely, since the increase in precautionary demand is contingent on there being some relative decrease in cash holdings.

5. A priori analysis of the precautionary and the speculative demands for cash is more difficult. In particular, there seems to be

556   *QUARTERLY JOURNAL OF ECONOMICS*

little we can say about the latter, important though it may be, except that it seems unlikely that it will work consistently in any special direction. In dealing with the precautionary demand, assumptions about probability distributions and expectations must be made.[2] It seems plausible offhand, that an increase in the volume of transactions will make for economies in the use of cash for precautionary as well as transactions purposes by permitting increased recourse to insurance principles.

Indeed, here we have a rather old argument in banking theory which does not seem to be widely known. Edgeworth,[3] and Wicksell[4] following him, suggested that a bank's precautionary cash requirements might also grow as the square root of the volume of its transactions (!). They maintained that cash demands on a bank tend to be normally distributed.[5] In this event, if it is desired to maintain a fixed probability of not running out of funds, precautionary cash requirements will be met by keeping on hand a constant multiple of the standard deviation (above the mean). But then the precautionary cash requirement of ten identical banks (with independent demands) together will be the same as that for any one of them multiplied by the square root of ten. For it is a well-known result that the standard deviation of a random sample from an infinite population increases as the square root of the size of the sample.

WILLIAM J. BAUMOL.

PRINCETON UNIVERSITY

2. See Arrow, Harris and Marschak, *op. cit.* for a good example of what has been done along these lines in inventory control analysis.

3. F. Y. Edgeworth, "The Mathematical Theory of Banking," *Journal of the Royal Statistical Society*, Vol. LI (1888), especially pp. 123–127. Fisher (*loc. cit.*) points out the relevance of this result for the analysis of the cash needs of the public as a whole. The result was independently rediscovered by Dr. Whitin (*op. cit.*) who seems to have been the first to combine it and (2) in inventory analysis.

4. K. Wicksell, *Interest and Prices* (London, 1936), p. 67.

5. The distribution would generally be approximately normal if its depositors were large in number, their cash demands independent and not very dissimilarly distributed. The independence assumption, of course, rules out runs on banks.

[2]

A MODEL OF THE DEMAND FOR MONEY BY FIRMS *

MERTON H. MILLER AND DANIEL ORR

I. Introduction, 413. — II. A model of cash flows and the costs of cash management for business firms, 416; assumptions underlying the model, 417; optimal values of the policy parameters, 420; some properties of the solution, 423; implications for the demand for money by firms, 425; extension to allow for non-zero drift, 427. — III. The applicability of the model; 429. — Appendix, 433.

I. INTRODUCTION

Economists have long recognized the similarity between the problem of managing a cash balance and that of managing an inventory of some physical commodity. An early attempt to exploit this analogy was provided by Baumol [1] who applied to cash holdings the classical "lot size" model of inventory management that Whitin [2] had earlier brought to the attention of economists. Since that time, the analysis of the firm's control of physical stocks has been vastly extended by economists and others; but no parallel advance has occurred on the cash balance front. The Baumol model in its original or some more refined version (such as that of Tobin [3]) has remained the dominant tool for analyzing the "transactions" demand for money at the micro level.

Since the Baumol model will serve as the point of departure and of contrast for the results to be presented in this paper, it will be helpful first to summarize briefly the main assumptions and properties of that model. In essence, the decision-maker is pictured as holding two distinct types of asset: (1) an earning asset such as a savings deposit or "bond" which bears interest at given rate of, say, v per dollar per day; and (2) a noninterest bearing cash balance into which periodic receipts of income are deposited and from which a steady flow of expenditures are made at the constant rate of, say, m dollars per day.[4] Transfers of funds between the two accounts

* We wish to thank Eugene Fama, Milton Friedman, William Kruskal, Franco Modigliani, John F. Muth, Victor Niederhoffer and Lester Telser for helpful suggestions and comments. Francis Nourie set up and carried out the computations upon which Table I is based.

1. W. J. Baumol, "The Transactions Demand for Cash: An Inventory Theoretic Approach," this *Journal*, LXVI (Nov. 1952).

2. T. M. Whitin, *The Theory of Inventory Management* (Princeton University Press, 1953).

3. J. Tobin, "The Interest Elasticity of Transactions Demand for Cash," *Review of Economics and Statistics*, XXXVIII (Aug. 1956).

4. The Baumol model may also be applied to the opposite situation in

are permissible at any time, but only at a cost which, in the simplest version of the model, is taken as a constant, γ, independent of the amount transferred.[5] The precise nature of this transfer cost will vary depending on the context to which the model is being applied, but in all cases it is to be interpreted as including both the direct expenses of effecting the transfer (such as postage or bank service charges) and any opportunity costs (such as time spent waiting at the teller's window or in making and communicating decisions about purchases and sales of portfolio assets).

Given these conditions, an optimal cash management policy will call for the investment of the periodic receipts in the earning asset followed by a regularly timed sequence of security sales that transfers M dollars every $L = M/m$ days from the earning to the cash account. The operating cash balance will thus have the "saw-tooth" form shown in Figure Ia. If the decision-maker assigns a

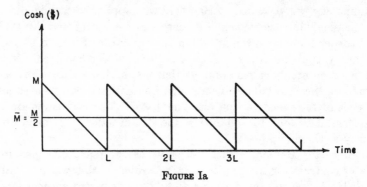

FIGURE Ia

relatively large value to M, transfers will be infrequent; but the average cash balance $\dfrac{M}{2}$ will also be high with a consequent sub-stantial loss of interest earnings. If he assigns a low value to M, then the interest loss on idle funds is reduced, but the gains thereby realized may be eaten up by the in-and-out costs. The minimum cost solution, balancing these opposing forces, is given by the famil-iar "square root rule," viz., transfer $M^* = \left(\dfrac{2\gamma m}{\nu}\right)^{1/2}$ dollars every $L^* = \left(\dfrac{2\gamma}{m\nu}\right)^{1/2}$ days, implying an average cash balance (or long-run

which receipts from operations flow steadily into the cash balance at a constant rate per day subject to periodic large withdrawals for operating expenditures.

5. Although γ represents what would ordinarily be called a "transaction cost" we shall refer to it throughout as a "transfer" cost, reserving the term "transactions" for the receipts and payments exogenous to the model.

THE DEMAND FOR MONEY BY FIRMS 415

demand for money) of $\overline{M}^* = \dfrac{M^*}{2} = \left(\dfrac{\gamma m}{2\nu}\right)^{1/2}.$[6]

Simple as it is, this inventory model of cash management, with its emphasis on the cost of putting idle cash to work, does capture the essence of one fundamental element underlying the demand for money — perhaps the single most important element in an economy such as ours with a wide variety of interest-bearing securities of very low risk and very quickly convertible to cash. Moreover, the assumptions with respect to cash flows underlying the Baumol model apply reasonably well to much of the household sector, particularly to salary-earning households. The model, however, is much less satisfactory, both from the positive and normative points of view when applied to business firms (and to entrepreneurial and professional households) who hold about half of the total money stock.

For many business firms, the typical pattern of cash management is not the simple, regular one of Figure Ia, but a more complex one which might appear as in Figure Ib. The cash balance fluctuates

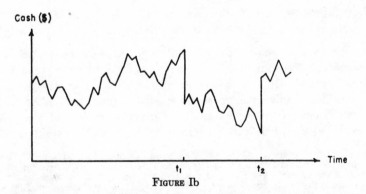

FIGURE Ib

irregularly (and to some extent unpredictably) over time in *both* directions — building up when operating receipts exceed expendi-

6. The expressions given are optimal only under the further assumption that the transfer costs under the policy are less than the interest earnings on the amounts transferred. If not, receipts should be kept entirely in cash and the average cash balance will be one-half the periodic receipt. Some additional difficulties arise with respect to the solution as developed by Baumol if the size of the periodic cash receipt is not an integer multiple of the optimal amount transferred. Tobin, *op. cit.*, presents a modified solution in which M is optimized subject to this "adding up" constraint. For further discussion and characterization of the minimum cost conditions see R. L. Teigen, "Demand and Supply Functions for Money in the United States: Some Structural Estimates," *Econometrica*, Vol. 32 (Oct. 1964) and H. G. Johnson, "Notes on the Theory of Transactions Demand for Cash," *Indian Journal of Economics*, XLIV (July 1963).

tures and falling off when the reverse is true. If the build-up is at
all prolonged, a point is eventually reached (such as that indicated
at t_1) at which the financial officer decides that cash holdings are
excessive, and transfers a sizable quantity of funds either to the
control of the portfolio staff for temporary investment or to loan
retirement. In the other direction, in the face of a prolonged net
drain, a level will be reached (as at t_2) at which the portfolio managers will be instructed to liquidate securities, or the firm will
borrow to restore the cash balance to an "adequate working level."

The main purpose of this paper is to develop a simple, analytic
model that incorporates both this "up and down" cash balance movement characteristic of business operations *and* the critical, lumpy
transfer cost feature of the Baumol model. Note that we say *a*
model, since for cash management as well as inventory management
a wide variety of models will ultimately have to be developed by
finance specialists and monetary theorists to cover all of the many
important and interesting variations.[7]

II. A Model of Cash Flows and the Costs of Cash Management for Business Firms

We shall begin by listing the main assumptions underlying
the model. Some of these will be recognized as mere technical
simplifications. Others, however, are of a more substantive nature
and will inevitably raise questions about the range of applicability
of the model. Although we shall comment on certain of the substantive assumptions briefly here in passing, fuller consideration

7. In fact, there are already in the literature models that advance matters
beyond the original Baumol model (such as Johnson, *op. cit.*), including some
which allow for both positive and negative net changes in the cash balance.
One such is the model developed by D. Patinkin in *Money, Interest, and Prices*
(Evanston: Row Peterson, 1956), Chap. VII and further elaborated by Dvo-
retzky in the appendix to that book. It is essentially a "buffer stock" model
focusing on the size of the initial cash balance needed to reduce the probability
of cash run-outs during a "period" to some given, small level (transfers from
other assets to cash being permitted only at the start of a period). The analysis
is also restricted by the assumptions that total cash flows net out to zero in
every period and that the total volume of transactions over the period is
known in advance. More recently, D. Orr and W. G. Mellon have developed
a model in the context of reserve holdings by banks, but otherwise similar in a
number of respects to the model to be developed here, "Stochastic Reserve
Losses and Expansion of Bank Credit," *American Economic Review*, LI (Sept.
1961). The main difference comes from the assumption in the Orr-Mellon
model of a fixed settlement period for reserves — the Federal Reserve bi-weekly
Wednesday call — which permits their problem to be treated as a series of
independent, one-period decisions rather than as a single problem, continuous
in time. Mention should also be made of a model for cash holdings by firms,
very similar in spirit to ours, developed independently by Melvin Greenball,
currently a student at the Graduate School of Business, University of Chicago.

THE DEMAND FOR MONEY BY FIRMS 417

of the matter of applicability is best postponed until Section III, after the model and its major empirical implications have been set forth.

1. *The Assumptions Underlying the Model*

A first group of assumptions represents the analogues and necessary extensions of those in the Baumol model. Specifically, we suppose: (1) that we continue to have a "two-asset" setting, one asset being the firm's cash balance and the other a separately managed portfolio of liquid assets (such as Treasury bills, certificates of deposit, commercial paper or other money market instruments) whose marginal and average yield is v per dollar per day; (2) that transfers between the two asset accounts may take place at any time at a given marginal cost of γ per transfer, independent of the size of the transfer, the direction of the transfer or of the time since the previous transfer; [8] and (3) that such transfers may be regarded as taking place instantaneously, i.e., that the "lead-time" involved in portfolio transfers is short enough to be ignored.

The third assumption serves, among other things, to eliminate the need for a precautionary "buffer stock" whose function in stochastic inventory problems is to protect against runouts during the lead-time. While an assumption of zero lead-time may seem quite strong at first glance, it is actually not unrealistic, at least for the larger firms with specialized staffs that monitor the cash balance and the portfolio closely. Transactions in most of the major money market instruments can be initiated by such firms merely by placing a telephone call, with delivery for the start of the next business day (and in some special cases even during the same day).[9]

8. Another cost component proportional to the amount transferred might be added to allow for the brokerage charges typically incurred when securities are sold before maturity. Such an extension is fairly easily handled in the context of the Baumol model. See Tobin, *op. cit.* Analytical results for the present problem, however, are much harder to obtain under that form of cost structure and would require methods different and considerably more complex than those to be used here.

9. To say that the model contains no buffer stock does not mean that we are ignoring the so-called "precautionary" motive for holding cash. While cash can be obtained instantaneously in the event of an unexpectedly large cash drain, it can only be obtained by incurring a transfer cost. Hence the possibility of such drains and consequent costs will affect the size of the optimal cash balance even though no specific part of the optimal holding can be separately identified as the precautionary balance. As for the so-called "speculative" motive, we would expect under present day conditions (where securities of very short maturity are always readily available) that most of any speculation on a fall in interest rates would take the form of shortening the maturity structure of the portfolio rather than of building up cash holdings. But the optimal cash holding might be affected indirectly by speculation, however, to the extent that the prospect of speculative gains were reflected in the value of v.

Consistent with present-day banking arrangements we shall further assume that there is a definite minimum level below which a firm's cash balance is not permitted to fall. Zero, of course, would be an absolute minimum since overdrafts are rarely allowed for business firms: even firms with open lines of credit must go through the formality (and expense) of a transfer to the cash balance before an overdrawn check will be cleared. In practice, required minimum balances are normally substantially greater than zero. The precise amount of the required minimum in any particular instance is negotiated between the parties and depends basically on the amount of banking services — mainly check processing and loan accommodation — that the firm actually uses. Since this required minimum is primarily a form of compensation to the bank in lieu of service charges we shall here regard it as completely exogenous to the problem of cash balance management and focus attention entirely on the discretionary holdings over and above the required minimum.[1] For further simplicity in notation we shall designate the required minimum level as zero.

A third group of assumptions specifies the nature of the fluctuations in the cash balance. In contrast to the completely deterministic Baumol model we shall here make the opposite extreme assumption that the net cash flows are completely stochastic; and, specfically, that they behave as if they were generated by a stationary random walk. Given this framework, it is convenient and yet sufficiently general for our purposes to suppose that the random behavior of the cash flows can be characterized as a sequence of independent Bernoulli trials. In particular, let $1/t$ = some small fraction of a working day such as 1/8, i.e., an "hour." We suppose that during any such hour the cash balance will either increase by m dollars with probability p, or decrease by m dollars with probability $q = 1 - p$.[2] Over a longer interval of, say, n days, the observable

1. Little of importance is lost, we feel, by treating the minimum as exogenous and "suboptimizing" in terms of the "discretionary" balance only. Although a firm can certainly affect its required minimum to some extent by altering its use of bank services, the interaction of policies is likely to be extremely weak since the cost trade-offs involved and the speed with which adjustments can be made are of a very different kind in the two cases.

To the extent that a firm's required minimum balance changes over time — and it will do so periodically in response to changes in the level of activity in the account as well as to changes in the agreed interest rate used for computing the stock-equivalent of the service charge flows — we assume in effect that the whole discretionary balance is instantly and costlessly moved up or down by an appropriate transfer to or from the portfolio.

2. These increments or decrements represent only "operating" cash transactions and are to be regarded as exclusive of cash flows stemming from the portfolio, either transfers or run-offs of securities held. The proceeds of matured individual securities are assumed to be immediately reinvested.

THE DEMAND FOR MONEY BY FIRMS 419

distribution of changes in the cash balance will thus have mean $\mu_n = ntm(p-q)$ and variance $\sigma_n^2 = 4ntpqm^2$; and this distribution in turn will approach normality as n increases. Most of the subsequent discussion in the text will focus on the special symmetric or zero-drift case in which $p = q = 1/2$ (with the derivations for more complicated nonsymmetric cases relegated to the Appendix).

For this special case, $\mu_n = 0$, $\sigma_n^2 = nm^2t$ and $\sigma^2 = \dfrac{\sigma_n^2}{n} = m^2t =$ the variance of daily changes in the cash balance.

The Bernoulli process is by no means as restrictive in this context as it may appear at first glance. The properties of the Bernoulli process that are crucial for present purposes are not the implied regular timing or constant size of transaction; the critical features are rather serial independence, stationarity and the absence of discernible, regular swings in the cash balance. Any of a number of other familiar generating processes with these features might equally well have been used, all leading to the same solution as the one we present.[3]

The final set of assumptions concerns the firm's objective function. Here, following a standard practice in inventory theory we shall assume that the firm seeks to minimize the long-run average cost of managing the cash balance under some "policy of simple form."[4] In the present context, the simplest and most natural such policy is the two-parameter control-limit policy illustrated in Figure II. That is, the cash balance will be allowed to wander freely until it reaches either the lower bound, zero, or an upper bound, h, at which times a portfolio transfer will be undertaken to restore the balance to a level of z.[5] Hence, the policy implies that when the upper bound

3. That the results are not dependent on the assumed Bernoulli process can be verified by reference to a forthcoming paper by G. Antelman and I. R. Savage, "Surveillance Problems: Wiener Processes," Technical Report No. 34, University of Minnesota, Department of Statistics, Jan. 1962, on the "surveillance problem," a special case of which is very similar to and has the same solution as our cash balance problem. The Antelman-Savage paper uses a Wiener process as the generating mechanism; in an earlier paper, "Surveillance Problems," *Naval Research Logistics Quarterly*, Vol. 9 (Sept. and Dec. 1962), Savage derives the same solution for a Poisson process. Our reason for relying on the Bernoulli process here is its great simplicity, which permits the solution to be developed with only the most elementary methods.

4. For the rationalization of this approach see S. Karlin, "Steady State Solutions," Chap. XIV in Arrow, Karlin, and Scarf, *Studies in the Mathematical Theory of Inventory and Production* (Stanford University Press, 1958), esp. p. 223.

5. Such a policy is simpler and more "natural" than, say, one involving different return points after a purchase and a sale — a policy form that might be appropriate if the transfer cost were assumed to differ depending on the direction of the transfer, or if the cost of transfer were in part proportional to the size of the transfer.

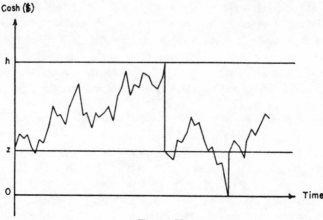

FIGURE II

is hit there will be a lump sum transfer *from* cash of $(h - z)$ dollars; and when the lower limit is triggered, a transfer *to* cash of z dollars.

Given this (h, z) policy structure, and our other assumptions, the expected cost per day of managing the firm's cash balance over any finite planning horizon of T days can be expressed formally as:

$$(1) \qquad \varepsilon(c) = \gamma \frac{\varepsilon(N)}{T} + \nu \, \varepsilon(M)$$

where $\varepsilon(N)$ = the expected number of portfolio transfers (in either direction) during the planning period; γ = the cost per transfer; $\varepsilon(M)$ = the average daily cash balance; and ν = the daily rate of interest earned on the portfolio.[6] The firm's objective is that of minimizing $\varepsilon(\overline{c})$ with respect to the control variables afforded by the chosen policy; the upper bound on cash holdings, h, and the intermediate return point, z.

2. The Optimal Values of the Policy Parameters

Turning now to the solution, consider first the term $\dfrac{\varepsilon(N)}{T}$, the expected number of transfers per day. The derivation of an expression for $\dfrac{\varepsilon(N)}{T}$ in terms of the decision variables z and h will be

6. The expression (1), like the loss functions in similar inventory models, is only an approximation, though normally a very close one (see G. Hadley, "A Comparison of Order Quantities Computed Using the Average Annual Cost and the Discounted Cost," *Management Science*, Vol. 10 (April 1964)) to the flow equivalent of the discounted present value of costs. The discrepancy comes from neglecting the interest on the transfer costs and on the interest itself as well as from averaging rather than integrating over the cash holdings.

THE DEMAND FOR MONEY BY FIRMS 421

performed in two parts. First the mean number of transfers will be expressed in terms of the average time interval between transfers; and then this average interval will be related to z and h.

As for the first part, suppose that the successive time intervals (measured in days) $x_1, x_2, \ldots$, between portfolio transfers are independent random drawings from a population with a well-defined probability distribution. In particular, let this distribution have mean D and finite variance. If T is a fixed planning horizon and N is a random variable denoting the number of transfers that occur during the horizon period, then (by the definition of N)

(1) $x_1 + x_2 + \ldots + x_N \le T < x_1 + x_2 + \ldots + x_{N+1}.$

Or, taking expectations

$\varepsilon(x_1 + x_2 + \ldots + x_N) \le T < \varepsilon(x_1 + x_2 + \ldots + x_{N+1}).$

Wald has proved [7] that under the assumed conditions on $\{x_i\}$

$\varepsilon(x_1 + x_2 + \ldots + x_N) = \varepsilon(x)\,\varepsilon(N) = D\,\varepsilon(N)$

from which the inequalities

$D\,\varepsilon(N) \le T < D\,\varepsilon(N) + D$

are seen to hold. These in turn imply

(2) $\dfrac{1}{D} - \dfrac{1}{T} < \dfrac{\varepsilon(N)}{T} \le \dfrac{1}{D}\,.$

Hence as T is allowed to grow unboundedly large, the ratio $\dfrac{\varepsilon(N)}{T}$,

the expected number of transfers per day, approaches $\dfrac{1}{D}$.[8]

We next seek an expression for D in terms of z and h, and here we can make direct use of classical results reviewed by Feller.[9] In particular, for a symmetric ($p = q = 1/2$) Bernoullian random walk with unit transaction "steps" originating at z and terminating at either 0 or h, Feller proves (a) that the duration of the walk is a random variable whose distribution has the properties we assumed to hold for the $\{x_i\}$; and (b) that the expected value of the duration, $D(z, h)$ is given by

(3) $D(z, h) = (z)(h - z).$

The above expression states the expected duration in terms of num-

---

7. A. Wald, *Sequential Analysis* (New York: Wiley, 1947), p. 52.

8. This result can be derived exactly rather than asymptotically if the cash balance changes are assumed to be generated by a continuous rather than a discrete probability mechanism. However, by maintaining a discrete framework, the stationary cash balance density, which underlies the calculation of holding cost, is far easier to derive; and since we are dealing with a steady state model, derivation of (2) as an asymptotic result is not in any sense a shortcoming.

9. W. Feller, *An Introduction to Probability Theory and Its Applications*, Vol. I (2d ed.; New York: Wiley, 1957), Chap. XIV.

ber of trials. To convert the time unit to days, we need merely divide by t, the number of operating cash transactions per day.[1] To convert z and h from unit steps to dollars we define new variables z' and h' in dollars with $z' = z \cdot m$ and $h' = h \cdot m$. Hence, the expected duration stated in days and with the bounds in dollar units is:

$$(4) \qquad D(z', h') = \frac{(z')(h' - z')}{m^2 t} .$$

Having shown that $\dfrac{\varepsilon(N)}{T}$ approaches $1/D(z, h)$ for sufficiently large T, the transfer cost term of the long-run average cost function (1.1) can thus be written as the product of γ and the reciprocal of the right-hand side of (4). (To simplify the notation we shall hereafter omit the primes on z and h in expressions based on (4) since the presence of m and t will indicate that dollar rather than transaction step units are the appropriate dimension.)

The second term of the cost function requires an expression for the long-run average cash balance in terms of z and h. This balance is simply the mean of the steady-state distribution of cash holdings. Following the usual procedure for deriving this distribution[2] the probability that the cash balance will contain precisely x units is obtained from the difference equations:

$$(5) \qquad f(x) = pf(x - 1) + qf(x + 1) \qquad\qquad x \neq z$$

with boundary conditions

$$(6) \qquad f(z) = p[f(z - 1) + f(h - 1)] + q[f(z + 1) + f(1)]$$

and

$$(7) \qquad f(0) = 0, \qquad f(h) = 0$$

and the density condition

$$(8) \qquad \sum_{x=0}^{n} f(x) = 1 .$$

For the special case $p = q = 1/2$, the system (5) has a solution of the form

$$(9) \qquad \begin{aligned} f(x) &= A_1 + B_1 x & 0 < x < z \\ f(x) &= A_2 + B_2(h - x) & z < x < h . \end{aligned}$$

The linearity of (9) and the conditions (6) and (7) imply that the steady-state distribution of cash holdings is of discrete triangular form with base h and mode z. The mean of such a distribution is

---

1. Cf. above, p. 418.
2. Feller, *loc. cit.*

THE DEMAND FOR MONEY BY FIRMS   **423**

$$\frac{h+z}{3}.$$ [3]

Combining both segments of the expected cost function, and letting $Z = h - z$, the problem can now be stated as:

$$(10) \quad \min_{Z,\, z} \varepsilon(c) = \frac{\gamma m^2 t}{zZ} + \frac{\nu(Z + 2z)}{3}.$$

The necessary conditions for a minimum are

$$\frac{\partial \varepsilon(c)}{\partial z} = -\frac{\gamma m^2 t}{z^2 Z} + \frac{2\nu}{3} = 0$$

$$\frac{\partial \varepsilon(c)}{\partial Z} = -\frac{\gamma m^2 t}{Z^2 z} + \frac{\nu}{3} = 0$$

which together yield the optimal values [4]

$$(11) \quad z^* = \left(\frac{3\gamma m^2 t}{4\nu}\right)^{1/3}$$

and

$$(12) \quad Z^* = 2z^*$$

or in terms of the original parameters

$$(13) \quad h^* = 3z^*.$$

3. *Some Properties of the Solution*

This solution has a number of interesting and in some respects quite surprising properties. Notice first that despite the symmetry of the generating process and of the cost of returning the system to z, the control rules turn out to be asymmetrical. The optimal return point lies substantially *below* the midpoint of the range over which the cash balance is permitted to wander. To put it another way, sales of portfolio assets will take place with greater average frequency and in smaller "lots" than purchases.[5] Some insight into the economic rationale of this result can be gained from Figure III in which

3. Derivations for the case $p \neq q$ are sketched in the Appendix.

4. Sufficient conditions also hold for these values.

5. Despite this asymmetry in the size and frequency of transfers, it is reassuring to note that no drift is thereby communicated to the volume of earning assets held in the firm's portfolio. This property follows directly from the probabilities of passage in a symmetric Bernoullian process; viz., Prob (first passage at 0 when process originates at z) $= \dfrac{h-z}{h}$ and Prob (first passage at h when process originates at z) $= 1 - \dfrac{h-z}{h} = \dfrac{z}{h}$. See Feller, *loc. cit.*

Although the portfolio has no drift, nothing in the model prevents the portfolio from becoming negative if the sales called for by the policy happen to precede or exceed the purchases over some period of time. In such cases, the firm is presumed to utilize a line of credit or some other short-term borrowing arrangement (i.e., the portfolio securities it sells are its own).

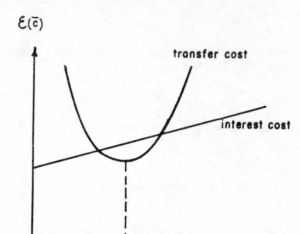

$\mathcal{E}(\bar{c})$

transfer cost

interest cost

$z = 1/2\ h_0$

FIGURE III

the transfer cost and the holding cost are plotted separately as
functions of z for some given $h = h_0$. The transfer cost is a symmetric U-shaped function with its minimum at the midpoint, $z =$
$1/2\ h_0$. The idle balance cost, by contrast, is a linear increasing
function of z throughout. Hence, it would obviously be uneconomical
to set z greater than $h_0/2$ since both costs would be increasing in
that range. But in the other direction some cost reduction can be
achieved by reducing z since the transfer cost function, though rising
as z moves below $1/2\ h_0$, is relatively flat in the region of its minimum.

An even more surprising aspect of the optimal solution is that
z^* always lies at $1/3\ h^*$, regardless of the relative magnitudes of
the cost coefficients γ and ν. Changes in these costs serve only to
shrink or dilate the system as a whole with no change in the internal
balance between z and h. The explanation of this result lies in the
structure of the cost function (2.10). Note that z and Z enter
symmetrically into the transfer cost component, but that z enters
with twice as much weight as Z in the holding cost component. This
means that if $Z > 2z$, we can add $\cdot$ small amount, $\triangle$, to z and subtract $2\triangle$ from Z with no resulting change in the holding cost term
$\nu(Z + 2z)/3$. These changes, however, will transform the denominator of the transfer cost term to

$$(Z - 2\triangle)(z + \triangle) = Zz + \triangle(Z - 2z) - 2\triangle^2 > Zz$$

the last inequality necessarily holding for some small value of $\triangle$

THE DEMAND FOR MONEY BY FIRMS   **425**

so long as $Z > 2z$. Thus, it would pay to increase z by $\triangle$ and to reduce Z by $2\triangle$ since the higher value of the denominator implies a lower value for the transfer cost term. Similar reasoning applies to the case of $Z < 2z$ so that only if $Z = 2z$ is no such cost-reducing substitution possible.

4. *Implications for the Demand for Money by Firms*

For economists, the major interest in the solution lies in its implications for the demand for money by firms. In the present context, that demand can be identified with the average cash balance realized when operating under a policy (h, z) and hence will be given by $\dfrac{h + z}{3}$. Substituting the optimal values of h^* and z^* from (2.11) and (2.13) and recalling (from page 419 above) that $\sigma^2 = \dfrac{\sigma_n^2}{n} = m^2 t =$ the variance of the daily change in the cash balance, we obtain

$$(1) \qquad \bar{M}^* = \frac{4}{3}\left(\frac{3\gamma m^2 t}{4\nu}\right)^{1/3} = \frac{4}{3}\left(\frac{3\gamma}{4\nu}\sigma^2\right)^{1/3}$$

as an expression for the firm's optimal average cash balance (or long-run average demand for money) in terms of the cost parameters γ and ν and the (observable) variance of daily cash flows, σ^2. As in the case of the Baumol model the demand for money is an increasing function of the cost of transferring funds to and from the earning portfolio, and a decreasing function of the interest rate or opportunity cost of the funds held in the cash balance. The novel aspect of the money demand equation (1) is the presence of σ^2, a term directly representing the variability of the cash balance, or the degree of the "lack of synchronization" between cash receipts and payments.

The fact that the variance of daily net cash flows serves as the "transactions" variable in the money demand function raises the question of how equation (1) is related to the kind of demand function typically used in empirical studies of money holdings by firms in which total sales or some closely related concept is taken as the measure of transactions. That there is a relation between total sales and the variance of changes in the cash balance is clear enough since total sales are approximately the positive changes in the cash balance summed over a time interval. But the relation is a loose one, and no precise value can be established for the elasticity of the demand for cash with respect to sales that is implied by our model. The difficulty in specifying the sales elasticity stems from the fact that even with unchanging prices sales may change in any of several ways, each with a different impact on the firm's need for cash. At one extreme, a doubling of sales may be due to a doubling of each separate receipt and expenditure invoice. In terms of the model, this is equivalent to raising the transaction step size from m to $2m$ and implies that the optimal average balance will rise by a factor of $2^{2/3}$. At the other extreme, a doubling of sales may take the form of a doubling in the frequency of transactions (i.e., a doubling of t), with the average invoice size unchanged. In this case, because of the increased opportunity for offsetting changes, the desired balance increases only by a factor of $2^{1/3}$. The range of elasticities, of course, becomes even larger when we allow for the possibility of increases in transaction magnitude accompanied by decreases in transaction frequency, or vice versa.

The existence of such a wide range for the sales elasticity in our (h, z) model is in sharp contrast to the prediction of the Baumol model where the elasticity of average cash holdings with respect to sales (assuming constant prices) is always and precisely 1/2. This uniformity of prediction is one of the most obvious weaknesses of Baumol-type models as applied to corporate cash balances. Studies of intersectoral velocities [6] show substantial differences between industries; and there is simply no convincing way of accounting for such differences in the Baumol framework. Whether our variability term provides the answer we cannot say; but it does at least offer a plausible (and testable) explanation for the observed systematic interindustry differences.

Further questions arise about the relation of our demand function (1) to the "classical" quantity theory of money and to the so-called "modern" quantity theory (running in terms of such variables as "permanent income" or wealth). As to the former, if we regard as the essence of the classical position that the demand for money in real terms be independent of the absolute price level, then equation (1) is consistent with that position. Like the Baumol model, it is homogeneous of degree one in prices, that is, it implies that a doubling of all prices (including those impounded in γ) will lead to a doubling of the quantity of money demanded. With respect to the modern quantity theory, however, the relation is much less clear. Certainly it is hard to see any direct relevance for concepts such as permanent income or wealth in the decision process at the level of the firm. But this, of course, does not rule out the possibility that

6. E.g., R. Selden, *The Postwar Rise in the Velocity of Money*, Occasional Paper 78 (New York: National Bureau of Economic Research, 1962).

THE DEMAND FOR MONEY BY FIRMS 427

aggregate permanent income or wealth might nevertheless be effective proxies for the level of transactions in macro models of the demand for money.

5. *Extension to Allow for Non-zero Drift*

Although the no-drift case is likely to be the one of greatest interest to monetary theorists, the model can be extended to incorporate systematic drift in the cash balance (in either direction).[7] The analytical expressions leading to the optimal solution values for h, z and $\overline{M}$ in the presence of drift turn out to be extremely cumbersome and hard to interpret,[8] but the main qualitative properties of

TABLE I

OPTIMAL SOLUTION VALUES AS A FUNCTION OF DRIFT

A. For $\gamma/\nu = 50$

p	z^*	h^*	$\overline{M}^*$	$|\mu|$	σ^2
1.0	1.0	11.0	5.5	1.0	0.00
0.9	1.2	10.6	5.3	0.9	0.36
0.8	1.5	10.0	5.1	0.8	0.64
0.7	1.9	9.5	4.8	0.7	0.84
0.6	2.5	9.4	4.6	0.6	0.96
0.5	3.3	10.0	4.5	0.5	1.00
0.4	4.7	11.7	4.4	0.6	0.96
0.3	6.3	13.9	4.4	0.7	0.84
0.2	7.7	16.1	4.7	0.8	0.64
0.0	11.0	—	5.5	1.0	0.00

B. For $\gamma/\nu = 500$

p	z^*	h^*	$\overline{M}^*$	$|\mu|$	σ^2
1.0	1.0	32.6	16.3	1.0	0.00
0.9	1.6	30.4	15.4	0.9	0.36
0.8	2.2	27.4	14.0	0.8	0.64
0.7	2.9	24.1	12.4	0.7	0.84
0.6	4.1	20.9	10.6	0.6	0.96
0.5	7.2	21.6	9.6	0.5	1.00
0.4	14.2	31.0	9.6	0.6	0.96
0.3	20.0	44.7	11.2	0.7	0.84
0.2	24.5	—	13.1	0.8	0.64
0.0	32.6	—	16.3	1.0	0.00

7. Drift models might be appropriate even where there was no overall net drift in the operating cash balance, but simply a heavy concentration of receipts or expenditures at regularly recurring intervals. If a firm, for example, gets 75 per cent of its monthly receipts on the tenth of the month, then the process over the remaining days might be characterized as one with $p = .25$ and $q = .75$. And similarly, in the other direction, for cases involving large, regularly recurring payments such as tax or dividend payments.

8. Cf. the Appendix.

428   *QUARTERLY JOURNAL OF ECONOMICS*

the solutions as a function of drift can easily be seen from constructed numerical examples. Two sets of such numerical results are presented in Table I, the first for a case in which the critical cost ratio γ/ν has the extremely low value of 50; and the second for one in which it has the higher and more reasonable value of 500 (the values of m and t being taken as unity in both cases).

For extreme positive drift (the case $p = 1$) the stochastic element in the cash flow vanishes and we are, in effect, dealing with a Baumol model of the pure uniform-flow-of-receipts variety. The cash balance builds up steadily to h and then is returned to its lowest possible value (which is zero, in principle, but which we have had to set at one unit for purposes of computer calculation). As p falls, and hence as the upward drift becomes less pronounced and then changes to downward drift, the optimal "return point" z^* increases steadily in value. The behavior of the optimal upper bound, h^*, however, is somewhat surprising. As p falls, h^* first falls slowly; reaches a minimum while still in the zone of net upward drift (in the neighborhood of $p = .6$); then rises again at an increasing rate once the zone of downward drift ($p < q$) is entered. As the downward drift increases and p approaches zero, the probability of ever hitting h^* becomes microscopic, and when p reaches zero, h^* becomes entirely irrelevant to the solution. We have returned to the one-parameter Baumol model, this time of the pure uniform-flow-of-expenditures variety.

The column headed $\bar{M}^*$ in the table relates the average cash balance to drift. Starting from $p = 1$ (extreme upward drift) the optimal cash balance declines steadily with p, and is still falling in the neighborhood of the no-drift case. The minimum of $\bar{M}^*$ actually occurs somewhat beyond the no-drift point and within the zone of net downward drift (at about $p = .4$ in both panels).[9] Thereafter the optimal average balance rises again reaching the same level at $p = 0$ as obtained at $p = 1$ (which is as expected since the extreme cases are Baumol models differing only in the direction of the cash flow).

Some insight into why cash holdings are a U-shaped function of drift can be gained by relating drift to the mean and variance of the distribution of cash balance changes (shown in the last two columns of the table). In these terms, our no-drift case can be thought of as an "all variance — no mean" model; while the pure

9. The fact that the minimum occurs in both cases very near the value $p = .4$ is entirely an artifact of the particular numbers used. As successively higher values of the ratio γ/ν are used, the minimum tends to move steadily closer to the no-drift point, $p = .5$.

THE DEMAND FOR MONEY BY FIRMS **429**

Baumol models for extreme drift are essentially "all mean — no variance" models. Starting near a zero value for the drift, increases in drift (in either direction) imply smaller values for the variance of daily changes in cash and this, by itself, would tend to reduce cash needs. But higher values of drift also imply larger mean daily changes in cash and this, by itself, would tend to raise average holdings. Since the mean rises faster than the variance falls; and since the responsiveness of cash holdings to the mean is greater (a square-root as opposed to a cube-root effect), the net effect of substantial amounts of drift in either direction is to increase optimal average cash balances.

III. The Applicability of the Model

Now that the model of cash management by business firms has been developed and the main properties and implications of that model have been sketched, we may turn to consider the previously postponed questions regarding the realism and empirical relevance of the model. As noted earlier, the various assumptions underlying the model fall into two categories. On the one hand are those that define the basic framework; the assumptions of a "two-asset" structure, of a lumpy component in the cost of transfers between the assets; of a negligible lead time in transfers; and, especially, of a stationary random walk for the cash flows. On the other are the special assumptions introduced primarily to simplify either the proofs or the economic interpretation of the results, such as the assumption of a constant marginal transfer cost independent of the size or direction of the transfer, or the assumption that the cash balance changes by a constant positive or negative amount at regular intervals. Insofar as the latter assumptions are concerned, many interesting variations with respect to the cost structure or the distribution of cash changes can and should be explored. Such variations will certainly lead to more complicated control rules and change other matters of detail, but the general qualitative picture is unlikely to be much altered as long as the basic framework is maintained.[1] Attention here will therefore be focused primarily on the more fundamental question of whether the framework itself constitutes a useful and meaningful way of describing the demand for money by business firms.[2]

1. This has certainly proved to be the case with the Baumol model and, in fact, with classes of inventory models generally.
2. In one sense, the single most crucial assumption in shaping the whole analysis is that substantial lump sum portfolio transfer costs exist. Here, how-

430   *QUARTERLY JOURNAL OF ECONOMICS*

In this connection some reservations must certainly be entered with respect to the realism of the simple two-asset dichotomy. Business firms typically hold many different liquid securities in their portfolios, frequently even at the same time that they are issuing short-term claims such as commercial paper or bank loans. If this were the only problem, however, we doubt that it would constitute any very serious limitation for present purposes. In principle, it is possible to extend the model to allow for more than one portfolio asset each with its own γ and ν (and, presumably, with γ higher for those with higher yields). Analytical results for such extensions are hard to obtain, but from such limited experimentation as we have conducted with models of this type we would conjecture that the system will turn out to be very loosely coupled.

Much more serious than lumping all earning assets into a single portfolio asset is the lumping of all cash holdings into a single cash balance. Most firms do maintain an identifiable central bank balance, but they also hold many separate smaller accounts. This is particularly true of large, divisionalized firms.[3] Transfers take place not only between the field accounts and the central balance but also among the local balances and between these balances and the port-folio. For such a setting, a more appropriate inventory model might be one of the multi-stage factory-warehouse system variety — though models of the general type developed here might still be expected to govern the behavior of some of the separate components of the system. How much a multi-stage approach would affect our main conclusions is hard to say — because results to date in inven-tory theory with such models have been meager, and because we still have very little precise information about the relative importance of field and central balances or the cost savings that field balances permit. At the very least, however, we would expect to find smaller economies of scale than those implied under our single-balance framework.

Many will regard the assumption that the cash generating

ever, we feel that no extended defense is really necessary even though we would concede that those costs may be hard to estimate in practical applications. Their existence seems amply demonstrated by the very large minimum trading units in all the standard money market instruments (e.g., currently $100,000 for commercial bank negotiable Certificates of Deposit).

3. The results of a recent survey of cash balances practices of large cor-porations by W. E. Gibson, "Compensating Balance Requirements," *National Banking Review*, Vol. 2 (March 1965), indicate that the average number of separate bank balances maintained is currently about 200 per firm with some firms actually holding more than 2,300 individual accounts. Gibson's data, how-ever, give no indication of the size distribution of the balances and many ac-counts undoubtedly are of only nominal size. Even so, the extent of significant multiple holding is clearly quite substantial.

THE DEMAND FOR MONEY BY FIRMS 431

mechanism is entirely stochastic as an even more serious limitation on the approach taken here. And certainly this can hardly be defended as being literally descriptive. The size and timing of many of the important individual transactions comprising the cash flow are under the direct control of the management (e.g., dividend payments). Other transactions are the foreseeable fulfillments of past commitments (such as payments on trade accounts or tax payments). Even where genuinely random changes do occur they are usually superimposed on some systematic and at least partially forecastable movements (e.g., payroll disbursements).[4] This is, however, not a very useful way of evaluating the random walk assumption or the model based on it. The decisive question is how well the assumption serves on an "as if" basis; and here the case against it is by no means an obvious one.

For normative applications, models can certainly be developed to utilize available information about local "patterns" in the cash flow. The lumpy component of transfer cost, however, may present a serious obstacle to the derivation of optimal decision rules under some kinds of programming approaches and the derivation of rules under any such approach would definitely be greatly complicated by the presence of both stochastic and deterministic elements in the cash flow. Because of these difficulties it is by no means certain here, as elsewhere in inventory theory, that the gains from exploiting more of the local information about the flows are large enough to offset the added costs of model development and implementation.

For positive applications, the usefulness of a simple stochastic model of cash management depends mainly on how closely its conditional predictions of the average frequency and size of transfer and of average cash balances correspond to those actually observed. Tolerably accurate predictions of these items are entirely possible even though firms use more complicated, *ad hoc* decision procedures based on detailed forecasts or cash budgets. In terms of operating characteristics, the main effect of such procedures and forecasts is likely to be to transform the bounds on cash holdings into zones rather than the simple limits as in our model. For example, there will be occasions when the firm will not transfer funds to the portfolio, even though current cash holdings are larger than h, because it knows or predicts that a "turnaround" will occur in the very near

---

4. To the extent that the systematic component is in the form of a simple trend then a non-zero drift model might meet the need. Even seasonal components might be incorporated by an alternating sequence of drift models, provided the seasonal movements persisted long enough relative to the mean time between transfers to avoid excessive violence to the steady-state assumptions that underlie the objective function (II. 2.10).

future. In the other direction, it may pay the firm to make a transfer even when holdings are below h if a reasonably long "quiet" period is anticipated. Because these tendencies are partially offsetting, no decisive case against a stochastic model with single-valued bounds can be established on a priori grounds.[5] Final judgment must await the results of empirical testing.

Some may argue that the empirical decision has already been rendered by recent cross-sectional studies of the corporate demand for money.[6] The failure of these studies to find any significant economies of scale in cash holdings with respect to total sales or total assets is seen as running directly counter to predictions based on inventory models either of the Baumol variety or of the (h, z) type developed here. Such a conclusion, however, would be unwarranted. Quite apart from the difficulties noted previously in the use of sales or assets as measures of transactions,[7] recall that our (h, z)

5. Another possibility that might more seriously affect the predictive power of the model would be systematic efforts to obtain closer synchronization between receipts and payments by influencing the timing of receipts and payments (e.g., by increasing discounts for early payment when interest rates rise). Such direct adjustments in timing are admittedly quite common among small firms where there is often no alternative to such brute force methods of synchronization as delaying payments to some creditors until sufficient cash receipts have been accumulated. For larger firms, however, it is unlikely to be economic to tinker with the details of the receipt and payment structure in the short run though from time to time the whole system will be re-examined (and of course, such re-examinations are likely to be made more frequently in periods of high interest rates).

6. E.g., A. H. Meltzer, "The Demand for Money: A Cross-Section Study of Business Firms," this *Journal*, LXXVII (Aug. 1963).

7. See Section II. 4, p. 425 above. On a priori grounds, one would suspect that within any given industry the variance of daily cash changes would probably tend to increase less than proportionally with sales, thus strengthening the presumption of scale economies with respect to size under the inventory approach. The "industries" studied tend to be quite heterogeneous, however, so that it may be well to withhold judgment until some direct empirical evidence on variability in relation to size is available.

Although our concern in this paper is primarily with the demand for money by business firms it may perhaps be worth pointing out that somewhat similar problems with respect to interpreting cross-sectional elasticities arise in the case of households. In particular, it does not follow that a finding of an elasticity of money holdings with respect to *income* of unity or even greater is inconsistent with the "inventory" approach. For one thing, many (perhaps most) households have incomes too small or too frequently received to justify moving off the "corner solution" (cf. fn. 6, p. 415) and over this range the implied income elasticity is unity. For those with incomes large enough to warrant temporary investment of idle cash, income will be the relevant "transactions" variable provided that the only portfolio purchases and sales made by the household are those transfers required by the inventory model. Where, however, the household engages in autonomous portfolio activity (such as switching in and out of investments) an additional "transactions" demand for cash balances is generated over and above that involved in spending income on current account. If the amount and frequency of such autonomous financial transactions tend to rise more than proportionally with income (which is certainly not improbable), then an income elasticity of cash holdings greater than unity might well be observed over this range even though substantial economies of scale were present with respect to total transactions.

model is intended to explain only the "discretionary" part of the firm's cash balance over and above its required minimum balance. Despite the fact that such minimum balance requirements in lieu of service charges have long been a conspicuous feature of banking arrangements for business firms in this country, little precise information is available about the absolute size of such balances or how they vary between firms and over time. As was noted earlier, however, it is at least clear that the cost-trade-offs and other strategic elements involved in determining minimum balances differ in important respects from those relating to the active transactions balances. Consequently, the empirical cross-sectional elasticities of money holdings with respect to sales represent only an average (with unknown weights) over the two very different processes.[8] In the absence of evidence, therefore, either that the negotiated minimum balances are a considerably smaller part of the total than the finance literature would lead one to believe; or that minimum balances increase substantially less than proportionally with size of firm, the issue of the validity of inventory models in representing the transactions demand for money by firms must be regarded as still very much an open one.[9]

APPENDIX

In general, the occupancy probabilities of a Bernoullian cash balance which drifts between 0 and h, and is returned instantly to z upon encountering either barrier, are given by the difference equation

$$f(x, t + 1) = pf(x - 1, t) + qf(x + 1, t)$$

and the boundary conditions

$$f(z, t + 1) = p[f(z - 1, t) + f(h - 1, t)] + q[f(z + 1, t) + f(1, t)]$$

8. Although the functions governing the two kinds of balances are different, they are likely to have some arguments in common. In particular, our transaction-frequency variable t is closely related to the "activity" variable used in negotiating minimum balances. Both functions also contain an interest rate variable, though not necessarily the same one for the two cases.

9. For the sake of argument, we accept here the proposition that existing cross-section studies do not show significant economies of scale in cash holdings though, in fact, we have some reservations about these findings. The main one is that these studies typically fit a single money demand relation over the whole range of available size classes of firms including the very smallest sizes; whereas inventory models of the type developed here are at best applicable only for reasonably large firms. With respect to the larger size classes, the case for the existence of economies of scale does seem to be somewhat stronger (cf. Selden, *op. cit.*), though there are too few cells in the usual *Statistics of Income* or F.T.C.-S.E.C. tabulations to permit any reliable estimates of the elasticity in this range of size classes.

$$f(0, t + 1) = 0$$
$$f(h, t + 1) = 0$$
$$\sum_{x=0}^{h} f(x, t + 1) = 1.$$

To ascertain the steady-state occupancy probabilities, we pass to the limit in time, to obtain the system

(1) $f(x) = pf(x - 1) + qf(x + 1)$

(2) $f(z) = p[f(z - 1) + f(h - 1)] + q[f(z + 1) + f(1)]$

$$f(0) = f(h) = 0, \qquad \sum_{x=0}^{h} f(x) = 1.$$

The general solution for the case $p \neq q$

(3) $f(x) = A + B(p/q)^x \qquad 0 \leq x \leq z$
$\quad\; f(x) = C + D(p/q)^x \qquad z \leq x \leq h$

contains four arbitrary constants, which are evaluated via the four boundary conditions.

Since $f(0) = 0$, it follows that

(4) $0 = A + B, \qquad B = -A.$

Similarly,

(5) $D = -C(p/q)^{-h}.$

Substitution of (3), (4) and (5) in (2) yields the relation

(6) $C = A \left[\dfrac{1 - (p/q)^z}{1 - (p/q)^{z-h}} \right].$

Finally, the density condition on the summed occupancy probabilities

$$1 = \sum_{x=0}^{h} f(x) = \sum_{x=0}^{z} A[1 - (p/q)^x]$$
$$+ \sum_{x=z+1}^{h} [1 - (p/q)^{x-h}] A \left[\frac{1 - (p/q)^z}{1 - (p/q)^{z-h}} \right]$$

yields the result

(7) $A = \dfrac{1 - (p/q)^{z-h}}{z[1 - (p/q)^{z-h}] + (h - z)[1 - (p/q)^z]}.$

The values (6) and (7) may be combined to obtain a specific expression for the stationary occupancy probabilities of x, in terms of p and q.

Expression of the density permits explicit evaluation of the expected steady-state cash balance:

$$E(x) = \sum_{x=0}^{h} xf(x) = \sum_{x=0}^{z} xA[1 - (p/q)^x]$$
$$+ \sum_{x=z+1}^{h} xC[1 - (p/q)^{x-h}].$$

THE DEMAND FOR MONEY BY FIRMS 435

Use of the values (6) and (7), and resort to the identity

$$\sum_{x=1}^{h-1} x(p/q)^{x-1} \equiv d/d(p/q) \sum_{x=0}^{h} (p/q)^x$$

$$\equiv \frac{1 - h(p/q)^h - (p/q)^h - h(p/q)^{h+1}}{[1 - (p/q)]^2}$$

for $q > p$, yields the value

$$E(x) = \frac{1}{2} \left\{ \frac{1}{q-p} + h + z \right.$$

$$\left. - \frac{hz[1 - (p/q)^{z-h}]}{z[1 - (p/q)^{z-h} + (h-z)[1 - (p/q)^z]} \right\} .$$

For the other segment of the cost function, the expression for the expected duration between passages of either 0 or h is derived in Feller, *loc. cit.*: it is

$$D(z) = \frac{z}{q-p} - \frac{h}{q-p} \cdot \frac{1 - (p/q)^z}{1 - (p/q)^h} \qquad q > p .$$

GRADUATE SCHOOL OF BUSINESS, UNIVERSITY OF CHICAGO

UNIVERSITY OF CALIFORNIA, SAN DIEGO

[3]

THE USELESSNESS OF TRANSACTIONS DEMAND MODELS

CASE M. SPRENKLE*

I. INTRODUCTION

THE BAUMOL-TOBIN TREATMENT of the transactions demand for money by large economic units has by now become so well accepted that it might well be called the "traditional" theory.[1] The purpose of this paper is to point out how little the theory really explains, how subject to error the results of the theory are, and how fruitless more sophisticated versions of the theory are apt to be. In addition, some light is shed on the directions future research should take to better understand the nature of the transactions demand. In particular it will be shown that differences in decentralization and timing will make enormous differences in optimal cash holdings. These differences are so great that the simple models literally explain nothing. Moreover more sophisticated versions of the model will be equally unhelpful without substantial additional information and knowledge which is currently unavailable.

At the outset it should be emphasized that the discussion here is concerned *solely* with the transactions demand. This exclusion of other possible demands for money immediately raises questions as to means of empirical investigation. If large economic units have demands for money for other than transactions purposes, the usual means of verification—cross section studies of large economic units—will be misleading. This point was, of course, recognized in the various empirical papers.[2] The rationale for treating observed balances as being essentially transactions balances was usually that the Keynesian speculative and precautionary demands would undoubtedly be very low. Few qualms were felt about excluding the possibility of speculative cash balances since it was felt that these balances would be held in short-term assets other than money. Although there may have been more qualms about excluding precautionary balances, it was felt that the level of them would be low in relation to transactions balances. Some recent work provided stronger support for this assumption. It has been shown that using the (overly) simple Baumol-Tobin model, the precautionary demand will be negative—less money will be demanded with uncertainty than without it.[3] In addition, it should by now be clear that the only uncertainty involved in a precautionary demand for *money*

* Associate Professor of Economics, University of Illinois.

1. William J. Baumol, "Transactions Demand for Cash—An Inventory Theoretic Approach," *Quarterly Journal of Economics*, Nov. 1952; James Tobin, "The Interest Elasticity of Transactions Demand for Cash," *Review of Economics and Statistics*, Aug. 1956.

2. See for example: Alan Heston, "An Empirical Study of Cash, Securities, and Other Current Accounts of Large Corporations," *Yale Economic Essays*, Spring 1962; Allan H. Meltzer, "The Demand for Money: A Cross Section Study of Business Firms," *Quarterly Journal of Economics*, Aug. 1963.

3. Case M. Sprenkle, "Is the Precautionary Demand for Money Negative," *Journal of Finance*, Mar. 1967; Robert W. Resek, "Uncertainty and the Precautionary Demand for Money," *Journal of Finance*, Dec. 1967.

is the uncertainty of payments and receipts between the present and next planned purchase or sale of short-term assets. For a large economic unit this period can be as little as one day. The amount of uncertainty over such a short period is apt to be small indeed, and thus the precautionary demand for money should also be very low.

What is not generally understood, however, is that although the precautionary and speculative demands for money are very low or nonexistent, there are other demands for money which in fact are huge in comparison with any conceivable transactions demand. These demands are basically caused by the fact that institutional arrangements in the U.S. are such that large economic units pay for bank services by holding deposits rather than paying fees. The profession seems to have been misled by thinking of such service balances solely in connection with bank loans. Since large economic units rarely have need for such loans, the implication was that service (compensating) balances would be low or nonexistent. The fact is, however, that most service balances have nothing to do with bank loans. They are instead held to pay for the great array of bank services used by the large units.[4] One of the results of this paper is that although the degree of decentralization of cash management and the timing of receipts and/or payments make large differences in the transactions demand for money, no conceivable assumptions can be made for which the transactions demand is more than a small fraction of observed cash balances.

The implication of this is that empirical verification of any transactions demand model is hopeless through the use of the usual kinds of cross-section analysis. Only through data on day-to-day deposits in the various accounts of a firm along with data on purchases and sales of short-term assets will there be any progress toward an understanding of large economic unit cash holdings for transactions purposes.

II. DECENTRALIZATION OF CASH MANAGEMENT

To start, consider the simple Baumol-Tobin model which assumes one lump sum receipt and a steady stream of payments.[5] Using Tobin's notation, let

$T =$ dollars of *yearly* transactions, possibly measured by sales or receipts

$r =$ *yearly* interest rate on short-term assets; possibly the Treasury Bill rate or possibly an average of that rate and other relevant short-term rates

$a =$ fixed cost in dollars of making one purchase or one sale of short-term assets

$n =$ number of sales and purchases of short-term assets per *year*, $n = 2, 3, \ldots$

Since $\dfrac{T}{2n} =$ the average cash balance, and $\dfrac{T}{2} - \dfrac{T}{2n} =$ the average holding of

---

4. For some indication of this, see W. E. Gibson, "Compensating Balance Requirements," *National Banking Review*, Mar. 1965. Merton H. Miller and Daniel Orr, "A Model of the Demand for Money by Firms," *Quarterly Journal of Economics*, Aug. 1966, point out the possible importance of service balances as well as of decentralization, but chose to ignore them in order to concentrate on the effects of uncertainty—a concentration which seems to be unjustified in light of the shortness of the relevant period.

5. The model is equally applicable where it is appropriate to assume a steady flow of receipts and a lump sum payment at the end of the period.

short-term securities, net profit, Z, from investing part of the transactions balance will be,

$$Z = r \left(\frac{T}{2} - \frac{T}{2n} \right) - na \gtreqless 0. \tag{1}$$

The optimal n is found to be,

$$n^* = \left(\frac{Tr}{2a} \right)^{\frac{1}{2}} \tag{2}$$

optimal cash holdings are,

$$C^* = \frac{T}{2n^*} = \left(\frac{Ta}{2r} \right)^{\frac{1}{2}} \tag{3}$$

and optimal short-term security holdings are,

$$B^* = \frac{T}{2} - \left(\frac{Ta}{2r} \right)^{\frac{1}{2}}. \tag{4}$$

All of these well-known results are based on the assumption that the economic unit has complete centralization of its cash management. All receipts and payments are assumed to flow directly into one office; no branch or other office ever has anything to do with the flow of cash. Not only that, but the central office maintains and manages only one account. There are no special accounts for any purposes, and presumably there are also no holdings of currency or coin —no "petty cash". Such an assumption is, of course, completely unrealistic.

Consider now a large economic unit with some degree of decentralization of cash management. Suppose there are J branches, separate accounts, etc., and the jth branch or account receives x_j per cent of total receipts T. Assume also that it makes x_j per cent of total payments. The optimal cash holding of the jth branch will be

$$C_j^* = \left(\frac{x_j Ta}{2r} \right)^{\frac{1}{2}} \tag{5}$$

if the branch does indeed optimize its cash holdings, that is, if optimal n for each branch is $\geqslant 2$. The sum of the optimal cash holdings of all branches will be

$$C_j^* = \sum_{j=1}^{J} \left(\frac{x_j Ta}{2r} \right)^{\frac{1}{2}} = \left(\frac{Ta}{2r} \right)^{\frac{1}{2}} \sum_{j=1}^{J} (x_j)^{\frac{1}{2}} = C^* \sum_{j=1}^{J} (x_j)^{\frac{1}{2}}. \tag{6}$$

The extent to which optimal cash holdings under decentralization, C_J^*, differ from completely centralized cash holdings, C^*, thus depends on the degree of decentralization. Under complete centralization obviously $C_J^* = C^* (1)^{\frac{1}{2}} = C^*$.

Under what might be called complete decentralization, where $x_j = \frac{1}{J}$ for all j,

$$C_J{}^* = C^* \sum_{j=1}^{J} \left(\frac{1}{J}\right)^{\frac{1}{2}} = C^*J \left(\frac{1}{J}\right)^{\frac{1}{2}} = C^* (J)^{\frac{1}{2}}. \qquad (7)$$

That is, optimal cash holdings under complete decentralization will be greater than under complete centralization by a factor equal to the square root of the number of branches or accounts. A firm with 25 branches and complete decentralization will have 5 times the optimal cash holdings of a firm identical in all respects to it except having complete centralization. Complete decentralization, of course, yields the maximum possible optimal cash balances.[6]

Both extremes are unlikely to be realistic. Consider the possibly more realistic case under which the largest branch has $\frac{1}{2}$ the receipts, the next largest $\frac{1}{4}$, and so on. Then

$$C_J{}^* = C^* \sum_{j=1}^{J} \left(\frac{1}{2^j}\right)^{\frac{1}{2}} = C^* [1 + 2^{\frac{1}{2}}] \left[1 - \frac{1}{2^J + \frac{1}{2}}\right]. \qquad (8)$$

If J is large, then

$$C_J{}^* = C^*(2.414). \qquad (9)$$

Whether J is large or small, however, there will be $\frac{1}{2^J}$ T receipts and payments unaccounted for. These can be thought of as being connected with branches or accounts for which no switches in and out of short-term securities are made.

The average cash holdings of these funds will, therefore, be $\frac{1}{2^J + 1}$ T which must be added to $C_J{}^*$ to obtain the total cash holdings.

Probably a still more realistic case is one in which there is one central account which is closely managed and a substantial number of small accounts which are not. If $1 - x$ is the percentage of T received by the central account, then the average cash balance will be

$$C_J{}^* = \left[\frac{(1-x)Ta}{2r}\right]^{\frac{1}{2}} + \frac{xT}{2}. \qquad (10)$$

It is easy to see that for large T and reasonable values of a and r, x does not have to be very large before the total cash holdings in the small accounts become much larger than the average holding in the central account.

The argument has proceeded so far under the assumption that all receipts are received annually. Before continuing with an analysis of the effects of decentralization, it is necessary to consider the effect of the timing of receipts on cash management.

III. Timing and Cash Management

Consider the case where receipts are obtained k evenly spaced times per year, where $k = 1, 2, \ldots, = 250$ (the number of banking days per year).

6. Only under the critical assumption that $n \geqq 2$ for all the branches, however. See below.

Then receipts per period are $\dfrac{T}{k}$, and the interest rate per period is $\dfrac{r}{k}$. The optimal average cash balance for a centralized firm with $n \geqq 2$ is

$$C^* = \left(\frac{\frac{Ta}{k}}{\frac{2r}{k}} \right)^{\frac{1}{2}} = \left(\frac{Ta}{2r} \right)^{\frac{1}{2}}. \tag{11}$$

That is, the optimal cash balance is independent of the timing of payments. Note that the number of sales and purchases of securities per period, n_k, is

$$n_k = \left(\frac{\frac{Tr}{k^2}}{2a} \right)^{\frac{1}{2}} = \frac{1}{k} \left(\frac{Tr}{2a} \right)^{\frac{1}{2}} = \frac{n}{k} \tag{12}$$

where n is the number of sales and purchases per year.

Although the optimal average cash balance is unaffected by frequency of receipts, this does not imply that the frequency is of no importance. Optimal average short-term security holdings will be

$$B^* = \frac{T}{2k} - C^*. \tag{13}$$

Since B^* is dependent on k, the profits from cash management will be affected. This result can easily be generalized to cases in which various percentages of yearly receipts are received at various frequencies per year. If $y_1 =$ percentage of T which is received k_1 evenly spaced times per year, then

$$B^* = \frac{1}{2} \left[\frac{y_1}{k_1} + \frac{y_2}{k_2} + \ldots + \frac{y_n}{k_n} \right] T - C^* = \frac{T}{2} \sum_{i=1}^{n} \frac{y_1}{k_1} - C^*. \tag{14}$$

Note that $y_1 T$ is the total amount received over the year in receipts coming in k_1 times; therefore, the size of each of the receipts is $\dfrac{y_1}{k_1} T$. The profits from cash management are thus heavily dependent upon the percentages of T coming in infrequent receipts. For example if once a year receipts are one half the total and quarterly receipts one half, then $B^* = \dfrac{T}{2} [\dfrac{1}{2} + \dfrac{1}{2} (\dfrac{1}{4})] - C^* = \dfrac{5}{16} T - C^*$. But if quarterly and monthly receipts are each one half the total, $B^* = \dfrac{T}{2} [\dfrac{1}{2} (\dfrac{1}{4}) + \dfrac{1}{2} (\dfrac{1}{12})] - C^* = \dfrac{T}{12} - C^*$.[7]

---

7. The effects of timing on optimal cash and bond holdings can be generalized to cases where receipts are not evenly spaced throughout the year. Consider, for example, the case of equal receipts twice a year, but instead of being evenly spaced suppose they are received at the start of the first and second quarters. Assume that payments are at a constant rate throughout the year. The first

Although C* is invariant over a wide range of assumptions with respect to timing, this conclusion is subject to an important qualification. It holds only if T is large enough and/or k is small enough to ensure that it is profitable to buy and sell securities during the period. From (1)

$$Z = \frac{r}{k}\left(\frac{T}{2k} - \frac{T}{2kn_k}\right) - n_k a \geqq 0, \tag{15}$$

for switching to occur. For minimal switching $n_k = 2$ and thus

$$\frac{r}{k}\left(\frac{T}{2k} - \frac{T}{4k}\right) - 2a \geqq 0$$

$$T \geqq \frac{8k^2 a}{r}. \tag{16}$$

The minimal size T for switching to occur is thus dependent upon the frequency of receipts. It is instructive to consider the effects of the frequency of receipts on the size T must be to have switching occur. Suppose $a = \$20$ and $r = .05$.[8] Then to have switching occur,

for yearly receipts	$k = 1$ and $T \geqq$	3,200;
for twice yearly receipts	$k = 2$ and $T \geqq$	12,800;
for quarterly receipts	$k = 4$ and $T \geqq$	51,200;
for monthly receipts	$k = 12$ and $T \geqq$	460,800;
for weekly receipts	$k = 52$ and $T \geqq$	8,652,800.

Thus if there are frequent receipts, T must be large indeed before any gains from cash management will occur.

If there is no switching between cash and short-term securities, we are back to the simple pre-inventory model world. The average cash balance will be

---

receipt is thus adequate to meet all the payments for the first half year. Therefore, all the second receipt will be invested throughout the second quarter. Optimal cash balances will again not have been changed, but optimal bond holdings will go up by the size of each receipt times one quarter of a year. This result can be generalized to include any number of unevenly spaced receipts per year. If $M =$ length of time the receipts are speeded up in units of length $\frac{1}{n}$, where $M = 1, 2, \ldots$, n_{k-1}; and $m =$ number of times per year the speeded up receipts occur, $m = 1, 2, \ldots, k$; then the average bond holdings per year (B') will be

$$B' = B* + \frac{2mM}{k(n_{k-1})} B*$$

where B* is the equally spaced receipts solution. For example, if receipts are monthly and the number of purchases and sales per month is four, suppose twice a year the monthly receipts arrive one week early, then $n_k = 4$, $k = 12$, $m = 2$, $M = 1$ and $B' = 1\frac{1}{6}B*$. The implication of this result is that although average cash holdings remain independent of the frequency as well as the evenness of receipts, average bond holdings, and thus profits, increase with lower frequency and more unevenness.

8. These would seem to be not unreasonable values for a and r. With short-term money at about 5%, some firms with as little to invest as $100,000 are going into the market over weekends. The return on $100,000 invested at 5%, for three days is $41.67. Since there are two transactions involved, the transactions cost must be somewhat less than half this amount.

$$C = \frac{T}{2k} \tag{17}$$

and since for this to occur, $T < \dfrac{8k^2a}{r}$

$$C < \frac{4ka}{r}. \tag{18}$$

For $a = \$20$ and $r = .05$ the average cash balance can be as high as:

$$
\begin{array}{ll}
\text{for } k = 1 & C = \$\ 1{,}600 \\
\text{for } k = 2 & C = \$\ 3{,}200 \\
\text{for } k = 4 & C = \$\ 6{,}400 \\
\text{for } k = 12 & C = \$19{,}200 \\
\text{for } k = 52 & C = \$83{,}200
\end{array}
$$

Although these results with no switching may seem irrelevant since we are not dealing here with small economic units, the results are equally applicable to branches or separate accounts of large economic units. In fact it will be shown that by far the greatest part of a large economic unit's cash balances for transaction purposes may very well be held in relatively small accounts for which switching does not occur.

IV. DECENTRALIZATION AND TIMING OF RECEIPTS

Consider a large economic unit with x per cent of T received by branches or accounts which are too small to optimize, and $1 - x$ per cent of T received by branches or accounts which optimize. From (6) and (17), the average cash balance will be,

$$C_0 = \left(\frac{Ta}{2r} \right)^{\frac{1}{2}} \sum_{j=1}^{J} (x_j)^{\frac{1}{2}} + \frac{xT}{2k} \tag{17}$$

where $\displaystyle\sum_{j=1}^{J} x_j = 1 - x$. The average cash balance, C_0, will thus partially follow the square root law and partially follow a linear relationship with respect to T. In order to estimate the relative importance of optimized and non-optimized cash balances on the total balance, consider first the two extremes of complete centralization (of the optimized portion) and complete decentralization.

With complete centralization of the optimized balances, from (10),

$$C_0 = \left[\frac{(1 - x)\, Ta}{2r} \right]^{\frac{1}{2}} + \frac{xT}{2k}. \tag{10a}$$

Given x, (10a) yields the smallest optimized cash balance, and thus the smallest C_0. With complete decentralization, from (7)

$$C_0 = \left[\frac{J\,(1 - x)\, Ta}{2r} \right]^{\frac{1}{2}} + \frac{xT}{2k}. \tag{10b}$$

Given x, (10b) yields the largest optimized cash balance, and thus the largest C_0.

Consider the minimum that x could be to have non-optimized cash equal to or greater than the optimized cash. For (10a)

$$\frac{xT}{2k} \geqq \left[\frac{(1-x)\,Ta}{2r} \right]^{\frac{1}{2}}$$

or

$$\frac{x^2}{1-x} \geqq \frac{2ka}{Tr}. \tag{18}$$

For our usual assumptions of $a = \$20$ and $r = .05$, and with $k = 12$ (monthly receipts),

$$\frac{x^2}{1-x} \geqq \frac{9600}{T}.$$

For very small x, $\dfrac{x^2}{1-x} = x^2$, and thus

$$x^2 \geqq \frac{9600}{T}.$$

It is easy to see the effects of the non-optimized cash balances on the total cash balances of a large economic unit. For example, for a firm with transactions of \$9.6 million per year, $x \geqq .03$ for non-optimized cash balances to be greater than optimized cash balances. For a firm with \$96 million, $x \geqq .01$, and for a firm with \$960 million (about 90th in size of sales on the *Fortune* 500 list), $x \geqq .001$. Thus for very large economic units, the size of the non-optimized balances in various branches and accounts may easily be much greater than the size of the optimized balances.[9]

This result casts grave doubt, to say the least, on the by now traditional transactions demand theory. According to the traditional theory, the cash balances of large economic units will follow the square root law with respect to T, and the cash balances will be interest elastic. The larger the economic unit, presumably the more likely are these results to occur. But the larger the economic unit, the greater the need for branches and special accounts, etc. Thus x is likely to increase with firm size, and, therefore, the size of non-optimized balances will become increasingly greater compared with optimized balances. The square root law will not be followed and there will be little or no interest elasticity. In fact rather than a square root law, we may find that average cash

9. This result is strengthened further for very large economic units which enter the market on a day-to-day basis. For units this large the observed balances will not be the average balance, but rather the end-of-day balance, which is, of course, also the end-of-period balance. The average balance, in fact, is of no concern since it occurs at some immeasurable point during the day. End-of-day balances will consist solely in whatever is left over after the day's switches into and out of short-term assets are made, and thus will be very small. In fact from footote 8 and with no uncertainty, the maximum that optimized balances can be at the end of a day is \$300,000. Thus the end-of-day balance should not increase with firm size. The relations among average cash balances, end-of-day cash balances and size of economic unit are considered in some detail in Case M. Sprenkle, "The Transactions Demand for Money Revisited," mimeo (submitted for publication).

balances increase more than proportionately with firm size, not because money is a "luxury," but rather because x may rise substantially with firm size.

It may be instructive to consider the explanatory power of the traditional theory as well as several of the various extensions of it suggested here, when applied to several examples.

V. Applications

Consider first the explanatory power of the traditional Baumol-Tobin model applied to very large industrial firms. Actual cash holdings at the end of 1966 were obtained from Moody's for 475 of the largest 500 industrial firms as listed by *Fortune;* the 25 other firms did not separate cash and short term assets in their accounts. Optimal cash holdings under complete centralization for each firm were obtained by using sales as a proxy for T and our usual assumptions that $a = \$20$ and $r = .05$. The ratio of the optimal cash holding to the actual cash holding for each firm was then obtained. The results, shown in Table I, indicate just how little the simple theory explains. For the largest 50 firms, on the average only 1.0% of firms' cash balances were explained by the simple model, and the greatest amount explained was 3.7%. For all the firms the median amount explained was only 2.5%, and for only 2 firms was more than 20% explained. Thus, on the average, 97.5% of the actual cash holdings of these large firms is unexplained by the simple Baumol-Tobin model with complete centralization, in only 8 cases is less than 90% unexplained, and in only 2 cases as little as 80%. Even if the transactions cost were significantly higher or the interest rate lower, the results would not be changed much. A quadrupling of a to $80, for example, would only double the percentages explained, so that for the largest 50 firms on the average 2% would be explained, and for the largest 500 only 5%.

Table I indicates that there is a very definite relationship between size of firm and percentage of cash balances explained. As size of firm increases, the percentage explained decreases. This result is suggestive in several ways. First it indicates that actual cash holdings increase by more than the square root of sales over this size range of firms. In fact, as will be shown below, cash holdings seem to increase approximately linearly with respect to sales. Second, the decrease in explanatory power as firm size increases suggests that the necessity for increased numbers of branches as firm size increases may be of some real importance in determining cash balances.

Consider first the case of complete specialization. Since we do not know J, the number of branches for any firm, we cannot determine $C_J{}^*$, the optimal cash balance for a completely decentralized firm. However, we can ask the question, how large would J have to be in order to explain the actual cash holdings? Equation (7) can be rewritten

$$J = \left(\frac{C_J{}^*}{C^*} \right)^2.$$

To explain the actual cash holdings, we in effect let $C_J{}^*$ equal the actual cash, and thus J is equal to the square of the inverse of the percentage of the actual cash explained by the simple centralized Baumol-Tobin model. The number of branches necessary to explain the actual cash holdings for the average firm in each size group is shown in the second-to-last line of Table 1. Thus to explain the actual cash holdings of the average firm of the largest 50, there must be 10,000 equal sized branches, etc. However, the median sales for the largest 50 firms is $2.25 billion, thus each of the 10,000 branches would have to have

TABLE 1

PERCENTAGE OF ACTUAL CASH BALANCES EXPLAINED BY THE TOBIN-BAUMOL MODEL

Number of firms with percentage		Rank of Firms by size of sales, 1966						
from	to	1-50	51-100	101-200	201-300	301-400	401-500	All 500
0	.5%	7		1		2		10
.5	1.0%	19	8	11	2	3	3	46
1.0	2.0%	13	21	46	23	17	13	133
2.0	3.0%	6	11	21	24	17	9	88
3.0	4.0%	4	2	10	24	25	24	89
4.0	5.0%		3	3	9	13	11	39
5.0	6.0%		1	2	5	6	8	22
6.0	7.0%				4	5	7	16
7.0	8.0%			1			7	8
8.0	9.0%		1		1	2	7	11
9.0	10.0%			1	1	1	2	5
10.0	20.0%			1	2	2	1	6
Over	20%				1		1	2
Median percentage		1.0	1.6	1.9	2.9	3.1	3.9	2.5
Mean percentage		1.3	2.1	2.2	3.3	3.6	4.4	3.0
No. of firms observed		49	47	97	96	93	93	475
No. of branches necessary		10,000	3910	2780	1190	1040	660	1600
Percentage not optimized		66%	63%	80%	66%	72%	72%	

yearly receipts of only $225,000. This level of receipts might easily be so low as to preclude any optimization of cash. Explaining the actual level of cash balances by the necessity for branches is thus seen to be impossible.

Although the level of actual cash balances cannot be explained by the necessity for branches, branches may be able to explain the differences in cash holdings among the different size groups. The fact that as firm size decreases the percentage of actual cash explained by the simple models increases, suggests that the difference in percentage explained may be caused by the increased necessity for branching for larger firms. The median yearly sales for the largest 50 firms is 15.1 times the sales for the median firm in the 401-500 size group. The number of branches necessary to explain actual cash for the largest 50 firms is precisely 15.1 times the number of branches for the 401-500 size group. Thus if the necessity for branching increases at the same rate as sales, the difference in percentage of actual cash explained will be accounted for. Although the relation between median sales and branches necessary is not in general as precise as this, it is close enough no matter what size groups are being compared to suggest that the differences in necessary branching determine the differences in the percentage of actual cash explaind by the simple model.

We might also consider the case in which the firms are assumed to have one central account which is optimized, and a number of small branches or accounts which are not. The question now is, how large would X (the percentage of T not optimized) have to be in order to explain the size of the balance. This can be obtained from equation (10a) for any firm using actual cash for C_0 and assuming k to be 12 (monthly receipts). The results for the median firm for each size group are shown in the last line of Table I. They show that in order to explain cash holdings in this manner, from two-thirds to four-fifths of all receipts must be put into non-optimal accounts. In addition there seems to be little if any effect of size of firm on these results. The lack of size effects on X is equivalent to the result of a linear relation between sales and cash holdings. In equation 10a the first term on the right is very small in relation to C_0 no matter the size of X. At most (when $X = 0$), this term would equal the optimal cash balance under the simple Baumol-Tobin assumptions and will thus be a very small percentage of C_0. The second term of the equation will thus essentially determine C_0, and if X is a constant over the size range considered here, the relation between sales and cash is linear.

The large values for X also seem absurd. With all the effort spent by large firms to speed the flow of receipts into centralized, optimized balances, it seems entirely unreasonable that such large proportions of funds would go into non-optimized balances.

The conclusion seems clear with respect to large firms: the transactions demand for money has little or nothing to do with the actual cash holdings of firms. As stated in the introduction, the level of actual cash balances can only be explained by the fact that firms pay for bank services by leaving deposits rather than by paying fees. If banks earn the market rate on deposits (actually they should earn somewhat less since a portion of the deposits must be held as reserves), and if *all* cash balances are to pay for bank services, then the $62 million of cash held by the median size firm in the largest 50 will buy $3.1 million of bank services per year. With annual sales of $2250 million, this would not seem to be entirely unreasonable as an upper limit to the amount of bank services this size firm might need per year.

The second application concerns the cash balances of state and local governments. In a recent article,[10] Aronson estimated the average optimal cash balances for state and local governments in each state, assuming complete centralization. That is, he assumed that for each state all receipts for the state and for all local governments in the state go into one account. He then compares these optimal balances with the actual balances of state and local governments in each state, and concludes that the state and local governments are mismanaging their cash and, therefore, foregoing substantial amounts of interest income. In most cases the optimal transaction balances he estimates are

10. J. Richard Aronson, "The Idle Cash Balances of State and Local Governments: An Economic Problem of National Concern," *Journal of Finance*, June 1968.

between one half of one percent and one percent of the actual balances. That is, they are similar to the results obtained above with respect to large firms assuming complete centralization.

The results obtained by Aronson are, of course, meaningless. In 1962, the year of his data, there were over 91,000 local governmental units in the U.S.— an average of over 1800 per state.[11] In addition, it is clear that not all state receipts go into one centralized account. Consider what optimal balances might be for the average state under some reasonable assumptions as to decentralization and the timing of receipts.

Expenditures by state governments are on the average about one third and expenditures by local governments about two thirds the total[12] expenditures per state. The average state and local expenditures per state in 1962 was about $1300 million[13] of which about $435 million was spent by the state government and $870 million by the (on the average) 1800 local units. The total cash balances for all state and local governments in 1962 was about $9500 million or an average of $190 million per state. Can this level of cash balances be explained by use of the various transactions demand models?

Assume first that for the hypothetical average state all receipts and expenditures are centralized in one account. In 1962 interest rates were lower than they are now, so assume $r = .04$. With a still $20 and T of $435 million,[14] the average cash balance of the state government will be about $1,040,000.

The size of the local government's cash balances, of course, will depend upon the size distribution of the 1800 units, and on the frequency of receipts if some of them are too small to optimize their cash balances. Suppose all the 1800 units are the same size. With total expenditures of $870 million, the average expenditure per unit will be slightly less than $500,000. With monthly receipts, this will be less than the minimum necessary to have switching occur [see (16) and the results below (16) but with $r = .04$ rather than .05]. With monthly receipts, local cash balances will be

$$C = \frac{T}{2k} = \frac{\$870 \text{ million}}{24} = \$36,250,000.$$

Thus total cash balances for the state and local governments should be approximately $37,300,000. The model has explained about 20% of the actual balances of $190 million compared with the less than one percent explained by the model using complete centralization. This is the largest cash balance which can be explained by decentralization, given k and given the assumption of complete centralization by the state government. With complete decentralization of the state cash balances and with $k = 12$, the total cash balances for the state and the local governments would be

$$C = \frac{T}{2k} = \frac{\$1300 \text{ million}}{24} = \$54,166,667.$$

11. See *Facts and Figures on Government Finance*, 14th Biennial Edition, 1967, Tax Foundation, New York, Table 2.

12. *Ibid.*, Table 103, data are for fiscal year 1965.

13. Aronson, *loc. cit.*, Table I.

14. Aronson assumes $a = \$100$ which would seem to be a gross misestimate which will overestimate the optimal cash balance for the completely centralized case.

That is, the cash balances that could be explained with complete decentralization and k = 12 amount to less than 30% of the actual balances.[15] In order to have the actual balances explained, k would have to be greater than four. If this were the case, however, it is clear that even with all local governments the same size, they would then be able to optimize their cash holdings. With only one purchase and one sale of short-term securities per quarter, their average cash balance would be halved, and again the size of the actual cash balances would be unexplained.

The implication of these results is that decentralization and timing cannot explain anywhere near the actual cash balances of state and local governments. The conclusion drawn from this result by Aronson that state and local governments mismanage their cash and forego substantial interest earnings does not necessarily follow, however. We have seen that large firms' cash balances also cannot be explained by transactions needs. If state and local governments receive bank services equal in value to bank earnings from their deposits, there would be no reason to conclude that mismanagement exists.[16] Without knowledge of the details of such possible services, no analysis of the transactions demand yields much in the way of evidence as to mismanagement.

VI. Conclusions

The simple transactions demand for money models have been shown to explain such a small proportion of actual cash balances for large economic units as to be totally useless. Transactions demand models which consider the effects of decentralization of cash management and the timing of receipts (or payments) can explain larger proportions of the actual balances, but the variations in results of the models are so great, depending on the specific assumptions made, that they are useless at present. Until substantial detailed knowledge of centralization and timing is known, there is no prospect of improved results. At present we cannot estimate the transactions demand for money for any large economic unit with any accuracy. Depending on the assumptions used, the largest estimate may be 50 or more times the smallest estimate. Even the largest estimate (with *a priori* unreasonable assumptions) cannot explain more than a small proportion of the actual balances. Therefore, it is clear that most cash balances are held for other than transactions purposes; they are, in fact, held to pay banks for their services. Until more is known as to the costs and demands for bank services, we will know next to nothing about the demand for money of large economic units. Since the cash balances of these large units account for about one-quarter to one-third of the total money supply, and since in addition they are most likely to vary with economic conditions with the least lag (in comparison with the cash balances of households), our lack of knowledge of the determinants of these balances is especially critical.

15. With k = 12 in this case the average cash balance would be equal to expenditures during a two-week period. Aronson uses a one week balance as an alternative measure of optimal transactions balances. This is equivalent to receipts every two weeks, or monthly receipts with one purchase and one sale of securities per month. His result for this case would be one half the result obtained here for the average balance if he had used the same value for a.

16. Of course, it may be that some of the bank services are services to particular politicians or public officials rather than to the governmental unit itself, in which case mismanagement of a different sort occurs.

[4]

NEW CALCULATIONS OF INCOME AND INTEREST ELASTICITIES IN TOBIN'S MODEL OF THE TRANSACTIONS DEMAND FOR MONEY

George A. Akerlof and Ross D. Milbourne*

Introduction

IN 1952 Baumol presented a simple inventory-theoretic approach to the transactions demand for money. If Y denotes the predetermined value of transactions, with an interest rate of r, and a constant transactions cost of a, the individual chooses equally spaced withdrawals of C to minimize total holding cost of cash. This cost is $aT/C + r(C/2)$, where $C/2$ is the average money holding and $r(C/2)$ is the opportunity cost of holding it. This total cost is minimized, if C is continuous, when

$$C = \sqrt{\frac{2aY}{r}},\qquad(1)$$

in which case the average money holding is

$$M = \sqrt{\frac{aY}{2r}}.\qquad(2)$$

This has become known as the "square root law" for money holding. It implies that the interest and income elasticities of the demand for money are, respectively,

$$\xi_r = \frac{dM}{dr}\frac{r}{M} = -\frac{1}{2}\qquad(3)$$

$$\xi_Y = \frac{dM}{dY}\frac{Y}{M} = \frac{1}{2}.\qquad(4)$$

However, if withdrawals are evenly spaced, then T/C must be an integer, in which case C is not continuous, and the calculus that yielded (1), and hence (2), (3), and (4), is not applicable.

A more appropriate framework of analysis was provided by Tobin (1956), who permitted the number of transactions to take on only integral values. In addition, he considered the individual as maximizing the net benefit from the timing of bond-money transactions.[1] At the start of the payments period, when income is received, the individual may transfer some of his money into bonds, earn interest, and hence transfer back into money when required for transactions. If r is the annual rate of interest, and there are T such payments periods in a year, then r/T is the rate of interest for each such payments period. It can be easily shown that if n transactions are made, the optimal policy is to transfer $((n - 1)/n)\,Y$ initially into bonds and make $n - 1$ further transactions of $(1/n)Y$ bonds into money. The revenue from this policy in each period is

$$R_n = \frac{r}{T}\left(\frac{n-1}{2n}\right)Y,\qquad(5)$$

and with fixed transfer costs of a, net revenue is[2]

$$\Pi_n = R_n - C_n = \frac{r}{T}\left(\frac{n-1}{2n}\right)Y - na.\qquad(6)$$

For n transactions to be profitable, $\Pi_n > \Pi_{n-1}$, or

$$Y > \frac{2aTn(n-1)}{r},\ n \geq 2.\qquad(7)$$

For example, if we assume that income is paid monthly, and $a = \$2$, $r = .05$, then for two transactions to be optimal (namely, a conversion each way), Y would have to be at least $\$1,920$ per month. A monthly salary below this figure would mean that the optimal policy would be never to transact.

Many economists have associated the preceding description of cash holding with the Baumol

* University of California, Berkeley, and London School of Economics; and Queens University, respectively.

The authors thank Marcelle Arak, Olivier Blanchard, and an anonymous referee for valuable comments. They would also like to thank the National Science Foundation for financial assistance under Research Grant SOC 75-23076 administered by the Institute of Business and Economic Research, University of California, Berkeley. This paper was revised while the first author was Visiting Research Economist at the Board of Governors of the Federal Reserve System.

[1] Tobin and others have referred to the alternative to money as "bonds," although that terminology may be a bit misleading. Actual real-world alternatives are savings and time deposits, certificates of deposit, bills, etc.

[2] The Tobin model also considered a variable cost of transactions proportional to amounts transacted, b_1. This paper will ignore the added complication due to such variable costs. We do not expect such addition to alter significantly the elasticities that are calculated, or the conclusions of the paper.

model, implicitly believing that the Tobin model, as just another transactions model, also has an implied interest elasticity of -0.5. One of the purposes of this paper is to demonstrate that this is certainly not true. The reason can be argued intuitively as follows. Equation (7) and the above example illustrate that only very high wage earners would transact at all during any one period. For small changes in r, only those people in the neighborhood of (7) and above would be likely to alter their money holdings by changing the number of transactions that they make. Consequently, the changes in aggregate money holdings will be due to changes by only a few people at the margin, and the interest elasticity is likely to be much closer to zero.

This has been somewhat pointed out in a recent paper by Barro (1976), which was brought to our notice only after our own analysis and results had been completed. He uses an approach similar to ours. However, it differs in two quite important respects. In the first instance, there appears to be an internal inconsistency in Barro's analysis. He derives average money holdings from Tobin's framework by applying an income distribution function. By choosing the gamma distribution, this gives a neat relation between average money holdings and average income. However, he substitutes this average income into the *Baumol* square-root formula to obtain the average (Baumol) number of transactions, which is used parametrically to describe the resulting elasticity values. His analysis is therefore not free of Baumol's procedure. We also follow a more intuitive approach of presenting elasticities in terms of exogenous parameters, rather than the endogenously determined Baumol average number of transactions.[3]

In the second case, and perhaps more importantly, ours is a multi-period model. We allow the individual to optimize over a period larger than each payment—in particular, to carry savings forward, and to decide upon the optimal timing of savings transfers to bonds, as well as upon conversions for transactions. In reality, many bond transactions are made for savings purposes.

The Model

Assume that households are paid income in equally spaced periods and save a constant frac-

[3] For a demonstration that Barro's procedure can be misleading, see footnote 10.

tion, s, of this income, which they can accumulate forward as money balances until it is optimal to transfer it into bonds.[4] If the transactions rate is constant, and all received income is held as money balances, the money-balance profile will be as in figure 1, where the sawtooth pattern rises

FIGURE 1.—MONEY BALANCES AS A FUNCTION OF TIME

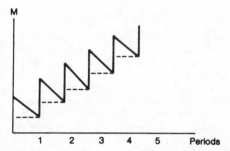

at a slope of s. Assume that income is received T times during some time interval, which for expositional purposes we take to be a year. This is then a T-period horizon model with income received at the start of each period. To find the optimal number and timing of transactions between bonds and money, consider two categories of households.

Category I consists of those households whose income is sufficient to warrant bond-money transfers during each period to meet transactions requirements—that is, those whose income satisfies (7) for $n = 2$. Category II consists of those households whose income is below this level, and that make no transfers for transactions purposes, but that may still transfer accumulated savings into bonds at certain periods.

We deal first with category II. An optimal policy for savings transactions can be established by the following observations. Consider a particular period, say, the first. Let W denote the income per period.[5]

1. Any transfer of savings into bonds during this period cannot exceed sW. If this were

[4] "Saving" here is at least a slight misnomer. Some savings, for example, social security payments, are taken directly out of the weekly paycheck. Other savings such as life insurance are paid monthly. Such "contractual savings" are not included in the ratio s. It is largely for this reason that table 1 calculates income and interest elasticities for rather low values of s. For expositional purposes we shall, however, refer to s as the "savings ratio."

[5] We change notation, since $W \neq$ Tobin's Y, since Y is total transactions.

not the case, there would have to be a reverse transaction of bonds to money before the end of the period, which is not optimal for category II households.

2. If a transfer of savings into bonds is optimal during this period, it will not be less than sW. This follows, since there is a positive opportunity cost of holding excess money balances, given that a transfer is being made in this period. As a consequence of 1 and 2, the amount of savings transferred for the first transfer (at any point in time) is given by the horizontal dashed lines in figure 1.

3. A savings transfer, if made at all, will be made at the start of, and never during, any period. This is obvious, since the full amount of transferable savings is available at the start of any period, implying an opportunity cost in the case of a later transfer.

The optimal policy is then to select, for the given level of income, the optimal number of times during the year to transfer savings, and to transfer the full amount of accumulated savings at that time. If a household transfers λ times during the T periods, at spaces of $m = T/\lambda$ periods (m an integer), it involves a transfer each time of msW. The first transfer will occur at the start of period m, and hence interest will be earned for $T + 1 - m$ periods. Revenue from transferring λ times is then[6]

$$R_\lambda = rmsW \left(\frac{T + 1 - m}{T} + \frac{T + 1 - 2m}{T} \right.$$

$$\left. + \ldots + \frac{1}{T} \right)$$

$$= rmsW \sum_{i=1}^{\lambda = T/m} \left(\frac{T + 1 - im}{T} \right),$$

which, after summing and rearranging, yields

$$R_\lambda = rsW \left(\frac{T + 2}{2} - \frac{T}{2\lambda} \right). \qquad (8)$$

Net revenue is then

$$\Pi_\lambda = rsW \left(\frac{T + 2}{2} - \frac{T}{2\lambda} \right) - \lambda a, \qquad (9)$$

and, hence, at least λ transactions will be profitable when

$$\Pi_\lambda > \Pi_{\lambda - 1},$$

[6] Since transferring at the start of the last period will still yield the interest for that period.

or

$$W > \frac{2a\lambda(\lambda - 1)}{rsT}, \qquad \lambda \geq 1. \qquad (10)$$

The average money holdings from carrying savings over the m periods between transfers $(M_{\lambda, m}{}^s)$ will then be

$$\frac{1}{m} \sum_{i=0}^{m-1} isW = \frac{sW(m - 1)}{2},$$

or

$$M_{\lambda, m}{}^s = \frac{sW(T - \lambda)}{2\lambda} \qquad (11)$$

on substituting for m.

The average money balance from transactions demand is just $(1 - s)W/2$, since households in category II make no transfers for transactions purposes. Consequently, average money demand for households in category II, with λ optimal savings transfers, is

$$M_\lambda = \frac{sW(T - \lambda)}{2\lambda} + \frac{(1 - s)W}{2}. \qquad (12)$$

We now consider households in category I. Clearly, any household that finds it optimal to transfer transactions money into bonds at the beginning of a period will also transfer any savings then, since the transactions cost has already been met, and the marginal cost in doing so is therefore zero. That is, households in category I will transfer each period's savings at the beginning of the period, and the contribution of savings to average money balances is consequently zero for this category. For one conversion from money to bonds, and n conversions back the other way, we have, by the same process that led to (7), these n transactions being optimal if

$$\frac{2aTn(n + 1)}{r(1 - s)} < W < \frac{2aT(n + 1)(n + 2)}{r(1 - s)}, \qquad (13)$$

whereupon the average money demand is

$$M_n = \frac{(1 - s)W}{2(n + 1)}. \qquad (14)$$

Given a density $f(W)$ over the income per period, money demand can then be aggregated. Substituting $n = 1$ in the left-hand side of (13) gives $4aT/r(1 - s)$ as the income boundary between categories I and II. Consequently, average money holdings from transactions for all households in category I is

$$\int_0^{4aT/r(1-s)} \frac{(1-s)W}{2} f(W)dW, \qquad (15)$$

which follows from the second term in (12). The first term in (12) gives the average money demand from savings transfers for those in category II. Denote the values of λ such that T/λ is an integer as $\lambda_1, \ldots, \lambda_k$ ordered so that $\lambda_1 = 1, \lambda_k = T$. For notational convenience, define

$$\alpha = \frac{2a\lambda_i}{rsT}, \quad \beta = \frac{2aT(n+1)}{r(1-s)}. \qquad (16)$$

Average money demand from all households transferring savings λ_i times is

$$\int_{\alpha(\lambda_i-1)}^{\alpha(\lambda_i+1)} \frac{sW(T-\lambda_i)}{2\lambda_i} f(W)dW, \qquad (17)$$

where $\alpha(\lambda_i - 1)$, $\alpha(\lambda_i + 1)$ are the applicable income bounds for making λ_i transactions (from (10)). Finally, total demand for those in category I making n transactions is

$$\int_{\beta n}^{\beta(n+2)} \frac{(1-s)W}{2(n+1)} f(W)dW, \qquad (18)$$

which follows from (13) and (14), and substitution of (16).

Thus, from (15), (17), and (18), aggregate money demand is

$$M^d = \int_0^{4aT/r(1-s)} \frac{(1-s)W}{2} f(W)dW$$

$$+ \sum_{i=1}^m \int_{\alpha(\lambda_i-1)}^{\alpha(\lambda_i+1)} \frac{sW(T-\lambda_i)}{2\lambda_i} f(W)dW$$

$$+ \sum_{n=1}^\infty \int_{\beta n}^{\beta(n+2)} \frac{(1-s)W}{2(n+1)} f(W)dW. \qquad (19)$$

The endogenous parameters in (19) are a, r, s, and T, and hence one can calculate exact elasticities for different ranges of these parameters. When $s = 0$, the pure Tobin case is obtained, and reworking the analysis yields (19) without the second term, with $s = 0$ in the first and third terms.

Calculated Values of Elasticities

Data from the 1970 U.S. Census of Population on income of families in the previous year were used to estimate the elasticities.[7] A piecewise

linear distribution function was fitted, except for the final open-ended class interval, where a Pareto distribution was fitted.[8] The interest elasticities were computed using (19) and the derivative of (19) with respect to r.

For the income elasticity, there are factors working in opposite directions. An increase in income will induce some people in category I to switch from n to $n + 1$ bond-money transactions, hence *lowering* their average money balances. Similarly, there will be some households in category II induced to transfer their savings more frequently, hence lowering their money balances; in addition, an increase in income will shift some people from category II to category I, which results in lower money holdings. Offsetting this will be the (much more frequent) increase in money balances of those not induced to change their number of transactions. In this type of aggregate model, the income elasticity of the demand for money depends upon to whom the income increase is given. For the calculations here, it has been assumed that the increase has applied to all households equally.

We selected $T = 12$,[9] giving monthly income payments. Values of income and interest elasticities are displayed in table 1 for selected values of a, r, and s. The negative sign of the interest elasticities has been suppressed.

Comments and Conclusions

(1) For the pure Tobin case $s = 0$, the interest elasticities are extremely small, unless there are both very high interest rates and low transactions costs. The notion that has prevailed since Tobin's seminal paper in 1956—namely, that such transactions demand models provide a theoretical justification for interest elasticity of the demand for money—can thus be seen to require also severe restrictions on the ranges of a and r.

---

[7] The year 1969 was selected because of the accuracy of data for a census year. The liquidity crunch in 1969 must have depressed actual holdings below desired. For the predictions of aggregate money holdings there would be an even greater

discrepancy between desired holdings and the predictions of these transactions demand models than between realized and predicted values. This strengthens the conclusions.

[8] Estimation of the two Pareto parameters requires two pieces of information. The total density of the last class gave one. For the second, we assumed that the density at the lower boundary equaled the density at the upper boundary of the previous class interval.

[9] Higher values of T would decrease interest elasticities and increase income elasticities. Since payments at intervals greater than one month are quite uncommon, the elasticity calculations in table 1 can therefore be considered lower bounds for η_w and upper bounds for $-\eta_r$.

INCOME AND INTEREST ELASTICITIES 545

TABLE 1.—CALCULATED INTEREST (η_r) AND INCOME (η_w) ELASTICITIES

	a	$2.50		$5.00		$7.50		$10.00	
s	r	η_r	η_w	η_r	η_w	η_r	η_w	η_r	η_w
0	.025	.0006	.8489	.0000[a]	.7047	.0000[a]	.6017	.0000[a]	.5251
	.05	.1401	.7934	.0006	.8489	.0000[a]	.7705	.0000[a]	.7047
	.075	.2971	.4912	.0152	.9046	.0006	.8498	.0000[a]	.7953
	.10	.4945	.4837	.1401	.7934	.0060	.8934	.0006	.8498
.025	.025	.0399	.8217	.0112	.6836	.0004	.5825	.0000[a]	.5435
	.05	.1801	.7622	.0399	.8217	.0778	.7234	.0112	.6835
	.075	.3124	.5380	.0807	.8463	.0399	.8217	.0641	.7543
	.10	.4932	.4839	.1800	.7622	.0860	.8265	.0399	.8217
.05	.025	.1386	.7514	.0584	.7023	.1088	.5846	.0151	.5496
	.05	.1832	.7707	.1386	.7514	.1264	.6966	.0584	.7022
	.075	.3360	.5524	.0762	.8523	.1386	.7514	.1103	.7271
	.10	.2403	.4899	.1832	.7707	.0854	.8324	.1386	.7514
.075	.025	.0893	.7900	.1361	.6451	.0695	.6320	.0162	.5459
	.05	.1403	.7923	.0893	.7900	.1753	.6663	.1361	.6466
	.075	.3786	.5599	.1269	.8237	.0893	.7900	.1460	.7001
	.10	.2614	.4823	.1403	.7923	.1506	.7948	.0893	.7900
.10	.025	.1786	.7395	.2022	.6039	.1736	.5569	.0769	.5858
	.05	.1545	.7906	.1786	.7395	.1211	.7090	.2022	.6039
	.075	.3914	.5686	.1076	.8263	.1786	.7395	.1054	.7386
	.10	.3179	.4421	.1567	.8867	.1281	.7995	.1786	.7395

[a] Significant only in the fifth decimal place or beyond.

Note: a = transactions cost; r = interest rate; s = savings ratio. For a constant value of s, the ratio a/r actually is sufficient to determine the elasticities, as can be seen by examining (19). Consequently, the diagonal pairs for each s turn out to be equivalent. We think it more intuitive, however, to present the table as it is.

It seems more plausible to argue the reverse. The incorporation of savings behavior does, however, raise the interest elasticities, though not necessarily monotonically.

(2) Because of the complex nature of (19), one cannot get monotonic changes in the elasticities by varying the parameters. For example, an increase in s increases the boundaries and decreases the integrand in the first and third terms, and has the reverse effect on the second. Moreover, such changes affect the derivatives and values of M in the same way. These considerations are reflected in the calculations. However, the following observations seem fairly general:

a. The highest interest elasticity occurs when the savings ratio and transactions costs are extremely low, simultaneously with very high rates of interest. In these situations, the average money demand is very low (approximately one-third of average monthly income), and hence (r/M) is very high. No other combination of a and s, given a high interest rate, is able to produce such an effect.

b. For low values of a, higher rates of interest have lower income elasticities, while the reverse is the case for higher values of a. This is true for the same reasons as the result of (a), above. When transactions costs are low, high interest rates shift the boundaries between transactions much closer to the lower end of the distribution. Consequently, a greater number of people switch optimal policy, which has a substantial negative effect upon η_w.

c. In general, the interest elasticities are substantially below 0.5, and income elasticities vary between 0.5 and unity.[10] The variation

[10] Barro proves in his article that $0 < |\eta_r| < 0.5$ and $0.5 < \eta_w < 1.0$. However, unfortunately this is not true in general, and is dependent upon the combination of his definition of the average number of transactions, and the gamma distribution for income. For example, one could exhibit an income distribution that yields negative income elasticity, namely, a density that has support only near each boundary separating optimal numbers of transactions. An increase in each household's income pushes everyone to transact more and lowers everyone's average demand for money. In reality, most reasonable income distributions will not do this, but the income elasticity can certainly fall below 0.5. Cases in point are the exact elasticities above for $a = 2.5$ and $r = 0.10$ over every value of s.

The difficulty with using a Baumol substitution is shown precisely by this example, where the fact is hidden that there are a number of people who will actually reduce money demand.

is quite substantial and certainly not uniform.

(3) The model's predictions for aggregate household demand for money, given optimal holding of cash balances, are presented in table 2.

TABLE 2.—PREDICTED AGGREGATE MONEY DEMAND
($ billions 1969), $r = 7.5\%$
(actual = $123.347)

s \ a	2.5	5.0	7.5	10.0
0	25.064	29.993	32.252	34.473
.025	28.365	35.267	39.468	43.007
.05	28.900	36.071	40.499	45.003
075	29.266	36.327	41.345	45.624
.10	29.317	36.599	41.652	46.595

Currency plus demand deposits in 1969 for the household sector were $123.347 billion.[11] The rate on commercial paper in 1969 was 7.83%.[12] The predictions of aggregate demand are given for $r =. 7.5\%$, over different values of a and s. They predict, on average, approximately 30% of actual cash balances, with the highest, $s = 0.1$, $a = 10$, predicting only 38%.

As is well known, the size of cash holdings in general is difficult to explain, one important complication being the hoarding of currency, and the use of currency for illegal transactions and tax evasion. However, currency in circulation in July 1969 was $45.2 billion,[13] so that hoarding practices cannot account for the large discrepancy between the predictions of such transactions models and actual holdings. One explanation is the holding of buffer stocks to deal with uncertain flows in expenditures and receipts,

which are not a feature of the models considered here. Nevertheless, the degree of discrepancy between predicted and actual holdings for households seems to agree with Sprenkle's (1969) finding for firms, namely, that transactions models substantially underpredict actual balances. In summary, we offer the following conclusions:

i. Interest elasticities in the Tobin model are very close to zero, except for a combination of high rates of interest and low transactions costs, and are certainly much less than 0.5 as in the original formulation of Baumol;

ii. both income and interest elasticities vary widely with the "square root law" significantly overestimating interest and, in general, underestimating income, elasticities;

iii. the inclusion of savings behaviour, that is, positive drift in the cash balance, raises the interest elasticities; and

iv. transactions demand models appear to underpredict significantly actual aggregate household demand for money.

REFERENCES

Barro, Robert J., "Integral Constraints and Aggregation in an Inventory Model of Money Demand," *Journal of Finance* 31 (Mar. 1976), 77–87.
Baumol, William J., "The Transactions Demand for Cash—An Inventory Theoretic Approach," *Quarterly Journal of Economics* 66 (Nov. 1952), 545–556.
Board of Governors of the Federal Reserve System, *Federal Reserve Bulletin* 56(6) (June 1970).
——, *Flow of Funds Accounts, 1945–1972* (Aug. 1973).
Sprenkle, Case M., "The Uselessness of Transactions Demand Models," *Journal of Finance* 24 (Dec. 1969), 835–847.
Tobin, James, "The Interest-Elasticity of Transactions Demand for Cash," this REVIEW 38 (Aug. 1956), 241–247.
U.S. Department of Commerce, Social and Economic Statistics Administration, *Census of Population* (1970).

[11] Board of Governors of the Federal Reserve System (1973), p. 84. The figure includes personal trusts and nonprofit organizations.
[12] Board of Governors of the Federal Reserve System (1973), p. 260.
[13] Board of Governors of the Federal Reserve System (1970).

Part II
The Portfolio Approach

[5]

A Suggestion for Simplifying the Theory of Money[1]

By J. R. HICKS

AFTER the thunderstorms of recent years, it is with peculiar diffidence and even apprehension that one ventures to open one's mouth on the subject of money. In my own case these feelings are particularly intense, because I feel myself to be very much of a novice at the subject. My education has been mostly in the non-monetary parts of economics, and I have only come to be interested in money because I found that I could not keep it out of my non-monetary problems. Yet I am encouraged on reflection to hope that this may not prove a bad approach to the subject: that some things at least which are not very evident on direct inspection may become clearer from a cross-light of this sort.

It is of course very largely by such cross-fertilisation that economics progresses, and at least one department of non-monetary economics has hardly emerged from a very intimate affair with monetary theory. I do not, however, propose to resume this particular liaison. One understands that most economists have now read Böhm-Bawerk; yet whatever that union has bred, it has not been concord. I should prefer to seek illumination from another point of view—from a branch of economics which is more elementary, but, I think, in consequence better developed—the theory of value.

To anyone who comes over from the theory of value to the theory of money, there are a number of things which are rather startling. Chief of these is the preoccupation of monetary theorists with a certain equation, which states that the price of goods multiplied by the quantity of goods equals the amount of money which is spent on them. This equation crops up again and again, and it has all sorts of ingenious little arithmetical tricks performed on it. Sometimes it comes out

[1] A paper read at the Economic Club, November 1934. The reader is asked to bear in mind the fact that the paper was written to be read aloud, and to excuse certain pieces of mischief.

I

2   ECONOMICA   [FEBRUARY

as $MV = PT$; and once, in its most stupendous trans-figuration, it blossomed into $P = \dfrac{E}{O} + \dfrac{I' - S}{R}$. Now we, of the theory of value, are not unfamiliar with this equation, and there was a time when we used to attach as much importance to it as monetary theorists seem to do still. This was in the middle of the last century, when we used to talk about value being " a ratio between demand and supply." Even now, we accept the equation, and work it, more or less implicitly, into our systems. But we are rather inclined to take it for granted, since it is rather tautologous, and since we have found that another equation, not alternative to the quantity equation, but complementary with it, is much more significant. This is the equation which states that the relative value of two commodities depends upon their relative marginal utility.

Now, to an *ingénu*, who comes over to monetary theory, it is extremely trying to be deprived of this sheet-anchor. It was marginal utility that really made sense of the theory of value; and to come to a branch of economics which does without marginal utility altogether! No wonder there are such difficulties and such differences! What is wanted is a " marginal revolution "!

That is my suggestion. But I know that it will meet with apparently crushing objections. I shall be told that the suggestion has been tried out before. It was tried by Wicksell, and though it led to interesting results, it did not lead to a marginal utility theory of money. It was tried by Mises, and led to the conclusion that money is a ghost of gold—because, so it appeared, money as such has no marginal utility.[1] The suggestion has a history, and its history is not encouraging.

This would be enough to frighten one off, were it not for two things. Both in the theory of value and in the theory of money there have been developments in the twenty or thirty

---

[1] A more subtle form of the same difficulty appears in the work of Marshall and his followers. They were aware that money ought to be subjected to marginal utility analysis ; but they were so dominated by the classical conception of money as a " veil " (which is valid enough at a certain level of approximation) that they persisted in regarding the demand for money as a demand for the things which money can buy— " real balances." As a result of this, their invocation of marginal utility remained little more than a pious hope. For they were unable to distinguish, on marginal utility lines, between the desire to save and the desire to hoard ; and they necessarily overlooked that indeterminateness in the " real balance " (so important in some applications of monetary theory), which occurs when the prices of consumption goods are expected to change. On the other hand, I must admit that some versions of the Marshallian theory come very close to what I am driving at. Cf. Lavington, *English Capital Market,* ch. vi.

years since Wicksell and Mises wrote. And these developments have considerably reduced the barriers that blocked their way.

In the theory of value, the work of Pareto, Wicksteed, and their successors, has broadened and deepened our whole conception of marginal utility. We now realise that the marginal utility analysis is nothing else than a general theory of choice, which is applicable whenever the choice is between alternatives that are capable of quantitative expression. Now money is obviously capable of quantitative expression, and therefore the objection that money has no marginal utility must be wrong. People do choose to have money rather than other things, and therefore, in the relevant sense, money must have a marginal utility.

But merely to call that marginal utility X, and then proceed to draw curves, would not be very helpful. Fortunately the developments in monetary theory to which I alluded come to our rescue.

Mr. Keynes' " Treatise," so far as I have been able to discover, contains at least three theories of money. One of them is the Savings and Investment theory, which, as I hinted, seems to me only a quantity theory much glorified. One of them is a Wicksellian natural rate theory. But the third is altogether much more interesting. It emerges when Mr. Keynes begins to talk about the price-level of investment goods; when he shows that this price-level depends upon the relative preference of the investor—to hold bank-deposits or to hold securities. Here at last we have something which to a value theorist looks sensible and interesting! Here at last we have a choice at the margin! And Mr. Keynes goes on to put substance into our X, by his doctrine that the relative prefer-ence depends upon the " bearishness " or " bullishness " of the public, upon their relative desire for liquidity or profit.

My suggestion may, therefore, be re-formulated. It seems to me that this third theory of Mr. Keynes really contains the most important part of his theoretical contribution; that here, at last, we have something which, on the analogy (the appropri-ate analogy) of value theory, does begin to offer a chance of making the whole thing easily intelligible; that it is from this point, not from velocity of circulation, natural rate of interest, or Saving and Investment, that we ought to start in con-structing the theory of money. But in saying this, I am being more Keynesian than Keynes; I must endeavour to defend my position in detail.

II

The essence of the method I am proposing is that we should take the position of an individual at a particular point of time, and enquire what determines the precise quantity of money which he will desire to hold. But even to this simple formulation of the problem it is necessary to append two footnotes.

1. " Point of Time." We are dealing with an individual decision to hold money *or* something else, and such a decision is always made at a point of time. It is only by concentrating on decisions made at particular points of time that we can apply the theory of value to the problem at all. A very large amount of current controversy about money seems to me to be due to the attempt, superficially natural, but, in fact, highly inconvenient, to establish a close relation between the demand for money and *income*. Now the simple consideration that the decision to hold money is always made at a point of time shows that the connection between income and the demand for money must always be indirect. And in fact the whole conception of income is so intricate and beset by so many perplexing difficulties, that the establishment of any connection with income ought only to be hoped for at a late stage of investigation.[1]

2. " Money." What sort of money are we considering ? For the present, any sort of money. The following analysis will apply equally whether we think of money as notes, or bank deposits, or even metallic coins. It is true that with a metallic currency there is an ordinary commodity demand for the money substance to be considered, but it is relatively unimportant for most of our purposes. Perhaps it will be best if we take as our standard case that of a pure paper currency in a community where there are no banks. What follows has much wider application in reality. Only I would just ask you to keep this standard case in mind, since by using it as a basis for discussion, we may be able to save time a little.

An individual's decision to hold so much money means that he prefers to hold that amount of money, rather than either less or more. Now what are the precise contents of these displaced alternatives ? He could reduce his holding of money in three ways:

[1] Cf. Lindahl, *The Concept of Income* (Essays in honour of Gustav Cassel).

1935] SUGGESTION FOR SIMPLIFYING THE THEORY OF MONEY 5

1. by spending, i.e. buying something, it does not matter what;
2. by lending money to someone else;
3. by paying off debts which he owes to someone else.

He can increase his holding of money in three corresponding ways:

1. by selling something else which he owns;
2. by borrowing from someone else;
3. by demanding repayment of money which is owed by someone else.

This classification is, I think, complete. All ways of changing one's holding of money can be reduced to one of these classes or a combination of two of them—purchase or sale, the creation of new debts or the extinction of old.

If a person decides to hold money, it is implied that he prefers to do this than to adopt any of these three alternatives. But how is such a preference possible ?

A preference for holding money instead of spending it on consumption goods presents no serious difficulty, for it is obviously the ordinary case of a preference for future satisfactions over present. At any moment, an individual will not usually devote the whole of his available resources to satisfying present wants—a part will be set aside to meet the needs of the future.

The critical question arises when we look for an explanation of the preference for holding money rather than capital goods. For capital goods will ordinarily yield a positive rate of return, which money does not. What has to be explained is the decision to hold assets in the form of barren money, rather than of interest- or profit-yielding securities. And obviously just the same question arises over our second and third types of utilisation. So long as rates of interest are positive, the decision to hold money rather than lend it, or use it to pay off old debts, is apparently an unprofitable one.

This, as I see it, is really the central issue in the pure theory of money. Either we have to give an explanation of the fact that people do hold money when rates of interest are positive, or we have to evade the difficulty somehow. It is the great traditional evasions which have led to Velocities of Circulation, Natural Rates of Interest, *et id genus omne.*[1]

[1] I do not wish to deny that these concepts have a use in their appropriate place—that is to say, in particular applications of monetary theory. But it seems to me that

Of course, the great evaders would not have denied that there must be some explanation of the fact. But they would have put it down to "frictions," and since there was no adequate place for frictions in the rest of their economic theory, a theory of money based on frictions did not seem to them a promising field for economic analysis.

This is where I disagree. I think we have to look the frictions in the face, and see if they are really so refractory after all. This will, of course, mean that we cannot allow them to go to sleep under so vague a title.

III

The most obvious sort of friction, and undoubtedly one of the most important, is the cost of transferring assets from one form to another. This is of exactly the same character as the cost of transfer which acts as a certain impediment to change in all parts of the economic system; it doubtless comprises subjective elements as well as elements directly priced. Thus a person is deterred from investing money for short periods, partly because of brokerage charges and stamp duties, partly because it is not worth the bother.

The net advantage to be derived from investing a given quantity of money consists of the interest or profit earned less the cost of investment. It is only if this net advantage is expected to be positive (i.e. if the expected rate of interest ± capital appreciation or depreciation, is greater than the cost of investment) that it will pay to undertake the investment.

Now, since the expected interest increases both with the quantity of money to be invested and with the length of time for which it is expected that the investment will remain untouched, while the costs of investment are independent of the length of time, and (as a whole) will almost certainly increase at a diminishing rate as the quantity of money to be invested increases, it becomes clear that with any given level of costs of investment, it will not pay to invest money for less than a certain period, and in less than certain quantities. It will be profitable to hold assets for short periods, and in relatively small quantities, in monetary form.

Thus, so far as we can see at present, the amount of money a person will desire to hold depends upon three factors: the

they are a nuisance in monetary theory itself, that they offer no help in elucidating the general principles of the working of money.

dates at which he expects to make payments in the future, the cost of investment, and the expected rate of return on investment. The further ahead the future payments, the lower the cost of investment, and the higher the expected rate of return on invested capital—the lower will be the demand for money.

However, this statement is not quite accurate. For although all these factors may react on the demand for money, they may be insufficient to determine it closely. Since the quantity of available money must generally rise to some minimum before it is profitable to invest it at all, and further investment will then proceed by rather discontinuous jumps for a while, we shall expect to find the demand for money on the part of private individuals, excepting the very well-to-do, fairly insensitive to changes of this sort. But this does not mean that they are unimportant. For among those who are likely to be sensitive, we have to reckon, not only the well-to-do, but also all business men who are administering capital which is not solely their own private property. And this will give us, in total, a good deal of sensitivity.

IV

Our first list of factors influencing the demand for money— the expected rate of interest, the cost of investment, and the expected period of investment—does, therefore, isolate some factors which are really operative; but even so, it is not a complete list. For we have also to take into account the fact, which is in reality of such enormous importance, that people's expectations are never precise expectations of the kind we have been assuming. They do not say to themselves " this £100 I shall not want until June 1st " or " this investment will yield 3·7 per cent"; or, if they do, it is only a kind of shorthand. Their expectations are always, in fact, surrounded by a certain penumbra of doubt ; and the density of that penumbra is of immense importance for the problem we are considering.

The risk-factor comes into our problem in two ways : first, as affecting the expected period of investment ; and second, as affecting the expected net yield of investment. There are certain differences between its ways of operation on these two lines ; but, as we shall see, the resultant effects are broadly similar.

Where risk is present, the *particular* expectation of a riskless situation is replaced by a band of possibilities, each of which is considered more or less probable. It is convenient to represent these probabilities to oneself, in statistical fashion, by a mean value, and some appropriate measure of dispersion. (No single measure will be wholly satisfactory, but here this difficulty may be overlooked.) Roughly speaking, we may assume that a change in mean value with constant dispersion has much the same sort of effect as a change in the particular expectations we have been discussing before. The peculiar problem of risk therefore reduces to an examination of the consequences of a change in dispersion. Increased dispersion means increased uncertainty.

If, therefore, our individual, instead of knowing (or thinking he knows) that he will not want his £100 till June 1st, becomes afflicted by increased uncertainty; that is to say, while still thinking that June 1st is the most likely date, he now thinks that it will be very possible that he will want it before, although it is also very possible that he will not want it till after ; what will be the effect on his conduct ? Let us suppose that when the date was certain, the investment was marginal—in the sense that the expected yield only just outweighed the cost of investment. With uncertainty introduced in the way we have described, the investment now offers a chance of larger gain, but it is offset by an equal chance of equivalent loss. In this situation, I think we are justified in assuming that he will become less willing to undertake the investment.

If this is so, uncertainty of the period for which money is free will ordinarily act as a deterrent to investment. It should be observed that uncertainty may be increased, either by a change in objective facts on which estimates are based, or in the psychology of the individual, if his temperament changes in such a way as to make him less inclined to bear risks.

To turn now to the other uncertainty—uncertainty of the yield of investment. Here again we have a penumbra; and here again we seem to be justified in assuming that spreading of the penumbra, increased dispersion of the possibilities of yield, will ordinarily be a deterrent to investment. Indeed, without assuming this to be the normal case, it would be impossible to explain some of the most obvious of the observed facts of the capital market. This sort of risk, therefore, will ordinarily be another factor tending to increase the demand for money.

V

So far the effect of risk seems fairly simple; an increase in the risk of investment will act like a fall in the expected rate of net yield; an increase in the uncertainty of future out-payments will act like a shortening of the time which is expected to elapse before those out-payments; and all will ordinarily tend to increase the demand for money. But although this is what it comes down to in the end, the detailed working of the risk-factor is not so simple; and since these further complications have an important bearing upon monetary problems, we cannot avoid discussing them here.

It is one of the peculiarities of risk that the total risk incurred when more than one risky investment is undertaken, does not bear any simple relation to the risk involved in each of the particular investments taken separately. In most cases, the " law of large numbers " comes into play (quite how, cannot be discussed here), so that the risk incurred by undertaking a number of separate risky investments will be less than that which would have been incurred if the same total capital had been invested altogether in one direction. When the number of separate investments is very large, the total risk may sometimes be reduced very low indeed.

Now in a world where cost of investment was negligible, everyone would be able to take considerable advantage of this sort of risk-reduction. By dividing up his capital into small portions, and spreading his risks, he would be able to insure himself against any large total risk on the whole amount. But in actuality, the cost of investment, making it definitely unprofitable to invest less than a certain minimum amount in any particular direction, closes the possibility of risk-reduction along these lines to all those who do not possess the command over considerable quantities of capital. This has two consequences.

On the one hand, since most people do not possess sufficient resources to enable them to take much advantage of the law of large numbers, and since even the large capitalist cannot annihilate his risks altogether in this manner, there will be a tendency to spread capital over a number of investments, not for this purpose, but for another. By investing only a proportion of total assets in risky enterprises, and investing the remainder in ways which are considered more safe, it will be possible for the individual to adjust his whole risk-situation to that which he most prefers, more closely than he could do by investing in any single enterprise. It will be possible, for example, for him to feel fairly certain that in particular unfavourable eventualities he will not lose more than a certain amount. And, since, both with an eye on future commitments with respect to debt, and future needs for consumption, large losses will lay upon him a proportionately heavier burden than small losses, this sort of adjustment to the sort of chance of loss he is prepared to stand will be very well worth while.

We shall, therefore, expect to find our representative individual distributing his assets among relatively safe and relatively risky investments; and the distribution will be governed, once again, by the objective facts upon which he bases his estimates of risk, and his subjective preference for much or little risk-bearing.

On the other hand, those persons who have command of large quantities of capital, and are able to spread their risks, are not only able to reduce the risk on their own capital fairly low—they are also able to offer very good security for the investment of an extra unit along with the rest. If, therefore, they choose to become borrowers, they are likely to be very safe borrowers. They can, therefore, provide the safe investments which their fellow-citizens need.

In the absence of such safe investments, the ordinary individual would be obliged to keep a very considerable proportion of his assets in monetary form, since money would be the only safe way of holding assets. The appearance of such safe investments will act as a substitute for money in one of its uses, and therefore diminish the demand for money.

This particular function is performed, in a modern community, not only by banks, but also by insurance companies, investment trusts, and, to a certain (perhaps small) extent, even by large concerns of other kinds, through their prior charges. And, of course, to a very large extent indeed, it is performed by government stock of various kinds.

Banks are simply the extreme case of this phenomenon ; they are enabled to go further than other concerns in the creation of money substitutes, because the security of their promises to pay is accepted generally enough for it to be possible to make payments in those promises. Bank deposits

1935] SUGGESTION FOR SIMPLIFYING THE THEORY OF MONEY 11

are, therefore, enabled to substitute money still further, because the cost of investment is reduced by a general belief in the absence of risk.

This is indeed a difference so great as to be properly regarded as a difference in kind ; but it is useful to observe that the creation of bank credit is not really different in its economic effects from the fundamentally similar activities of other businesses and other persons. The significant thing is that the person who deposits money with a bank does not notice any change in his liquidity position; he considers the bank deposit to be as liquid as cash. The bank, on the other hand, finds itself more liquid, if it retains the whole amount of the cash deposited; if it does not wish to be more liquid, but seeks (for example) to restore a conventional reserve ratio, it will have to increase its investments. But substantially the same sort of thing happens when anyone, whose credit is much above the average, borrows. Here the borrowing is nearly always a voluntary act on the part of the borrower, which would not be undertaken unless he was willing to become less liquid than before ; the fact that he has to pay interest on the loan means that he will be made worse off if he does not spend the proceeds. On the other hand, if the borrower's credit is good, the liquidity of the lender will not be very greatly impaired by his making the loan, so that his demand for money is likely to be at least rather less than it was before the loan was made. Thus the net effect of the loan is likely to be " inflationary," in the sense that the purchase of capital goods or securities by the borrower is likely to be a more important affair than any sale of capital goods or securities by the lender, made necessary in order for the lender to restore his liquidity position.

Does it follow that all borrowing and lending is inflationary in this sense ? I do not think so; for let us take the case when the borrower's credit is very bad, and the lender is only tempted to lend by the offer of a very high rate of interest. Then the impairment of the lender's liquidity position will be very considerable; and he may feel it necessary to sell rather less risky securities to an even greater capital sum in order to restore his liquidity position. Here the net effect would be " deflationary."

The practical conclusion of this seems to be that while *voluntary* borrowing and lending is at least a symptom of monetary expansion, and is thus likely to be accompanied by rising prices, " distress borrowing " is an exception to this rule; and it follows, further, that the sort of stimulation to lending, by persuading people to make loans which they would not have made without persuasion (which was rather a feature of certain phases of the world depression), is a dubious policy—for the lenders, perhaps without realising what they are doing, are very likely to try and restore their liquidity position, and so to offset, and perhaps more than offset, the expansive effects of the loan.

VI

It is now time for us to begin putting together the conclusions we have so far reached. Our method of analysis, it will have appeared, is simply an extension of the ordinary method of value theory. In value theory, we take a private individual's income and expenditure account; we ask which of the items in that account are under the individual's own control, and then how he will adjust these items in order to reach a most preferred position. On the production side, we make a similar analysis of the profit and loss account of the firm. My suggestion is that monetary theory needs to be based again upon a similar analysis, but this time, not of an income account, but of a capital account, a balance sheet. We have to concentrate on the forces which make assets and liabilities what they are.

So as far as banking theory is concerned, this is really the method which is currently adopted; though the essence of the problem is there somewhat obscured by the fact that banks, in their efforts to reach their " most preferred position " are hampered or assisted by the existence of conventional or legally obligatory reserve ratios. For theoretical purposes, this fact ought only to be introduced at a rather late stage; if that is done, then my suggestion can be expressed by saying that we ought to regard every individual in the community as being, on a small scale, a bank. Monetary theory becomes a sort of generalisation of banking theory.

We shall have to draw up a sort of generalised balance sheet, suitable for all individuals and institutions. It will have to be so generalised that many of the individual items will, in a great many cases, not appear. But that does not matter for our purposes. Such a generalised balance sheet will presumably run much as follows.

1935] SUGGESTION FOR SIMPLIFYING THE THEORY OF MONEY 13

Assets.	*Liabilities.*
Consumption goods —perishable	
Consumption goods —durable	
Money	
Bank deposits	
Short term debts	Short term debts
Long term debts	Long term debts
Stocks and shares	
Productive equipment (including goods in process)	

We have been concerned up to the present with an analysis (very sketchy, I am afraid) of the equilibrium of this balance sheet. This analysis has at least shown that the relative size of the different items on this balance sheet is governed mainly by anticipation of the yield of investments and of risks.[1] It is these anticipations which play a part here corresponding to the part played by prices in value theory.[2]

Now the fact that our " equilibrium " is here determined by subjective factors like anticipations, instead of objective factors like prices, means that this purely theoretical study of money can never hope to reach results so tangible and precise as those which value theory in its more limited field can hope to attain. If I am right, the whole problem of applying monetary theory is largely one of deducing changes in anticipations from the changes in objective data which call them forth. Obviously, this is not an easy task, and, above all, it is not one which can be performed in a mechanical fashion. It needs judgment and knowledge of business psychology much more than sustained logical reasoning. The arm-chair economist will be bad at it, but he can at least begin to realise

---

[1] As we have seen, these risks are as much a matter of the period of investment as of the yield. For certain purposes this is very important. Thus, in the case of that kind of investment which consists in the starting of actual processes of production, the yield which is expected if the process can be carried through may be considerable; but the yield if the process has to be interrupted will be large and negative. Uncertainty of the period for which resources are free will therefore have a very powerful effect in interrupting production. Short-run optimism will usually be enough to start a Stock Exchange boom ; but to start an industrial boom relatively long-run optimism is necessary.

[2] I am aware that too little is said in this paper about the liabilities side of the above balance sheet. A cursory examination suggests that the same forces which work through the assets side work through the liabilities side in much the same way. But this certainly requires further exploration.

the necessity for it, and learn to co-operate with those who can do it better than he can.

However, I am not fouling my own nest; I do not at all mean to suggest that economic theory comes here to the end of its resources. When once the connection between objective facts and anticipations has been made, theory comes again into its rights; and it will not be able to complain of a lack of opportunities.

Nevertheless, it does seem to me most important that, when considering these further questions, we should be well aware of the gap which lies behind us, and that we should bring out very clearly the assumptions which we are making about the genesis of anticipations. For this does seem to be the only way in which we can overcome the extraordinary theoretical differences of recent years, which are, I think very largely traceable to this source.

VII

Largely, but not entirely; or rather a good proportion of them seem to spring from a closely related source, which is yet not quite identical with the first. When we seek to apply to a changing world any particular sort of individual equilibrium, we need to know how the individual will respond, not only to changes in the price-stimuli, or anticipation-stimuli, but also to a change in his total wealth.[1] How will he distribute an increment (or decrement) of wealth—supposing, as we may suppose, that this wealth is measured in monetary terms?

It may be observed that this second problem has an exact counterpart in value theory. Recent work in that field has shown the importance of considering carefully, not only how the individual reacts to price-changes, but also how he reacts to changes in his available expenditure. Total wealth, in our present problem, plays just the same part as total expenditure in the theory of value.

In the theory of money, what we particularly want to know is how the individual's demand for money will respond to a change in his total wealth—that is to say, in the value of his

---

[1] The amount of money demanded depends upon three groups of factors : (1) the individual's subjective preferences for holding money or other things ; (2) his wealth : (3) his anticipations of future prices and risks. Changes in the demand for money affect present prices, but present prices affect the demand for money mainly through their effect on wealth and on price-anticipations.

1935] SUGGESTION FOR SIMPLIFYING THE THEORY OF MONEY 15

net assets. Not seeing any *a priori* reason why he should react in one way rather than another, monetary theorists have often been content to make use of the simplest possible assumption—that the demand for money will be increased in the same proportion as total net assets have increased.[1] But this is a very arbitrary assumption; and it may be called in question, partly for analytical reasons, and partly because it seems to make the economic system work much too smoothly to account for observed fact. As one example of this excessive smoothness, I may instance the classical theory of international payments ; as another, Mr. Harrod's views on the "Expansion of Bank Credit" which have recently been interesting the readers of *Economica* and of the *Economist*.[2] It would hardly be too much to say that one observed fact alone is sufficient to prove that this assumption cannot be universally true (let us hope and pray that it is sometimes true, nevertheless)—the fact of the trade cycle. For if it were true, the monetary system would always exhibit a quite straightforward kind of stability; a diminished demand for money on the part of some people would raise the prices of capital goods and securities, and this would raise the demand for money on the part of the owners of those securities. Similarly an increased demand for money would lower prices, and this would lower the demand for money elsewhere. The whole thing would work out like an ordinary demand and supply diagram. But it is fairly safe to say that we do not find this straightforward stability in practice.

The analytical reason why this sort of analysis is unsatisfactory is the following: The assumption of increased wealth leading to a proportionately increased demand for money is only plausible so long as the value of assets has increased, but other things have remained equal. Now, as we have seen, the other things which are relevant to this case are not prices (as in the theory of value) but anticipations, of the yield of investment and so on. And since these anticipations must be based upon objective facts, and an unexpected increase in wealth implies a change in objective facts, of a sort very likely to be relevant to the anticipations, it is fairly safe to assume that

[1] Of course, they say "income." But in this case "income" can only be strictly interpreted as "expected income." And in most of the applications which are made, this works out in the same way as the assumption given above.

[2] The above was written before reading Mr. Harrod's rejoinder to Mr. Robertson. As I understand him, Mr. Harrod is now only maintaining that the expansion of bank credit *may* work smoothly. With that I am in no disagreement.

very many of the changes in wealth with which we are concerned will be accompanied by a change in anticipations. If this is so, the assumption of proportionate change in the demand for money loses most of its plausibility.

For if we assume (this is jumping over my gap, so I must emphasise that it is only an assumption) that an increase in wealth will very often be accompanied by an upward revision of expectations of yield, then the change will set in motion at least one tendency which is certain to diminish the demand for money. Taking this into account *as well as* the direct effect of the increase in wealth, the situation begins to look much less clear. For it must be remembered that our provisional assumption about the direct effect was only guess-work; there is no necessary reason why the direct effect should increase the demand for money proportionately or even increase it at all. So, putting the two together, it looks perfectly possible that the demand for money may either increase or diminish.

We are treading on thin ice; but the unpleasant possibilities which now begin to emerge are sufficiently plausible for their examination to be well worth while. What happens, to take a typical case, if the demand for money is independent of changes in wealth, so that neither an increase in wealth nor a diminution will affect the demand for money ?

One can conceive of a sort of equilibrium in such a world, but it would be a hopelessly unstable equilibrium. For if any single person tried to increase his money holdings, and the supply of money was not increased, prices would all fall to zero. If any person tried to diminish his money holdings, prices would all become infinite. In fact, of course, if demand were so rigid, the system could only be kept going by a continuous and meticulous adaptation of the supply of money to the demand.

Further, in such a world, very curious results would follow from saving. A sudden increase in saving would leave some people (the owners of securities) with larger money balances than they had expected; other people (the producers of consumption goods) with smaller money balances. If, in their efforts to restore their money holdings, the owners of securities buy more securities, and the producers of consumption goods buy less consumption goods, a swing of prices, consumption goods prices falling, security prices rising, would set in, and might go on indefinitely. It could only be stopped, either by the owners of securities buying the services of producers, or by the producers selling securities. But there is no knowing when this would happen, or where prices would finally settle; for the assumption of a rigid demand for money snaps the connecting link between money and prices.

After this, we shall be fairly inured to shocks. It will not surprise us to be told that wage-changes will avail nothing to stop either an inflation or a deflation, and we shall be able to extend the proposition for ourselves to interference with conventional or monopolistic prices of any kind, in any direction. But we shall be in a hurry to get back to business.

VIII

These exercises in the economics of an utterly unstable world give us something too mad to fit even our modern *Spätkapitalismus*; but the time which economists have spent on them will not have been wasted if they have served as a corrective to the too facile optimism engendered by the first assumption we tried. Obviously, what we want is something between the two—but not, I think, a mere splitting of the difference. This would give the assumption that an increase in wealth always raises the demand for money, but less than proportionately; if we had time, it might be profitable to work out this case in detail. It would allow for the possibility of considerable fluctuations, but they would not be such absurd and hopeless fluctuations as in the case of rigid demand.

However, I think we can do better than that. The assumption which seems to me most plausible, most consistent with the whole trend of our analysis, and at the same time to lead to results which at any rate look realistic, is one which stresses the probable differences in the reactions of different members of the community. We have already seen that a considerable proportion of a community's monetary stock is always likely to be in the hands of people who are obliged by their relative poverty to be fairly insensitive to changes in anticipations. For these people, therefore, most of the incentive to reduce their demand for money when events turn out more favourably will be missing; there seems no reason why we should not suppose that they will generally react " positively " to changes in their wealth—that an increase in wealth will raise their demand for money more or less proportionately, a fall in their wealth will diminish it. But we must also allow for the probability that other people are much more *sensitive*—that an increase in wealth is not particularly likely to increase their demand for money, and may very well diminish it.

If this is so, it would follow that where the sensitive trade together, price-fluctuations may start on very slight provocation; and once they are under way, the rather less sensitive would be enticed in. Stock exchange booms will pass over into industrial booms, if industrial entrepreneurs are also fairly sensitive; and, in exactly the same way, stock exchange depressions will pass into industrial depressions. But the insensitive are always there to act as a flywheel, defeating by their insensitivity both the exaggerated optimism and the exaggerated pessimism of the sensitive class. How this comes about I cannot attempt to explain in detail, though it would be an interesting job, for one might be able to reconcile a good many apparently divergent theories. But it would lead us too deeply into Cycle theory—I will only say that I think the period of fluctuation turns out to depend, in rather complex fashion, upon the distribution of sensitivity and the distribution of production periods between industrial units.

Instead, I may conclude with two general reflections.

If it is the insensitive people who preserve the stability of capitalism, people who are insensitive (you will remember) largely because for them the costs of transferring assets are large relatively to the amount of assets they control, then the development of capitalism, by diminishing these costs, is likely to be a direct cause of increasing fluctuations. It reduces costs in two ways: by technical devices (of which banks are only one example), and by instilling a more " capitalistic " spirit, which looks more closely to profit, and thus reduces subjective costs. In doing these things, capitalism is its own enemy, for it imperils that stability without which it breaks down.

Lastly, it seems to follow that when we are looking for policies which make for economic stability, we must not be led aside by a feeling that monetary troubles are due to " bad " economic policy, in the old sense, that all would go well if we reverted to free trade and *laisser-faire*. In so doing, we are no better than the Thebans who ascribed the plague to blood-guiltiness, or the supporters of Mr. Roosevelt who expect to reach recovery through reform. There is no reason why policies which tend to economic welfare, statically considered, should also tend to monetary stability. Indeed, the presumption is rather the other way round. A tariff, for example, may be a very good instrument of recovery on occasion, for precisely the reason which free-traders deplore; that it harms a great many people a little for the conspicuous benefit of a few. That may be just the sort of measure we want.

These will be unpalatable conclusions; but I think we must face the possibility that they are true. They offer the economist a pretty hard life, for he, at any rate, will not be able to have a clear conscience either way, over many of the alternatives he is called upon to consider. His ideals will conflict and he will not be able to seek an easy way out by sacrificing either.

[6]

A General Equilibrium Approach To Monetary Theory

JAMES TOBIN

I WILL TAKE THE OPPORTUNITY provided by the first issue of a journal devoted to monetary economics to set forth and illustrate a general framework for monetary analysis. It is not a new approach, but one shared at least in spirit by many monetary economists. My purpose here is exposition and recapitulation.[1]

1. *The capital account.*—The approach focuses on the capital accounts of economic units, of sectors of the economy, and of the economy as a whole. A model of the capital account of the economy specifies a menu of the assets (and debts) that appear in portfolios and balance sheets, the factors that determine the demands and supplies of the various assets, and the manner in which asset prices and interest rates clear these interrelated markets. In this approach, monetary assets fall into place as a part, but not the whole, of the menu of assets; and the commercial banking system is one sector, but not the only one, whose balance sheet behavior must be specified.

Treatment of the capital account separately from the production and income account of the economy is only a first step, a simplification to be justified by convenience rather than realism. The strategy is to regard income account

[1] Among my many debts, I will acknowledge here a special one to my colleague and, on occasion, collaborator, William C. Brainard, who has helped to develop and clarify the approach here expounded. He is not responsible, however, for errors and confusions that may remain in this particular exposition. See also Tobin and Brainard, "Financial Intermediaries and the Effectiveness of Monetary Controls," *American Economic Review*, 53 (May, 1963), pp. 383–400 and Brainard, "Financial Intermediaries and a Theory of Monetary Control," *Yale Economic Essays*, 4 (Fall, 1964), pp. 431–482. These papers are reprinted as Chapters 3 and 4 in *Financial Markets and Economic Activity*, ed. Hester and Tobin. Cowles Foundation Monograph 21, (New York: Wiley, 1967).

JAMES TOBIN *is Sterling Professor of Economics at Yale University and has been chairman of the department of economics at Yale since February, 1968.*

16 : MONEY, CREDIT, AND BANKING

variables as tentatively exogenous data for balance-sheet behavior, and to find equilibrium in the markets for stocks of assets conditional upon assumed values of outputs, incomes, and other flows. Of course the linkages run both ways. Some of the variables determined in asset markets affect the flows of spending and income. In a complete equilibrium the two sides of the economy —one is tempted to call them "financial" and "real"—must be mutually consistent. That is, the financial inputs to the real side must reproduce the assumed values of the real inputs to the financial side.

A familiar and simple example of this strategy is the "*LM* curve." Macroeconomics texts and lectures have immortalized Hicks's decomposition of the Keynesian system into sub-models. One of these tells what asset stock equilibrium corresponds to any tentative assumption about aggregate real income and the commodity price level. In this conditional equilibrium "the" interest rate equates the demand and supply of money and clears the markets for other assets. Of the many *LM* equilibria, only one is in general consistent with the other relationships in the complete system.

The key behavioral assumption of this procedure is that spending decisions and portfolio decisions are independent—specifically that decisions about the accumulation of wealth are separable from decisions about its allocation. As savers, people decide how much to add to their wealth; as portfolio managers, they decide how to distribute among available assets and debts the net worth they already have. The propensity to consume may depend upon interest rates, but it does not depend *directly* on the existing mix of asset supplies or on the rates at which these supplies are growing.

Figure 1 illustrates schematically the approach just sketched.

2. *Accounting framework.*—The general accounting framework for a theory of the capital account is indicated in Table 1. Rows represent assets or debts. A row might be labeled "money" or "physical capital," or in a finer classification "demand deposits" or "producers' durable equipment." Columns represent sectors of the economy: for example, commercial banks, central government, nonbank financial institutions, public. Entries in cells, in general, can be positive, negative, or zero. A negative entry means that the sector in question is a debtor in the kind of asset indicated by the row. All holdings must be valued in the same numéraire, e.g., either in the monetary unit of account or in terms of purchasing power over consumer goods. The sum across a row is the net exogenous supply of the asset to the economy as a whole. For stocks of goods, this exogenous supply is the economy's inheritance from the past. For internally generated financial assets the net exogenous supply is, of course, zero. If from the sums in the final column the central government's holdings of an asset are subtracted (or its debt added), the net holdings of the private economy result. The sum of a column represents the net worth of a sector. The sum of the final column is national wealth. As indicated, private wealth differs from this total by the amount of the government's net worth. If the

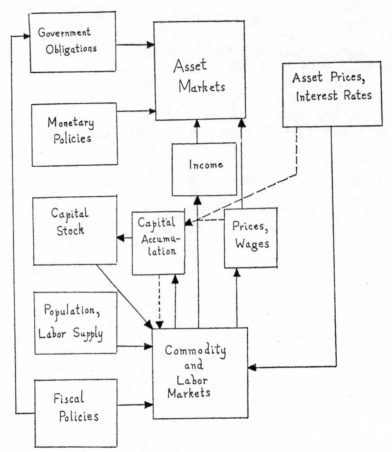

FIG. 1. Capital Account Approach (Schematic).

TABLE 1

GENERAL ACCOUNTING FRAMEWORK

Assets	Sectors of the Economy							Central Government	Net Total Holdings = Exogenous Supply
	1	2	3	.	.	.	m		
1									
2									
3									
.									
.									
.									
n									

Net Worth	Total Private Wealth (= National Wealth less Government Net Worth)	Government Net Worth	National Wealth

government is a net debtor, as will typically be the case, at least if its stocks of goods are ignored, then private wealth exceeds national wealth. The framework illustrated by Table 1 is intended for a closed economy, although it could be extended to include capital-account relations with the rest of the world.

3. *The analytical framework.*—The accounting framework of Table 1 can be brought to life as a framework for monetary analysis by (a) assigning to each asset a rate of return r_i, $(i = 1, 2, \cdots n)$ and (b) imagining each sector $j(j = 1, 2, \cdots m)$ to have a net demand for each asset, f_{ij}, which is a function of the vector r_i and possibly of other variables as well. Of course in practice many of the cells are empty; certain sectors are just not involved with certain assets, either as holders or as debtors.

Each sector is, at any moment of time, constrained by its own net worth. Its members are free to choose their balance sheets—the entries in the columns of Table 1—but not to choose their net worth—the sum of the column entries. This is determined by their past accumulations of assets and by current asset prices. The individual economic unit can neither change the legacy of the past nor, it is assumed, affect by his own portfolio choices the current market valuations of his assets. Of course, as time passes the individual may save and may make capital gains or losses. A year later his net worth will be different, but it will be once again a constraint on his portfolio behavior.

This adding-up requirement has certain obvious and simple implications. For any sector, the sum over all assets of responses to a change in any rate of return r_k is zero:

$$\sum_{i=1}^{n} \frac{\partial f_{ij}}{\partial r_k} = 0.$$

This is also true for any other variable that enters the sector's asset demand functions. The exception is the sector's net worth itself; clearly the sum of asset changes due to a change in wealth is equal to one:

$$\sum_{i=1}^{n} \frac{\partial f_{ij}}{\partial W_j} = 1.$$

These same properties will hold for demand functions aggregated over sectors, that is for $f_i = \sum_{j=1}^{m} f_{ij}$.

Each row in Table 1 corresponds to one market-clearing equation, by which the net demands of the m private sectors add up to the available supplies, whether issued by the government or otherwise exogenous. But these n equations are not independent. Whatever the values of the determining variables, the left-hand sides (net private demands) of these n asset equations sum to the same value as the right-hand sides (supplies), namely to aggregate private wealth. Therefore, contrary to superficial first impression, the n equations will not determine n rates of return but only $n - 1$ at most.

The value of aggregate or sectoral wealth may depend on asset prices, which are themselves related to the r_i, the market rates of return, determined by the system of equations. This will be true of all assets whose life exceeds the length of the assumed period of portfolio choice. For example, the outstanding supplies of durable physical capital and of long-term government bonds change in value as their market rates of return change. Consequently, the $n - 1$ market-clearing equations actually include rates of return in two roles, as arguments in the asset demand functions and as determinants of the values of existing asset supplies and total wealth.

In some applications of the analysis there are fewer than $n - 1$ rates of return free to be determined. There are fewer endogenous rates of return than there are independent market-clearing equations. Some rates are institutionally or legally fixed—consider the conventional zero own-rate of interest on currency, the prohibition of interest on demand deposits, effective ceilings on interest paid on time and savings accounts. Some are constrained, at least in the long run, by real factors—for example, by the technological marginal productivity of physical capital assets. In these cases the capital account equations cannot be satisfied unless some asset supplies are not exogenous but adjust to clear the markets, or unless some relevant variables from the real side of the economy—income, price level, price expectations—assume appropriate values. I will return to these problems in the illustrations that follow.

4. *A money-capital economy.*—I turn now to some simple applications of the approach just described. First, consider an economy with only one private sector and only two assets: money issued by the government to finance its budget deficits, and homogeneous physical capital. Let p be the price of currently produced goods, both consumer goods and capital goods. I shall, however, allow the value of existing capital goods, or of titles to them, to diverge from their current reproduction cost—let qp be the market price of existing capital goods. Let r_M and r_K be the real rates of return available from holding money and capital respectively. Let $\rho_p{}^e$ be the expected rate of change in commodity prices, let r_M' be the nominal rate of interest on money (generally, zero), and let R be the marginal efficiency of capital relative to reproduction cost. Let W be wealth and Y income, both measured in commodity prices.

Model I is as follows:

Wealth definition:

$$W = qK + M/p \qquad (I.0)$$

Balance equations:

$$f_1(r_K, r_M, Y/W)W = qK \qquad \text{capital } (r_K) \qquad (I.1)$$

$$f_2(r_K, r_M, Y/W)W = M/p \quad \text{money } (r_M) \tag{I.2}$$

Rate-of-return equations:

$$r_K q = R \quad \text{capital} \tag{I.3}$$

$$r_M = r_M' - \rho_p^e \quad \text{money} \tag{I.4}$$

The two portfolio behavior functions have been written in a special form. They are homogeneous in wealth; the proportions held in the two assets are independent of the absolute scale of wealth. The "adding-up" requirement tells us that $f_1 = 1 - f_2$; therefore, one of the two balance equations, let it be I.1, can be omitted. It is natural to assume the own-rate derivatives $\partial f_1/\partial r_K$ and $\partial f_2/\partial r_M$ to be positive and the cross-derivatives therefore to be negative.

The ratio of income to wealth appears in both asset demand functions; if it appears in one, it must be in the other one too. The conventional assumption is that more money will be "needed for transactions purposes" at higher income levels. The implication is that the demand for capital will, other things equal, be reduced by a rise in income. However, "other things" will not be equal if on the real side of the economy there is a positive connection between Y and R, and therefore between Y and r_K.

Whether income falls with wealth constant or wealth rises with income constant, a smaller fraction of wealth is needed to meet transactions requirements. The demand for money will fall relative to the demand for capital. I shall make the usual Keynesian assumption that the partial elasticity of demand for money with respect to income is positive but does not exceed one. The reasoning is that transactions demand is, at most, proportional to income (elasticity equal to one), but transactions balances are only part of money holdings. The assumption is, then, that

$$0 < \left\{ \frac{\partial(f_2 W)}{\partial Y} \middle/ \frac{f_2 W}{Y} = \frac{\partial f_2}{\partial(Y/W)} \middle/ \frac{f_2}{Y/W} \right\} \leq 1.$$

Equation I.3 expresses an inverse relation between the market valuation of capital equity and the market rate of return upon it. Suppose that the perpetual real return obtainable by purchasing a unit of capital at its cost of production p is R. If an investor must pay qp instead of p, then his rate of return is R/q. The consol formula of I.3 applies strictly only for perfectly durable capital. For depreciating capital, or physical assets of finite life, the relation of r_K and q will not be so simple or so pronounced. But there will still be an inverse relation.

Note that the commodity price level p does not affect the real rate of return on capital, calculated either on reproduction cost or on market value. However, the expected rate of inflation of commodity prices does enter portfolio behavior, as one of the constituents of the real rate of return on money in I.4.

With I.1 omitted as redundant, Model I consists of four equations. The interpretation of the model depends on which four variables are taken as endogenous.

5. *Short-run interpretation of the money-capital model.*—One interpretation (IA) is the following:

Endogenous variables: r_K, r_M, W, q

Exogenous variables: K, M, Y, p, R, $\rho_p{}^e$, $r_M{}'$

Then, by (I.4) r_M is, in effect, exogenous. By various substitutions the model can then be expressed as a single equation in q:

$$f_2\left(R/q, r_M, \frac{Y}{qK + M/p}\right)(qK + M/p) = \frac{M}{p} \tag{I.5}$$

The assumptions made in the previous section are sufficient, not necessary, to assure that $\partial q/\partial M > 0$, in words that an increase in the quantity of money is expansionary, causing a rise in the valuation of existing capital and stimulating investment. The same conditions assure that $\partial q/\partial R > 0$, i.e., that an increase in the marginal efficiency of capital pulls up its price; that $\partial q/\partial r_M < 0$, i.e., that an increase in the real rate of interest on money diminishes the valuation of capital; and that $\partial q/\partial Y < 0$, i.e., that asset equilibrium requires a lower valuation of capital the higher the level of income relative to asset stocks.

This last result leads to the observation that, as part of a short-run model of income determination, equation (I.5) can be interpreted as a species of the standard Keynesian *LM* curve. That is, it tells what combinations of real income Y and the rate of return on capital equity, r_K or R/q, are compatible with equilibrium in asset markets (Figure 2). Like the textbook *LM* curve, this relationship shifts to the right when M increases or p diminishes. The difference is that the interest rate on the vertical axis here is the return on capital equity rather than Keynes's long-term bond rate. However, Keynes was assuming the two rates to be equal, or to differ only by a constant risk premium. If this assumption is dropped, R/q is the appropriate variable for the diagram, which needs to be completed by an *IS* curve. The *rate* of investment—the speed at which investors wish to increase the capital stock—should be related, if to anything, to q, the value of capital relative to its replacement cost.

The *LM* curve of Figure 2 was drawn on the assumption of a fixed marginal efficiency of capital, R. If R rises with Y, $\partial q/\partial Y$ will be smaller than with R constant, and may even be negative. In Keynesian theory there has always been ambivalence on this point, between the apparent view of Keynes himself that investors' estimate of the marginal efficiency of capital is related to a future largely independent of the current level of income and the view that

22 : MONEY, CREDIT, AND BANKING

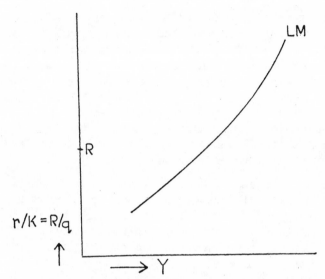

Fɪɢ. 2. *LM* Curve Drawn from Equation (I.5).

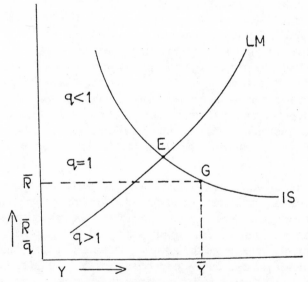

Fɪɢ. 3. *LM* Curve Plotted with *IS* Curve.

investors simply expect the current rate of profit on capital to continue. If, in line with the second view, some dependence of R on Y is built into the *LM* curve, there is no one-to-one relation between r_K and q.

Consequently, Figure 3 plots the *LM* curve against $\bar{R}/q$, where $\bar{R}$ is the marginal efficiency of the existing capital stock K at a standard real income $\bar{Y}$. This standard income $\bar{Y}$ is the level at which saving would just suffice to increase the capital stock at the natural rate of growth of the economy. For example, let this growth rate be g and the saving ratio s; then $gK = s\bar{Y}$. Investment at this rate will, under the usual assumptions of neo-classical growth theory, keep $\bar{R}$ unchanged. Consequently, investment at this rate is compatible with $q = 1$, $rK = \bar{R}$. In other words, the *IS* curve goes through the point $(\bar{R}, \bar{Y})$.[2] At an income lower than $\bar{Y}$, this normal rate of investment will exceed saving; therefore, investment-saving equality requires a q less than one. The short-run equilibrium—for a given real money supply M/p—is shown as E in Figure 3; in this illustration it occurs at a lower income level and equity valuation than the steady growth position G.

6. *Long-run equilibrium in the money-capital model.*—An alternative interpretation of Model I(IB) requires that capital be valued at its reproduction cost, i.e., that $q = 1$. This may be regarded as a condition of equilibrium in the long run. In a long-run growth equilibrium, E and G in Figure 3 must coincide; moreover this income $\bar{Y}$ must also represent equilibrium of labor supply and demand. Then if M/p, R, Y, and K are given, they determine r_K and W. Equation I.2 must then determine r_M, the real rate of interest on money. That is, either expectations of price change ρ_{p^e} or the own-rate on money r_M' must be market-determined rather than institutionally or legally fixed. Otherwise, there is no way of reconciling wealth-owners to the supplies of capital and real balances that history and policy have determined.

Alternatively, if r_M is fixed, the supplies of capital and money, measured in real terms, must be free to adjust to public portfolio preferences. Models of the role of outside money in long-run growth show how this adjustment can occur.[3] One mechanism is flexibility in the price level p, which assures that any nominal supply of money M can be turned into the real supply that the public wants at the prevailing set of real interest rates. Another possible mechanism is fiscal policy itself, adjusting the size and rate of expansion of the government debt so as to achieve equilibrium.

7. *A money-securities-capital model.*—In Model I there is no monetary policy as this term is generally understood. The supply of money is identical with the government debt. It is not possible to increase money by a dollar without simultaneously increasing private wealth by a dollar. They rise together in money value when the government runs a budget deficit and prints money to cover it, or in real value when the price level falls. An increase in the nominal money stock is a monetary consequence of fiscal policy rather than-monetary policy in the usual sense. The closest conceivable thing to monetary policy in model IA is variation of r_M', the institutionally determined rate of interest on money.

---

[2] Jerome Stein has insisted on this property of the short-run investment schedule. See his paper, "Money and Capacity Growth," *Journal of Political Economy*, 74 (October, 1966), 451–65.

[3] See Tobin, "Money and Economic Growth," *Econometrica*, Vol. 33, No. 4 (October, 1965), pp. 671–84.

24 : MONEY, CREDIT, AND BANKING

Monetary policy can be introduced by allowing some government debt to take non-monetary form. Then, even though total government debt is fixed at any moment of time, at least in terms of its original money value, its composition can be altered by open market operations—or by debt management operations, which are really the same thing. Model II makes this emendation of Model I: (Let $\hat{r}$ stand for the vector of real rates of return (r_K, r_M, r_S)). Wealth definition:

$$W = qK + \frac{M + S}{p} \tag{II.0}$$

Balance equations:

$$f_1(\hat{r}, Y/W)W = qK \qquad \text{capital } (r_K) \tag{II.1}$$

$$f_2(\hat{r}, Y/W)W = M/p \qquad \text{money } (r_M) \tag{II.2}$$

$$f_3(\hat{r}, Y/W)W = S/p \qquad \text{gov't. securities } (r_S) \tag{II.3}$$

Rate-of-return equations:

$$r_K q = R \qquad \text{capital} \tag{II.4}$$

$$r_M = r_M' - \rho_p^e \qquad \text{money} \tag{II.5}$$

$$r_S = r_S' - \rho_p^e \qquad \text{gov't. securities} \tag{II.6}$$

Here it is assumed for simplicity that securities are short-term, so that their market value is independent of their interest rate r_S'. Otherwise a relationship between the two could be introduced, playing the same role as II.4 for capital, and allowed for in the calculation of wealth.

An interpretation analogous to IA takes as exogenous Y, M, S, K, R, r_M', ρ_p^e, and p, leaving q, W, r_K, r_S, r_M, r_S' to be determined by the six independent equations. Consolidation gives the following two equations, along with the definition of W, to determine q and r_S:

$$f_2(R/q, r_M, r_S, Y/W)W = M/p \tag{II.7}$$

$$f_3(R/q, r_M, r_S, Y/W)W = S/p \tag{II.8}$$

It is assumed, as before, that the own derivatives of the f_i

$$\left(\frac{\partial f_1}{\partial r_K}, \frac{\partial f_2}{\partial r_M}, \frac{\partial f_3}{\partial r_S} \right)$$

are positive, and that all the cross-derivatives are non-positive. (It will be remembered also that $\sum_i \partial f_i / \partial x = 0$ for any x that appears as an argument in the functions f_i.) In other words, the assets are gross substitutes: the demand for each asset varies directly with its own rate and inversely with other rates.

It is also assumed, as before, that the partial elasticity of demand for money with respect to income is positive but does not exceed one. Moreover, now that government securities are available, it is assumed that they, rather than capital, absorb changes in transactions requirements for money. That is,

$$\frac{\partial f_3}{\partial(Y/W)} = -\frac{\partial f_2}{\partial(Y/W)} \quad \text{and} \quad \frac{\partial f_1}{\partial(Y/W)} = 0.$$

These assumptions lead to the conclusions presented in Table 2.

The first two columns represent increases in government debt taking one form or the other. The third column represents monetary policy in the shape of open market purchases. Here, unlike Model IA, it is possible to shift the *LM* curve of Figures 2 and 3 to the right by monetary policy in the usual sense. The fourth column represents monetary policy in the guise of an increase in the legally-determined interest rate on money.

What is the feature of money that leads to the results tabulated in the first three columns? That is, why does an increase in government debt in monetary form have a more expansionary effect than increase in government debt in the form of securities? And why is substitution of money for securities via open market purchases expansionary?

It is not because asset No. 1 has been called "money" and asset No. 2 "securities." It is not because asset No. 1 is a means of payment or has any other intrinsic properties asset No. 2 lacks. It is not that asset No. 1 bears no interest—it may or may not. These properties have nowhere entered the analysis, except in the general sense that they explain why the assets are not perfect substitutes for each other.

The essential characteristic—the only distinction of money from securities

TABLE 2

EFFECTS ON ENDOGENOUS VARIABLES OF INCREASE IN SPECIFIED EXOGENOUS VARIABLES,
WITH ALL OTHERS HELD CONSTANT

ENDOGENOUS VARIABLES	EXOGENOUS VARIABLES							
	M	S	M at expense of S	$r_{M'}$	Y	R	p	$\overset{\bullet}{p}_p$
q	$+$	?	$+$	$-$	$-$	$+$	$-$	$+$
r_S	$-$	$+$	$-$	$+$	$+$	?	?	$-$
r_K	$-$	?	$-$	$+$	$+$	$+$	$+$	$-$

26 : MONEY, CREDIT, AND BANKING

that matters for the results given above—is that the interest rate on money is exogenously fixed by law or convention, while the rate of return on securities is endogenous, market-determined. If the roles of the two assets in this respect were reversed, so also would be the economic impacts of changing their supplies. Conceivably the government could fix the interest rate on its time obligations and let the rate on its demand debts be determined in the market. Then the way for the central bank to achieve an expansionary monetary impact would be to buy money with securities!

When the supply of any asset is increased, the structure of rates of return, on this and other assets, must change in a way that induces the public to hold the new supply. When the asset's own rate can rise, a large part of the necessary adjustment can occur in this way. But if the rate is fixed, the whole adjustment must take place through reductions in other rates or increases in prices of other assets. This is the secret of the special role of money; it is a secret that would be shared by any other asset with a fixed interest rate.

As observed above, an n-asset economy will provide no more than $n - 1$ independent market-clearing equations. The system will determine, therefore, no more than $n - 1$ real rates of return. If the rate on one asset, "money," is fixed, then the market rate of return on capital can, indeed must, be among the $n - 1$ rates to be determined. This enables the monetary authority to force the market return on physical capital to diverge from its technological marginal efficiency—or, what is the same thing, to force the market valuation of existing capital to diverge from its reproduction cost. By creating these divergences, the monetary authority can affect the current rate of production and accumulation of capital assets. This is the manner in which the monetary authority can affect aggregate demand in the short run—diagrammatically, by moving the *LM* curve of Figure 3 to the left or right and changing its intersection with the *IS* curve.

If the interest rate on money, as well as the rates on all other financial assets, were flexible and endogenous, then they would all simply adjust to the marginal efficiency of capital. There would be no room for discrepancies between market and natural rates of return on capital, between market valuation and reproduction cost. There would be no room for monetary policy to affect aggregate demand. The real economy would call the tune for the financial sector, with no feedback in the other direction. As previously observed, something like this occurs in the long run, where the influence of monetary policy is not on aggregate demand but on the relative supplies of monetary and real assets, to which all rates of return must adjust.

8. *A model with bank deposits and loans.*—As a third and final illustration of the approach, consider an economy with two sectors rather than one. Model III has a banking system as well as a general public sector and adds two new assets—deposits and private loans—to the economy's menu of assets. There are also two new real rates of interest to be determined, r_D on deposits

and r_L on loans, and two new nominal rates, r_D' on deposits and r_L' on loans, to be established either exogenously or endogenously. A new interest rate relevant to the banks, the central bank discount rate d', (d in real terms) can also be introduced; this is another instrument of monetary control.

Let $\hat{r}$ be the vector of real interest rates (r_K, r_M, r_S, r_D, r_L, d). For convenience, both bank and public portfolio choices will be written as functions of $\hat{r}$. But it will be understood that the discount rate d is irrelevant to the public, and that the market rate on capital r_K is irrelevant to the banks, which are assumed not to hold such equity. For the same reason, the banks' asset demands could be expressed equally well in money values and related to money interest rates rather than real. The legal reserve requirement enters as k.

Asset No. 2 is still the demand debt of the government, inclusive of the central bank. The size of this debt, net of the banks' borrowings from the central bank at the discount window, is the supply of currency and unborrowed reserves to the banks and the public. But of course M no longer corresponds to the quantity of money as conventionally defined. Rather it represents "high-powered" money. The money stock would include the public's share of M plus bank deposits (or perhaps only demand deposits if, as is not done here, time deposits were distinguished from them). Thus the money stock would be an endogenous quantity.

Wealth definition:

$$W = qK + \frac{M + S}{p} \qquad\qquad (\text{III.0})$$

Balance equations:

Sector:
    Banks   Public

$$f_{1P}(\hat{r}, Y/W)W = qK \text{ (capital } (r_K)) \qquad (\text{III.1})$$

$$kD + f_{2B}(\hat{r})D(1 - k) + f_{2P}(\hat{r}, Y/W)W = M/p \text{ (currency and} \qquad (\text{III.2})$$
$$\text{reserves) } (r_M, d)$$

$$f_{3B}(\hat{r})D(1 - k) + f_{3P}(\hat{r}, Y/W)W = S/p \text{ (government} \qquad (\text{III.3})$$
$$\text{securities } (r_S))$$

$$f_{4B}(\hat{r}) + f_{4P}(\hat{r}, Y/W)W = 0 \text{ (deposits } (r_D)) \qquad (\text{III.4})$$

$$D = f_{4P}(\hat{r}, Y/W)W \text{ (definition of } D) \qquad (\text{III.4a})$$

$$f_{5B}(\hat{r})D(1 - k) + f_{5P}(\hat{r}, Y/W)W = 0 \text{ (loans } (r_L)) \qquad (\text{III.5})$$

Rate-of-return equations:

$$r_K q = R \text{ (capital)} \tag{III.6}$$

$$r_M = r_M' - \rho_p^e \text{ (currency and reserves)} \tag{III.7}$$

$$r_S = r_S' - \rho_p^e \text{ (government securities)} \tag{III.8}$$

$$r_D = r_0' - \rho_p^e \text{ (deposits)} \tag{III.9}$$

$$r_L = r_L' - \rho_p^e \text{ (loans)} \tag{III.10}$$

$$d = d' - \rho_P^e \text{ (discount rate)} \tag{III.11}$$

The equity of bank shareholders is ignored, so that the items in the bank column sum to zero, just as the items in the public column sum to private net worth W.

There are eleven independent equations. As before, Y, M, S, K, R, r_M', ρ_P^e, p, d', and K may be taken as exogenous and the system solved for the eleven variables q, W, r_K, r_M, r_S, r_S', r_0, r_D', r_L, r_L', and d. In this interpretation of model III, the interest rate paid on deposits is endogenous, market-determined. The banks' deposit supply function f_{4B} tells, for given values of other interest rates, the quantity of deposits banks wish to accept at any given deposit rate. In equilibrium this must be equal to the quantity of deposits the public wishes to hold at this same set of rates.

As before, the effects of various instruments of monetary policy and of other exogenous variables on the key variable q represents their impact on aggregate demand. With the same assumptions about asset substitution, and about income-elasticity of demand for high-powered money, the results will be qualitatively the same as in the other models. They will be quantitatively very different, of course. Fractional reserve banking means that a bigger reshuffling of portfolios and larger changes in rates of return are needed to absorb a given increase in the supply of high-powered money. To the extent the banks are not induced to add the new supply to their excess reserves, the public must be induced to hold some multiple of it as deposits. The change in rates of return necessary to accomplish either of these results, or any combination of them, may be very large in comparison with the 100 per cent money regime depicted in models I and II.

An alternative interpretation is to take the deposit rate r_D' as institutionally or legally fixed. Adding it to the list of exogenous variables means that one equation must be deleted. The one to delete, of course, is III.4. With an effective ceiling on the interest banks are allowed to pay, banks fall short of their supply curve $(-f_{4B})$. They accept all the deposits the public is willing to leave with them at the prevailing set of interest rates, and they would gladly accept more. Thus III.4 becomes an inequality: $f_{4B} + f_{4P} > 0$. The remaining equations in the model, including III.4a, still apply.

This interpretation is the one customarily made. It accords with United

States institutions—prohibition of interest on demand deposits and a ceiling on time deposit interest. Once again the effects on q of policy measures and other exogenous changes can be analyzed. Here, however, there is a new possible source of abnormal results. The "gross substitutes" assumption may be violated in the market as a whole even though it is satisfied by each sector—banks and public—separately. For example, an increase in the deposit rate or a reduction in the securities rate might increase rather than diminish the net demand for currency or government securities. While the public's direct demands fall as they shift into deposits, the banks' demands may increase simply because they have more deposits.[4]

This formulation adds the deposit rate ceiling to the list of monetary policy instruments and permits analysis of the question whether an increase in the ceiling is expansionary or contractionary.

9. *Concluding remarks.*—The models discussed here were meant to be illustrative only, and to give meaning to some general observations about monetary analysis. The basic framework is very flexible. It can be extended to encompass more sectors and more assets, depending on the topic under study. Other financial intermediaries can be introduced. More distinctions can be made among categories of government debts and types of private debts. Equally important, the assumption that physical capital is homogeneous can be dropped, and a number of markets, prices, and rates of return for stocks of goods introduced—distinguishing among houses, plant, equipment, consumers' durables, etc.

According to this approach, the principal way in which financial policies and events affect aggregate demand is by changing the valuations of physical assets relative to their replacement costs. Monetary policies can accomplish such changes, but other exogenous events can too. In addition to the exogenous variables explicitly listed in the illustrative models, changes can occur, and undoubtedly do, in the portfolio preferences—asset demand functions—of the public, the banks, and other sectors. These preferences are based on expectations, estimates of risk, attitudes towards risk, and a host of other factors. In this complex situation, it is not to be expected that the essential impact of monetary policies and other financial events will be easy to measure in the absence of direct observation of the relevant variables (q in the models). There is no reason to think that the impact will be captured in any single exogenous or intermediate variables, whether it is a monetary stock or a market interest rate.[5]

---

[4] These problems are analyzed in the Tobin-Brainard and Brainard papers cited above.

[5] This point has been illustrated in simulation of a numerical model on the order of Model III above. See Brainard and Tobin, "Pitfalls in Financial Model Building," *American Economic Review*, 58 (May, 1968), pp. 99–122.

[7]

Excerpt from J. Tobin, 'An Essay on the Principles of Debt Management', Commission on Money and Credit, *Fiscal and Debt Management Policies*, 149–67

II. MONETARY EFFECTS OF CHANGES IN SIZE AND STRUCTURE OF DEBT

A. Net Private Wealth and its Composition

Suppose that at a given moment of time the net worth of every economic unit in the United States other than the federal government is calculated. Net private[1] wealth is the aggregate of these net worths. In the aggregation private debts wash out. They appear as assets on the balance sheets of some units, but in equal amount on the liability side of other balance sheets. What remains? There are three basic components of net private wealth: (1) claims against the federal government, i.e., the federal debt defined in Section I; (2) the value of the United States physical capital stock, other than capital owned by the federal government, and (3) net claims of United States economic units, again excepting the federal government, against the rest of the world. The first component grows with federal deficits or declines with federal surpluses, as explained in Section I. The second component grows with net investment in plant and equipment, residential construction, and stock of goods. It changes also with market valuations of existing capital goods and real estate. The third component grows when United States residents acquire claims against foreigners or invest in property and capital abroad; it declines when foreigners acquire claims against us or equity in property here.[2] In what follows, the third category will be

---

[1]The word "private" is not altogether appropriate, since among the economic units in the aggregate would be state and local governments. "Private" should be interpreted, in this context, as nonfederal.

[2]One implication of the concept of federal debt adopted in Section I should be noted. When the United States finances a balance of trade deficit by selling gold or by foreign acquisition of U.S. Government securities, it is the federal debt component of private wealth that declines. When the same deficit is financed by United States banks' incurring deposit obligations to foreigners, it is the third component of private wealth that declines.

ignored, or consolidated with the second. The net capital position of the United States vis-a-vis the rest of the world is an important topic in its own right, but it is not the subject here. It will not distort the analysis of debt management to assume a closed economy in order to focus attention on the relative magnitudes of the first two components of net private wealth.

B. Stabilization Policy and the Supply Price of Capital

Control of the course of aggregate economic activity—economic stabilization—is the principal purpose of monetary and debt management. What is the route by which management of money and public debt may affect economic activity? Ultimately its effectiveness depends on its ability to influence the terms on which investors will hold the existing stock of real capital and absorb new capital. If investors demand a higher rate of return on capital than the existing stock can yield, given the state of technology and the supplies of labor and other factors of production, investment will decline and the economic climate will be deflationary. If investors are willing and anxious to expand their holdings of capital at a rate of return lower than the marginal productivity of the capital stock, investment will tend to outrun saving and the outlook will be inflationary. The same point may be expressed in another way. If investors are content with a low rate of return on equity in real capital, relative to its marginal productivity, their bids for existing capital will cause its valuation to exceed its replacement cost; the difference will be an incentive to expand production of capital goods. But if investors require a relatively high rate of return on equity in real capital, the valuation of capital in place will be low relative to its replacement cost and will deter further production of investment goods. The course of economic activity, then, depends on the difference between two rates of return on ownership of capital. One is the anticipated marginal productivity of capital, determined by technology, factor supplies, and expectations about the economy. This cannot be controlled by the managers of money and public debt, except in the indirect sense that if they somehow successfully control the economy they control all economic magnitudes. The second rate of return on capital equity is that rate at which the public would be willing to hold the existing stock of capital, valued at current prices. It is this rate of return, the supply price of capital, which the monetary and debt authorities may hope to influence through changing the supplies and yields of assets and debts that compete with real capital for place in the portfolios and balance sheets of economic units.

Broadly speaking, the authorities can lower the supply price of capital by lowering the yields of competing assets. But it is important to remember that these yields—interest rates on national debt instruments, bank loan rates, mortgage rates, etc.—are means rather than ends. The target is the supply price of capital. This rate, although influenced by the yields of other assets, is not identical with any of them. It is a mistake to use the rate on long-term Government or corporate bonds, for example, as an unerring gauge of the tightness of monetary control of the economy. The differential between a long-term bond interest rate and the rate of return investors require of equity is surely as variable as any differential in the whole gamut of the structure of interest rates. Lowering the long-term Government bond rate is not expansionary if the premium above it required for investment in real capital is at the same time commensurately increased. Increasing the long-term bond rate is not deflationary if the means that increase it at the same time lower in equal degree the equity-bohd differential.

What is the monetary effect of an increase in the public debt? Other things equal, what difference does the size of the debt make to the supply price of capital? Will a larger debt change the rate of return that the community of private investors require in order to hold a given stock of capital? The answer of this section is that the monetary effect of an increase in the debt is to lower the required rate of return on capital, to make it easier to absorb a growing capital stock into portfolios and balance sheets. The magnitude of the effect depends on the form that the increase in debt takes. The expansionary effect is strongest, of course, if the increment of debt is "monetized," i.e., if it takes the form of demand debt. The effect is weaker for short debt and still weaker for long debt. But, it is argued here, the direction of the effect is unambiguous. Given the present assortment of debt instruments, the enduring monetary effect of increase in government debt is expansionary. To have a neutral or restrictive effect on the demand for capital, an increase in debt would have to take unconventional form. This is a principal motivation for the proposal set forth in Section IV below for new debt instruments geared to the purchasing power of the dollar.

A $1 billion increase in public debt, while the value of the capital stock is given, means a $1 billion increase in net private wealth. At given rates of return on debt instruments and on equity in capital, owners of wealth would be unlikely to choose to concentrate the whole of a billion dollar increase in wealth on public debt. Rather they would choose a balanced expansion of their holdings. Their new acquisitions would be divided between public debt and capital. Consequently to induce the community to absorb the whole of an increase in wealth in the form of public debt, yields of public debt instruments must rise relative to the rate of return on capital. The differential of capital equity over public debt must fall. If the public debt were homogeneous and the yield on the uniform debt instrument were fixed, the result of debt expansion would be perfectly clear. The differential in favor of capital would have to fall; otherwise the public would not be content with portfolios in which capital forms a smaller proportion and government debt a larger proportion.

Given a fixed yield on government debt, the differential could fall only if the supply price of capital were to fall.

In practice, the public debt is not homogeneous, and the yields on debt instruments are not absolutely fixed. However, there are certain fixed anchors to the structure of yields on public debt. First, the rate on the transferable demand debt of the government—currency for nonbank holders, reserve balances in Federal Reserve banks for banks—is zero. The rate on demand deposits is likewise legally set at zero; every dollar of public holding of deposits is indirectly a holding of a fraction of a 'dollar, the required reserve ratio, for government demand debt. Second, banks can obtain additional holdings of demand debt at the Federal Reserve discount rate. So long as it is maintained constant, the discount rate provides another fixed pivot for the structure of rates.

About a quarter of the marketable U.S. federal debt is demand debt, subject to legally or administratively fixed yield. The rest takes the form of instruments whose yields are determined in the market. Although they are market-determined, these yields cannot stray too far from the fixed yields of the demand debt. The time obligations of the government—the Treasury or the Federal Reserve—are more or less substitutable for its demand obligations, and an effective chain of substitution keeps the yields even of long maturities in line. Therefore, if yields on public debt must rise relative to the rate of return on capital, the main brunt of the adjustment falls on the latter. The inducement to increase the proportion of wealth held as public debt, decreasing the share held as capital equity, must be in substantial part a fall in the yield of equity.

To say that an increase in debt is expansionary, and likewise that debt retirement has a deflationary monetary effect, is not to say that neutralization of these effects is beyond the powers of the monetary and debt authorities. The assertion is merely that effects in the indicated direction will occur, in the absence of deliberate action to offset them. The Federal Reserve may be able to neutralize the expansionary influence of an increase in debt by raising the discount rate. Or the effect of a change in the size of the debt may be counteracted by a change in the composition of the initial debt. For example, expansion of long-term debt might be neutralized by a tighter monetary policy, open market sales substituting short debt for demand debt. The effects of changes in the composition of debt of a given total size are discussed in Section II.G.

C. Effects of Change in the Supply of Demand Debt

The expansionary effect of an increase in debt is clearest and strongest when it takes the form of demand debt. Suppose that federal demand debt is increased by $1 billion, while the quantities of short and long government debt outside the Treasury and the Federal Reserve are unchanged. Assume that the Federal Reserve discount rate remains unchanged. Take the money value of the stock of capital, and the prices of goods, as given also. (Of course, in fact the stock of capital is always changing both in real amount and in money value at the same time as the federal debt. The assumption of a fixed amount and value of capital is made for analytical purposes, because the gauge of the impact of change in debt is what it does to the rate of return investors require of a <u>given</u> quantity of capital. As is usual in comparative static analysis, the purpose is to describe the difference it makes whether a parameter—in this case demand debt—is smaller or larger. The analysis is timeless, even though it would be impossibly puristic to try to explain it without chronological language.)

Private wealth increases by $1 billion, and interest rates must adjust so that owners of wealth are content to put the whole increment into demand debt, either directly or through banks and other intermediaries. Public currency holdings are quite inelastic; it will not strain fact too much to assume them constant. Then the whole of the billion dollars must find its home with the banks, either as required reserves or as free reserves. Initially the deposits of the public in the banks will increase by the same amount as the increment in private wealth, and the free reserves of the banks will increase by a large fraction—five-sixths if the required reserve ratio is one-sixth—of that amount. As banks try to convert these excessive holdings of free reserves into earning assets, they bid government and private debt away from the public. The nonbank holders of these assets are induced to sell them, and to hold bank deposits instead, by a fall in their yields. Banks are willing to acquire them in spite of their reduced yields because they are, within limits, more profitable than free reserves. How far this process of expansion of banks' deposits and assets goes depends on the banks' preferences for cash and for freedom from debt to the Federal Reserve, relative to the yields of less liquid assets. If the banks' equilibrium demand for free reserves is constant, deposits and earning assets will expand by the textbook multiples of the original accretion of reserves. For example, if the average required reserve ratio is one to six, deposits will expand by six billions and earning assets by five billions, from an increase in demand debt of one billion dollars. However, these classic multiples probably overstate the expansion. The expansion is inevitably accompanied by a fall in the yields of government and private debts. With the Federal Reserve discount rate unchanged, this fall diminishes the inducement to borrow from the Federal Reserve. It increases the attractiveness of excess reserve balances. As a result, banks' equilibrium demand for free reserves will be higher. A part of the increment in demand debt will serve to satisfy an enhanced appetite for free reserves; not all of the billion will go into higher required reserves.

What is the adjustment of the public outside the banks? Suppose, provisionally, that in the end the banks keep free reserves unchanged. In order to absorb as required bank reserves a billion dollar increase in demand debt, the public must absorb a multibillion dollar increase in bank deposits. At the assumed required reserve ratio, the public must increase deposits by six times the increase in its wealth. Here is the significance of fractional-reserve banking. A substantial change in yields is required to effect a drastic shift in portfolio composition. A part of the increase in public willingness to hold bank deposits will be induced by reduction in yields of interest-bearing government debt. Short debt, in particular, is regarded by many corporations and institutions as a close substitute for cash. But it is hardly likely that these yields can fall enough to make the public reduce its holdings of federal debt by anything like five or six times the increase in net private wealth. In the balance sheet of the public, most of the room for the multiple expansion of deposits must come from an increase in the debt of the public to the banks, in response to a reduction in interest rates on private loans. This adjustment is a shift by private lenders from direct lending or from lending through nonbank intermediaries, which become less profitable, to bank deposits; the banks acquire the loan business given up. But unless the rate of return on capital falls too, the reduction in loan rates will stimulate new borrowing to finance new capital investment. But in the hypothetical example the stock of capital is assumed constant. To prevent the demand for capital from exceeding the existing stock, the yield of capital must fall. Its fall is the measure of the expansionary effect of the increase in debt.

Even if banks increase their equilibrium free reserve holdings, deposits will in all probability expand by a multiple—though smaller than the reciprocal of the required reserve ratio—of the increment of demand debt. Substantial reduction in the yields of alternative assets, including capital equity, would be necessary to induce the public to make this shift in the composition of their balance sheets.

Is it conceivable that banks' demand for free reserves would be so elastic with respect to yields on earning assets that they would absorb as free reserves five-sixths of the increment of demand debt? If so, the expansion of deposits would be limited to the growth of private wealth. Even an expansion of deposits thus limited would require, in general, some reductions in yields on other assets. Without the inducement provided by lower yields elsewhere, the public would not wish to keep even as little as 100 percent of an increase in its net worth in deposits. Conceivably the reduction in yields that would accomplish this reallocation of assets by the public might be sufficient to persuade the banks to hold their initial gain idle in free reserves. Something like this happened in the thirties when yields on earning assets were low and the banks were saturated with reserve funds. In normal times, and in the usual range of interest rates, the banks' demand for free reserves is much more easily satisfied.

Table III-2 is a hypothetical illustration of the change in bank and public balance sheets necessary to absorb an increment of demand debt and private wealth equal to 1 percent of initial wealth. The Table is meant to be indicative of behavior and circumstances between the extremes discussed above. That is, a multiple expansion of deposits occurs, but not the full textbook multiple. Free reserves also increase.

TABLE III-2

Hypothetical Illustration

Assets (+) and Liabilities (-) of Banks and Public Before and After

An Increment of Demand Debt and Private Wealth Equal to 1% of Wealth

	Banks			Public			Total		
	Before	After	Change	Before	After	Change	Before	After	Change
Currency	0	0	0	+30	+30	0			
Required Reserves	+20	+27	+7						
Free Reserves	0	+3	+3						
Demand Debt Total	+20	+30	+10	+30	+30	0	+50	+60	+10
Short Debt	+20	+30	+10	+60	+50	-10	+80	+80	0
Long Debt	+10	+15	+5	+60	+55	-5	+70	+70	0
Private Debt	+80	+97	+17	+320 / -400	+303 / -400	-17	0	0	0
Deposits	-120	-162	-42	+120	+162	+42	0	0	0
Capital	-10	-10	0	+810	+810	0	+800	+800	0
TOTAL	0	0	0	+1000	+1010	+10	+1000	+1010	+10

D. Change in the Supply of Short Debt

Suppose that private wealth is increased by government deficit financed by short debt. Demand debt, long debt, and the capital stock remain constant in supply, and the Federal Reserve maintains a fixed discount rate.

An extreme assumption will provide a useful point of departure for analysis of this case. The assumption is that the banks do, and the public does not, regard bills and free reserves as perfect substitutes at the prevailing bill rate. (Not all short debt is in the form of Treasury bills, but since the differences among short debt instruments are not of great moment, it is not misleading to use "bills" as a convenient synonym for short debt.) In this case an increase in bank holdings of short debt would have the same consequences as an equal increase in bank holdings of demand debt. In the "after" column of the example of Table III-3 banks have absorbed an extra 9 of short debt. Net free reserves have become -6; banks have to borrow to meet reserve requirements. But banks

act the same as if their free reserves had been increased by 3(9-6).
They expand loans and deposits. The public makes room for part
of the expansion of deposits, which exceeds the increment in private
wealth, by selling long debt to the banks, but for most of it by re-
linquishing private loan business to the banks. Reductions in the
long rate, loan rate, and return on capital equity are necessary to
achieve this reconstitution of bank and public balance sheets. Because of the assumed perfect substitutability of short debt for cash
in bank portfolios, the short rate remains unchanged. For this
reason, the public increases its holdings of shorts (+1) as well as
of bank deposits.

The assumption behind Table III-3 is far-fetched but it is instructive. Short debt is not a perfect substitute for demand debt in
bank portfolios, but it is within limits a good substitute. A bank
needs a defensive buffer between its commercial loans and its required reserves. The purpose of the buffer is to enable it to with-
stand a loss of deposits and reserves, on the one hand, or compelling
demands for loan accommodation, on the other hand. In neither case
does the bank wish the necessity of meeting the reserve requirement to force it to disappoint customers, many of whom have earned
the right to loan accommodation by faithfulness as depositors. Excess reserve balances are the most obvious defensive asset. Over-
night loans of such balances—federal funds—to other banks are
another. Treasury bills fill the defensive function almost as well.
They can be sold quickly in a well organized market. Since they are
of short maturity, they subject the bank to very little risk of capital
loss. Indeed by staggering maturities the bank can contrive to meet
most reserve stringencies by letting bills "run off" and need worry
very little about the chance that it would have to sell bills in a
declining market. In any case bills can be used, like other Government securities, as collateral for advances from the Federal Reserve. This further reduces the chance of capital loss involved in
using them as secondary reserves; if the bill market is down when
the bank needs reserves, the bank may find it advantageous not to
sell bills but to borrow the needed reserves, repaying the loan when
its bills mature or its reserve position is replenished.

These considerations suggest that for the banking system as a
whole, short Treasury debt is a good though imperfect substitute
for net free reserves. When the bill is very low, banks will prefer
excess reserves in order to avoid the slight risks and transactions
costs involved in using bills as secondary reserves. This preference
will be very little affected by the discount rate. Even at a very low
discount rate, banks would not find it profitable to borrow in order
to acquire or to retain bills. But at higher rates, banks' demand
for bills relative to net free reserves will be sensitive to the differential between the discount rate and the bill rate. When the bill rate
is high relative to the discount rate, banks short of reserves will

borrow rather than sell bills, and banks with free funds will buy bills rather than repaying debt or adding to excess reserves. When the bill rate is low relative to the discount rate, banks short of reserves will sell bills rather than incur debt to the Federal Reserve and banks with free funds will repay debt or hold cash rather than buy bills.

TABLE III-3

Hypothetical Illustration

Assets (+) and Liabilities (-) of Banks and Public Before and After
An Increment of Short Debt and Private Wealth Equal to 1% of Wealth
Assuming Short Debt a Perfect Substitute for Free Reserves

	Banks			Public			Total		
	Before	After	Change	Before	After	Change	Before	After	Change
Currency	0	0	0	+30	+30	0			
Required Reserves	+20	+26	+6						
Free Reserves	0	-6	-6						
Demand Debt	+20	+20	0	+30	+30	0	+50	+50	0
Short Debt	+20	+29	+9	+60	+61	+1	+80	+90	+10
Long Debt	+10	+16	+6	+60	+54	-6	+70	+70	0
Private Debt	+80	+101	+21	+320 −400	+299 −400	-21	0	0	0
Deposits	-120	-156	-36	+120	+136	+36	0	0	0
Capital	-10	-10	0	+810	+810	0	+800	+800	0
TOTAL	0	0	0	+1000	+1010	+10	+1000	+1010	+10

TABLE III-4

Hypothetical Illustration

Assets (+) and Liabilities (-) of Banks and Public Before and After
An Increment of Short Debt and Private Wealth Equal to 1% of Wealth

	Banks			Public			Total		
	Before	After	Change	Before	After	Change	Before	After	Change
Currency	0	0	0	+30	+30	0			
Required Reserves	+20	+23	+3						
Free Reserves	0	-3	-3						
Demand Debt	+20	+20	0	+30	+30	0	+50	+50	0
Short Debt	+20	+27	+7	+60	+63	+3	+80	+90	+10
Long Debt	+10	+10	0	+60	+60	0	+70	+70	0
Private Debt	+80	+91	+11	+320 −400	+309 −400	-11	0	0	0
Deposits	-120	-138	-18	+120	+138	+18	0	0	0
Capital	-10	-10	0	+810	+810	0	+800	+800	0
TOTAL	0	0	0	+1000	+1010	+10	+1000	+1010	+10

Table III-4 is a hypothetical illustration of the absorption of an increase in the supply of short debt, on the assumption that bills are a good but imperfect substitute for free reserves in bank port- folios. Here the short rate must rise slightly to provide banks the incentive to reduce net free reserves. Banks add to their holdings of short debt by more than they lower their free reserves. With their over-all defensive position thus strengthened, they expand private loans and deposits, lowering the loan rate. The rate on long government debt also falls; there may be some reallocation of long debt between banks and public, but none is assumed in Table III-4. The fall in the rate on private debt induces the public to switch to deposits, surrendering loan business to the banks. As before, the rate of return on equity capital—the supply price of capital—must fall to prevent an increase in demand for capital, as against the fixed supply, resulting from the reduction in long and private loan rates and from the increment of wealth.

How great the expansionary effect of short debt is depends cru- cially on whether the banks regard short debt as a better substitute for cash than the public does, or vice versa. The reason is that substitution of short debt for bank reserves economizes "high- powered money," demand debt, while public substitution of short debt for deposits economizes "low-powered money." In one case a dollar of bills takes the place of a dollar of demand debt. In the other case a dollar of bills takes the place of one-sixth of a dollar of demand debt. To take an example that is in a sense the opposite of Table III-3, suppose that the public will substitute bills for cash without a change in the bill rate but that the banks will not. Banks will have no incentive to reduce their net free reserve position, since public demand will keep the bill rate from rising. Deposits will not increase. The only reductions in other interest rates, in- cluding the supply price of capital, will be those that suffice to in- duce the public to concentrate the increase in their wealth on hold- ings of short debt.

E. Change in the Supply of Long Debt

On the direction of the effects discussed in Sections II.C and II.D there is general agreement, although on their magnitudes there is of course great uncertainty and disagreement. In respect to the monetary effect of a change in the supply of long debt, other things equal, there is not even general agreement as to direction. It is sometimes argued that the monetary effect of an increase in the supply of long-term debt is deflationary, the effect of retirement of long-term debt expansionary. After all, an increase in long debt will raise the long-term rate of interest, and retirement of long debt will lower it; many economists are accustomed to judge the direction of impact on aggregate demand of any monetary event by what happens to "the" rate of interest, approximated by the yield of long-term Government bonds. However, the differential of the yield of equity over the long rate may not be constant but systematically variable. If an increase in long debt lowers this differential more than it raises the long rate, it lowers the supply price of capital and is expansionary.

The effects of an increase in the supply of long-term Government securities, keeping the supplies of other components of public debt constant, depend on whether these securities are directly and indirectly a better substitute for demand and short debt, on the one hand, or for ownership of capital, on the other hand. The concept of "better substitute" can be given precision, and this is done below. The meaning can be conveyed by considering two extreme models: A) in which long-term securities are a perfect substitute for demand debt, and not for capital, and B) in which long-term securities are a perfect substitute for capital, and not for demand debt. In the case of either pair, the term "perfect substitute" means that the two yields are held in a certain relation to each other—not necessarily equal—by the fact that investors will make wholesale substitutions of one asset for the other in their portfolios if the yield differential deviates in the slightest degree from normal.

Model (A) amounts to the case discussed above (Section II.B), where the public debt is homogeneous, at a fixed rate. For even though there are a variety of debt instruments, the structure of yields is not affected by the relative supplies of the various kinds of debt. Long securities are such a good substitute for cash, either directly or through the substitution chain of intermediate and short-term securities, that the rate on long securities cannot be changed by altering their supply. In a given state of market expectations, with a given Federal Reserve discount rate, the long rate is as good as pegged. On the other hand, the expansion of debt means that the equity-bond differential must change in favor of debt; capital and long-term debt are not perfect substitutes, and capital has become relatively more abundant. In Model (A), therefore, the supply price of capital must fall.

In Model (B) it is the differential between capital and long-term government bond yields which substitution maintains unchanged. Issue of long-term bonds is essentially an increase in the combined supply of capital and capital substitutes. Meanwhile the supply of assets, government short and demand debt, which are imperfect substitutes for capital and long-term bonds is maintained. Accordingly the yield differential of capital over demand debt must rise. The rates on demand debt being fixed, the supply price of capital must rise. Likewise the rate on long-term securities must rise.

Is the world better approximated by (A) or by (B)? There are good reasons for believing that (A) is the better approximation, that

debt instruments of varying maturities are better substitutes for
each other than for equity in physical capital. The argument will
be presented below. Economics has, however, been dominated by
the tradition of Model (B), and the trained intuition of economists
faced with a problem such as analyzing the monetary effects of deficit financing by long-term debt is to apply that model. The tradition
of Model (B) is involved in the proposition, common to Keynesians
and anti-Keynesians, that investment in capital will be carried to the
point where the marginal efficiency [or productivity] of capital
equals "the rate of interest." "The rate of interest" is identified
with the rate on long-term Government bonds. The equality need
not be taken strictly; some premium for risk may be subtracted
from the expected return on capital to obtain the rate that is to be
equated to the bond yield. Nevertheless implicitly or explicitly capital investment and bond holding are regarded as perfect substitutes
for each other at the proper rate differential. The risk premium,
whatever else it depends on, does not vary systematically with the
relative supplies of capital and long securities. Just as it conforms
to Model (B) in regarding capital and long securities as perfect
substitutes, so the prevailing theoretical tradition regards cash and
long securities as quite imperfect substitutes. The theory of liquidity preference, and of the maturity structure of interest rates,
explains the differential of long rates over the yields of short securities and demand debt. In this explanation the relative supplies of
the various imperfect substitutes play a crucial role. In the simple
Keynesian model "the rate of interest"—the very same one to which
the marginal efficiency of capital must be equated—is wholly determined by the supply of cash relative to the supply of bonds. It
is quite remarkable that Keynes devoted so much attention to the
cash-bond yield differential and so little to the capital-bond differential, and that he failed to apply to the second the principle, that
yield differentials depend on relative supplies, he developed for the
first. It is perhaps even more surprising that the general theoretical
tradition of economics has followed him in these regards so closely
so long.

If Model (A) is the better approximation, though an imperfect
one, the consequences of issue of long-term government debt may
be described as follows: The public and the banks together have
greater over-all net worth, with the same holdings of capital equity,
short debt, and demand debt as before but larger holdings of long-
term government debt. It is of course highly unlikely that the public
will wish to absorb the increase in net worth entirely in an increase
of holdings of long-term Government securities unless there is
some change in the structure of yields and asset prices. The saving
corresponding to the government deficit would not automatically
take the permanent form of investment in long-term Government
bonds. As the public attempts to maintain portfolio balance, with
their larger net worth, they will try to sell long-term Governments

in order to buy equity, private debt, short-term government debt, and deposits. Yields of long-term securities will rise relative to those of competing assets: this process will continue until the change in structure of yields reconciles investors to the new structure of relative asset supplies. Since long securities are good substitutes for short debt, the short rate may be pulled up too. The improvement in yields of interest-bearing debt will induce the banks to diminish net free reserves and the public to hold more debt relative to deposits and currency. Banks, with an over-all increase in their holdings of defensive assets, may expand loans and reduce the loan rate even though the yields on these assets are higher. In any case it takes a decrease in the rate of return on equity to induce the public to increase their holdings of liquid assets, deposits plus government debt, by more even than the increase in their wealth. What might happen to bank and public balance sheets is illustrated in Table III-5.

TABLE III-5

Hypothetical Illustration

Assets (+) and Liabilities (-) of Banks and Public Before and After

An Increment of Long Debt and Private Wealth Equal to 1% of Wealth

	Banks			Public			Total		
	Before	After	Change	Before	After	Change	Before	After	Change
Currency				+30	+30	0			
Required Reserves	+20	+21	+1						
Free Reserves	0	-1	-1						
Demand Debt	+20	+20	0	+30	+30	0	+50	+50	0
Short Debt	+20	+22	+2	+60	+58	-2	+80	+80	0
Long Debt	+10	+12	+2	+60	+68	+8	+70	+80	+10
Private Debt	+80	+82	+2	+320	+318	-2	0	0	0
				-400	-400				
Deposits	-120	-126	-6	+120	+126	+6	0.	0	0
Capital	-10	-10	0	+180	+810	0	+800	+800	0
TOTAL	0	0	0	+1000	+1010	+10	+1000	+1010	+10

In the end the long-term rate is higher absolutely, and higher relative to the yield on capital equity and to the rates on shorter-term Government securities. However, the rise in the long rate is limited by the readiness with which many holders will substitute long debt for shorter securities or cash. The short-long differential will not have to change much to induce banks and other institutional investors to shorten the average maturity of their holdings. Short securities are in turn a close substitute for cash; for banks, government bills are a close substitute for excess reserves or for reduction of debt to the Federal Reserve. Consequently short rates are fairly firmly anchored to the Federal Reserve discount rate and to the zero rate on demand debt and on deposits. Given these basic rates, the yields of short-term Government securities can be changed

substantially only by considerable shift in the relative supplies of
demand and short debt. Here these supplies are taken to be constant. The rise in the long rate is, for these reasons, limited. But
the differential of equity yield—the supply price of capital—over the
long rate must fall. Indeed this differential must fall more than the
differential, positive or negative, of short rates over long. That is
a consequence of the assumption of Model $(B)^A$ that long debt is a
better substitute for other government debt than for capital. Accordingly the supply price of capital must fall.

Debt issue is on balance expansionary, in spite of the fact that
the long-term rate rises. Instead of being an indication that the
operation has deflationary results, the rise in the long-term rate
is in large part a symptom of the expansionary impact of the transaction. It results mainly from the effort to restore portfolio balance
between capital equity and government debt. Another result of the
same effort is a decrease in the supply price of capital.

The argument applies in reverse, of course, for retirement of
government debt. Other things equal, a decrease in government
debt due to budget surplus has an enduring deflationary monetary
effect, superimposed on its transient deflationary fiscal effect. This
is true even if debt retirement is concentrated entirely on long-term
bonds. Given the supplies outstanding of short debt and demand debt,
and given the discount rate, retirement of long-term securities from
budget surplus will raise the supply price of capital.

F. Correlations of Risks Among Debt Instruments and Capital Equity

What are the reasons for believing that government debt instruments are better substitutes for each other than any of them, even
those of long maturity, are for equity in physical capital?

In general, an asset which is a candidate for an investor's portfolio may be characterized by two attributes of his estimate of the
probability distribution of gains and losses from holding the asset
for a given period ahead. One is the expectation of return, the mean
of the distribution. The other is a measure of dispersion or risk,
the standard deviation of returns. Considering a number of assets
together, the investor may be imagined to estimate a joint probability distribution, with possible positive or negative correlations
in the returns on any pair of assets.

In general two assets are good substitutes for each other to the
extent that they share the same risks, i.e., to the extent that their
future rates of return are positively correlated with each other. If
the same future contingencies that would make asset X turn out more
profitably than expected on average would also make asset Y exceptionally remunerative, then X and Y are good substitutes. If the

correlation is perfect, holding both X and Y in a portfolio does not accomplish any spreading of risk or hedging, in comparison with concentrating the same total investment on either asset alone. Considering two assets with high positive correlation of returns, which asset the investor chooses to concentrate on, or the proportions in which he holds the two assets, will be very sensitive to the difference between his expectations of return on the two assets.

When two assets have uncorrelated rates of return, the investor can reduce his risk by dividing his investment between them. The worst may happen to one, but it will be very unlikely to happen to both at the same time. This is, of course, the basic reason for portfolio diversification. To reduce over-all risk, a portfolio manager balances his holdings of assets by seeking independent risks. Some assets he holds have less expected return than others; the justification for their inclusion in the portfolio is reduction of risk. To maintain balance and diversification as wealth grows, an investor will expand the risk-independent components of his portfolio together in rough proportion. He will sacrifice risk-spreading and diversification only under the inducement of a higher expected rate of return on the riskier assets. A larger expected return differential is required for two reasons. There is an increase in over-all risk due to the simple fact that one asset is riskier than the other. Added to this, in the case where the risks are independent, is an increase in risk due to loss of risk-pooling.

When two assets have returns with negative correlation–i.e., events that would make X a big loser would more or less surely make Y a big winner–then real hedging is possible to reduce risk.

What are the risks of holding government obligations? All categories of government debt are free of risk of default. All categories of government debt, including demand debt, share their principal risk, namely uncertainty about the purchasing power of the dollar. Presumably each investor assigns to cash and to other obligations fixed in units of currency a real rate of return based on his expectation of the change in the price level. If his mean expectation is inflation at a rate of 3 percent per annum, his expected real rate of return on cash is -3 percent per annum. Likewise he will subtract 3 percent from the expected money return on any other obligation of fixed money value, in order to arrive at its expected real rate of return. But no one is sure about the price level. It may rise more than the expected 3 percent, or it may rise less, even fall. This is a risk in holding any asset of this kind. It is shared equally by all government debt instruments. If inflation takes away 50 percent of the value of cash during the next decade, it will also take away 50 percent of the value of a 10-year bond. If deflation adds 20 percent to the value of cash, it will also add 20 percent to the value of a bond. An investor cannot defend himself against risks of this kind by spreading investments among different kinds or maturities of government obligations.

The second risk of government obligations is due to uncertainty about future interest rates. This risk affects differently obligations of different maturities. An investor interested in the money value of his asset three months from now can be perfectly sure of it by holding cash or an obligation with maturity of three months or less. If he holds a debt of longer maturity, the value of his investment in three months will depend on the vagaries of the market. If the interest rate rises, he will suffer a capital loss; if it falls, he will gain. The degree of this uncertainty depends on the length of maturity. A one point change in interest rate cannot alter very much the capital value of an obligation due in another three months or a year. It can alter considerably the capital value of a distant maturity. If interest rates for various maturities are expected most probably to move together, the prospects of short-period return on obligations of different maturities are positively correlated, with greater risks on greater maturities. For investors of short horizon, therefore, the risk associated with interest rate changes works in the same direction as the risk associated with price level changes. It makes government obligations of different maturities good substitutes for each other.

Some investors have long horizons; they are interested in their aggregate return over ten or twenty or thirty years, or more. They anticipate little or no probability that they will need to consume their capital at an earlier date. Accordingly they attach little importance to the value of their investments at intervening dates but concentrate on their ultimate value. For long horizon investors, so far as risks of interest rate change are concerned, the ranking of maturities with respect to risk is reversed. One can be more certain of the amount of money he will have in twenty years by buying a twenty-year bond than by buying a ten-year bond and planning to reinvest in a second ten-year bond when the first one matures. Uncertainty about the level of interest rates ten years from now affects the second strategy but not the first. Uncertainty about the future of interest rates adds even more to the risk of a shorter initial investment, a five-year or one-year maturity instead of a ten-year bond. If interest rates fall next month and stay down, the long-horizon investor with a twenty-year bond will nevertheless earn the original higher rate over the twenty-year period. If he has a ten-year bond, he will at least enjoy the higher interest over a ten-year period. With a one-year obligation, he will be stuck with a low rate of return over the nineteen subsequent years. Similarly the long-horizon investor will gain more from a rise in interest rates the shorter his initial investment.

Although the ranking of maturities with respect to risk is reversed for a long-horizon investor, the risks of the various maturities are positively correlated. As in the case of short-horizon investment, this positive correlation makes obligations of different maturities good substitutes for each other. Investors will be sensitive to the structure of yields in choosing among alternative ways of accumulating a sum of money for a target date twenty years in the future. If the current rate on ten-year bonds is enough higher than that on twenty-year bonds, they will buy ten-year bonds and take their chances on the interest rate ten years from now. After all the absolute worst that can happen is that they will hold cash at zero interest for the last ten years.

There is a third situation, in which the target date is neither at the beginning nor at the end of the maturity spectrum. Maturities both longer and shorter than the horizon entail risk, the more risk the more they diverge from the target date. But longer and shorter maturities can be combined as an imperfect hedge; and in this situation they are complements, rather than substitutes. Suppose an investor is holding both, and a rise in interest rates occurs before the target date. He suffers a capital loss on the longer maturities, but makes this up by increased earnings of interest as he reinvests the proceeds of his shorter maturities. Similarly, if interest rates fall, he loses as he reinvests the proceeds of the short maturities but makes a capital gain on the longer maturities. Hedging combinations of short and long securities are, of course, a substitute for the simple matching of maturity with timing of obligation or need. Likewise there are various possible hedging combinations—very short and very long, moderately short with moderately long, etc. Which procedure is followed depends on which promises the highest yield. In this sense various maturities are again substitutes for each other.

Gains or losses from ownership of capital depend on quite a different set of events and contingencies. To begin with, capital ownership is specific. It requires betting on particular kinds of capital goods, particular industries, particular managements. The risks of a poor specific choice are of the same nature as the risks of default of private obligations of fixed money value. Government obligations are free of such risk. It is true that the specific risks of capital ownership can be reduced, though not wholly eliminated, by diversification. The rise of mutual funds and of agglomerate corporations tends to make diversified portfolios generally available, even to small investors. What diversification cannot begin to do, of course, is to eliminate the risks common to capital ownership of all kinds. Though there are tremendous variations in the fortunes of specific equities, they are variations on a common theme. To judge the prospects, either short-run or long-run, of a particular equity investment, one must guess not only its specific merits relative to other equities but also the course of "the market" in general.

The long-run prospects of capital ownership in general depend upon what happens to the relative prices of capital and consumption goods, rather than what happens to the absolute consumers' price level. In the short run there can, of course, be considerable discrepancy between the market's valuation of capital in place and the replacement cost of capital, even of the most up-to-date technological vintage. Market valuations fluctuate violently and erratically as investors speculate regarding the prospects of the economy and regarding each others' speculations. Whether in the stock market or in the markets for real capital goods, the terms of trade between capital ownership and consumption-goods may turn in favor of owners of capital or against them. But what happens to these terms of trade is quite independent of what happens to the terms of trade between consumption goods and money. The main sources of inflation or deflation cause both capital goods and consumption goods prices to rise. Ownership of capital is therefore a good though incomplete hedge against the risks of changes in the consumer price index. Ownership of government debt or its equivalent avoids the risks due to changes in the relative prices of investment goods, either as measured day to day in the stock market valuations of capital in place or as measured by the real cost of new capital equipment.

Another risk of capital ownership is due to uncertainty about the rate of technological obsolescence. All capital may be expected to decline in value in relation to its replacement cost as time and technological advance bring better ways of doing the same things. The anticipated rate of return on replacement cost that initially induces investors to acquire a capital item contains some allowance for the expected decline in value of the item due to obsolescence. If obsolescence is slower than anticipated, the net return on the item will be better than anticipated. But if obsolescence occurs faster than this guess, the return on the investment will be disappointing. Diversification of capital investments is a way of avoiding the consequences of miscalculation of obsolescence prospects in a particular line. But uncertainty about the rate of technological progress in the economy as a whole remains. Again, this is a risk that is not shared by government debt instruments nor correlated with their characteristic risks.

The conclusion is that there is substantial independence of risk between ownership of capital and ownership of government obligations. In contrast, there is considerable positive correlation of real rates of return within each of the two categories, among different kinds of government debt, on the one hand, and among different capital equities, on the other. The public will use government debt and capital equity to balance each other in diversified portfolios. They will shift the proportions of this balance only in response to changes in the differential real rates of return expected on the two categories. If, for example, the public must absorb a greater proportion of capital equity, the expected rate of return on capital equity must rise relatively to the expected rate on government debt. The rise must be sufficient to induce investors not only to assume more of the intrinsic risks of capital ownership but also to forego some of the defense against these risks afforded by a balanced holding of claims fixed in money value.

G. Changes in the Composition of a Given Debt

Previous sections have discussed the monetary effects of increasing the debt in each of the three forms: demand, short, and long. If those sections are shifted into reverse gear, they describe the effects of reducing the debt outstanding in each of these forms. Most of the operations of the monetary and debt management authorities involve changes in the composition of a given debt, i.e., increasing the supply of one kind of debt and reducing the supply of another. The effects of such operations are already implicitly described in the previous sections. For example, the effects of open market purchases of bills can be inferred from Section II.C with the hypothetical example of Table III-2, which describes an increase in the supply of demand debt, and from a reverse reading of Section II.D and the hypothetical example of Table III-4, which would describe an equal decrease in short debt. The assumptions about substitutabilities among assets made in the preceding sections already imply: (1) substitution of demand debt for short debt is expansionary, (2) substitution of demand debt for long debt is even more expansionary, and (3) substitution of short debt for long debt is expansionary, but probably less so, dollar for dollar, than either of the other two operations. These conclusions all assume that no category of debt is a perfect substitute for another, either in bank portfolios or public balance sheets. If, contrary to this view, banks regarded bills as perfect substitutes for free reserves, open market purchases and sales of bills would have little effect. Or, if the public, say, regarded short and long debt as perfect substitutes, it would not matter whether open market operations were conducted in the one kind of security or the other [operations (1) and (2) would have the same effect] and lengthening or shortening the interest-bearing debt [operation (3)] would make no difference to the state of aggregate demand.

Tables III-6, III-7, and III-8 provide hypothetical examples of each of the three shifts in debt composition mentioned. These examples are consistent with those of Tables III-2, III-4, and III-5.

[8]

1. COMMENTS ON BRUNNER AND MELTZER

Rudiger DORNBUSCH*

1. Introduction

The work by Brunner and Meltzer over the last fifteen years has become an important part of monetarism and macroeconomics. From their earlier work on the transmission mechanism[1] to the more recent work on an integrated macroeconomic model,[2] they have given consistent emphasis to a unified view of the operation of the economy, the sources of disturbances, and the patterns of responses. The model that has evolved exhibits considerable analytical detail, in particular in the modeling of the asset markets. That detail is designed primarily to provide a framework for the analysis of specific effects in the asset markets – say, disintermediation induced by inflation in the presence of regulatory constraints on the banking system – and is less critical to an analysis of the broad macroeconomic problem of the determination of output and prices. It will therefore be helpful to separate out in the form of a brief exposition the main elements of the Brunner–Meltzer model (B–M) as it pertains to these issues. In section 2, accordingly a restatement of the key features of the B–M model is provided. In the third section, I extend the analysis to a steady-state model that is implicit in some of the B–M conjectures and that further highlights important aspects of their approach. In section 4, finally, some comments are offered and the question is raised to what extent the B–M model is "monetarist".

2. The Brunner–Meltzer Model: An Exposition

In this section I propose to develop a brief exposition of the B–M model. In so doing, I shall not consider those aspects of the model that arise from steady-state

* I am indebted to Karl Brunner, Thomas Mayer and Michael Mussa for their very helpful comments on an earlier draft and for a number of specific suggestions that I have followed.
[1] See Brunner and Meltzer (1963).
[2] Such models are developed in Brunner (1974) and Brunner and Meltzer (1972, 1974).

1. Comments on Brunner and Meltzer   105

inflation and trend growth.[3] I shall attempt to modify the treatment somewhat to accord with the standard macroeconomic literature, and to do so it will be helpful to derive the reduced form aggregate demand function the properties of which, together with the budgetary process, form the core of the B–M model.

The model will be analyzed in terms of the asset markets – the markets for money, debt, and capital – and the goods market. The exogenous variables can be grouped into two sets. One set comprises the money wage rate and the physical stock of capital – along with technology and the like – and is considered given at a point in time. Another set of exogenous variables, again parametrically given at a point in time, is at the discretion of the government. This set, summarized in the vector z, contains the tax structure, t, real government spending, g, the nominal stock of public debt, S, and the nominal quantity of base money, B,

$$z = z(t, g, S, B). \tag{1}$$

For given values of these exogenous variables, we determine at a point in time the equilibrium prices of goods and assets as well as the level of real output. Along with the determination of current prices and the rate of supply, we determine the rate at which the government, through the budgetary process, creates assets and the rate at which the money wage rate and expected prices are revised. These changes in the state variables govern the dynamics of the system.

The analysis distinguishes four time periods differentiated by the state variables that are allowed to adjust. To study the impact or *short-run* effect of disturbances, all state variables are held constant. In the *intermediate run*, financial asset supplies are endogenous but the capital stock and money wage rate are held constant. In the *long run*, the money wage rate is fully endogenous and an invariance of output along with budgetary balance characterizes that state. There is a *final run*, or steady state, in which the capital stock is endogenous and in which the detail of fiscal and financial interventions affects the productive structure of the economy.

2.1. The Asset Markets

A key feature of the B–M model is a distinction between debt and real capital; capital, or equity, and debt are imperfect substitutes and are therefore not aggregated into "bonds" in the manner that has proved so convenient in the Hicksian apparatus summarized in the *LM* schedule. Rather, we have to distinguish now three assets and accordingly require to study the equilibrium in asset

[3] Issues of steady-state inflation and trend growth are not raised in the paper under discussion here but are developed in an essentially similar framework in Brunner (1974).

markets in terms of two separate markets. Since it will be convenient to study alternative pairs, we lay down here all the equilibrium conditions although it should be obvious that, because of the budget constraint attaching to asset demands, only two equilibrium conditions will be independent.

In the market for debt, the supply of loans by the banking system has to equal the stock of public debt outstanding plus the private sector's net demand for loans, V,

$$a(i, \ldots)B = S/i + V(r, i, W), \tag{2}$$

r = the yield on equity,
i = the yield on debt,
B = the monetary base,
W = nominal wealth,
a = the bank asset multiplier,
S = the number of permanent income streams yielding each a dollar a year
     indefinitely,

and where nominal wealth is equal to the value of the capital stock, PK, plus the value of the public debt, S/i, plus the monetary base, B,

$$W \equiv PK + S/i + B. \tag{3}$$

It is assumed that an increase in the yield on debt (or loans which are assumed to be perfect substitutes for debt) raises the banks supply of loans as would an increase in the monetary base. The public's demand for loans is an increasing function of the yield on capital and a decreasing function of yield on debt. An increase in wealth, following B–M, is assumed to raise the private sector's desired net indebtedness or, equivalently, to reduce the private sector's demand for debt holdings.

Equilibrium in the money market requires that the equilibrium supply of money, mB, be equal to the demand for nominal balances,

$$m(i, \ldots)B = L(r, i, W). \tag{4}$$

The bank money multiplier, $m(\cdot)$, is an increasing function of the yield on earning assets, while the demand for money is a decreasing function of the yield on both debt and capital. An increase in wealth, on the contrary, raises the demand for money. Finally, in the capital market equilibrium requires that the existing stock of capital be held or that the value of the capital stock, PK, be equal to the nominal demand for equity, E,

$$PK = E(r, i, W). \tag{5}$$

The stock of capital, K, is given and the price of capital assets, P, is endogenous. The demand for equity is an increasing function of the yield on equity and of wealth and a decreasing function of the yield on debt.

To close the model of the asset markets, we require a determination of the yield on equity. The yield on equity, r, is defined as the ratio of nominal earnings to the price of a unit of capital,

$$r = pe(w/p, K)/P, \tag{6}$$

e = real rental on capital,
p = the price of output,
w = money wage rate,
P = the price of capital.

From equation (6), the yield on capital is an increasing function of the price of output and a decreasing function of the price of capital. Alternatively, using (6) we can write the price of capital as a function of the yield on capital and the price of output,

$$P = pe/r = \pi(p)/r, \quad \pi \equiv pe(w/p, K). \tag{7}$$

Using the relation between the price of equity, the yield on capital and the price of output, we can rewrite the wealth definition in terms of (7) as

$$W \equiv \pi(p)K/r + S/i + B. \tag{8}$$

From (8) we observe that the price of output will have effects in the asset markets through wealth: an increase in the price of output raises nominal wealth and thereby creates an excess supply of equity and loans and an excess demand for money at initial asset yields.[4]

Consider next the equilibrium in the asset markets for a given level of output prices, P_0, and given values of asset supplies. In figure 1 we show the asset market equilibrium schedules, having imposed the assumption of gross substitutability. Along *LM* the money market clears, along *KK* the capital market is in equilibrium, and along *SS* the market for debt and loans is in equilibrium. To characterize the nature of disequilibria off the curves, we note that at point A_1 there is an excess supply of money, an excess supply of debt, and an excess demand for capital.

Consider next the effect of variations in the price of output on the equilibrium asset yields. An increase in the price of output at the initial yield on capital will

---

[4] This effect does not depend on the assumption that the wage rate is fixed. The latter assumption serves rather to reinforce the effect since it implies that the nominal value of capital rises proportionately more than the price of output due to the increase in the real rental on capital.

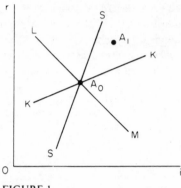

FIGURE 1

raise the value of the capital stock and hence wealth. The increase in the value of capital and wealth will create an excess supply of capital and debt and an excess demand for money. To eliminate this disequilibrium, the yield on both debt and capital will have to rise. In terms of figure 1, the market equilibrium schedules shift to intersect at point A_1.[5]

In figure 2, we consider the effect of an increase in the public debt. An increase in the public debt will create an excess demand for money and capital and an excess supply of debt or equivalently an excess demand for loans. The excess

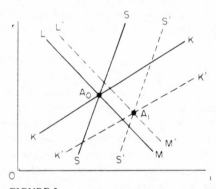

FIGURE 2

[5] The assumption that an increase in wealth raises the private sector's desired indebtedness is of relevance here since it implies that the *SS* schedule shifts to the right, thereby contributing to the unambiguity of our conclusion. If an increase in wealth, on the contrary, caused the private sector to purchase rather than issue debt there would be an excess supply of debt, the *SS* schedule would shift to the left and the equilibrium yield on debt could fall.

supply of debt arises from the increase in debt directly and from the effect of higher wealth on the desired indebtedness of the private sector. The excess supply of debt, therefore, is in excess of the increase in the public debt to the extent that the private sector in response to higher wealth increases their desired indebtedness with a view of using the proceeds to increase their holdings of money and equity. The remaining disequilibrium is resolved by an increase in the yield on debt and a change in the yield on capital the direction of which is ambiguous without further restrictions. The relevant restriction that will determine the direction in which the equilibrium yield on capital will move concerns the *relative* substitutability between assets and the *relative* size of the wealth effects on asset demands. Following B–M, we show in figure 2 the case where money and debt are closer substitutes than debt and capital so that the equilibrium yield on capital falls and the equilibrium price of equity rises.[6] The fact that in the B–M model an increase in the public debt raises stock prices is a key feature of their model and is one they share with Tobin (1961, 1969) and that differentiates their treatment from the body of thinking that would draw a distinction between money on one hand and all other assets on the other hand. The latter line of thinking implicitly assumes a relatively high substituability between debt and capital and would imply that an increase in debt would raise the yield on both debt and capital, although raising the yield on debt relative to that on capital.

Finally, consider the effect of an increase in the monetary base. This will create an excess supply of money – the money multiplier exceeds the marginal propensity to hold money out of wealth – an excess demand for capital, and an excess supply of debt. The equilibrium yields on both debt and equity will therefore decline.

The conclusions of the preceding paragraphs are summarized in the reduced form solutions that express *equilibrium* interest rates as functions of asset supplies and the price of output,

$$r = \alpha(p, S, B, \ldots), \quad \alpha_p > 0, \quad \alpha_S < 0, \quad \alpha_B < 0, \quad (9)$$

and

$$i = \beta(p, S, B, \ldots), \quad \beta_p > 0, \quad \beta_S > 0, \quad \beta_B < 0. \quad (10)$$

The value of wealth, too, is determined by the equilibrium condition in asset

---

[6] The relative shifts in the *KK* schedule and *LL* schedule depend on both the wealth effect and the responsiveness to the yield on debt. At a constant yield on capital, the *KK* schedule will shift more than the *LL* schedule the larger the wealth effect on capital demand relative to money demand and the smaller the responsiveness of capital demand, as compared to money demand, with respect to the yield on debt.

markets, and we can write equilibrium wealth as a function of the output price level and asset supplies. The effect of various parameter changes on *equilibrium* real wealth is somewhat ambiguous,

$$W/p = \phi(p, S, B), \qquad \phi_p > 0, \quad \phi_S > 0, \quad \phi_B > 0. \tag{11}$$

We will follow B–M in assuming that an increase in the price of output or the stock of debt raises wealth. The effect of an increase in the base on real wealth is unambiguous since here the quantity increase is accompanied by a decline in asset yields and hence an increase in asset prices.

This completes the dicussion of asset markets, and we can now proceed to use these equilibrium reduced forms in the determination of goods market equilibrium.

2.2. The Goods Market

In the goods market we assume in the short run, because of a fixed money wage, that the supply of output is an increasing function of the current price of output,

$$y = y(p/w), \qquad y' > 0. \tag{12}$$

The demand for output will depend on asset yields, real wealth, and real disposable income, $\bar{y}$,[7]

$$d = d(r, i, W/p, \bar{y}). \tag{13}$$

In addition, the government spends on real output at the given rate, g.

Real disposable income is an increasing function of the level of output and a decreasing function of the level of prices if taxation is progressive on nominal income.

Equilibrium in the goods market requires that the supply of output equal private aggregate demand plus real government spending,

$$y(p) = d(r, i, W/p, \bar{y}) + g. \tag{14}$$

If we further impose the condition of simultaneous asset market equilibrium, we can use the equilibrium asset yields and real wealth derived in the preceding section and substitute into the aggregate demand function to obtain the *reduced*

---

[7] We depart here marginally from the B–M model by including real disposable income rather than non-human wealth as an argument in aggregate demand. The variable is included in order to have taxes show up somewhere and without the need to raise the issue of the capitalization of labor income.

1. Comments on Brunner and Meltzer   111

form aggregate demand, x, that embodies asset market equilibrium,

$$d(\alpha, \beta, \phi, \bar{y}) \equiv x(p, S, B, t), \qquad x_p < 0, \quad x_S > 0, \quad x_B > 0. \tag{15}$$

In assigning restrictions to the effects of output price changes and debt changes on (reduced form) aggregate demand we have used further restrictions on the relative magnitude of yield and wealth effects. The assumption that an increase in the price of output lowers real aggregate demand arises because the combined effects of higher real taxes and higher asset yields dominate the (possible) positive wealth effects. For the case of an increase in debt the situation is considerably more ambiguous since now the yield on debt increases as does wealth while the yield on equity declines. It is assumed here that the yield on debt does not dominate and that accordingly an increase in debt will *raise* aggregate demand.[8] We note next that an increase in the monetary base will quite unambiguously raise the level of aggregate demand since such a change raises wealth and lowers asset yields. Finally an open market operation – a purchase of debt and sale of money – has a net expansionary effect on aggregate demand. This is another way of noting that while an increase in debt is expansionary with respect to aggregate demand the effect is small relative to the expansionary effects of a monetary increase.

In figure 3 we show, following B–M, the short-run equilibrium of the system for given values of all the state variables, in particular, supplies of debt and base and the money wage rate. The aggregate demand curve is shown downward sloping as a function of the price level, while the supply schedule is upward sloping, given the money wage rate.[9]

Consider next the budget. The real budget deficit, D, is equal to the excess of government spending plus debt service over real tax collections,

$$D = g + S/p - \theta, \tag{16}$$

where real tax collection is an increasing function of real income plus income from

[8] The ambiguity that surrounds the effect of an increase in debt on aggregate demand, given that the asset market(s) clears, is not peculiar to the B–M model but actually obtains, too, in the standard Keynesian model where the wealth effect in the demand for money will raise the interest rate at the initial level of income, thereby depressing aggregate demand while at the same time the wealth effect on expenditure will tend to raise aggregate demand. The larger the direct wealth effect relative to the interest rate effect the more expansionary is a debt increases. See, for a further discussion Blinder and Solow (1974, pp. 52–55).

The reader will note too, that in assigning an expansionary effect to debt issue B–M decidedly do *not* espouse the view that debt-financed increases in government spending are ineffective because of crowding-out effects resulting from the debt issue. On the contrary in the short run the debt issue reinforces the effects of higher government spending. The long-run effect will, however, involve crowding out. For a further discussion see below section 3.

[9] For early use of such a graphical representation, see Tobin and Hall (1971) and Marschak (1965).

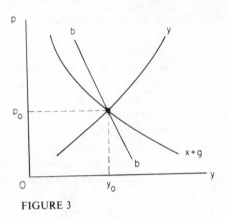

FIGURE 3

debt which is part of the tax base. If the tax structure is progressive on nominal income, an increase in the price level will raise real taxes. Finally, the parameter t denotes the tax structure,

$$\theta = \theta(y + S/p; p, t), \qquad \theta_1 > 0, \quad \theta_2 \geqq 0, \quad \theta_3 > 0. \qquad (17)$$

In figure 3 we show the schedule bb along which the budget is balanced, given the tax structure, the level of real government spending, and the number of consols outstanding. The schedule is negatively sloped since an increase in the price level raises real taxes while it lowers real government outlays by reducing the real value of interest payments. We require therefore an accompanying decline in real income in order to lower real taxes. The position of the *bb* schedule is determined by the tax structure, government spending, and the debt outstanding.

When the budget is not balanced, the resulting disequilibrium will be financed by increasing or decreasing the stocks of debt and/or base outstanding. Budgetary balance is obviously not necessary in short-run equilibrium and in fact is the prime element of the dynamics in the B–M model. The budgetary imbalance feeds assets into the system which in turn moves the equilibrium position over time.

As part of intermediate- and long-run equilibrium, we assume on the contrary that the budget is balanced. The only distinction between intermediate- and long-run equilibrium in fact lies in the supply of output. We assume that in the short and intermediate run output is supplied according to (12), while in the long run, because of wage flexibility, output is independent of the price level and equal to y_0. Accordingly, in the long run we have a vertical supply curve.[10] This

---

[10] There is a further difference in the long run that is suppressed by the reduced form in (15). In the long run, the real rental on capital is independent of the price level and therefore an increase in the price of output has a smaller effect on real wealth and asset yields. This will not, however, change any conclusions.

1. Comments on Brunner and Meltzer   113

completes the discussion of the model, and we can now turn to some applications
to illustrate its implications.

2.3. Comparative Statics

Consider now the effect of an increase in government spending assuming that any
budgetary imbalance is entirely financed by money creation. We show in figure 4
the effect of increased government spending as a shift in the aggregate demand
for goods and as a shift in the balanced budget line; the latter shifts to the right
since budgetary balance requires higher real taxes to match the higher level of
real government spending.

The impact effect of the increased spending is to move the system to point A_1,
where goods and asset markets clear and where both the price level and real output
have risen. Furthermore, at point A_1 we have a budget deficit so that the nominal
quantity of base money is expanding.

The expansion in the monetary base, by (15) raises aggregate demand at each
level of prices since it causes asset yields to decline and real wealth to rise.[11]
It therefore shifts the aggregate demand schedule upward over time until the
intermediate-run equilibrium at point A_2 is reached. At that point, real taxes

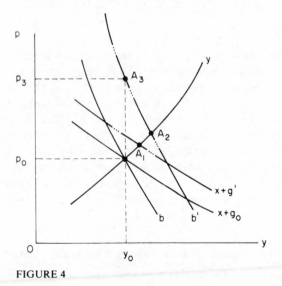

FIGURE 4

---

[11] We are using here the properties of the reduced form aggregate demand function developed
in section 2.1 above.

114   *R. Dornbusch*

have risen sufficiently, and the real value of interest payments has declined enough for the budget to be balanced. In fact, the economy would remain at that point if it were not for wage flexibility.

The flexibility of wages implies that over time the supply schedule shifts upward, or better, rotates and becomes in the long run a vertical schedule at the level of output y_0. This has the effect of raising prices further and reducing output until a long-run equilibrium at point A_3 is reached.

The manner in which the economy accommodates an increased level of real government spending is by an increase in the price level. An increase in the price level will serve to balance the budget through a higher real tax yield from progressive taxation of nominal income and through reduced real debt service. The goods market will be cleared via a price increase by crowding out private real aggregate demand.

It is perhaps peculiar that in our formulation the long-run equilibrium is determined exclusively by the long-run level of output and the balanced budget line but is entirely independent of private behavior such as aggregate demand or asset demands. There are several reasons. First, the interest rate on debt is excluded from the budget constraint by the assumption that all debt issue is in the form of consols so that no refunding is required and therefore the issue price – related to the rate of interest – does not appear.[12] Second, the long-run level of output is assumed independent of the tax yield. Third, the tax yield is dependent only on the level of output but is independent of microeconomic details that are aggregated away.

Assume now that rather than financing the budget by money creation it were financed by creation of debt. The impact effect of increased government spending would be identical both in terms of the shift in aggregate demand and the shift in the balanced budget line. The impact effect of increased government spending is therefore entirely independent of the mode of financing. The stability problem arises, however, the moment we actually start creating debt. Now both the aggregate demand schedule *and* the balanced budget line shift to the right; the latter will shift because of the increased debt service as part of government outlays. This raises then the question of stability – the question whether the balanced budget line outruns the aggregate demand schedule.[13]

---

[12] B–M actually use a broader assumption where the maturity structure of the debt is finite and accordingly they would use the full system to determine the long-run level of prices.

[13] The stability of the system with debt-financed deficits can be determined as follows. The *equilibrium* short-run price of output is a function of the parameters, in particular, the stock of debt outstanding: $p = \bar{p}(S, B, g, t, \ldots)$. The rate of increase of debt is equal to the deficit, or $\dot{S} = i[\bar{p}(g - \theta) + S]$, where the equation is evaluated at the balanced budget equilibrium. Taking

1. Comments on Brunner and Meltzer 115

If debt-financed deficits raise a stability question while money-financed decifits conspicuously do not, then we can be sure that mixed financing, in the right proportions, will be consistent with stability. To the extent that the debt component of deficit financing shifts the balanced budget line to the right, we can conclude that the long-run price effects of a given increase in government spending are larger the higher the share of debt creation in the budget-financing process. This point can be ascertained from inspection of figure 4. The intuition is simply that we now require a larger price change to reduce the real value of the larger debt service liability that is created in the transition period.

3. Steady-State Equilibrium

The model of the very long run, in which the capital stock itself is endogenous, is not developed in the B–M model except for some conjectures and two key features of such a model:

(i) Capital and output are the same in the sense that their prices are equalized, i.e., $P = p$.

(ii) Capital and debt are perfect substitutes and accordingly their real rate of return is equalized. In the absence of inflationary expectations this implies $i = r$.

This section is designed to fill the gap in B–M's treatment. Such an extension is of interest because it provides an interesting perspective on the implications of the budgetary process. In the shortest run, the manner in which the budget is financed – by debt or money creation – is of no consequence. In the very long run, the manner in which it is financed is all important for the real structure of the economy. Emphasis on this point and conjectures about the role of debt in this long-run context are an important aspect of the B–M model and approach.

We shall assume a neoclassical one-sector technology so that for a given labor force the equilibrium stock of capital, and hence the rate of output, is a decreasing function of the rate of interest,

$$y = y(K), \qquad r = r(K). \tag{18}$$

Footnote 13 continued
the derivative of that equation, we have

$$d\dot{S}/dS = i\left[\bar{p}'(g - \theta + \theta_1 S/\bar{p}^2 - \bar{p}\theta_2) + 1 - \theta_1/\bar{p}\right].$$

For stability we want the expression to be negative. This is the more likely, given that $\bar{p}' > 0$, the larger the initial excess of tax receipts over spending, $g - \theta$, and the more progressive the tax structure.

The equilibrium conditions characterizing the asset markets can be developed entirely in terms of the money market because of the assumed perfect substitution between debt and equity,

$$m(r, \ldots) (B/p) = L(r, W/p),$$ (19)

where real wealth, W/p, is defined as

$$W/p \equiv K + B/p + S/rp.$$ (20)

The rate of increase in the capital stock will equal the excess of output over consumption expenditure, c, plus government spending, and in the steady state will equal zero,[14]

$$\dot{K} = y(K) - c(r, W/p, y-\theta) - g = 0.$$ (21)

Finally, for budgetary equilibrium we require that the budget deficit, D, be equal to zero so that there is no net creation or destruction of financial assets,

$$D = g + S/p - \theta(y + S/p, p, t) = 0.$$ (22)

Equations (18) to (22) define the steady-state equilibrium of the model. Several important characteristics of that long-run equilibrium should be noted:

(i) In the long run, money is not neutral in the sense that a doubling in the nominal quantity of money leaves all real variables unchanged. This is so because there are systematic non-homogeneities built into the system. These non-homogeneities arise in part from the public debt and in part from progressive taxation of nominal income. In fact, it will be true that a doubling in both the nominal stock of debt and money will have real effects unless the tax structure is defined relative to real income.

(ii) There is a further sense in which homogeneity is relevant. Even if the tax structure does not give rise to non-homogeneities, we require restrictions on the manner in which the budget is financed in order to achieve long-run neutrality from changes in the nominal supplies of assets. In particular, the financing process

---

[14] The reader will note that in (21) we have shifted from aggregate demand, used so far, to consumption spending, c. The reason is that in a one-sector model we do not have an independent investment function. In fact, investment is identically equal to the excess of output over consumption plus government demand. An alternative treatment, perhaps more in line with the short-run model, would be to assume an explicit two-sector model such as developed in Foley and Sidrauski (1971) and Mussa (1976). While the detail of the productive structure, no doubt, affects the particulars of comparative statics the present structure would seem adequate for the points to be made.

1. Comments on Brunner and Meltzer   117

has to be able to undo the real affects of a change in the composition of assets. Thus an open market purchase of money and sale of debt would have no long-run real effects if the budget was entirely financed by money creation. In the long run, the nominal quantity of debt and money would increase in the same proportion and leave the real equilibrium unaffected, provided $\theta_2 = 0$.

(iii) Comparative static analysis across long-run equilibria requires that we specify which of the assets, base or debt, is endogenous or equivalently whether transitory budget disequilibria are financed by money or debt. The stocks of base and/or debt are endogenous in the long run. This very important point is an implication of the budgetary process which makes at least one of the assets fully endogenous. To put the same point in a slightly different manner: the authorities can fix the quantity of money or the quantity of debt but not both – unless, of course, the tax structure is changed along with the change in parameters.

Consider now the question whether this model indeed generates the B – M conclusion that an increase in government spending eventually raises prices and lowers the capital stock and output? This question can be analyzed with the help of figure 5. The money market equilibrium is represented by the down-ward-sloping *LM* curve along which the nominal quantity of debt and money are held constant. The schedule is downward sloping since an increase in the capital stock via the wealth effect and the lowering of interest rates creates an excess demand for money that has to be compensated by a lowering of the price level. The balanced budget schedule, for the initial level of government spending, debt, and tax structure, is shown as the $D_0 = 0$ schedule. It is downward sloping since an in-

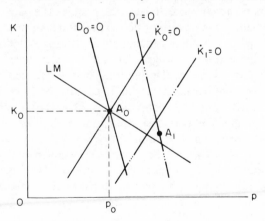

FIGURE 5

crease in the capital stock raises the tax base, and hence collection, and therefore requires a lower price level so as to raise the real value of the debt service liability.[15] Finally, along $\dot{K} = 0$, the capital stock is stationary. That schedule is positively sloped on the assumption that an increase in the capital stock raises consumption demand, via interest and wealth effects, relative to the level of output and therefore causes capital to be decreasing unless compensated by the expenditure-reducing effect of an increase in the price level.

The initial full equilibrium obtains at point A_0, with the markets clearing and stationary stocks of capital and financial assets. An increase in the rate of government spending will shift the balanced budget line to the right to $D_1 = 0$ since a higher price level and therefore lower real debt service is required to compensate for the higher real spending. The zero investment schedule shifts similarly to the right since at A_0 the higher real government spending reduces capital investment by exactly that amount.

The position to which the economy will move in the long run will depend both on how the budget deficit is financed and on the relative response of consumption and the budget to changes in the price level – the relative shifts of the D and $\dot{K}$ schedules. In figure 5 we consider the case of money finance in which case the economy will move in equilibrium to a lower stock of capital and a higher price level. To note this point, we just need to recognize that the deficit at point A_0 will cause money creation which shifts to the right both the LM and $\dot{K}_1 = 0$ schedules until they intersect along the balanced budget line.

For the case shown in figure 5, it is true that the long-run effect of increased government spending is to depress output and raise prices as, indeed, B–M suggest. This need not, however, be the case as can be noted from the alternative where the D schedule shifts relatively more than the $\dot{K}$ schedule – the budget is less responsive to price level changes than consumption expenditure. In that case we may end up with a higher price level and a higher stock of capital and flow of output. This case is more likely the less progressive is the tax structure.

Consider next the case where some of the budget deficit is financed by debt creation. The analysis now becomes significantly more cumbersome because the balanced budget line, too, will shift with debt issue. A relatively simple case, though, is provided by the assumption that the proportions in which the budget is financed by money and debt are such that the LM schedule will stay put. Equivalently, the budget financing is *neutral* in its portfolio effects. Given that assumption, the new long-run equilibrium must lie along the initial LM schedule. By inspection of figure 5, it is obvious that the new equilibrium will imply a higher

---

[15] We assume for the present that $\theta_2 = 0$.

price level and lower capital stock than point A_1. This is so because the debt issue will shift the balanced budget line from $D_1 = 0$ up and to the right.[16]

From the preceding analysis, we can infer that the steady-state reduction in the capital stock and output will be larger the larger the share of the budget that is financed by debt creation. It is true, too, that instability becomes more likely the larger that share.

4. Comments

In these comments I shall focus on three essential issues raised by the B–M model. They are, respectively, the adequacy of discussing their model in terms of comparative statics, the need for disaggregation, and the extent to which their analysis can be judged "monetarist".

4.1. Dynamics, Stability, and Comparative Statics

The B–M analysis of the process of adjustment of the economy relies essentially on a comparative static analysis. The economy adjusts to a disturbance over various runs where for each run a further state variable is treated as endogenous or a further constraint is imposed. Thus, in the short run all state variables other than the one causing a disturbance are treated as given; in the inter run financial assets are endogenous; in the long run money wages and expectations adjust; and in the final-run equilibrium the stock of capital itself is endogenous. The problem with such a formulation is that in fact most of the described states would actually never be observed because the state variables are *jointly* endogenous. To put the same point somewhat differently, we note that capital accumulation, wage revisions, and budget financing are concurrent processes. This implies that in terms of comparative statics we can only study the impact effect of a disturbance and the steady state but not the intermediate and long run. Alternatively with a complete dynamic specification the entire equilibrium path of the system can be considered.

There is a further respect in which the splitting up of essentially concurrent processes is misleading, and this concerns the stability properties of the model.

---

[16] If the budget was entirely financed by debt creation, the *LM* schedule must shift down and to the left in the financing process. The case of mixed finance such that the *LM* schedule stays put is therefore a benchmark case in between a deficit that is entirely money-financed and one that is entirely debt-financed; it is in this sense that the financing is "neutral".

If, in fact, revisions in money wages and capital accumulation occur concurrently with budget financing, then the appropriate dynamic system is not restricted to the goods market equilibrium conditions and the evolution of financial asset supplies but rather is to be augmented by a theory of investment and a wage formation process as part of the dynamic model.

Such an extension has two implications. One is that the B–M model does not possess enough "allocative detail" to discuss the actual time path of the economy and is therefore limited to statements that can be made relative to the static equations that govern the impact effect and the steady state. Contrary to B–M, their neglect of a distinction between consumption and investment spending is a shortcoming rather than a superior method.[17]

A second implication concerns their inference that "the economic system is stable" and that "cumulative movements of price or output result mainly from the decisions or actions of governments, not individuals or private institutions. The private sector has a stabilizing influence, so that the economy adjusts to any maintained policy". There is quite obviously no support in the B–M model for such a statement. There is surely little doubt that for a sustained period of time the motion of the economy can be entirely dominated by capital formation and expectations or, for that matter, that shifts in private behavior can induce budgetary imbalance.

A final remark in the context of dynamics and stability concerns the adjustment of the economy to a debt-financed budget deficit. B–M show, by imposing sufficient conditions on the structural equations, that the system may be stable provided an increase in debt expands aggregate demand. It is not obvious why one would want to restrict behavior, somewhat arbitrarily perhaps, to generate stability under all kinds of experiments. In particular, why should the economy not blow up if the government persistently feeds debt into the system? The answer, in all likelihood, is that the economy would come to expect the debt creation and that the relevant system of behavioral equations changes to accomodate the systematic behavior of the government.

No doubt, B–M are aware of the above limitations of their model and in fact are arguing, implicity, that their modeling of the economy reflects empirical judgments about the relative speeds and dominance of various processes and about the relative contributions to stability of the government and the private sector. Viewed in this perspective the private sector is relatively stable and aggregate demand changes and the budgetary process are dominant relative to the influence of expectations and capital accumulation in the initial phases of a disturbance induced by a change in government spending. It is important for an understanding of the

---

[17] See, however, Brunner and Meltzer (1974, p. 46).

present paper to remember that these empirical judgments that characterize much of the B–M work are implicit in their modeling.

4.2. Aggregation in Asset Markets and Channels of Transmission

A key feature of the work on macroeconomics by B–M has been an emphasis on disaggregated asset markets – a distinction between debt, money, and capital. Their models have the feature that "substitution is not limited to two assets but includes the entire spectrum of assets. Adjustment is not limited to 'the interest rate' but includes the relative prices of real capital and financial assets". They further claim that "contrary to frequent assertions, the major issues in aggregative analysis cannot be reduced to propositions about the relative slopes of the *IS* and *LM* curves".

I believe it is important to distinguish two separate and distinct issues. One concerns the value added of disaggregated asset markets as opposed to the judicious aggregation using the concept of "the rate of interest" to reflect a broad range of substitution across financial and real assets. If such an aggregation is possible – and it is if debt and capital are relatively close substitutes – the issue is one of exposition and there is considerable advantage in the use of aggregation. The second issue is concerned with the *reduced form* aggregate demand function and the question whether the only channel of transmission is the interest rate or whether, in addition, wealth effects act on real aggregate demand. This issue is substantitive, indeed, but I am certain entirely un-contested at the theoretical level and in more recent empirical work.[18]

Consider first the question of aggregation in asset markets. For that purpose assume for a moment that money, debt, and capital were gross substitutes, as B–M do. Assume, too, contrary to B–M, that debt and capital were relatively close substitutes so that an increase in debt raises the equilibrium yield on *both* debt and capital. We have shown above already that an increase in the price of output – and therefore an increase in the value of capital – would raise the yield on both assets and that an increase in the base would lower the yield on both. It follows, therefore, that the yields on both debt and equity would, for the relevant experiments, move in the same direction so that we could without any loss of generality talk about "the rate of interest" as a function of the relative quantities of money and other assets where, for the purpose

---

[18] See, for example, Modigliani (1971). That such agreement has been achieved is perhaps largely due to theoretical work on the consumption function and perhaps the limited effects of transitory tax cuts.

of discussing the *level* of the yield structure, we aggregate debt and capital and oppose it to the monetary base. For purposes of determining *relative* asset yields, we will be concerned with the composition of assets between capital and debt, and we know that an increase in the quantity of debt relative to capital will raise the yield on debt relative to that on capital. If need be, we can therefore go behind the aggregate concept of "the interest rate" and enquire into allocative detail such as relative interest rates.

The concept of "the rate of interest" is therefore in no manner incompatible with a broad spectrum of assets and a wide-ranging substitution effect induced by changes in the relative supplies of assets. It certainly takes account, too, of changes in the relative prices of assets since these are reflected in changes in their rates of return. In fact, the aggregation of all non-monetary assets and a consequent distinction between money and all other assets strikes me as far more "monetarist" an approach than the B–M procedure.[19]

I should like to question briefly what such an aggregtion would do to the B–M conclusions. The only change I can see would be in the effect of a change in debt on the price of capital or the rate of return on capital. B–M assume that the debt issue will cause an increase in the value of stocks while the approach suggested above implies the obverse. The proposed aggregation does not, however, affect any of the substantive conclusions concerning the effects of policies on prices and output. This is so because these effects depend on the reduced form properties of the aggregate demand function that embodies the effect of changes in wealth and all asset yields and because these properties have to be imposed by assumption because of ambiguities.[20]

There is a further reason why aggregation of non-monetary assets is indicated and why the asumption that debt and capital are *relatively* close substitutes is not too unfounded. This arises from the B–M assumption that in the very long run debt and capital are perfect substitutes and, indeed, are actually fully aggregated in that run. Given that there is no theory as to the time path of substitution possibilities, one might as well start aggregating right away. I conclude therefore that for the issues at hand the disaggregated asset market model yields no significant insights and that the analysis could be fruitfully developed in terms of more aggregative concepts.

The second issue concerns the manner in which monetary and fiscal actions are translated into changes in prices and output. As should be obvious from section 2,

---

[19] The aggregation of non-monetary assets does obviously not assume that these assets are perfect substitutes; it only assumes that their relative yields are well behaved. For a further discussion, see Tobin (1961, 1969).

[20] See above, section 2.2.

1. Comments on Brunner and Meltzer 123

these transmission channels are summarized in the reduced form aggregate demand function and derive from interest rate effects and wealth effects.[21] It is not entirely correct to argue that the adjustment of assets and output to policy changes is more pervasive than in Keynesian models, unless one wishes to take an unduly narrow view of the set of models that qualify as "Keynesian". Surely the "interest rate" is quite universally recognized as a channel of transmission, and wealth effects, too, are now enjoying broad use across schools of thought – from Metzler to Modigliani.[22] Since there are no further channels of transmission in the B–M model, I believe the claim to a more pervasive adjustment mechanism must be discounted. What this means, however, is that macroeconomic literature has to a considerable extent espoused a view that B–M, and a few "Keynesians", have advocated for more than a decade.

4.3. Monetarism?

In this subsection, I propose to question to what extent the B–M model may qualify as "monetarist". B–M propose three features without which a theory does not qualify as "monetarist":[23]

(i)   The long-run position to which the system moves is determined by stocks, particularly the stock of money, and not by flows.
(ii) The adjustment to a change in money involves substitution between money, other assets, and new production. Adjustment is not confined to a narrow range of assets, called bonds, or a single price, "the" interest rate.
(iii) The economic system is stable.

I have argued above that the development of the stability properties is not without problems and is inadequate as a basis for the inference that the economy is stable. An alternative interpretation of the stability issue, and one I believe closer to the B–M hypothesis, is that in a stochastic setting the money supply, via the behavior of the monetary authorities, is a source of variability in the aggregate rather than private behavior. While such a view may be perfectly justified, and in fact is an important question, it is a consideration altogether extraneous to the present model.

[21] There is no distinct role for "asset prices [to] join interest rates in the transmission of monetary changes"; asset prices affect aggregate demand either via asset yields or interest rates or else through a wealth effect.

[22] For a recent treatment, see Blinder and Solow (1974). See, too, Teigen (1970).

[23] See, too, Brunner (1970).

I have argued, too, that a proper interpretation of the concept of "the rate of interest" is perfectly consistent with a multiplicity of assets – in fact many more than three – and is therefore in no way inconsistent with a broad view of the adjustment process. I shall add here that the notion that money operates on a broad spectrum of assets and generates "a ripple throughout the economy" is in no manner particular to a monetarist approach but rather constitutes the common core of any general equilibrium approach to macroeconomics, although it should be recognized that the time structure of these ripples may differ quite drastically across models.[24]

The statement that is perhaps most controversial is the first proposition. The assertion that money plays a particular role in the analysis is in no way substantiated. Surely the stock of public debt outstanding plays at least as critical a role in the analysis. To show that point, consider the experiment of a helicopter increase in money under conditions where budgetary imbalance is entirely financed by money creation. The long-run effects of such a money increase are precisely zero – the increase in money causes transitorily an increase in output and prices that gives rise to a budget surplus and destruction of money until the initial stock of nominal balances is restored. In fact, the public debt plays a significantly more critical role since changes in public debt are not self-liquidating in the manner that monetary changes may be. There is another respect in which the public debt plays a special role in the analysis and one that accords poorly with one's conception of monetarism. As shown in section 2, the B–M model implies that an increase in public debt exerts an expansionary effect on aggregate demand and causes an increase in the price of capital. This is perhaps the exact opposite of what has been construed as a monetarist position where debt finance exerts a deflationary effect, if any.

I believe, in part, that B–M may have adopted their formulation out of a concern to ensure the stability of their model. In part the feature is due to the fact that the public debt is entirely undiscounted. As it stands, I believe the suggestion advanced by B–M that an increase in debt stimulates economic activity in the intermediate run and is inflationary must be considered the most controversial implication of their paper.

The departure from a narrow monetarist orthodoxy is obvious, too, in the analysis of an open market increase in the base and purchase of debt. Such a policy – if the budget is financed by money creation – will *lower* in the long run the price level, although it is expansionary in the short run. The departure from inherited thinking is largely, if not entirely, due to an explicit consideration of the budgetary process and the implied endogeneity of assets.

[24] See, for example, Tobin (1961), Modigliani (1971) and Cagan (1958).

5. Conclusion

The review and discussion of the B–M model has provided an opportunity to lay out the key elements of their approach. It has provided, too, an opportunity to question the extent to which their approach can be called "monetarist". It is appropriate now to ask what the significance of their model is. I believe it is correct to argue that their model is in the best tradition of eclectic macroeconomics. It embodies the Keynes–Metzler emphasis on portfolio balance, the Keynesian concern for aggregate demand as a determinant of output, the monetarist concern for the endogeneity of the price level, and a more novel concern with the role of the budget in macroeconomic dynamics. Were it not for their particular treatment of the effects of debt on the economy, one might wish to refer to the B–M model as a representation of the consensus view of macroeconomics, or of what one likes to think it should be.

Bibliography

Blinder, A. and R. Solow, 1974, Analytical foundations of fiscal policy, in: The economics of finance (Brookings, Washington, D.C.).

Brunner, K., 1970, The monetarist revolution in monetary theory, Weltwirtschaftliches Archiv, no. 1.

Brunner, K., 1974, Inflation, money and the role of fiscal arrangements: An anayltical framework for the inflation problem, unpublished manuscript (University of Rochester, Rochester, N.Y.).

Brunner, K. and A. Meltzer, 1963, The role of financial intermediaries in the transmission of monetary policy, American Economic Review, May.

Brunner, K. and A. Meltzer, 1972, Money, debt and economic activity, Journal of Political Economy, Sept./Oct.

Brunner, K. and A. Meltzer, 1974, An aggregate theory for a closed economy, unpublished manuscript.

Cagan, P., Why do we use money in open market operations? Journal of Political Economy, Feb.

Foley, D. and M. Sidrauski, 1971, Monetary and fiscal policy in a growing economy (Macmillan, New York).

Marschak, J., 1965, Income, employment and the price level (Kelley, Clifton, N.Y.).

Modigliani, F., 1971, Monetary policy and consumption, in: Consumer spending and monetary policy: The linkages, FRBB Conference Series, no. 5 (Federal Reserve Band of Boston, Boston, Mass.).

Mussa, M., 1976, A study in macroeconomic dynamics (North-Holland, Amsterdam).

Teigen, R., 1970, The Keynesian-monetarist debate in the U.S.: A summary and evaluation, Statsøkonomisk Tidskrift, no. 1.

Tobin, J., 1961, Money, capital and other stores of value, American Economic Review, May.

Tobin, J., 1969, A general equilibrium approach to monetary theory, Journal of Money, Credit and Banking, Feb.

Tobin, J. and C. Hall, 1971, Income taxation, output and prices, in: J. Tobin, ed., Essays in macroeconomics, vol. 1 (North Holland, Amsterdam).

Journal of Monetary Economics 11 (1983) 281–319. North-Holland Publishing Company

MONEY AND ECONOMIC ACTIVITY, INVENTORIES AND BUSINESS CYCLES

Karl BRUNNER*

University of Rochester, Rochester, NY 14627, USA

Alex CUKIERMAN*

University of Tel-Aviv, Ramat-Aviv, Tel-Aviv, Israel

Allan H. MELTZER*

Carnegie–Mellon University, Pittsburgh, PA 15213, USA

Incomplete information is a necessary condition for any real effects produced by monetary impulses. An alternative to the local–global inference problem is explored in this paper. Agents are confronted with permanent and transitory shocks. Even with full knowledge about the stochastic structure their best perception at any particular time will usually be erroneous. Prices for each period are set at the beginning of the period on the basis of market conditions. The realization of the shock process thus creates a short-run 'disequilibrium' absorbed by inventory adjustments. This adjustment translates perceived transitory monetary shocks into serially correlated output movements. The analysis proceeds within the context of rational expectations. It offers a generalization of equilibrium analysis in two respects. Prices are always in equilibrium relative to perceived conditions, but they do not reflect *all* ongoing shocks. Quantity adjustments reflect the perceived transitory shocks. The framework used involves moreover a stock-flow interaction operated by inventory adjustments. The stock-flow interaction imposes at any time a future expected adjustment path (for price-level and quantities) to the system's unique stock equilibrium. A major implication of the analysis resolves a puzzle experienced in a recent paper by Robert Hall. It reconciles intertemporal substitution with lagged effects of monetary impulses. It also reconciles small and inconclusive cyclic movements in real wages with the occurrence of production function and large variations in unemployment. Lastly, the nature of the inference problem determined by the pattern of incomplete information produces serially correlated movements conditioned on large permanent shocks.

1. Introduction

The observation that unanticipated changes in money cause fluctuations in real wages, inventories and economic activity is almost as old as systematic

*We are indebted to Alan Blinder, Benjamin Eden, Lars Hansen, Dorit Hochbaum, Edi Karni, Finn Kydland, Leo Leiderman, Michael Parkin, Walter Wasserfallen and to the participants of the NBER summer institute group on inventories for helpful comments. An earlier version of this paper was presented at the 1980 Konstanz conference.

discussion of economics.[1] Currently, two hypotheses are offered. One uses nominal wage contracts to explain the real effects of money. Gordon (1976), Fischer (1977), and Phelps and Taylor (1977) are examples. Increases in money can induce increases in real output by raising prices and thereby reducing real wages earned under prevailing contracts. Studies of cyclical changes in real wages by Cargill (1969) and others do not find evidence that this pattern is dominant. A second hypothesis emphasizes that wages (or prices) are set in local markets. Expectations are formed rationally, using all available information, but the information available in local markets does not permit people to separate absolute and relative price changes promptly. The confusion between relative and absolute price changes is responsible for the short-term responses of real output to money.[2] This class of models implies that unemployment and deviations of output from capacity or 'normal' output are serially uncorrelated, contrary to common observations.[3] More recently Blinder and Fischer (1981) resurrect the idea that inventories can lead to persistence when people confuse absolute and relative price changes; increasing marginal costs of production, at the level of the industrial firm, make it profitable to smooth production by partially accommodating demand out of inventories.

This paper reopens the analysis of business cycles in a monetary economy with inventories. All markets are expected to clear each period, and expectations are formed rationally using available information and knowledge of the deterministic and stochastic structure. Product and labor markets differ from financial markets, however, in the speed with which they adjust to new information. Prices, wages and employment are set at the start of the period using all information available at the time. Once set, these variables remain unchanged until the beginning of the next period. They are then reset in light of new, available information. Financial markets clear within the period. Nominal stocks of money and bonds are willingly held at a market rate of interest that reflects both beliefs about all shocks that occur during the period and the actual values of the shocks.

The deterministic segment of the economy is dichotomized. All real variables, including the real rate of interest, depend only on real values and are independent of the money stock. The price level is fixed each period,

[1]Henry Thornton (1802, pp. 118–120) refers to a 'very great and sudden reduction' of money instead of an 'unanticipated reduction in money' and develops the consequences for inventories, employment and production. The core of his argument is that if the fall in prices is believed to be temporary money wages change less than prices, and manufacturers accumulate (unintended) inventories.

[2]This line of argument was developed in Lucas (1972, 1973) and extended in Sargent (1973), Barro (1976), Cukierman (1979) and elsewhere.

[3]Lucas (1975) demonstrates that an accelerator effect on the demand for capital transforms serially uncorrelated errors into serially correlated deviations of real variables from 'normal' values. Sargent and Wallace (1975) also obtain serially correlated errors through the capital stock. Other models with persistence include Sargent (1979) and Kydland and Prescott (1983).

however, so real and monetary shocks that occur within the period change interest rates and cause unintended changes in inventories. Firms hold inventories to increase expected profits by decreasing the probability of stockouts.[4] Within the period they accommodate demand passively, within some range.[5] Production technology is linear in labor so there is no production smoothing at the level of the individual firm.

Gradual adjustment of inventories and production smoothing develops for macroeconomic reasons that are related to the intertemporal substitution of labor supply. The model reconciles the intertemporal substitution theory of labor supply with the observed effects of lagged money on output and employment after allowing for the effect of intertemporal substitution.[6] A depletion of inventories at the aggregate level increases aggregate labor demand. The labor market clears at a higher real wage rate and higher employment; workers substitute current for future leisure as in Lucas and Rapping (1969). The higher real wage rate also makes it profitable to rebuild inventory over several periods. As a result, a given unanticipated monetary shock induces a cycle in inventories, employment and output. The duration and amplitude of the cycle is systematically related to the magnitude of the effects of the real wage on labor demand and supply and other parameters of the macroeconomy.

The adjustment of inventories gives rise to several characteristic features of modern business cycles. Monetary and real shocks have persistent effects on output and employment. Unemployment rates and deviations of output from 'normal' or 'capacity' output are serially correlated. Real wages move procyclically and adjust more slowly than unemployment.[7] Prices move in direct proportion to money only when inventories have settled at their permanent, steady-state level. In other states, prices depend on both money and on the cyclical position of the economy.

The plan of the paper is as follows. Section 2 sets out the deterministic and stochastic features of the macroeconomic environment and develops the implications for aggregates of individual firm's behavior. Aggregate labor demand and product supply are derived from an underlying model of firm's optimizing choices in section 3. This section also establishes the internal consistency or 'rationality' of the model. Section 4 shows that aggregate inventories follow a partial adjustment process and characterizes the behavior of planned and unintended changes in inventories. A general framework for analyzing the cyclical fluctuations set off by real and nominal shocks is presented. This framework is then specialized to focus on the

---

[4]The contribution of inventories to expected profits is modeled directly rather than through a downward sloping inventory carrying cost function as is customary in some of the inventory literature. [See, for example, Maccini (1976).]

[5]The range is set by the optimal choices of the individual firm.

[6]Evidence is presented in Hall (1980).

[7]For evidence on the relative sluggishness of wages and unemployment see Hall (1977).

channels through which money affects economic activity. A conclusion completes the paper.

2. The macroeconomy: Fast clearing versus fixed price markets and the dynamic behavior of expectations

In the economy, we consider the macrostructure and the microstructure are interrelated, but they are presented separately. The demand facing each firm depends on aggregate demand and on factors specific to the firm. Each firm solves a dynamic optimization problem to determine its expected sales and its demand for labor. Firms hold inventories to reduce the (negative) effect of stockouts on expected profits. The individual firm's decisions are derived in section 3. This section uses the aggregate of the expected sales and labor demand functions derived in section 3 as aggregate expected sales and labor demand functions. The macro model determines the level of aggregate demand and the prices and interest rates on which the individual firm's decisions depend. These macro results become inputs for the micro decisions analyzed in the next section.

The underlying framework of the macroeconomy is conventional. There are four markets: The goods market, the labor market, the money market and the bond market.[8] The first two markets clear in an ex ante or 'contract' sense while the last two markets clear continuously and reflect the realization of shocks that occur during the current period. There is a fixed number of firms, N, in the economy; each is endowed with the simple production function

$$y_i = l_i,$$

where y_i is the ith firm's homogeneous output and l_i its labor input.[9]

2.1. The commodity market

Aggregate demand in period t, D_t is

$$D_t^a = \alpha Y^p + \beta(r_t^a - \pi_{t+1}) + \varepsilon_t, \qquad \alpha > 0, \quad \beta < 0, \tag{1}$$

where Y^p is (constant) permanent income, r_t^a is the nominal rate of interest, ε_t

---

[8]Since these markets are related through the budget constraint, one market can be eliminated from the analysis. We chose to drop the bond market.

[9]In general, we will denote by the corresponding upper case letters the aggregate values of these variables.

is a stochastic shock to current demand, with expected value of zero, and $\pi_{t+1} = P_{t+1}/P_t^a - 1$ is the rate of inflation expected to occur between t and $t+1$ as of the beginning of period t. The superscript 'a' on a variable designates the *actual* value of that variable. A variable without the superscript 'a' designates the value of that variable rationally expected by individuals at the beginning of the period for that period.[10] P_t^a is period t's price level and P_{t+1} is the price level expected for period $t+1$.[11]

Firms hold inventories, so the commodity market clears when aggregate demand is equal to expected sales rather than to current output. Expected aggregate sales, $\bar{S}_t$, reflects the combined, optimal supply decisions of firms,

$$\bar{S}_t = K_0 + K_1(H_t^a + Y_t^a) + K_2 D_t, \qquad 0 < K_1, \quad K_2 < 1, \tag{2}$$

where H_t^a is economy wide finished good inventories at the beginning of period t, Y_t^a is period t's income and D_t is the forecast of aggregate demand for the period using all the information available to firms at the beginning of the period.

Eq. (2), including the restrictions on K_1 and K_2, results from optimization and an aggregation over all firms in the economy. Each firm chooses its optimal level of employment and production for the period by maximizing the present value of expected future profits. Demand facing the individual firm depends on aggregate demand as well as on factors specific to the firm. All firms have the same average size. Given D_t, the demand facing an individual firm is stochastically distributed around the firm's average share of aggregate demand. The more the individual firm decides to produce at the beginning of the period, and the larger its inventories, the smaller the probability that it will stockout during this period and the larger its expected sales. As a result, expected sales of the indidual firm depend on opening inventories and, its optimally chosen, current production level. Expected average demand per firm is given by

$$\mu_t = D_t/N. \tag{3}$$

---

[10]Since much of the discussion involves these expectations, this notational choice economizes on the use of symbols. Whenever the time at which an expectation is formed is not mentioned explicitly, it should be understood as refering to the beginning of the period.

[11]Several of the structural variables of the economy, e.g., income, appear in three forms: (1) as an actual value with the superscript 'a', Y^a; (2) as an expected value without any superscript, Y; (3) as a permanent or steady-state value, Y^p. For *some* variables — output, employment, the real wage rate and the price level — the actual and the expected value of the variable for the current period are equal. For sales, demand and the interest rate actual and expected values are not necessarily equal, as explained below. Precise definitions of expectations and permanent values appear in the subsections on ex ante equilibrium and permanent values later in this section. The notational rule does not apply to random shocks. Realizations of shocks do not carry any superscripts.

2.2. The labor market

The aggregate demand for labor at the beginning of period t is

$$L_{dt} = \bar{L}_d + (\gamma_1 \beta + \gamma_2) v_t + \gamma_3 w_t - H_t^a, \qquad 1 > \gamma_1 > 0, \quad \gamma_2, \gamma_3 < 0, \tag{4}$$

where L_{dt} is aggregate demand for labor in period t, $\bar{L}_d$ is a constant, γ_1 is the sensitivity of labor demand with respect to average expected demand per firm, γ_2 is the direct sensitivity of labor demand with respect to the expected real rate of interest, γ_3 is the sensitivity of labor demand with respect to the real wage rate, w_t, and

$$v_t \equiv r_t - \pi_{t+1} \tag{5}$$

is the expected value of the real interest rate.[12] Each firm chooses its optimal labor input. Aggregation of the individual demands leads to eq. (4) including the restrictions on the coefficients. Note that the demand for labor is inversely related to the opening level of inventories and to the relative prices, v and w.

Aggregate supply of labor is given by

$$L_{st} = \bar{L}_s + \omega(w_t - w^p), \qquad \bar{L}_s > 0, \quad \omega > 0, \tag{6}$$

where L_{st} is aggregate labor supply in period t and w^p is the (time independent) permanent value of the real wage rate. The supply function embodies the main idea of the Lucas and Rapping (1969) intertemporal substitution theory of labor supply. Workers substitute leisure in low wage periods for leisure in high wage periods.[13] If we interpret the real wage rate as an index or proxy for all dimensions of the employment agreement, eq. (6) states that the supply of labor increases when a suitably weighted average of all the benefits a worker anticipates from a current offer of employment increases relative to the permanent value of the benefits he expects to command.

The dependence of labor supply on current and permanent real wage rates leads to the same definition of unemployment as in Brunner, Cukierman and Meltzer (1980). When the current wage rate is below the rate believed to be permanent, part of the labor force finds it profitable to abstain from accepting employment. These workers appear in the statistics as unemployed until actual and permanent real wage rates are equal. Within the context of the model, unemployment is defined as the difference between labor supply

---

[12]r_t is the expected value of the nominal rate.
[13]We assume for simplicity that equal changes in actual and permanent wage rates do not change the supply of labor. Qualitative results do not depend on this assumption.

when $w_t = w^p$ and labor supply when actual and permanent wages differ. The number of unemployed workers is given by[14]

$$n_t^a = \omega(w^p - w_t). \tag{7}$$

The steady-state rate of unemployment is zero by definition, but the actual rate of unemployment may be positive or negative.

In the models of Friedman (1968), Phelps (1967) and Lucas (1973), unemployment is a consequence of faulty perceptions about the price level. Here workers are unemployed when they expect their labor to command more benefits than the market currently offers.[15]

2.3. The money market

The demand for nominal money is

$$P_t^a[Y^p + g(Y_t^a - Y^p) + br_t^a - \theta\varepsilon_t], \qquad g, \theta > 0, \quad b < 0. \tag{8}$$

Eq. (8) makes the demand for real money balances an increasing function of both permanent and transitory income and a decreasing function of the nominal rate of interest. We assume that g is relatively small. The term $\theta\varepsilon_t$ shows that any shock to aggregate demand is partly a shock to the demand for money in the opposite direction. The parameter θ measures how much of the shock to aggregate demand individuals desire to finance by changes in their money holdings.[16]

Money supply at the beginning of period $t+1$ is given by

$$M_{t+1}^a = M_t^a(1 + m_t), \tag{9}$$

where m_t is the stochastic rate of growth of money supply between the beginning of period t and the beginning of period $t+1$. m_t has a time independent expected value denoted $\bar{m}$.[17]

---

[14]Recall that in eq. (4) the demand for labor is set at the beginning of the period and does not respond to changes in v_t that occur within the period. We do not mean to imply that this is the only kind of unemployment reflected in the statistics. However, it is probably an important element in the cyclical component of the measured rate of unemployment.

[15]A more complete analysis of unemployment requires discussion of the pecuniary and non-pecuniary components of w^p and of changes in w^p.

[16]The rest is financed in the bond market.

[17]More generally, imperfectly perceived permanent changes could occur in $\bar{m}$ over time. The implications of this case for the cycle are briefly investigated at the end of section 4.

2.4. Financial versus real markets and ex post versus ex ante equilibrium

A basic feature of the economy is that employment, output the real wage rate and the price level are set at the beginning of each period at levels which clear all markets in an ex ante sense before the realization of the aggregate shocks (ε and m) and the individual demand shocks. By contrast, the nominal rate of interest, r_t^a, is determined after the realization of these shocks by the clearing of the money market. The actual values of both aggregate and individual demands reflect the shocks that occur during the period. This assymetry is designed to capture the more rapid clearing of markets for nominal stocks relative to markets for real product and labor. Recontracting in real markets within the period is prohibitively costly because of the complex nature of production and distribution activities. By contrast, the relative ease with which financial obligations are exchanged makes it possible for financial markets to clear more frequently. We assume, along the lines of Alchian (1969), that because of the informational efficiency to buyers of a fixed price for the period, firms that do not post price in advance lose customers to firms that do. Furthermore, alteration of the price, within the period after it has been posted, is prohibitively costly to the firm. As a consequence, all firms post a price for the product at the beginning of each period and adhere to it for at least one period.[18,19]

The demand for labor and expected sales depend on opening inventories, so the ex ante equilibrium of the economy also depends on these inventories. Shocks occur after the decisions about employment, output, the real wage and the price level have been made. Generally, firms respond to the shocks passively, selling from opening inventories and current production until they stockout.[20] Since the realization of demand and the ex post equilibrium usually differ from the forecast at the beginning of the period, end of period inventories differ in general from the ex ante plan made at the beginning of the period. The new, and partly unanticipated, level of inventories affects firms' decisions in the next period. Unanticipated inventories are the channel through which current unanticipated shocks affect the future equilibrium of the economy.

---

[18]This temporary price fixity can be viewed as an implicit contract between firms and buyers. Several models with a temporary fixity of the *nominal* wage have appeared in the recent literature. See Fischer (1977) and Phelps and Taylor (1977). In these models, monetary policy affects real variables by temporarily decreasing the real wage rate. This channel of monetary policy is absent here since the *real* wage rate is determined along with the level of employment and the price level at the beginning of the period. Unlike the above-mentioned models, our 'contract' is immune to the criticism raised by Barro (1977), since both the real wage rate and employment are determined concurrently at ex ante market clearing values. Costs of adjustment prevent employment from adjusting to shocks within the period.

[19]Since the price level is fixed for the period, it does not matter whether the contract is made in terms of the nominal wage rate or not. In either case, the real wage rate and employment are predetermined and independent of the current monetary shock.

[20]The condition under which such behavior is optimal is shown at the end of section 3.

We now show the nature of these adjustments and the way in which they occur. Firms set plans. Aggregations of the planned values yields the market ex ante equilibrium values. The ex ante values, the expected permanent values and the unforeseen shocks that occur during the period determine the ex post realizations. Firms adjust plans using the new information.

2.5. The ex ante equilibrium

All firms and individuals know the deterministic and stochastic structure of the economy. At the beginning of period 0 each obtains information on the aggregate level of inventories, H_0^a, and on the money supply, M_0^a, inherited from the previous period. Information about the aggregate level of inventories and the money supply at the end of period 0 (or beginning of period 1) does not become available until the beginning of period 1. The ex ante market clearing values of the various variables are obtained by equating demand and supply in all markets after setting the shocks' values equal to their respective expected values. This yields the system[21]

$$D_0 = \alpha Y^p + \beta v_0 = a(H_0^a + L_0) + \frac{K_0}{1 - K_2}, \qquad 1 > a \equiv \frac{K_1}{1 - K_2} > 0, \qquad (10a)$$

$$\bar{L}_d + (\gamma_1\beta + \gamma_2)v_0 + \gamma_3 w_0 - H_0^a = \bar{L}_s + \omega(w_0 - w^p) = L_0, \qquad (10b)$$

$$M_0^a(1 + \bar{m}) = P_0[(1 - g)Y^p + gY_0 + br_0], \qquad (10c)$$

$$r_0 = v_0 + P_1/P_0 - 1, \qquad (10d)$$

where use has been made of the fact that $Y_0 = L_0$. Eq. (10a) and (10b) constitute a system of three equations from which the ex ante market clearing values v_0, w_0 and $L_0 = Y_0$ can be solved in terms of H_0^a and the known, constant values of Y^p and w^p. Given these values, (10c) and (10d) determine P_0 and r_0 in terms of P_1 and $\bar{m}$.[22] The ex ante equilibrium of the economy is dichotomized, so real variables like employment, production, the real wage and the real rate of interest are determined by the subsystem (10a)–(10b). The price level and the nominal rate of interest are determined by (10c) and (10d) as functions of expected inflation and the quantity of money.

The ex ante market clearing values are the values that individuals expect the respective variables to take in period 0 given the (identical) information

---

[21]Eq. (10a) is obtained by equating (1) and (2), putting $D_0 = D_0^a$, $\varepsilon_0 = 0$ and rearranging. Eq. (10b) is obtained by equating (4) and (6). Eq. (10c) is obtained by equating (8) and (9) after putting $\varepsilon_0 = 0$ and $m_0 = \bar{m}$. Eq. (10d) is just the Fisher relation in (5) rewritten explicitly. The restriction $a < 1$ follows from micro considerations established in section 3.

[22]The solution appears below.

they have at the beginning of the period. For Y, L, w and P, as we saw earlier, expectations are equal to actual values. ($Y_0^a = Y_0$, etc.) The common expected value of sales, $\bar{S}_0$, and of aggregate demand, D_0, can also be solved in terms of H_0^a by substituting the solution for v_0 into eq. (1) with $\varepsilon_0 = 0$. The solutions for some of the expectations for period 0 are

$$Y_0 = L_0 = \bar{Y} - C_y H_0^a, \tag{11a}$$

$$w_0 = \bar{w} - (C_y/\omega) H_0^a, \tag{11b}$$

$$v_0 = \bar{v} + (a/\beta)(1 - C_y) H_0^a, \tag{11c}$$

$$D_0 = \bar{S}_0 = \bar{S} + a(1 - C_y) H_0^a, \tag{11d}$$

where $\bar{Y}$, $\bar{v}$, $\bar{w}$ and $\bar{S}$ are some constants which depend on Y^p, w^p and the parameters of the model and

$$0 < C_y \equiv \frac{\omega[\beta(1 - a\gamma_1) - a\gamma_2]}{-\beta\gamma_3 + \omega[\beta(1 - a\gamma_1) - a\gamma_2]} < 1. \tag{12}$$

The inequalities in (12) hold, provided the commodity market is dynamically stable in the sense that an increase in the real rate of interest decreases excess demand on this market.[23] The intuitive meaning of this condition can be understood as follows: Ceteris paribus, an increase in the real rate of interest decreases both aggregate demand and expected sales. The latter reflects the supply behavior of firms. Dynamic stability requires that the decrease in demand be larger than the decrease in supply. Eq. (11a) through (11d) imply that employment, output, the real wage rate and the expected real rate are all lower the higher the initial level of inventories. By contrast, expected sales are higher the higher the initial level of inventories.

2.6. Determination of permanent values

The permanent values are the values generated by the general equilibrium of the economy when the exogenous shocks are their expected values — $\bar{m}$ and 0 — and inventories are at their permanent level H^p. Operationally, the permanent values of all real variables can be obtained from eqs. (11) by replacing H_0^a with H^p and using eqs. (10),

$$Y^p = K_0 + K_1(H^p + Y^p) + K_2(\alpha Y^p + \beta v^p) = D^p = \bar{S}^p, \tag{13a}$$

$$\alpha Y^p + \beta v^p = a(H^p + Y^p) + K_0/(1 - K_2), \tag{13b}$$

$$\bar{L}_d + (\gamma_1\beta + \gamma_2)v^p + \gamma_3 w^p - H^p = \bar{L}_s = L^p = Y^p. \tag{13c}$$

[23]For a proof, see part A.1 of the appendix.

Eq. (13a) is the steady-state condition which states that no inventory change is planned, so output and expected sales are equal. The solutions to the five eqs. (13a)–(13c) are the permanent values H^p, Y^p, L^p, w^p and v^p. The solutions are omitted for brevity.

2.7. The ex post equilibrium

The market interest rate, aggregate demand and sales are affected by shocks that occur within period, so the actual values of these variables differ from the values expected at the beginning of the period. The interest rate, determined by clearing of the money market within the period, depends on the price level. The path of interest rates depends on the path of prices, analyzed below. After rearrangement of the demand for money,

$$r_0^a = \frac{1}{b}\left[\frac{M_0(1+m_0)}{P_0^a} + \theta\varepsilon_0 - (1-g)Y^p - gY_0^a\right]. \tag{14}$$

The actual value of aggregate demand is given by eq. (1). Actual sales are

$$S_0 = \min[D_0^a, H_0^a + Y_0^a] = \min[\alpha Y^p + \beta(r_0^a - \pi_1) + \varepsilon_0, H_0^a + Y_0^a]. \tag{15}$$

As long as aggregate demand is less than current production plus carryover stocks of inventories, $H_0^a + Y_0^a$, actual sales equal aggregate demand.[24] If aggregate demand exceeds $H_0^a + Y_0^a$, sales are constrained to equal $H_0^a + Y_0^a$. The actual level of inventories at the beginning of period 1 is then

$$H_1^a = H_0^a + Y_0^a - \min[D_0^a, H_0^a + Y_0^a]. \tag{16}$$

2.8. The dynamic behavior of expected inventories

The expected change in inventories during period 0 is the difference between the sum of output planned by individual firms and the expected level of sales or demand. H_1 is the level of inventories that firms in the

---

[24]Writing actual sales in this way involves three assumptions. First, whenever a particular firm stockouts and other firms have merchandise for sale, customers find the other firms within the period. Customers fail to complete purchases only if there are stockouts at the aggregate level. Second, the real rate is non-negative. Third, observation of the within period value of the interest rate, r_0^a, does not alter expected inflation for the period. This assumption is made for simplicity and without much loss of generality since, as demonstrated in part A.2 of the appendix, its removal does not change the qualitative results to be discussed in the text. Explicit incorporation of the informational value of r_0^a in the model increases the effect of unanticipated money on aggregate demand. This fact also constitutes an answer to Siegel's (1981) criticism of a similar mechanism presented in Cukierman (1981). Those who believe that stockouts are unimportant can disregard the minimum throughout.

292   K. Brunner et al., *Money and economic activity, inventories and business cycles*

aggregate currently expect to hold at the start of period 1,[25]

$$H_1 = H_0^a + Y_0^a - D_0. \tag{17}$$

Substituting (11a) and (11d) into (17) and rearranging terms gives

$$H_1 = \bar{H} + (1-a)(1-C_y)H_0^a, \tag{18}$$

where $\bar{H}$ depends on the constant values of Y^p and w^p and on the model's parameters. Given H_1, (18) can be used to calculate H_2, since the level of inventories expected at the beginning of period 2 bears the same relationship to H_1 as H_1 bears to H_0^a. In general,

$$H_t = \bar{H} + AH_{t-1}, \quad \text{and} \tag{19a}$$

the permanent level of inventories is

$$H^p = \bar{H}/(1-A), \quad \text{where} \tag{19b}$$

$$0 < A \equiv (1-a)(1-C_y) < 1. \tag{20}$$

The solution for H^p is the same as the solution obtained from eqs. (13). Eq. (19a) is a monotonically convergent first order difference equation. The steady state level of expected inventories (which is also their permanent level) is obtained by setting $H_t = H_{t-1} = H^p$ for all t in (19a). The solution for the dynamic, expected behavior of future inventories is

$$H_t = H^p + A^t(H_0^a - H^p). \tag{21}$$

Eq. (21) shows that the expected level of inventories converges to its permanent value. If the current level of inventories is larger than H^p, the economy is expected to decumulate inventories. Similarly, if $H_0 < H^p$, (21) implies that inventories are expected to increase until they reach H^p.[26]

[25]Again, to avoid repeating information on timing, current expectations refer to expectations formed at the start of period 0. Footnote 38 below shows that firms never *plan* to stockout. Stockouts occur only because of unanticipated shocks. This assures that in eq. (17) H_1 is always strictly positive.

[26]The current level of inventories of any individual firm may deviate from the economy-wide average. A firm with inventories below their expected permanent level may at times expect its own inventories to go up while simultaneously expecting the aggregate level of inventories to go down.

2.9. The dynamic behavior of other expectations

By adding and subtracting the term $C_y H^p$ on the right-hand side of (11a) and leading by t periods, the level of output and employment expected for period t at the beginning of period 0 becomes

$$Y_t = L_t = Y^p - C_y(H_t - H^p). \tag{22a}$$

Proceeding similarly with eqs. (11b) to (11d),

$$w_t = w^p - \frac{C_y}{\omega}(H_t - H^p), \tag{22b}$$

$$v_t = v^p + \frac{a}{\beta}(1 - C_y)(H_t - H^p), \tag{22c}$$

$$\bar{S}_t = D_t = N\mu_t = \bar{S}_p + a(1 - C_y)(H_t - H^p). \tag{22d}$$

The time paths in eqs. (22a) through (22d) describe, in addition to expectations, the actual path that the economy follows if, after period 0, there are no further unanticipated shocks to demand or to money. Any shock that raises H_t above its steady-state value, H^p, reduces Y, w and v and raises $\bar{S}$. Adjustment to the shock continues until H_t converges to H^p. The deviation of each of the expected values from its permanent value is uniquely determined by the deviation of (expected) inventories from its permanent value.

2.10. The path of prices and inflation

When inventories are at their permanent position, the demand for real money balances is constant. In this special circumstance, the price level is proportional to the permanent money stock. If the permanent money stock changes at the rate $\bar{m}$, prices are expected to change at the same rate. There is a unique path for expected permanent prices and for the permanent rate of inflation. The path can be computed from[27]

$$M_0(1 + \bar{m})^t = P_t^p[Y^p + b(v^p + \bar{m})]. \tag{23}$$

Generally, inventories are not at their permanent value, so the path of expected prices differs from the path of expected permanent prices. We

[27]Eq. (23) is obtained by substituting permanent instead of expected variables in (10c), using (10d) and noting that along the permanent path $P_t/P_{t-1} - 1 = \bar{m}$. The path of expected permanent prices is the path followed by the price level in the absence of unforeseen shocks once inventories have reached their permanent level.

294   *K. Brunner et al., Money and economic activity, inventories and business cycles*

showed above that because A is a proper fraction, planned inventories adjust gradually. The gradual adjustment of inventories causes gradual adjustment of expected output and other expected real variables, as shown by (22). The expected demand for money depends on expected output and interest rates, so the gradual adjustment of planned inventories causes gradual adjustment of expected real money balances (and prices) to the permanent or steady-state level.

Fig. 1 illustrates the adjustment of prices. The line labelled $\log P^p$ is the path of the permanent price level obtained from (23). The slope of $\log P^p$ is approximately $\bar{m}$; the permanent rate of inflation equals the maintained rate of money growth. The lines labelled $\log P_i$, $i = U, L$ are the paths of prices before the economy settles at its permanent position.[28]

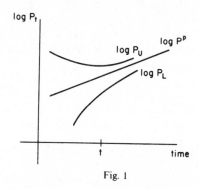

Fig. 1

Two cases are illustrated in fig. 1. Along $\log P_L$ the expected rate of inflation exceeds the rate of monetary growth: $\pi_t > \bar{m}$; P_t approaches P^p from below. The reason is that the response of income and interest rates to inventory adjustment lowers the real demand for money. The converse happens along $\log P_U$. Note that the slopes of the lines $\log P_U$ and $\log P_L$, which are approximately equal to the expected rate of inflation, approach the long-run rate of inflation $\bar{m}$ gradually.[29] In general, if P_t is a converging path, a necessary and sufficient condition for $P_t > P_t^p$ is $\pi_t < \bar{m}$.[30]

[28] Although the word 'expected' does not always appear here it should be understood that these are expected price paths or alternatively the actual paths on which P_t adjusts in the absence of any further unanticipated shocks.

[29] This is a direct consequence of the discussion on pp. 110–111 in Cukierman (1981). The statement presupposes convergence; see footnote 30.

[30] This statement can be proved by assuming the converse — that when $\pi_t < \bar{m}$, $P_t < P_t^p$ — and establishing a contradiction. Let $\pi_t < \bar{m}$. As shown in corollary to proposition 1, of Cukierman (1981) convergence is monotonic, so $\pi_{t+k} < \bar{m}$ for $k \geq 0$. If $P_t < P_t^p$, P never converges to P^p. (Similarly for $\pi_t > \bar{m}$ and $P_t > P_t^p$.) Economic reasoning excludes non-convergence of P to a unique equilibrium at P^p. The reason is, as we see from (23), that both P^p and the permanent

Substituting (11a), (11c) and (10d) into (10c) and rearranging

$$P_0^a = P_0 = \frac{M_0(1+\bar{m}) + |b|P_1}{B_0 + B_1 H_0^a} \equiv x_0 [M^0 \rho + |b|P_1], \tag{24}$$

where B_0 is a positive constant of no particular interest, $\rho \equiv 1 + \bar{m}$, x_0 is implicitly defined by the last equality of (24), and x_0 depends on H_0^a.

$$B_1 \equiv a\frac{b}{\beta}(1 - C_y) - gC_y. \tag{25}$$

We assume that g, the sensitivity of money demand with respect to transitory income, is relatively small, so $B_1 > 0$. Eq. (24) suggests that period 0's expected price depends on P_1, the price expected for period 1, which in turn through the same relation depends on P_2 and so on. Leading (24) by one period to express P_1 in terms of P_2, substituting the resulting expression into eq. (24) and continuing, eventually we get[31]

$$P_0^a = P_0 = M_0 [x_0\rho + x_0 x_1 |b|\rho^2 + \ldots + x_0 x_1 \ldots x_{t-1}|b|^{t-1}\rho^t]$$

$$+ |b|^t x_0 x_1 \ldots x_{t-1} P_t^p. \tag{26}$$

Here use has been made of the assumption that prices eventually converge to their permanent path.

Eq. (26) is a unique well-determined expression for the current period's price level in terms of the expected path of inventories and P_t^p. The uniqueness of the path contrasts with the multiple solutions for the price level found in some recent rational expectations models. [See Taylor (1977) and Blanchard (1979).] The two reasons that rational expectations do not give rise to non-unique solutions in our model are (1) the real economy is expected to converge eventually to fixed permanent values, and (2) stock equilibrium determines a unique permanent price level. If real balances always have a positive, finite value, the price level converges to its permanent value and is strictly proportional to the stock of money. Thus the current price level is pinned down by the permanent value of the demand for real money balances.

---

value of real balances have unique finite values when Y and v are at their permanent values, Y^p and v^p. We know also that Y, v, H and other real variables converge to permanent values. If P_{t+k} does not converge to P_{t+k}^p (in fact diverges) real balances approach zero or infinity as k increases. Non-convergence implies, therefore, that with all remaining real variables constant, real balances approach zero or infinity. An algebraic proof of convergence cannot be provided because the system is dichotomized. Using (26) below, it is easy to see that P approaches P^p, if there is convergence.

[31]Here, $x_t \equiv 1/(B_0 + B_1 H_t)$ for $t > 0$.

Eq. (21) shows that, ceteris paribus, an increase in H_0^a increases H_t for all $t \geq 0$. Since $B_1 > 0$, x_t falls. This leads to the following proposition:

Proposition 1.   An increase in beginning of period inventories reduces the price level for small g.

This result is reminiscent of a similar result at the micro level according to which upward deviations of actual from 'desired' inventories cause downward deviations of the current price set by a firm from its long-run price. [See, for example, Maccini (1980).] The reason is completely different, however. The micro result arises because the firm attempts to decrease its relative price. Our result concerns the general price level; ceteris paribus, a higher current level of inventories decreases expected real and nominal rates of interest, increases the expected demand for money and, thus reduces the current price level.

3. Microfoundations of the firms sector: Derivation of labor demand and expected sales

At the beginning of a period, each firm chooses employment, output, inventories and prices by maximizing the present value of expected real profits given its perceptions about the state of the economy in the current and future periods. Demand facing the representative firm depends on aggregate demand and on factors specific to the firm. Both components of demand are stochastic, but the uncertainty in the individual component of demand is large relative to macroeconomic uncertainty.

Expected average demand per firm at the beginning of period 0 is equal to μ of eq. (3). Firms use this expectation when setting price. At this level of demand and at the price $P_0^a = P_0$, from eq. (26), the representative firm faces a kinked demand curve. The kink is sufficiently strong that no firms sets its price higher or lower than P_0. As a consequence of this assumption, all firms in the economy post the same price, P_0. At the posted price, the stochastic demand facing the individual firm, given μ, is

$$d = z + \delta\mu, \qquad 0 < \delta < 1, \tag{27}$$

where z is the stochastic demand factor specific to the firm. The distribution of z is the same for all firms but its realizations differ across firms. Further, z is i.i.d. and is statistically independent of the macroeconomic shocks, m and ε. The expected value, Ez, is positive for all μ. This last assumption means that in the relevant range, part of the systematic demand facing the individual firm is not related to movements in the systematic part of aggregate demand.[32]

3.1. The single firm's optimization

The representative firm maximizes the present value of its stream of real expected profits, given the forecasts of the relevant macroeconomic variables from eq. (22). Formally, at the beginning of period 0, the firm's problem is

$$J_0(h_0) \equiv \max_{\{l_0, l_1, \ldots\}} E_{-1} \sum_{i=0}^{\infty} \left(\Pi_i(l_i) \bigg/ \prod_{s=0}^{i-1} (1+v_s) \right), \tag{28}$$

subject to

$$h_i = h_{i-1} + l_{i-1} - \delta \mu_{i-1} - z_{i-1}, \qquad i = 1, 2, \ldots,$$

$$h_i \geq 0, \qquad l_i \geq 0, \qquad\qquad i = 0, 1, 2,$$

$$h_0 \quad \text{given}$$

where l_i is the amount of labor employed by the firm in period i, h_i the level of its inventories at the beginning of period i. It is understood that $\prod_{s=\tau}^{i-1} (1+v_s) = 1$, for $i - 1 < \tau$.

$$\Pi_i(l_i) = \bar{s}_i(h_i + l_i) - w_i l_i \tag{29}$$

are the expected real profits of the firm in period i, measured in units of the product, $\bar{s}_i(h_i + l_i)$ the expected sales of the firm, and $h_i + l_i$, the total that the firm has available for sale.[33] The dependence of $\bar{s}_i$ on $h_i + l_i$ arises because the firm stocks out at realizations of demand above $h_i + l_i$. Stockouts truncate the positive effect of high realizations of demand on expectes sales, $\bar{s}_i(\cdot)$ and, thus, create a positive dependence of $\bar{s}_i(\cdot)$ on $h_i + l_i$. Each firm takes the macro forecasts of the real wage and the real rate of interest, w_i and v_i as determined from (22b) and (22c), given H_0^a.

Let $g(z)$ and $G(z)$ be respectively the probability density and the cumulative probability density of the specific demand shock z. We assume that the probability of zero sales at the firm's level is zero, so that

---

[32]The restriction $\delta < 1$ in (27) is implied by the assumption that $Ez > 0$ for all μ together with equilibrium in the commodity market. This is shown at the end of this section.

[33]The expected value operator E_{-1} in (28) is over the distribution of the firm specific demand shocks $z_0, z_1, z_2, \ldots$ given the information available to the firm at the beginning of period 0. Since this expectation is formed on the basis of information up to and including period -1, before the realizations of period 0's shocks are known, it carries the index -1. The latest information included in this information set is H_0^a, M_0 and h_0. Note that h_0 is an actual value whereas the h_i, $i > 0$, are random variables. The index 'a' for 'actual' is not attached to h_0 for simplicity.

$g(-\delta\mu) = G(-\delta\mu) = 0$, and that in the upper tail of z, $g(z)$, although small, is positive for large $z-s$. Backlogs are not permitted. The firm either sells in the period in which a given demand materializes or loses the sale. Let

$$x \equiv h + l \tag{30}$$

be the total amount of the product the firm has available for sale in a given period. Using eq. (27) and the distribution function of z, $\bar{s}$, the expected value of sales conditional on the forecast μ can be computed as[34]

$$\bar{s}(x) = \delta\mu + \int_{-\delta\mu}^{x-\delta\mu} z\,dG(z) + [1 - G(x-\delta\mu)][x-\delta\mu]$$

$$= G(x-\delta\mu)\delta\mu + [1 - G(x-\delta\mu)]x + \int_{-\delta\mu}^{x-\delta\mu} z\,dG(z). \tag{31}$$

Partial differentiation of $\bar{s}$ with respect to x yields

$$\partial\bar{s}/\partial x = 1 - G(x-\delta\mu) > 0. \tag{32}$$

Any increase in the total available for sale, x, increases expected sales by decreasing the probability of stockouts. Inventories are held, therefore, to increase expected sales and profits.

By the principle of optimality, eq. (28) can be rewritten

$$J_0(h_0) = \max_{l_0}\left[E_{-1}(\bar{s}_0(h_0 + l_0) - w_0 l_0) + \frac{T_1(h_0 + l_0 - \delta\mu_0)}{1 + v_0} \right], \tag{33}$$

where

$$J_1(h_1) = \max_{\{l_1, l_2, \ldots\}} E_0 \sum_{i=1}^{\infty}\left(\Pi_i(l_i) \Big/ \prod_{s=1}^{i-1}(1 + v_s) \right), \tag{34}$$

and

$$T_1(h_0 + l_0 - \delta\mu_0) \equiv E_{-1} J_1(h_0 + l_0 - \delta\mu_0 - z_0). \tag{35}$$

In the expected value, $E_{-1}J_1$, if $z_0 \geq h_0 + l_0 - \delta\mu_0$, $h_1 = 0$. Note that eq. (33) can be rewritten as a decision problem in $x_0 \equiv h_0 + l_0$, provided $h_0 \leq x_0$.[35]

---

[34]This expected value is always smaller than or equal to the expected value of demand, $Ed = Ez + \delta\mu$, which does not permit stockouts.

[35]If $h_0 > x_0$, x_0 is not a decision variable (negative production is not possible) so the firm's demand for labor is zero. We assume $h_0 \leq x_0$ to be the typical case. Tracing out the effects of $h_0 > x_0$ through the macroeconomy complicates the analysis without changing the qualitative nature of the results.

K. Brunner et al., Money and economic activity, inventories and business cycles 299

Each unit of labor produces one unit of the product. A necessary condition for positive production at the permanent position of the economy is that the permanent wage, per unit of labor supplied, is less than unity, so we assume $w^p < 1$. With this assumption, an interior maximum for x_0 in eq. (33) exists. (See part A.3 of the appendix.) The optimum that the firm chooses is the same whether x_0 or l_0 is the decision variable. The first order (necessary) condition [using (31) specialized to period 0] is

$$1 - G(h_0 + l_0 - \delta\mu_0) - w_0 + \frac{T_1'(h_0 + l_0 - \delta\mu_0)}{1 + v_0} = 0, \qquad (36a)$$

and the second order (sufficient) condition is

$$R'' \equiv -g(h_0 + l_0 - \delta\mu_0) + \frac{T_1''(h_0 + l_0 - \delta\mu_0)}{1 + v_0} < 0, \qquad (36b)$$

where T_1' and T_1'' are respectively the first and the second order partial derivatives of the function T_1. Eq. (36a) determines optimal l_0 for given initial inventories, h_0, or determines optimal x_0. All firms choose the same level of x_0 independently of their initial inventories.[36]

3.2. From individual to aggregate expected sales

This section derives eq. (2) in the macro problem. Differentiating $\bar{s}$ from eq. (31) partially with respect to μ, we have

$$\partial\bar{s}/\partial\mu = \delta G(x - \delta\mu). \qquad (37)$$

Eqs. (32) and (37) imply that

$$0 < \partial\bar{s}/\partial x < 1 \quad \text{and} \quad 0 < \partial\bar{s}/\partial\mu < 1. \qquad (38)$$

Furthermore,

$$\partial\bar{s}/\partial x + \partial\bar{s}/\partial\mu = 1 - (1 - \delta)G(x - \delta\mu) < 1, \qquad (39)$$

and

$$0 < \frac{\partial\bar{s}}{\partial x} \bigg/ \left(1 - \frac{\partial\bar{s}}{\partial\mu}\right) = \frac{1 - G(x - \delta\mu)}{1 - \delta G(x - \delta\mu)} < 1. \qquad (40)$$

Approximating $\bar{s}(x)$ linearly around the point $x = Ez + \delta\mu^p$ for $\mu = \mu^p$, we

[36]The last two statements are strictly true only when $h_0 \leq x_0$, and x_0 is the decision variable.

obtain

$$\bar{s} = k_0 + K_1 x + K_2 \mu, \quad \text{where} \tag{41}$$

$$k_0 \equiv \int_{-\delta\mu}^{Ez} z \, dG(z), \quad K_1 \equiv 1 - G(Ez), \quad K_2 \equiv \delta G(Ez). \tag{42}$$

From eqs. (38), (39), (40) and the definitions in (42), we see that

$$0 < K_1, \quad K_2 < 1, \quad 0 < K_1 + K_2 < 1, \quad 0 < a \equiv \frac{K_1}{1 - K_2} < 1. \tag{43}$$

Since all firms choose the same x, the aggregate level of expected sales for the whole economy is obtained by summing (41) over all (N) firms and using (3) to get

$$\bar{S} = N\bar{s} = K_0 + K_1 X^a + K_2 D, \tag{44}$$

where $K_0 \equiv Nk_0$ and $X^a \equiv Nx = H^a + Y^a$. Eq. (44) is the expected aggregate sales function that appears as eq. (2) of the macro model. Eq. (43) shows that the restrictions imposed on eq. (2) and (10a) of the macro model are implications of the micro model.

3.3. Comparative statics and the demand for labor

By differentiating the first order condition (36a) with respect to period 0's variables, we derive the restrictions on the coefficients of the aggregate labor demand function, eq. (4),

$$dl_0/dh_0 = -1, \tag{45a}$$

$$1 > \gamma_1 \equiv dl_0/d\mu_0 = \delta > 0, \tag{45b}$$

$$\gamma_2 \equiv dl_0/dv_0 = \frac{1}{R''} \left[\frac{T_1'(\cdot)}{(1 + v_0)^2} \right] < 0, \tag{45c}$$

$$\gamma_3 \equiv dl_0/dw_0 = \frac{1}{R''} < 0. \tag{45d}$$

The sign of γ_2 requires discussion. $T_1'(\cdot) = E_{-1}J_1'(h_1)$, where J_1' is the derivative of the optimized function in eq. (34) with respect to beginning inventory. An increase in beginning inventory increases expected sales and therefore expected profits, in some states of nature, but may not affect these

K. Brunner et al., Money and economic activity, inventories and business cycles   301

variables in others; so for all h_1, $J_1'(h_1) \geq 0$, and for some h_1 it is strictly positive. It follows that $T_1'(\cdot)$ [being a linear combination over states of nature of $J_1'(\cdot)$] is also positive.

The firm in our model has no reason to smooth inventories at the micro level.[37] Eq. (45a) shows that a unit increase in inventories decreases production (and the demand for labor) equiproportionally. This result differs from much of the micro literature on inventories. See Amihud and Mendelson (1982), Reagan (1982), Blinder and Fischer (1981) and Blinder (1981). There, a unit increase in inventories decreases production by less than one unit: diminishing marginal productivity and fluctuating demand induce firms to smooth production and hold inventories. In contrast, we have assumed constant returns to scale for labor. Our firm plans to hold a positive amount of inventory, on average, to increase expected profits.[38] Since the effects of an additional unit of current production and an additional unit of inventories on expected profits are the same, the firm treats current production and inventories as perfect substitutes.

Approximating labor demand of the jth firm linearly, we have[39]

$$l_{0j} = \tilde{\gamma}_0 + \gamma_1 \mu_0 + \tilde{\gamma}_2 v_0 + \tilde{\gamma}_3 w_0 - h_{0j}, \tag{46}$$

where in view of eq. (45), $0 < \gamma_1 = \delta < 1$, $\tilde{\gamma}_2 < 0$, $\tilde{\gamma}_3 < 0$. Summing eq. (46) over all firms, the aggregate demand for labor is

$$L_0^d \equiv \sum_{j=1}^{N} l_{0j} = N\tilde{\gamma}_0 + \gamma_1(N\mu_0) + N\tilde{\gamma}_2 v_0 + N\tilde{\gamma}_3 w_0 - \sum_{j=1}^{N} h_{0j}$$

$$= \gamma_0 + \gamma_1 D_0 + \gamma_2 v_0 + \gamma_3 w_0 - H_0^a, \tag{47}$$

where $\gamma_0 \equiv N\tilde{\gamma}_0$, $\gamma_2 \equiv N\tilde{\gamma}_2 < 0$, $\tilde{\gamma}_3 \equiv N\tilde{\gamma}_3 < 0$. Substituting expected aggregate demand from (10a) into (47) and rearranging, we obtain the aggregate demand for labor function postulated in eq. (4) of the macro section,

$$L_0^d = \bar{L}_d + (\gamma_1\beta + \gamma_2)v_0 + \gamma_3 w_0 - H_0^a, \qquad 0 < \gamma_1 < 1, \qquad \gamma_2, \gamma_3 < 0, \tag{47'}$$

where $\bar{L}_d \equiv \gamma_0 + \alpha\gamma_1 Y^p$.

---

[37]The macroeconomic model implies that $dY^a/dH^a = dL^a/dH^a > -1$, however, so there is 'smoothing' for macro reasons, as shown in section 4.

[38]That the firm plans to hold a positive amount of inventories, on average, can be seen from eq. (31). $\tilde{s}(x)$ is a weighted average of x and of demand which is lower than x, so it must be lower than x. Therefore, $h_1 = h_0 + l_0 - \mu_0 = x_0 - \tilde{s}(x_0) > 0$.

[39]l_{0j} also depends on the expected time paths of μ, v and w for future periods from period 1 on. We know that these time paths eventually converge to some constant permanent values, so we approximate the dependence of l_{0j} on those paths by making it a function of μ^p, v^p and w^p. The permanent values are constant over time, and the dependence is subsumed in the constant, γ_0 in (46).

3.4. Recapitulation of the linkages between the macro and the micro structures

In section 2 we postulated the forms of the aggregate expected supply function and the aggregate labor demand by firms, eqs. (2) and (4), and derived the expectations of firms concerning the future time paths of relevant economic variables. In this section, the individual firm chose its optimal employment and production, for given expectations. Then, we showed that aggregation of the individual firm's expected sales and labor demand functions, derived from their optimizing choices, yielded the aggregate functions postulated in the macro section. [Compare (44) with (2) and (47′) with (4).] This establishes the consistency between the macro and the micro structures as well as the rationality of the various expectations derived in the macro section.

Before closing this section, two remarks are in order. First, we note that whatever view the firm holds about future prices during period 0, it always chooses to carry out the plan made at the beginning of this period provided that the realized real rate is non-negative.[40] The firm does not alter its current price by assumption, but it can refrain from selling some of the product on hand in order to sell it in future periods. For small shocks the firm never finds it profitable to refuse sales. The reason is that one unit of the product not sold today decreases the present value of expected real profits by exactly one unit and increases the present value of future expected real profits by less than one unit. This can be seen by noting that, whatever the price level expected for period 1, the transfer of one unit of inventories to period 1 increases the present value of expected *real* profits by

$$\frac{1 - G(x_1 - \delta\mu_1)}{1 + r_0^a - \pi_1}, \tag{48}$$

which is always smaller than 1 for a positive real rate of interest. Transfer of this unit to more distant future periods increases the present value of expected profits by even less. Hence, as long as they do not stockout firms satisfy demand passively out of current production and opening inventories as assumed in the macro section.[41] Second, our claim that $Ez > 0$ for all μ, implies that $\delta < 1$ is demonstrated. Taking the expected value of (27) over the distribution of z,

$$Ed = Ez + \delta\mu. \tag{49}$$

[40]This also establishes that even if the firm changes its view about future prices within the period (along the lines of part A.2 of the appendix), it does not change behavior within the period.

[41]Note that speculation on future changes in relative prices is excluded since all firms charge the same price. A large shock to the money stock can make $r_0^a - \pi_1$ negative for a period by driving the nominal rate of interest below the expected rate of inflation. In this case, the value of eq. (48) can exceed unity. If this happens, optimizing behavior leads firms to withhold sales and carry inventory to the next period.

For the case $\mu = Ed$, the ex ante equilibrium condition in the commodity market together with (49) imply

$$\mu = Ed = Ez + \delta\mu, \tag{50}$$

which implies that $\delta < 1$ since both Ez and μ are positive.

4. Money, business cycles and macroeconomic aspects of inventory behavior

If real markets and financial markets clear simultaneously, money is neutral in our model. Non-neutrality of money results from a one period difference in the speed of response to unanticipated shocks. The nominal stock of money is always willingly held at the market clearing rate of interest, so the markets for money and securities reflect all shocks instantly. Efficient production and sales require advance planning of real output and expected sales. To plan production and sales, firms set prices and agree with workers on employment and real wages one period at a time. These 'contracts' are revised each period using all available information, but they remain fixed during the period for which they are set. Consequently unanticipated shocks to the growth rate of money change interest rates immediately but do not affect prices, employment and real wages until 'contracts' are revised. Unanticipated increases in the growth of money reduce interest rates, increase sales and reduce end of period inventories; unanticipated reductions in money growth raise interest rates, reduce sales and increase end of period inventories. At the start of each period, everyone knows the changes in money growth, sales and aggregate inventories that have occurred; prices, real wages, employment, output, planned inventories and expected rates of interest reflect the new information. Nevertheless, persistent deviations from permanent values occur, and the deviations are serially correlated.

Producers do not restore inventories to their (known) permanent value in the period following an unintended change but, instead, spread the response over several periods. A main reason is that the aggregate labor supply surve is positively sloped. Each firm knows that the larger the increase in the aggregate demand for labor, the larger is the rise in the real wage and the larger the cost of rebuilding inventories. The speed of response, and the length of time for which deviations from permanent values persist, depends not only on the slope of the labor supply function but also on the slope of the labor demand function and on the sensitivity of aggregate demand to the interest rate.

In this section we show that, despite the absence of production smoothing at the micro level, rational expectations provides a macro reason for aggregate inventories to follow a partial adjustment process. Then, we present a general analysis of the response of inventories to unanticipated changes. The analysis is specialized to the case in which there are only monetary shocks to analyze the cyclical responses of output, unemployment and other real variables to unanticipated money growth. We show that errors in judging the persistence of shocks to money growth contribute to the serial correlation. The section closes with a comparison of our results to some previous studies.

4.1. Production smoothing — macro versus micro considerations

Individual firms do not smooth inventories as shown by eq. (45a);

$$dy/dh = dl/dh = -1, \tag{51}$$

but, for the aggregate, we know from eq. (11a) of section 2 that

$$dY/dH^a = dL/dH^a = -C_y > -1. \tag{52}$$

A given decrease in economy-wide inventories increases aggregate production by less than the decrease in inventories.

The origin of the difference in response lies in the familiar distinction between a 'market' and an 'individual' experiment and depends on the rational expectations of producers who know the structure of the model and anticipate the aggregate response. An unexpected exogenous decrease in aggregate inventories increases the aggregate demand for labor as firms try to rebuild stocks. The increased demand for labor increases the real wage rate along the aggregate labor supply schedule in (6). At the higher real wage rate, firms spread the rebuilding of inventories over time, reducing the planned increase in current period output and employment. Because firms know that the increase in the aggregate demand for labor increases the real wage, they spread inventory rebuilding activity over time. Although there is no production smoothing at the level of the individual firm, there is production smoothing because of macroeconomic reasons under rational expectations. The intensity of the smoothing is inversely related to C_y and, thus, depends on structural parameters. The effects of these parameters on C_y are summarized in the following proposition.

Proposition 2. C_y *is smaller and macroeconomic smoothing stronger, the lower* ω , *the higher* $|\gamma_2|$ *and* $|\gamma_3|$ *and the lower* $|\beta|$.[42]

---

[42]These results follow directly from (12) and by noting that $\partial C_y/\partial \beta$ has the same (negative) sign as $-\omega a \gamma_2 \gamma_3$.

The less sensitive labor supply to the real wage rate (low ω), the more the real wage rate increases and the less employment and production increase following a decrease in inventories. The more sensitive labor demand (high $|\gamma_3|$) to the real wage, the more the increase in the real wage discourages production. As can be seen from (11d), lower initial inventories also partially reduce expected sales [since $0 < a(1 - C_y) < 1$]. To maintain commodity market equilibrium, aggregate demand falls. This is brought about by an increase in the real rate of interest. The rise in the real rate, ceteris paribus, decreases labor demand, employment and production. The less sensitive is aggregate demand to the real rate (low $|\beta|$), the larger is the necessary increase in the real rate; the more sensitive labor demand to the real rate (large $|\gamma_2|$), the stronger, ceteris paribus, is the negative effect of the higher real rate on current employment and production. Therefore, a low $|\beta|$ and a high $|\gamma_2|$ lead to a rather lengthy period of inventory rebuilding activity. Similar reasoning, later in this section, shows that the same parameters that determine the degree of macroeconomic smoothing play an important role in determining the amplitude and the length of the cycle.

4.2. The partial adjustment feature of aggregate inventories

By adding and subtracting AH^p to the right-hand side of (19a), we get, after rearrangement

$$H_t - H_{t-1} = (1 - A)(H^p - H_{t-1}), \tag{53}$$

where from (20), (42,) (43) and (45b)

$$A \equiv (1 - a)(1 - C_y) = (1 - a)\frac{-\beta\gamma_3}{-\beta\gamma_3 + \omega[\beta(1 - \delta a) - a\gamma_2]},$$

$$a \equiv \frac{1 - G(Ez)}{1 - \delta G(Ez)}. \tag{54}$$

Eq. (53) describes the anticipated path of aggregate inventories. In the absence of further unanticipated shocks, actual and anticipated inventories adjust to the permanent level by following a simple stock adjustment equation of the Koyck variety. The speed of adjustment is a decreasing function of A, which in turn is a decreasing function of C_y. Thus, the same factors that increase macro smoothing in Proposition 2 also increase the lag in the adjustment of inventories to their permanent or 'desired' value.

4.3. Unintended and planned inventory changes

Since decisions about production, employment and inventories are made at the beginning of each period, before the realizations of the shocks in that period, end of period inventories can differ from planned. As a result, total inventory investment has two components. The planned or anticipated component follows a path described by eq. (21). Unintended changes occur only if there are unanticipated shocks to aggregate demand or to money growth.[43] The unanticipated change in inventories is determined by the unanticipated component of demand which, [using eq. (1)], is

$$D_0^a - D_0 = \beta(r_0^a - r_0) + \varepsilon_0, \tag{55}$$

unanticipated demand depends on ε, the unanticipated component of aggregate demand, and on the unanticipated change in the normal rate of interest.[44] The latter is obtained by rearranging (10c) and subtracting from (14),

$$r_0^a - r_0 = \frac{1}{b}[(M_0^a/P_0^a)(m_0 - \bar{m}) + \theta\varepsilon_0] \tag{56}$$

so both shocks affect aggregate demand and unanticipated inventory change through their effect on interest rates. Substituting (56) into (55), and recalling that unanticipated inventory change is the mirror image of unanticipated shocks to demand, we can write the former as[45]

$$H_1^a - H_1 = -(D_0^a - D_0) = -\left[\frac{\beta}{b}\left(\frac{M_0^a}{P_0^a}(m_0 - \bar{m}) + \theta\varepsilon_0\right) + \varepsilon_0\right]. \tag{57}$$

Positive random shocks to either the rate of monetary growth or to aggregate demand cause unanticipated decumulations of inventories. The shock to money growth has this effect through the rate of interest. The shock to aggregate demand has this effect directly and, by changing the within period demand for money, through the interest rate as well.

Actual changes in inventory include planned and unintended changes,

$$H_1^a - H_0^a = H_1^a - H_1 + H_1 - H_0^a. \tag{58}$$

[43]By contrast, in the *macro* inventory model of Blinder and Fischer (1981), decisions are made after the resolution of uncertainty, so there is no room for unanticipated changes in inventories. In recent *micro* inventory models, that is not always the case. See, for example, Amihud and Mendelson (1980) and Blinder (1981).

[44]Firms accommodate demand within the period. Except for the case discussed in footnote 41, such behavior is optimal for the individual firm. We limit our analysis to the case in which there are no stockouts in the aggregate.

[45]If the effects of the information contained in r_0^a on aggregate demand are incorporated explicitly, the response of $H_0^a - H_0$ to unanticipated shocks increases. See part A.2 of the appendix and footnote 24.

K. Brunner et al., *Money and economic activity, inventories and business cycles*   307

The planned change is, using eq. (53),

$$H_1 - H_0^a = (1 - A)(H^p - H_0^a).$$

(59)

Planned changes in inventory are independent of current monetary shocks and depend only on actual and permanent values of real variables. Past monetary shocks continue to affect planned changes in inventory, however. The reason is that, as shown in (59), planned changes are a decreasing function of the inherited level of inventories, H_0^a. Since inventories adjust gradually, as shown in (53), the inherited level of inventories reflects the influence of past monetary (and real) shocks.

4.4. A general characterization of the cycle

The permanent values of the variables in our model are the values that rational individuals perceive as steady state, trend values. To characterize cyclical fluctuations, we use the deviations of actual values from (constant) permanent values as a measure of the cycle. These differences can be positive or negative.

Eqs. (21) and (57) specify the adjustment of inventories in any period, t, as the sum of two components — the planned adjustment toward the permanent value and the unanticipated shock that occurs in period t. Combining these terms, we have

$$H_t^a - H^p = -\left[\frac{\beta}{b}\frac{M_t^a}{P_t^a}(m_t - \bar{m}) + \left(1 + \theta\frac{1}{b}\right)\varepsilon_t\right] + A[H_{t-1}^a - H^p].$$

(60)

By lagging eq. (60) one period, and substituting the result into (60), we can write the cyclical deviation on the left in terms of the gradual adjustment that occurred in $t-2$ and the shocks in $t-1$. Continuing this procedure, we eventually obtain the cyclical amplitude of inventories expressed as a function of past unanticipated shocks,[46]

$$H_t^a - H^p = -\sum_{i=1}^{t} A^{i-1}\left[\frac{\beta}{b}\frac{M_{t-i}^a}{P_{t-i}^a}(m_{t-i} - \bar{m}) + \left(1 + \theta\frac{\beta}{b}\right)\varepsilon_{t-i}\right].$$

(61)

Eq. (61) suggests that the impact of past unanticipated shocks on the current cyclical deviation of inventories increases with the damping factor A. From (54), we know that A is larger the lower is C_y. A large A (low C_y) slows the adjustment of inventories to their permanent position. We find, therefore, that the same factors that increase the lag in the adjustment of inventories

---

[46]The term $A^t[H_0^a - H^p]$ is deleted since for large t, $A^t \rightarrow 0$.

308   *K. Brunner et al., Money and economic activity, inventories and business cycles*

also prolong the effect of past unanticipated shocks on the cyclical deviation of inventories. In view of proposition 2 and eq. (61), we have

Proposition 3.   The effect of past unanticipated shocks on the current cyclical deviation of inventories is larger and more durable the lower ω and the higher $|\gamma_2|$ and $|\gamma_3|$.

4.5. A monetary cycle

To focus on the effects of unanticipated money growth, we eliminate all uncertainty with respect to ε_t by setting it equal to its expected value (zero) for all t.[47] In this case, eq. (61) specializes to

$$H_t^a - H^p = -\frac{\beta}{b} \sum_{i=1}^{t} A^{i-1} \frac{d_{t-i}}{1+\bar{m}}(m_{t-1} - \bar{m}), \tag{62}$$

where $d_{t-i} \equiv M_{t-i}(1+\bar{m})/P_{t-i}^a$ is the expected value of real money balances in period $t-1$ as of the beginning of period $t-1$. By substituting (62) into eqs. (22) and using the definition of unemployment from (7), we get the effect of unanticipated money on the cyclical deviations of other variables. These are summarized in eqs. (63),[48]

$$Y_t^a - Y^p = L_t^a - L^p = \frac{\beta}{b} C_y \left[\sum_{i=1}^{t} A^{i-1} \frac{d_{t-i}}{1+\bar{m}}(m_{t-i} - \bar{m}) \right], \tag{63a}$$

$$w_t^a - w^p = \frac{\beta}{\omega b} C_y \left[\sum_{i=1}^{t} A^{i-1} \frac{d_{t-i}}{1+\bar{m}}(m_{t-i} - \bar{m}) \right], \tag{63b}$$

$$n_t^a = -\frac{\beta}{b} C_y \left[\sum_{i=1}^{t} A^{i-1} \frac{d_{t-i}}{1+\bar{m}}(m_{t-i} - \bar{m}) \right], \tag{63c}$$

$$v_t - v^p = -\frac{a}{b\beta}(1 - C_y) \times \left[\sum_{i=1}^{t} A^{i-1} \frac{d_{t-i}}{1+\bar{m}}(m_{t-i} - \bar{m}) \right], \tag{63d}$$

$$\bar{S}_t - D^p = -\frac{a}{b}(1 - C_y) \times \left[\sum_{i=1}^{t} A^{i-1} \frac{d_{t-i}}{1+\bar{m}}(m_{t-i} - \bar{m}) \right]. \tag{63e}$$

[47]The analysis in this section is easily generalizable to the case in which ε_t is stochastic.

[48]Note that the cyclical deviations of output, employment and unemployment are measured by deviations of actual values from permanent values while the real rate and sales are in terms of expectations of those variables as conceived at the beginning of each period. The cyclical deviation of actual sales is discussed below. Cyclical behavior of real rates is discussed at length in Cukierman (1981).

Eqs. (63) have four main implications for business cycles. First, cyclical deviations of all real variables are serially correlated. The reason is that the deviations depend on past, unanticipated shocks to the rate of money growth, and the responses to these shocks damp only gradually. Second, as sensitivity of money demand to the interest rate falls — as $|b|$ declines — the response of each of the real variables to an unanticipated monetary shock becomes larger in magnitude and persists longer. A small value of $|b|$ implies that the interest rate changes more, on impact, in response to a given monetary shock. A relatively large change in interest rates causes larger and more persistent cyclical deviations of real variables from their permanent values. Third, Proposition 3 applies to the cyclical deviations of all real variables in (63) since these deviations depend on the cyclical deviation of inventories. Fourth, the lower is the maintained rate of inflation, $\bar{m}$, the higher, ceteris paribus, real money balances, d_{t-i}, in every period, and the higher the impact of past unanticipated shocks to the rate of monetary growth on current cyclical deviations. Our analysis implies, therefore, that the dynamic Phillips curve is steeper in periods of high inflation and flatter in periods of low inflation. This effect depends on the properties of the money market, through d_{t-i}. Proposition 4 summarizes some principal determinants of the magnitude and duration of cycles in real variables.

Proposition 4. Ceteris paribus, the effects of monetary shocks on real variables is larger in magnitude and more persistent in time the smaller the maintained rate of inflation, $\bar{m}$, the smaller ω and $|b|$ and the larger $|\gamma_2|$ and $|\gamma_3|$.

The effect of past unanticipated monetary growth on the cyclical deviations of output, employment, the real wage rate and the expected real rate of interest is positive.[49] The effect on the cyclical deviations of unemployment and expected sales is negative. The directions of response accord with intuition. Past, unanticipated, positive shocks to money growth, reduce actual inventories and, therefore, start a process of inventory rebuilding. Current production and employment increase, so the real wage rate rises and unemployment falls. To bring actual and expected demand down to the level of the reduced supply (planned sales), the expected real rate of interest rises; the rise in the real rate reduces planned sales.

4.6. A monetary cycle with persistent errors about money growth

The model can be extended easily to incorporate uncertainty about the systematic rate of monetary expansion by respecifying the distribution of m_t,

---

[49]Inventory stocks are negatively related to the real rate of interest over the cycle. Further implications for interest rates appear in Cukierman (1981). For recent evidence on a negative relationship between target inventories and the cost of capital, see Irvine (1981a, b).

as

$$m_t = m_t^p + m_t^q, \qquad \Delta m_t^p \sim N(0, \sigma_p^2), \qquad m_t^q \sim N(0, \sigma_q^2). \tag{64}$$

The observed rate of monetary expansion is now the sum of a permanent (random walk) component and a transitory (white noise) component. The optimal predictor of future rates of monetary growth, given the information available at the end of period $t-1$, becomes

$$E_{t-1} m_{t+j} = \lambda \sum_{i=0}^{\infty} (1-\lambda)^i m_{t-1-i}, \qquad j \geqq 0, \tag{65}$$

where $0 < \lambda < 1$. λ is an increasing function of σ_p^2 / σ_q^2, the ratio of the variance of the permanent component to the variance of the transitory component.[50] All the analysis above, including, in particular, eqs. (61), (62) and (63) continues to hold with $m_{t-i} - \bar{m}$ replaced by the forecast errors,

$$m_{t-i}^a - E_{t-1-i} m_{t-i} \equiv m_{t-i}^a - m_{t-i}, \tag{66}$$

where the expected value in (66) is computed using (65). When a large permanent change in m^p occurs, forecast errors display ex post serial correlation for a number of periods after the change.[51] This phenomenon arises because individuals confuse permanent and temporary changes.

Fig. 2 shows the adjustment paths. Up to period t, the economy is at an equilibrium; $H_t = H_t^p$. During period t, there is an unanticipated increase in money growth. Interest rates fall; with prices fixed for the period, aggregate demand increases, and inventories are reduced. Inability to identify permanent shocks means that the perceived value of m changes as information about the rate of monetary expansion becomes available. Forecast errors remain on one side of zero for several periods. Forecast errors reinforce the cyclical deviation of inventories. A large permanent increase in money growth, that is not immediately recognized as permanent, increases m_t and adds to the cyclical deviation of inventories.

The reduction in inventories sets off a process of adjustment of output and inventories. The path along which inventories are expected to adjust at the onset of period $t+1$ is shown by the positively sloped line from H_{t+1}^a to the permanent level of inventories, H^p. Along this path, a typical firm plans to produce output in excess of expected sales and build inventories.[52] The expected value of inventories by the end of period $t+1$ is shown as H_{t+2}. If

---

[50]For further details, see Muth (1960), and Brunner, Cukierman and Meltzer (1980).

[51]In Brunner, Cukierman and Meltzer (1980) we discuss these errors more fully. Forecast errors are serially correlated in the sense that, looking back on the past, economists or historians can find evidence of serial correlation. At the time, no one is aware of serial correlation.

[52]Recall that all firms do not have the same inventories.

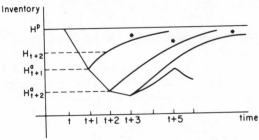

Fig. 2. (An asterisk, indicates the expected path of inventories. The outer envelope shows the actual path.)

the monetary shock is correctly perceived as transitory and there are no further shocks, firms adjust along the planned path and achieve the values of inventories, H_{t+2}, H_{t+3} in successive periods until the permanent value, H^p, is restored.

Suppose, however, that the increase in money growth persists. In period $t+2$, interest rates are again pushed below the value expected for the period, and actual inventories, H^a_{t+2}, are, again, below the value expected, H_{t+2}, as shown in fig. 2. At the beginning of period $t+2$ firms and households expect the economy to adjust along the new path, from H^a_{t+2} to H^p. The new path reflects all the available information about the shocks, including beliefs about the permanence of the change in money growth and knowledge of the structural parameters. The process shown in eq. (64) governs the speed with which people change their views about permanence or persistence of shocks. If the variance of the transitory component of money growth is large relative to the variance of the permanent component, adjustment to permanent changes is relatively slow. Inventories can fall below their expected value for several periods and, thus, move away from H^p.

Additional information about the permanence of the shock that first occurred in period t is revealed each period, so the path of adjustment toward H^p is not smooth. As time passes, however, the addition to information is small. After $t+3$ in fig. 2, inventories adjust toward H^p unless another shock — another unanticipated increase in money growth — lowers inventories and starts a new process of learning and adjusting.

Actual inventories follow the outer envelope in fig. 2; expected inventories, H, follow the adjustment paths that start at the actual values for each period. The figure shows principal features of our model of inventory behavior, augmented by the effect of permanent-transitory confusion. Deviations from H^p are on one side of H^p for several periods because of the slow adjustment of inventories. This feature occurs even if all shocks are white noise. In addition, information about the permanence of shocks becomes available gradually. People use all information and their beliefs about permanent values to determine the adjustment path, but they make unavoidable errors because they learn about the permanence of shocks gradually.

Obviously a similar analysis can be carried out for each of the real variables which appears in eqs. (63). This is not done for brevity. Instead, we conclude this discussion with the general observation that the model predicts that the effects of unanticipated money growth on the economy take the form of distributed lags of past money growth. Unanticipated changes in money causes procyclical movements in the levels of output, employment and real wages and countercyclical movements in unemployment. The path of each variable is qualitatively similar to the inventory adjustments shown in fig. 2. Even if money growth is underestimated in only one period — and is predicted without error in all subsequent periods — employment, output, real wages and real rates of interest are above their permanent values for a number of periods. Expected sales and unemployment are below their permanent values. In addition, persistent errors in the prediction of the money supply provide additional reason for serially correlated cyclical deviations.

The more slowly people learn about the permanent rate of money growth, the longer is the period during which permanent money growth is underestimated. The speed with which people learn about the rate of money growth depends on the variance of the permanent component, σ_p^2, relative to the transitory component, σ_q^2. Increases in σ_p^2/σ_q^2 reduce the length of time required to learn about the permanence of the change. When the ratio of variances is low, unanticipated permanent monetary acceleration induces a larger increase in output and employment. For the same reason, efforts to slow inflation cause more persistent unemployment as well as longer periods with high interest rates.

4.7. Unemployment and real wages during cycles

The permanent level of employment is a constant and, by definition, permanent unemployment is set at zero. Actual unemployment rises above the 'natural' or permanent rate when inventories are above their permanent value. Unemployment is lower than the natural rate when inventories are below their permanent value. As inventories are reduced or replaced, unemployment moves toward the natural rate.

In eq. (63c), the unemployment rate in any period, n_t^a, depends on the past history of monetary growth. An unanticipated increase in money growth pushes the actual rate of unemployment below the natural rate for several periods.[53] As the effect of the monetary shock on inventories decays, employment returns to L^p as shown in (63a), and unemployment returns to zero. During the adjustment, unemployment rates are serially correlated.

---

[53]Unanticipated real changes in demand have similar effects on real wages and unemployment.

Hall (1977) found that the real wage rate adjusts more slowly than the unemployment rate. Based on this finding, he concluded that real wage rates are not the only factor explaining unemployment. Hall interpreted his result as evidence of disequilibrium in the labor market.

In our model, employers and workers are always on their respective labor demand and labor supply curves. Changes in employment and unemployment are the result of changes in the real wage rate caused by past monetary acceleration and deceleration. Although workers respond only to market incentives, the model implies that the wage rate typically adjusts more slowly than the rate of unemployment. This can be seen by noting from eq. (7) that

$$n_t^a/n_{t-1}^a = (w^p - w_t)/(w^p - w_{t-1}).$$

Dividing numerator and denominator on the right-hand side of this equation by the product $w^p w_{t-1}$ and rearranging, we obtain

$$\left| \frac{w_t - w_{t-1}}{w_{t-1}} \right| = \left| 1 - \frac{w^p}{w_{t-1}} \right| \cdot \left| \frac{n_t - n_{t-1}}{n_{t-1}} \right|.$$

No separate, or additional explanation is required to reconcile our hypothesis with the observed sluggish response of real wages to unemployment. The percentage change in the real wage rate associated with a given change in the rate of unemployment is very likely to be considerably smaller than the percentage change in unemployment. For example, if over the cycle w_t does not deviate from w^p by more than 20 percent, percentage changes in the real wage rate are, at most, one-fifth of the associated percentage changes in unemployment. As w_t approaches w^p the relative response of real wages decreases monotonically towards zero.

4.8. Intertemporal substitution in the labor market

In a recent empirical study, Hall (1980) tested the intertemporal substitution model of labor supply. He (1980, p. 1) found that, 'This model stands up reasonably well on its own ground. The elasticity of labor supply is around one-half.' However, Hall also found that when a distributed lag on money is added to the pure intertemporal substitution model, the predictive power of the model of employment and real output increased substantially. Hall concluded that the pure substitution model is untenable in the light of this evidence.

The framework presented here suggests that the intertemporal substitution model is entirely consistent with the observation that current and lagged money affects output and employment. The resolution of the apparent puzzle raised by Hall's work comes from the response of labor *demand* to unanticipated money. Intertemporal substitution is the mechanism by which the effect of monetary shocks on the real rate increase the demand for labor, raise the real wage and increase employment. Rather than constituting a contradiction to the observed real effects of money, the substitution model is one of the links in the transmission mechanism through which current unanticipated monetary growth affects future employment and output.

5. Concluding comments

One of the challenges raised by the existence of a short-run trade-off between inflation and economic activity is to explain the trade-off within a consistent macroeconomic framework. Several alternative explanations have been offered. The oldest, used by Thornton (1802), Keynes (1936) and many others, relies on nominal wage rigidity but offers no explanation for wage rigidity. Modern formulations of this approach base the effects of money on output on the existence of nominally denominated labor contracts.[54]

The most articulate explanation of the short-run effects of money on output postulates that suppliers of labor services in localized markets react to nominal impulses because they confuse changes in the aggregate price level and changes in relative prices.[55] Blinder and Fischer (1981) present a macro model with inventories in which production smoothing by individual firms and confusion between aggregate and relative price changes leads to serially correlated deviations of output from trend. These authors also investigate the effects of perfectly anticipated money through the (Mundell) effect of inflation on real rates of interest.

Our explanation does not rely on the aggregate relative confusion; all individuals have identical information. Nor do we rely on prearranged *nominal* wage contracts; wage contracts are made in real terms.[56] Instead, we rely on two assumptions that are consistent with, and based upon, many economists' observations. First, the activities performed in real flow markets, like employment, production and distribution, require advance planning and commitment over some (possibly small) future discrete time period. Second, firms advertise prices in advance of the market period.[57] As a result of these assumptions, the real wage rate, employment and the price level are predetermined at the start of each period for one period; these variables do

[54]See Gray (1976), Fischer (1977), Phelps and Taylor (1977) and Cukierman (1980).

[55]See Lucas (1973, 1975), Barro (1976). Hall (1980) claims that in view of the speed with which information about aggregate variables becomes available, it is hard to believe that misperception of aggregate variables is an important source of non-neutrality in a modern economy.

[56]We also do not rely on the Mundell effect. The model does not have a real balance effect.

[57]For an argument for infrequent changes in prices as a mean of preserving the informational efficiency of the price system, see Alchian (1969).

K. Brunner et al., Money and economic activity, inventories and business cycles   315

not reflect shocks that occur during the market period. The clearing of financial markets, on the other hand, occurs continuously.

Monetary shocks change the real rate of interest and cause unanticipated inventory changes. These changes arise because prices are fixed for a period and financial markets clear continuously. Since all firms have the same constant returns to scale technology, there is no reason for production smoothing at the micro level. There is, however, production smoothing in the aggregate. The reason is that each firm recognizes that the cost of rebuilding inventories rises with the real wage. The real wage depends on the demand for labor and, therefore, on the speed with which firms in the aggregate choose to rebuild (or run down) inventories. More generally, the speed of adjustment to permanent values of real variables, the amplitude of business cycles, and the advantages of inventory smoothing at the macro level depend on structural parameters of the model.

All real variables reflect the influence of the inventory cycle and show sustained responses to monetary and real shocks. The longer or more persistent the deviations of the aggregate inventory from its permanent value, the longer or more persistent are the deviations of other real variables from their permanent values. And the larger the amplitude of inventory fluctuations, the larger are the cyclical deviations of other real variables from their permanent values.

Our model has a Keynesian, non-neutral, element in the very short-run since aggregate demand is satisfied, at a fixed price, out of buffer stock inventories. The price level fully reflects all information available at the beginning of each period, so prices change as new information becomes available. Everyone has the same information about the determinants of relative and absolute prices. Nevertheless, prices deviate persistently from their expected permanent value. The reason is that the demand for real balances responds to the induced changes in interest rates and income that result from shocks. Since the shocks have persistent real effects on all real variables, the demand for real balances changes cyclically.

The rate of price change fully reflects current monetary growth only in the long run. Elsewhere, price changes reflect all of the information the public has about current money growth and, in addition, reflect the lagged effects of past monetary growth on the demand for real balances. When all real variables are at their permanent values, the price level is at its permanent value.[58]

To keep the paper within manageable proportions, we have assumed, for the most part, that random shocks are completely transitory. We show that the model can be easily extended to the case in which there are persistent changes in the shocks that affect the economy. Within the extended

---

[58]Economic reasoning suggests that prices converge to their permanent level, but an algebraic proof cannot be supplied because the system is dichotomized.

framework, individuals cannot distinguish permanent and transitory shocks. Errors of forecast become serially correlated, in an ex post sense, whenever large permanent changes occur. When there is uncertainty about the permanence of monetary shocks, a permanent monetary change may produce, for a while, a bunching of overestimates or underestimates of money growth. The inability to separate permanent and transitory changes adds an additional cyclical disturbance to the disturbance produced by the slow adjustment of inventories.

Appendix

A.1. Proof that $0 < C_y < 1$

Using (1), (2) and (4), the systematic part of the excess demand for goods can be written

$$D - \bar{S} = \overline{ED} + (1 - K_2)[\beta(1 - a\gamma_1) - a\gamma_2]v - K_1\gamma_3 w,$$

where $\overline{ED}$ is a combination of constant parameters of no particular interest. We know from (43) that $1 - K_2 > 0$, so the excess demand for goods is a decreasing function of the real rate of interest, v, provided $\beta(1 - a\gamma_1) - a\gamma_2 < 0$. Since $\omega > 0$ and $-\beta\gamma_3 < 0$, this implies in conjunction with eq. (12) in the text that $0 < C_y < 1$.

A.2. Incorporation of the information contained in the within period observation on the interest rate

Eq. (56) of the text implies that $r_0^a - r_0$, the error in forecasting the nominal rate, conveys some information about m_0 and therefore about money growth at the beginning of period 1 and, thus, about the level of inventories at the beginning of period 1. In particular if $r_0^a < r_0$, rational individuals attribute at least part of this discrepancy to the excess of the actual over the anticipated rate of growth of money. They therefore revise their forecast of P_1^a upward. Defining $P_1^* \equiv E[P_1/(r_0^a - r_0)]$ this implies that $P_1^* > P_1$, where P_1 is the forecast of the price in period 1 as conceived at the beginning of period 0. The fact that $r_0^a < r_0$ allows individuals to infer that aggregate demand is higher than expected and therefore that the level of inventories at the beginning of period 1 is lower than had been expected. If g is relatively small, ceteris paribus, the relation between the price level and inventories is negative. (See Proposition 1 at the end of section 2.) This implies a further increase in $P_1^* - P_1$. It follows that $P_1^*/P_0 - P_1/P_0 = -\rho(r_0^a - r_0)$, where ρ is a positive coefficient. This implies that the expected rate of inflation goes up when the nominal rate is lower than expected so the effect of a decrease in the nominal rate on aggregate demand increases. More formally, when consumers are allowed to draw inferences from r_0^a, aggregate demand becomes

$$D_0^a = \alpha Y^p + \beta v_0 + \beta(1+\rho)(r_0^a - r_0) + \varepsilon_0.$$

The discussion in the text assumes $\rho = 0$ which weakens (but does not change the sign of) the effects of unanticipated shocks, through the interest rate channel, on aggregate demand.

A.3. Proof that for $w^p < 1$ there exists an interior maximum for x_0

$w^p < 1$ implies, using (6), that at zero unemployment the real wage demanded by a marginal unit of labor is always less than 1 since $w_t = w^p - \bar{L}_s/\omega < 1$ for $\bar{L}_s > 0$. Substituting the constraints in (28) and (29) and using the definition of x_i

$$\Pi_i(x_i, x_{i-1}) = \bar{s}_i(x_i) - w_i x_i + w_i \max[0, x_{i-1} - \delta \mu_{i-1} - z_{i-1}], \quad i = 1, 2, \ldots, \quad (A.1)$$

and

$$\Pi_0(x_0) = \bar{s}_0(x_0) - w_0(x_0 - h_0). \tag{A.2}$$

Let $x_0^*, x_1^*, x_2^*, \ldots$ be an optimal solution. We assume that $x_0^* = 0$ and prove by establishing a contradiction. From (A.2) and (32)

$$\partial \Pi_0(0)/\partial x_0 = 1 - w_0 > 0,$$

so a small increase in x_0^* at zero increases $\Pi_0(\cdot)$ and does not decrease $\Pi_i(\cdot)$ for $i \geq 1$ whatever the realization of z_{i-1}. It follows that x_0^* must be positive.

On the other hand $\bar{s}_0(x_0)$ is bounded by Ed. It follows from (A.2) that the optimal value of x_0 is finite. Hence $0 < x_0^* < \infty$.

References

Alchian, A.A., 1969, Information costs, pricing and resource unemployment, Economic Inquiry, June, 109–128.

Amihud, Y. and H. Mendelson, 1980, Monopoly under uncertainty: The enigma of price rigidity, Research working paper no. 305A, Graduate School of Business, Columbia University, March.

Amihud, Y. and H. Mendelson, 1982, The output inflation relationship: An inventory adjustment approach, Journal of Monetary Economics 9, March, 163–184.

Barro, R.J., 1976, Rational expectations and the role of monetary policy, Journal of Political Economy 84, Jan., 1–32.

Barro, R.J., 1977, Long term contracting, sticky prices and monetary policy, Journal of Monetary Economics 3, July, 305–316.

Blanchard, O.J., 1979, Backward and forward solutions for economies with rational expectations, American Economic Review, Papers and Proceedings 69, 114–118.

Blinder, A.S., 1977, A difficulty with Keynesian models of aggregate demand, in: A Blinder and P. Friedman, eds., Natural resources, uncertainty, and general equilibrium systems: Essays in memory of Rafael Lusky (Academic Press, New York).

Blinder, A.S., 1981, Inventories and sticky prices: More on the microfoundations of macroeconomics, manuscript, July.

Blinder, A.S. and S. Fischer, 1981, Inventories, rational expectations, and the business cycle, Journal of Monetary Economics 8, Nov., 277–304.

Brunner, K., A. Cukierman and A.H. Meltzer, 1980, Stagflation, persistent unemployment and the permanence of economic shocks, Journal of Monetary Economics 6, Oct., 467–492.

Cargill, T., 1969, An empirical investigation of the wage-lag hypothesis, American Economic Review 59, Dec., 806–816.

Cukierman, A., 1979, Rational Expectations and the role of monetary policy: A generalization, Journal of Monetary Economics 5, April, 213–229.

Cukierman, A., 1980, The effects of wage indexation on macroeconomic fluctuations; A generalization, Journal of Monetary Economics 6, April, 147–170.

Cukierman, A., 1981, Interest rates during the cycle, inventories and monetary policy — A theoretical analysis, in: K. Brunner and A. Meltzer, eds., The costs and consequences of inflation, Carnegie Rochester Conference Series on Public Policy, 15, Autumn (North-Holland, Amsterdam).

Fischer, S., 1977, Long term contracts, rational expectations and the optimal money supply rule, Journal of Political Economy 85, Feb., 191–205.

Friedman, M., 1968, The role of monetary policy, American Economic Review 58, March, 1–17.

Gordon, R., 1976, Recent developments in the theory of inflation and unemployment, Journal of Monetary Economics 2, April, 185–219.

Gray, J.A., 1976, Wage indexation: A macroeconomic approach, Journal of Monetary Economics 2, April, 221–236.

Hall, R.E., 1977, Expectation errors, unemployment and wage inflation, Center for Advanced Study in the Behavioral Science, Sept., manuscript.

Hall, R.E., 1980, Labor supply and aggregate fluctuations, in: K. Brunner and A. Meltzer, eds., On the state of macro-economics, Carnegie-Rochester Conference Series on Public Policy, 12, Spring (North-Holland, Amsterdam).

Irvine, Jr., F.O., 1981, A study of automobile inventory investment, Economic Inquiry 19, July.

Irvine, Jr., F.O., 1981, Retail inventory investment and the cost of capital, American Economic Review 71, Sept.

Keynes, J.M., 1936, The general theory of employment, interest and money (Macmillan, London).

Kydland, F. and E. Prescott, 1983, Time to build and aggregate fluctuations, Econometrica, forthcoming.

Lucas, Jr., R. and L. Rapping, 1969, Real wages, employment and inflation, Journal of Political Economy 77, Sept.–Oct., 721–754.

Lucas, Jr., R.E., 1972, Expectations and the neutrality of money, Journal of Economic Theory 4, April, 103–124.

Lucas, Jr., R.E., 1973, Some international evidence on output inflation tradeoffs, American Economic Review 63, June, 326–335.

Lucas, Jr., R.E., 1975, An equilibrium model of the business cycle, Journal of Political Economy 83, Dec., 1113–1144.

Maccini, L.J., 1976, An aggregate dynamic model of short run price and output behavior, Quarterly Journal of Economics 90, May, 177–196.

Maccini, L.J., 1980, On the theory of the firm underlying empirical models of aggregate price behavior, International Economic Review.

Muth, J.F., 1960, Optimal properties of exponentially weighted forecasts, Journal of the American Statistical Association 55, 299–306.

Phelps, E.S., 1967, Phillips curves, expectations of inflation and optimal unemployment over time, Economica, (NS), 34 Aug., 254–281.

Phelps, E.S. and J.B. Taylor, 1977, Stabilizing powers of monetary policy under rational expectations, Journal of Political Economy 85, Feb., 163–190.

Reagan, P., 1982, Inventory and price behavior, Review of Economics and Statistics 49, 137–142.

Sargent, T.J., 1973, Rational expectations, the real rate of interest and the natural rate of unemployment, Brookings Papers on Economic Activity 2, 429–480.

Sargent, T.J., 1979, Macroeconomic Theory (Academic Press, New York).

Sargent, T.J. and N. Wallace, 1975, Rational expectations, the optimal monetary instrument, and the optimal money supply rule, Journal of Political Economy 83, April, 241–254.

Siegel, J.J., 1981, Interest rates during the cycle, inventories and monetary policy — A theoretical analysis — A comment, in: K. Brunner and A. Meltzer, eds., The costs and consequences of inflation, Carnegie Rochester Conference Series on Public Policy, 15, Autumn (North-Holland, Amsterdam).

Taylor, J., 1977, Conditions for unique solutions in stochastic macro-economic models with rational expectations, Econometrica 45, Sept., 1377–1385.

Thornton, H., 1802, An enquiry into the nature and effects of the paper credit of Great Britain, reprinted in 1965 (Kelley, New York).

Part III
The Demand of Money, the Quantity Theory and Nominal Income

[10]

The Quantity Theory of Money—A Restatement

THE quantity theory of money is a term evocative of a general approach rather than a label for a well-defined theory. The exact content of the approach varies from a truism defining the term "velocity" to an allegedly rigid and unchanging ratio between the quantity of money—defined in one way or another—and the price level—also defined in one way or another. Whatever its precise meaning, it is clear that the general approach fell into disrepute after the crash of 1929 and the subsequent Great Depression and only recently has been slowly re-emerging into professional respectability.

The present volume is partly a symptom of this re-emergence and partly a continuance of an aberrant tradition. Chicago was one of the few academic centers at which the quantity theory continued to be a central and vigorous part of the oral tradition throughout the 1930's and 1940's, where students continued to study monetary theory and to write theses on monetary problems. The quantity theory that retained this role differed sharply from the atrophied and rigid caricature that is so frequently described by the proponents of the new income-expenditure approach—and with some justice, to judge by much of the literature on policy that was spawned by quantity theorists. At Chicago, Henry Simons and Lloyd Mints directly, Frank Knight and Jacob Viner at one remove, taught and developed a more subtle and relevant version, one in which the quantity theory was connected and integrated with general price theory and became a flexible and sensitive tool for interpreting movements in aggregate economic activity and for developing relevant policy prescriptions.

To the best of my knowledge, no systematic statement of this theory as developed at Chicago exists, though much can be read between the lines of Simons' and Mints's writings. And this is as it should be, for the Chicago tradition was not a rigid system, an unchangeable orthodoxy, but a way of looking at things. It was a theoretical approach that insisted that money does matter—that any interpretation of short-term movements in economic activity is likely to be seriously at fault if it neglects monetary changes and repercussions and if it leaves unexplained why people are willing to hold the particular nominal quantity of money in existence.

The purpose of this introduction is not to enshrine—or, should I say, inter—a definitive version of the Chicago tradition. To suppose that one

3

could do so would be inconsistent with that tradition itself. The purpose is rather to set down a particular "model" of a quantity theory in an attempt to convey the flavor of the oral tradition which nurtured the remaining essays in this volume. In consonance with this purpose, I shall not attempt to be exhaustive or to give a full justification for every assertion.

1. The quantity theory is in the first instance a theory of the *demand* for money. It is not a theory of output, or of money income, or of the price level. Any statement about these variables requires combining the quantity theory with some specifications about the conditions of supply of money and perhaps about other variables as well.

2. To the ultimate wealth-owning units in the economy, money is one kind of asset, one way of holding wealth. To the productive enterprise, money is a capital good, a source of productive services that are combined with other productive services to yield the products that the enterprise sells. Thus the theory of the demand for money is a special topic in the theory of capital; as such, it has the rather unusual feature of combining a piece from each side of the capital market, the supply of capital (points 3 through 8 that follow), and the demand for capital (points 9 through 12).

3. The analysis of the demand for money on the part of the ultimate wealth-owning units in the society can be made formally identical with that of the demand for a consumption service. As in the usual theory of consumer choice, the demand for money (or any other particular asset) depends on three major sets of factors: (*a*) the total wealth to be held in various forms—the analogue of the budget restraint; (*b*) the price of and return on this form of wealth and alternative forms; and (*c*) the tastes and preferences of the wealth-owning units. The substantive differences from the analysis of the demand for a consumption service are the necessity of taking account of intertemporal rates of substitution in (*b*) and (*c*) and of casting the budget restraint in terms of wealth.

4. From the broadest and most general point of view, total wealth includes all sources of "income" or consumable services. One such source is the productive capacity of human beings, and accordingly this is one form in which wealth can be held. From this point of view, "the" rate of interest expresses the relation between the stock which is wealth and the flow which is income, so if Y be the total flow of income, and r, "the" interest rate, total wealth is

$$W = \frac{Y}{r}. \tag{1}$$

Income in this broadest sense should not be identified with income as it is ordinarily measured. The latter is generally a "gross" stream with respect

The Quantity Theory of Money—A Restatement 5

to human beings, since no deduction is made for the expense of maintaining human productive capacity intact; in addition, it is affected by transitory elements that make it depart more or less widely from the theoretical concept of the stable level of consumption of services that could be maintained indefinitely.

5. Wealth can be held in numerous forms, and the ultimate wealth-owning unit is to be regarded as dividing his wealth among them (point [a] of 3), so as to maximize "utility" (point [c] of 3), subject to whatever restrictions affect the possibility of converting one form of wealth into another (point [b] of 3). As usual, this implies that he will seek an apportionment of his wealth such that the rate at which he *can* substitute one form of wealth for another is equal to the rate at which he is just willing to do so. But this general proposition has some special features in the present instance because of the necessity of considering flows as well as stocks. We can suppose all wealth (except wealth in the form of the productive capacity of human beings) to be expressed in terms of monetary units at the prices of the point of time in question. The rate at which one form can be substituted for another is then simply $1.00 worth for $1.00 worth, regardless of the forms involved. But this is clearly not a complete description, because the holding of one form of wealth instead of another involves a difference in the composition of the income stream, and it is essentially these differences that are fundamental to the "utility" of a particular structure of wealth. In consequence, to describe fully the alternative combinations of forms of wealth that are available to an individual, we must take account not only of their market prices—which except for human wealth can be done simply by expressing them in units worth $1.00—but also of the form and size of the income streams they yield.

It will suffice to bring out the major issues that these considerations raise to consider five different forms in which wealth can be held: (i) money (M), interpreted as claims or commodity units that are generally accepted in payment of debts at a fixed nominal value; (ii) bonds (B), interpreted as claims to time streams of payments that are fixed in nominal units; (iii) equities (E), interpreted as claims to stated pro-rata shares of the returns of enterprises; (iv) physical non-human goods (G); and (v) human capital (H). Consider now the yield of each.

(i) Money may yield a return in the form of money, for example, interest on demand deposits. It will simplify matters, however, and entail no essential loss of generality, to suppose that money yields its return solely in kind, in the usual form of convenience, security, etc. The magnitude of this return in "real" terms per nominal unit of money clearly depends on the volume of goods that unit corresponds to, or on the general price level, which we may designate by P. Since we have decided to take $1.00 worth as the unit for each form of wealth, this will be equally true for other forms of wealth as well, so P is a variable affecting the "real" yield of each.

(ii) If we take the "standard" bond to be a claim to a perpetual income stream of constant nominal amount, then the return to a holder of the bond can take two forms: one, the annual sum he receives—the "coupon"; the other, any change in the price of the bond over time, a return which may of course be positive or negative. If the price is expected to remain constant, then $1.00 worth of a bond yields r_b per year, where r_b is simply the "coupon" sum divided by the market price of the bond, so $1/r_b$ is the price of a bond promising to pay $1.00 per year. We shall call r_b the market bond interest rate. If the price is expected to change, then the yield cannot be calculated so simply, since it must take account of the return in the form of expected appreciation or depreciation of the bond, and it cannot, like r_b, be calculated directly from market prices (so long, at least, as the "standard" bond is the only one traded in).

The nominal income stream purchased for $1.00 at time zero then consists of

$$r_b(0) + r_b(0)\, d\,\frac{\left(\dfrac{1}{r_b(t)}\right)}{dt} = r_b(0) - \frac{r_b(0)}{r_b^2(t)} \cdot \frac{d\,r_b(t)}{dt}, \qquad (2)$$

where t stands for time. For simplicity, we can approximate this functional by its value at time zero, which is

$$r_b - \frac{1}{r_b}\frac{d\,r_b}{dt}. \qquad (3)$$

This sum, together with P already introduced, defines the real return from holding $1.00 of wealth in the form of bonds.

(iii) Analogously to our treatment of bonds, we may take the "standard" unit of equity to be a claim to a perpetual income stream of constant "real" amount; that is, to be a standard bond with a purchasing-power escalator clause, so that it promises a perpetual income stream equal in nominal units to a constant number times a price index, which we may, for convenience, take to be the same price index P introduced in (i).[1] The nominal return to the holder of the equity can then be regarded as taking three forms: the constant nominal amount he would receive per year in

1. This is an oversimplification, because it neglects "leverage" and therefore supposes that any monetary liabilities of an enterprise are balanced by monetary assets.

The Quantity Theory of Money—A Restatement 7

the absence of any change in P; the increment or decrement to this nominal amount to adjust for changes in P; and any change in the nominal price of the equity over time, which may of course arise from changes either in interest rates or in price levels. Let r_e be the market interest rate on equities defined analogously to r_b, namely, as the ratio of the "coupon" sum at any time (the first two items above) to the price of the equity, so $1/r_e$ is the price of an equity promising to pay \$1.00 per year if the price level does not change, or to pay

$$\frac{P(t)}{P(0)} \cdot 1$$

if the price level varies according to $P(t)$. If $r_e(t)$ is defined analogously, the price of the bond selling for $1/r_e(0)$ at time 0 will be

$$\frac{P(t)}{P(0)\, r_e(t)}$$

at time t, where the ratio of prices is required to adjust for any change in the price level. The nominal stream purchased for \$1.00 at time zero then consists of

$$r_e(0) \cdot \frac{P(t)}{P(0)} + \frac{r_e(0)}{P(0)} \cdot d\frac{\left[\frac{P(t)}{r_e(t)}\right]}{dt} = r_e(0) \cdot \frac{P(t)}{P(0)}$$

$$+ \frac{r_e(0)}{r_e(t)} \cdot \frac{1}{P(0)} \cdot \frac{dP(t)}{dt} - \frac{P(t)}{P(0)} \cdot \frac{r_e(0)}{r_e^2(t)} \cdot \frac{d\,r_e(t)}{dt}. \tag{4}$$

Once again we can approximate this functional by its value at time zero, which is

$$r_e + \frac{1}{P}\frac{dP}{dt} - \frac{1}{r_e}\frac{d\,r_e}{dt}. \tag{5}$$

This sum, together with P already introduced, defines the "real" return from holding \$1.00 of wealth in the form of equities.

(iv) Physical goods held by ultimate wealth-owning units are similar to equities except that the annual stream they yield is in kind rather than in money. In terms of nominal units, this return, like that from equities, depends on the behavior of prices. In addition, like equities, physical goods must be regarded as yielding a nominal return in the form of appreciation or depreciation in money value. If we suppose the price level P, introduced earlier, to apply equally to the value of these physical goods, then, at time zero,

$$\frac{1}{P}\frac{dP}{dT} \tag{6}$$

8   *Studies in the Quantity Theory of Money*

is the size of this nominal return per \$1.00 of physical goods.[2] Together with P, it defines the "real" return from holding \$1.00 in the form of physical goods.

(v) Since there is only a limited market in human capital, at least in modern non-slave societies, we cannot very well define in market prices the terms of substitution of human capital for other forms of capital and so cannot define at any time the physical unit of capital corresponding to \$1.00 of human capital. There are some possibilities of substituting non-human capital for human capital in an individual's wealth holdings, as, for example, when he enters into a contract to render personal services for a specified period in return for a definitely specified number of periodic payments, the number not depending on his being physically capable of rendering the services. But, in the main, shifts between human capital and other forms must take place through direct investment and disinvestment in the human agent, and we may as well treat this as if it were the only way. With respect to this form of capital, therefore, the restriction or obstacles affecting the alternative compositions of wealth available to the individual cannot be expressed in terms of market prices or rates of return. At any one point in time there is some division between human and non-human wealth in his portfolio of assets; he may be able to change this over time, but we shall treat it as given at a point in time. Let w be the ratio of non-human to human wealth or, equivalently, of income from non-human wealth to income from human wealth, which means that it is closely allied to what is usually defined as the ratio of wealth to income. This is, then, the variable that needs to be taken into account so far as human wealth is concerned.

6. The tastes and preferences of wealth-owning units for the service streams arising from different forms of wealth must in general simply be taken for granted as determining the form of the demand function. In order to give the theory empirical content, it will generally have to be supposed that tastes are constant over significant stretches of space and time. However, explicit allowance can be made for some changes in tastes in so far as such changes are linked with objective circumstances. For example, it seems reasonable that, other things the same, individuals want

2. In principle, it might be better to let P refer solely to the value of the services of physical goods, which is essentially what it refers to in the preceding cases, and to allow for the fact that the prices of the capital goods themselves must vary also with the rate of capitalization, so that the prices of services and their sources vary at the same rate only if the relevant interest rate is constant. I have neglected this refinement for simplicity; the neglect can perhaps be justified by the rapid depreciation of many of the physical goods held by final wealth-owning units.

The Quantity Theory of Money—A Restatement 9

to hold a larger fraction of their wealth in the form of money when they are moving around geographically or are subject to unusual uncertainty than otherwise. This is probably one of the major factors explaining a frequent tendency for money holdings to rise relative to income during wartime. But the extent of geographic movement, and perhaps of other kinds of uncertainty, can be represented by objective indexes, such as indexes of migration, miles of railroad travel, and the like. Let u stand for any such variables that can be expected to affect tastes and preferences (for "utility" determining variables).

7. Combining 4, 5, and 6 along the lines suggested by 3 yields the following demand function for money:

$$M = f\left(P, \; r_b - \frac{1}{r_b}\frac{d\,r_b}{dt}, \; r_e + \frac{1}{P}\frac{dP}{dt} - \frac{1}{r_e}\frac{d\,r_e}{dt}, \; \frac{1}{P}\frac{dP}{dt}; \; w; \; \frac{Y}{r}; u\right). \quad (7)$$

A number of observations are in order about this function.

(i) Even if we suppose prices and rates of interest unchanged, the function contains three rates of interest: two for specific types of assets, r_b and r_e, and one intended to apply to all types of assets, r. This general rate, r, is to be interpreted as something of a weighted average of the two special rates plus the rates applicable to human wealth and to physical goods. Since the latter two cannot be observed directly, it is perhaps best to regard them as varying in some systematic way with r_b and r_e. On this assumption, we can drop r as an additional explicit variable, treating its influence as fully taken into account by the inclusion of r_b and r_e.

(ii) If there were no differences of opinion about price movements and interest-rate movements, and bonds and equities were equivalent except that the former are expressed in nominal units, arbitrage would of course make

$$r_b - \frac{1}{r_b}\frac{d\,r_b}{dt} = r_e + \frac{1}{P}\frac{dP}{dt} - \frac{1}{r_e}\frac{d\,r_e}{dt}, \quad (8)$$

or, if we suppose rates of interest either stable or changing at the same percentage rate,

$$r_b = r_e + \frac{1}{P}\frac{dP}{dt}, \quad (9)$$

that is, the "money" interest rate equal to the "real" rate plus the percentage rate of change of prices. In application the rate of change of prices must be interpreted as an "expected" rate of change and differences of opinion cannot be neglected, so we cannot suppose (9) to hold; indeed,

10   *Studies in the Quantity Theory of Money*

one of the most consistent features of inflation seems to be that it does not.[3]

(iii) If the range of assets were to be widened to include promises to pay specified sums for a finite number of time units—"short-term" securities as well as "consols"—the rates of change of r_b and r_e would be reflected in the difference between long and short rates of interest. Since at some stage it will doubtless be desirable to introduce securities of different time duration (see point 23 below), we may simplify the present exposition by restricting it to the case in which r_b and r_e are taken to be stable over time. Since the rate of change in prices is required separately in any event, this means that we can replace the cumbrous variables introduced to designate the nominal return on bonds and equities simply by r_b and r_e.

(iv) Y can be interpreted as including the return to all forms of wealth, including money and physical capital goods owned and held directly by ultimate wealth-owning units, and so Y/r can be interpreted as an estimate of total wealth, only if Y is regarded as including some imputed income from the stock of money and directly owned physical capital goods. For monetary analysis the simplest procedure is perhaps to regard Y as referring to the return to all forms of wealth other than the money held directly by ultimate wealth-owning units, and so Y/r as referring to total remaining wealth.

8. A more fundamental point is that, as in all demand analyses resting on maximization of a utility function defined in terms of "real" magnitudes, this demand equation must be considered independent in any essential way of the nominal units used to measure money variables. If the unit in which prices and money income are expressed is changed, the amount of money demanded should change proportionately. More technically, equation (7) must be regarded as homogeneous of the first degree in P and Y, so that

$$f\left(\lambda P, \; r_b, \; r_e, \; \frac{1}{P}\frac{dP}{dt}; \; w; \; \lambda Y; \; u\right)$$
$$= \lambda f\left(P, \; r_b, \; r_e, \; \frac{1}{P}\frac{dP}{dt}; \; w; \; Y; \; u\right). \tag{10}$$

where the variables within the parentheses have been rewritten in simpler form in accordance with comments 7 (i) and 7 (iii).

3. See Reuben Kessel, "Inflation: Theory of Wealth Distribution and Application in Private Investment Policy" (unpublished doctoral dissertation, University of Chicago).

The Quantity Theory of Money—A Restatement 11

This characteristic of the function enables us to rewrite it in two alternative and more familiar ways.

(i) Let $\lambda = 1/P$. Equation (7) can then be written

$$\frac{M}{P} = f\left(r_b, \ r_e, \ \frac{1}{P}\frac{dP}{dt}; \ w; \ \frac{Y}{P}; \ u\right). \tag{11}$$

In this form the equation expresses the demand for real balances as a function of "real" variables independent of nominal monetary values.

(ii) Let $\lambda = 1/Y$. Equation (7) can then be written

$$\frac{M}{Y} = f\left(r_b, \ r_e, \ \frac{1}{P}\frac{dP}{dt}, \ w, \ \frac{P}{Y}, \ u\right)$$

$$= \frac{1}{v\left(r_b, \ r_e, \ \dfrac{1}{P}\dfrac{dP}{dt}, \ w, \ \dfrac{Y}{P}, \ u\right)}, \tag{12}$$

or

$$Y = v\left(r_b, \ r_e, \ \frac{1}{P}\frac{dP}{dt}, \ w, \ \frac{Y}{P}, \ u\right) \cdot M. \tag{13}$$

In this form the equation is in the usual quantity theory form, where v is income velocity.

9. These equations are, to this point, solely for money held directly by ultimate wealth-owning units. As noted, money is also held by business enterprises as a productive resource. The counterpart to this business asset in the balance sheet of an ultimate wealth-owning unit is a claim other than money. For example, an individual may buy bonds from a corporation, and the corporation use the proceeds to finance the money holdings which it needs for its operations. Of course, the usual difficulties of separating the accounts of the business and its owner arise with unincorporated enterprises.

10. The amount of money that it pays business enterprises to hold depends, as for any other source of productive services, on the cost of the productive services, the cost of substitute productive services, and the value product yielded by the productive service. Per dollar of money held, the cost depends on how the corresponding capital is raised—whether by raising additional capital in the form of bonds or equities, by substituting cash for real capital goods, etc. These ways of financing money holdings are much the same as the alternative forms in which the ultimate wealth-owning unit can hold its non-human wealth, so that the variables r_b, r_e, P, and $(1/P)(dP/dt)$ introduced into (7) can be taken to represent the cost to the business enterprise of holding money. For some purposes, however, it may be desirable to distinguish between the rate of return re-

12   *Studies in the Quantity Theory of Money*

ceived by the lender and the rate paid by the borrower; in which case it
would be necessary to introduce an additional set of variables.

Substitutes for money as a productive service are numerous and
varied, including all ways of economizing on money holdings by using
other resources to synchronize more closely payments and receipts, reduce
payment periods, extend use of book credit, establish clearing arrangements, and so on in infinite variety. There seem no particularly close substitutes whose prices deserve to be singled out for inclusion in the business
demand for money.

The value product yielded by the productive services of money per unit
of output depends on production conditions: the production function. It is
likely to be especially dependent on features of production conditions affecting the smoothness and regularity of operations as well as on those
determining the size and scope of enterprises, degree of vertical integration, etc. Again there seem no variables that deserve to be singled out on
the present level of abstraction for special attention; these factors can be
taken into account by interpreting u as including variables affecting not
only the tastes of wealth-owners but also the relevant technological conditions of production. Given the amount of money demanded per unit of
output, the total amount demanded is proportional to total output, which
can be represented by Y.

11. One variable that has traditionally been singled out in considering
the demand for money on the part of business enterprises is the volume of
transactions, or of transactions per dollar of final products; and, of course,
emphasis on transactions has been carried over to the ultimate wealth-
owning unit as well as to the business enterprise. The idea that renders
this approach attractive is that there is a mechanical link between a dollar
of payments per unit time and the average stock of money required to
effect it—a fixed technical coefficient of production, as it were. It is clear
that this mechanical approach is very different in spirit from the one we
have been following. On our approach, the average amount of money
held per dollar of transactions is itself to be regarded as a resultant of an
economic equilibrating process, not as a physical datum. If, for whatever
reason, it becomes more expensive to hold money, then it is worth
devoting resources to effecting money transactions in less expensive ways
or to reducing the volume of transactions per dollar of final output. In
consequence, our ultimate demand function for money in its most general
form does not contain as a variable the volume of transactions or of
transactions per dollar of final output; it contains rather those more basic
technical and cost conditions that affect the costs of conserving money,
be it by changing the average amount of money held per dollar of transac-

The Quantity Theory of Money—A Restatement 13

tions per unit time or by changing the number of dollars of transactions per dollar of final output. This does not, of course, exclude the possibility that, for a particular problem, it may be useful to regard the transactions variables as given and not to dig beneath them and so to include the volume of transactions per dollar of final output as an explicit variable in a special variant of the demand function.

Similar remarks are relevant to various features of payment conditions, frequently described as "institutional conditions," affecting the velocity of circulation of money and taken as somehow mechanically determined— such items as whether workers are paid by the day, or week, or month; the use of book credit; and so on. On our approach these, too, are to be regarded as resultants of an economic equilibrating process, not as physical data. Lengthening the pay period, for example, may save book-keeping and other costs to the employer, who is therefore willing to pay somewhat more than in proportion for a longer than a shorter pay period; on the other hand, it imposes on employees the cost of holding larger cash balances or providing substitutes for cash, and they therefore want to be paid more than in proportion for a longer pay period. Where these will balance depends on how costs vary with length of pay period. The cost to the employee depends in considerable part on the factors entering into his demand curve for money for a fixed pay period. If he would in any event be holding relatively large average balances, the additional costs imposed by a lengthened pay period tend to be less than if he would be holding relatively small average balances, and so it will take less of an inducement to get him to accept a longer pay period. For given cost savings to the employer, therefore, the pay period can be expected to be longer in the first case than in the second. Surely, the increase in the average cash balance over the past century in this country that has occurred for other reasons has been a factor producing a lengthening of pay periods and not the other way around. Or, again, experience in hyperinflations shows how rapidly payment practices change under the impact of drastic changes in the cost of holding money.

12. The upshot of these considerations is that the demand for money on the part of business enterprises can be regarded as expressed by a function of the same kind as equation (7), with the same variables on the right-hand side. And, like (7), since the analysis is based on informed maximization of returns by enterprises, only "real" quantities matter, so it must be homogeneous of the first degree in Y and P. In consequence, we can interpret (7) and its variants (11) and (13) as describing the demand for money on the part of a business enterprise as well as on the part of an

ultimate wealth-owning unit, provided only that we broaden our interpretation of u.

13. Strictly speaking, the equations (7), (11), and (13) are for an individual wealth-owning unit or business enterprise. If we aggregate (7) for
all wealth-owning units and business enterprises in the society, the result,
in principle, depends on the distribution of the units by the several variables. This raises no serious problem about P, r_b, and r_e, for these can be
taken as the same for all, or about u, for this is an unspecified portmanteau
variable to be filled in as the occasion demands. We have been interpreting $(1/P)(dP/dt)$ as the expected rate of price rise, so there is no reason
why this variable should be the same for all, and w and Y clearly differ
substantially among units. An approximation is to neglect these difficulties and take (7) and the associated (11) and (13) as applying to the
aggregate demand for money, with $(1/P)(dP/dt)$ interpreted as some kind
of an average expected rate of change of prices, w as the ratio of total
income from non-human wealth to income from human wealth, and Y as
aggregate income. This is the procedure that has generally been followed,
and it seems the right one until serious departures between this linear
approximation and experience make it necessary to introduce measures of
dispersion with respect to one or more of the variables.

14. It is perhaps worth noting explicitly that the model does not use
the distinction between "active balances" and "idle balances" or the
closely allied distinction between "transaction balances" and "speculative
balances" that is so widely used in the literature. The distinction between
money holdings of ultimate wealth-owners and of business enterprises is
related to this distinction but only distantly so. Each of these categories
of money-holders can be said to demand money partly from "transaction"
motives, partly from "speculative" or "asset" motives, but dollars of
money are not distinguished according as they are said to be held for one
or the other purpose. Rather, each dollar is, as it were, regarded as
rendering a variety of services, and the holder of money as altering his
money holdings until the value to him of the addition to the total flow of
services produced by adding a dollar to his money stock is equal to the
reduction in the flow of services produced by subtracting a dollar from
each of the other forms in which he holds assets.

15. Nothing has been said above about "banks" or producers of
money. This is because their main role is in connection with the supply of
money rather than the demand for it. Their introduction does, however,
blur some of the points in the above analysis: the existence of banks enables productive enterprises to acquire money balances without raising
capital from ultimate wealth-owners. Instead of selling claims (bonds or

The Quantity Theory of Money—A Restatement   15

equities) to them, it can sell its claims to banks, getting "money" in exchange: in the phrase that was once so common in textbooks on money,
the bank coins specific liabilities into generally acceptable liabilities. But
this possibility does not alter the preceding analysis in any essential way.

16. Suppose the supply of money in nominal units is regarded as fixed
or more generally autonomously determined. Equation (13) then defines
the conditions under which this nominal stock of money will be the
amount demanded. Even under these conditions, equation (13) alone is
not sufficient to determine money income. In order to have a complete
model for the determination of money income, it would be necessary to
specify the determinants of the structure of interest rates, of real income,
and of the path of adjustment in the price level. Even if we suppose interest
rates determined independently—by productivity, thrift, and the like—
and real income as also given by other forces, equation (13) only determines
a unique equilibrium level of money income if we mean by this the level
at which prices are stable. More generally, it determines a time path of
money income for given initial values of money income.

In order to convert equation (13) into a "complete" model of income
determination, therefore, it is necessary to suppose either that the demand
for money is highly inelastic with respect to the variables in v or that all
these variables are to be taken as rigid and fixed.

17. Even under the most favorable conditions, for example, that the
demand for money is quite inelastic with respect to the variables in v,
equation (13) gives at most a theory of money income: it then says that
changes in money income mirror changes in the nominal quantity of
money. But it tells nothing about how much of any change in Y is reflected in real output and how much in prices. To infer this requires bringing in outside information, as, for example, that real output is at its
feasible maximum, in which case any increase in money would produce
the same or a larger percentage increase in prices; and so on.

18. In light of the preceding exposition, the question arises what it
means to say that someone is or is not a "quantity theorist." Almost
every economist will accept the general lines of the preceding analysis on
a purely formal and abstract level, although each would doubtless choose
to express it differently in detail. Yet there clearly are deep and fundamental differences about the importance of this analysis for the understanding of short- and long-term movements in general economic activity.
This difference of opinion arises with respect to three different issues:
(i) the stability and importance of the demand function for money; (ii)
the independence of the factors affecting demand and supply; and (iii)
the form of the demand function or related functions.

16   *Studies in the Quantity Theory of Money*

(i) The quantity theorist accepts the empirical hypothesis that the demand for money is highly stable—more stable than functions such as the consumption function that are offered as alternative key relations. This hypothesis needs to be hedged on both sides. On the one side, the quantity theorist need not, and generally does not, mean that the real quantity of money demanded per unit of output, or the velocity of circulation of money, is to be regarded as numerically constant over time; he does not, for example, regard it as a contradiction to the stability of the demand for money that the velocity of circulation of money rises drastically during hyperinflations. For the stability he expects is in the functional relation between the quantity of money demanded and the variables that determine it, and the sharp rise in the velocity of circulation of money during hyperinflations is entirely consistent with a stable functional relation, as Cagan so clearly demonstrates in his essay. On the other side, the quantity theorist must sharply limit, and be prepared to specify explicitly, the variables that it is empirically important to include in the function. For to expand the number of variables regarded as significant is to empty the hypothesis of its empirical content; there is indeed little if any difference between asserting that the demand for money is highly unstable and asserting that it is a perfectly stable function of an indefinitely large number of variables.

The quantity theorist not only regards the demand function for money as stable; he also regards it as playing a vital role in determining variables that he regards as of great importance for the analysis of the economy as a whole, such as the level of money income or of prices. It is this that leads him to put greater emphasis on the demand for money than on, let us say, the demand for pins, even though the latter might be as stable as the former. It is not easy to state this point precisely, and I cannot pretend to have done so. (See item [iii] below for an example of an argument against the quantity theorist along these lines.)

The reaction against the quantity theory in the 1930's came largely, I believe, under this head. The demand for money, it was asserted, is a will-o'-the-wisp, shifting erratically and unpredictably with every rumor and expectation; one cannot, it was asserted, reliably specify a limited number of variables on which it depends. However, although the reaction came under this head, it was largely rationalized under the two succeeding heads.

(ii) The quantity theorist also holds that there are important factors affecting the supply of money that do not affect the demand for money. Under some circumstances these are technical conditions affecting the supply of specie; under others, political or psychological conditions determining the policies of monetary authorities and the banking system. A stable

The Quantity Theory of Money—A Restatement 17

demand function is useful precisely in order to trace out the effects of changes in supply, which means that it is useful only if supply is affected by at least some factors other than those regarded as affecting demand.

The classical version of the objection under this head to the quantity theory is the so-called real-bills doctrine: that changes in the demand for money call forth corresponding changes in supply and that supply cannot change otherwise, or at least cannot do so under specified institutional arrangements. The forms which this argument takes are legion and are still widespread. Another version is the argument that the "quantity theory" cannot "explain" large price rises, because the price rise produced both the increase in demand for nominal money holdings and the increase in supply of money to meet it; that is, implicitly that the same forces affect both the demand for and the supply of money, and in the same way.

(iii) The attack on the quantity theory associated with the Keynesian underemployment analysis is based primarily on an assertion about the form of (7) or (11). The demand for money, it is said, is infinitely elastic at a "small" positive interest rate. At this interest rate, which can be expected to prevail under underemployment conditions, changes in the real supply of money, whether produced by changes in prices or in the nominal stock of money, have no effect on anything. This is the famous "liquidity trap." A rather more complex version involves the shape of other functions as well: the magnitudes in (7) other than "the" interest rate, it is argued, enter into other relations in the economic system and can be regarded as determined there; the interest rate does not enter into these other functions; it can therefore be regarded as determined by this equation. So the only role of the stock of money and the demand for money is to determine the interest rate.

19. The proof of this pudding is in the eating; and the essays in this book contain much relevant food, of which I may perhaps mention three particularly juicy items.

On cannot read Lerner's description of the effects of monetary reform in the Confederacy in 1864 without recognizing that at least on occasion the supply of money can be a largely autonomous factor and the demand for money highly stable even under extraordinarily unstable circumstances. After three years of war, after widespread destruction and military reverses, in the face of impending defeat, a monetary reform that succeeded in reducing the stock of money halted and reversed for some months a rise in prices that had been going on at the rate of 10 per cent a month most of the war! It would be hard to construct a better controlled experiment to demonstrate the critical importance of the supply of money.

On the other hand, Klein's examination of German experience in World

18   *Studies in the Quantity Theory of Money*

War II is much less favorable to the stability and importance of the demand for money. Though he shows that defects in the figures account for
a sizable part of the crude discrepancy between changes in the recorded
stock of money and in recorded prices, correction of these defects still
leaves a puzzlingly large discrepancy that it does not seem possible to
account for in terms of the variables introduced into the above exposition
of the theory. Klein examined German experience precisely because it
seemed the most deviant on a casual examination. Both it and other wartime experience will clearly repay further examination.

Cagan's examination of hyperinflations is another important piece of
evidence on the stability of the demand for money under highly unstable
conditions. It is also an interesting example of the difference between a
numerically stable velocity and a stable functional relation: the numerical
value of the velocity varied enormously during the hyperinflations, but
this was a predictable response to the changes in the expected rate of
changes of prices.

20. Though the essays in this book contain evidence relevant to the
issues discussed in point 18, this is a by-product rather than their main
purpose, which is rather to add to our tested knowledge about the characteristics of the demand function for money. In the process of doing so,
they also raise some questions about the theoretical formulation and suggest some modifications it might be desirable to introduce. I shall comment on a few of those without attempting to summarize at all fully the
essays themselves.

21. Selden's material covers the longest period of time and the most
"normal" conditions. This is at once a virtue and a vice—a virtue, because
it means that his results may be applicable most directly to ordinary
peacetime experience; a vice, because "normality" is likely to spell little
variation in the fundamental variables and hence a small base from which
to judge their effect. The one variable that covers a rather broad range is
real income, thanks to the length of the period. The secular rise in real
income has been accompanied by a rise in real cash balances per unit of
output—a decline in velocity—from which Selden concludes that the income elasticity of the demand for real balances is greater than unity—
cash balances are a "luxury" in the terminology generally adopted. This
entirely plausible result seems to be confirmed by evidence for other
countries as well.

22. Selden finds that for cyclical periods velocity rises during expansions and falls during contractions, a result that at first glance seems
to contradict the secular result just cited. However, there is an alternative
explanation entirely consistent with the secular result. It will be recalled

The Quantity Theory of Money—A Restatement 19

that Y was introduced into equation (7) as an index of wealth. This has important implications for the measure or concept of income that is relevant. What is required by the theoretical analysis is not usual measured income—which in the main corresponds to current receipts corrected for double counting—but a longer term concept, "expected income," or what I have elsewhere called "permanent income."[4] Now suppose that the variables in the v function of (13) are unchanged for a period. The ratio of Y to M would then be unchanged, provided Y is *permanent* income. Velocity as Selden computes it is the ratio of *measured* income to the stock of money and would not be unchanged. When measured income was above permanent income, measured velocity would be relatively high, and conversely. Now measured income is presumably above permanent income at cyclical peaks and below permanent income at cyclical troughs. The observed positive conformity of measured velocity to cyclical changes of income may therefore reflect simply the difference between measured income and the concept relevant to equation (13).

23. Another point that is raised by Selden's work is the appropriate division of wealth into forms of assets. The division suggested above is, of course, only suggestive. Selden finds more useful the distinction between "short-term" and "long-term" bonds; he treats the former as "substitutes for money" and calls the return on the latter "the cost of holding money." He finds both to be significantly related to the quantity of money demanded. It was suggested above that this is also a way to take into account expectations about changes in interest rates.

Similarly, there is no hard-and-fast line between "money" and other assets, and for some purposes it may be desirable to distinguish between different forms of "money" (e.g., between currency and deposits). Some of these forms of money may pay interest or may involve service charges, in which case the positive or negative return will be a relevant variable in determining the division of money holdings among various forms.

24. By concentrating on hyperinflations, Cagan was able to bring into sharp relief a variable whose effect is generally hard to evaluate, namely, the rate of change of prices. The other side of this coin is the necessity of neglecting practically all the remaining variables. His device for estimating expected rates of change of prices from actual rates of change, which works so well for his data, can be carried over to other variables as well and so is likely to be important in fields other than money. I have already used it to estimate "expected income" as a determinant of consumption,[5]

4. See Milton Friedman, *A Theory of the Consumption Function*, forthcoming publication of the Princeton University Press for the National Bureau of Economic Research.

5. See *ibid*.

20   *Studies in the Quantity Theory of Money*

and Gary Becker has experimented with using this "expected income" series in a demand function for money along the lines suggested above (in point 22).

Cagan's results make it clear that changes in the rate of change of prices, or in the return to an alternative form of holding wealth, have the expected effect on the quantity of money demanded: the higher the rate of change of prices, and thus the more attractive the alternative, the less the quantity of money demanded. This result is important not only directly but also because it is indirectly relevant to the effect of changes in the returns to other alternatives, such as rates of interest on various kinds of bonds. Our evidence on these is in some way less satisfactory because they have varied over so much smaller a range; tentative findings that the effect of changes in them is in the expected direction are greatly strengthened by Cagan's results.

One point which is suggested by the inapplicability of Cagan's relations to the final stages of the hyperinflations he studies is that it may at times be undesirable to replace the whole expected pattern of price movements by the rate of change expected at the moment, as Cagan does and as is done in point 5 above. For example, a given rate of price rise, expected to continue, say, for only a day, and to be followed by price stability, will clearly mean a higher (real) demand for money than the same rate of price rise expected to continue indefinitely; it will be worth incurring greater costs to avoid paying the latter than the former price. This is the same complication as occurs in demand analysis for a consumer good when it is necessary to include not only the present price but also past prices or future expected prices. This point may help explain not only Cagan's findings for the terminal stages but also Selden's findings that the inclusion of the rate of change of prices as part of the cost of holding money worsened rather than improved his estimated relations, though it may be that this result arises from a different source, namely, that it takes substantial actual rates of price change to produce firm enough and uniform enough expectations about price behavior for this variable to play a crucial role.

Similar comments are clearly relevant for expected changes in interest rates.

25. One of the chief reproaches directed at economics as an allegedly empirical science is that it can offer so few numerical "constants," that it has isolated so few fundamental regularities. The field of money is the chief example one can offer in rebuttal: there is perhaps no other empirical relation in economics that has been observed to recur so uniformly under so wide a variety of circumstances as the relation between substantial

The Quantity Theory of Money—A Restatement 21

changes over short periods in the stock of money and in prices; the one is invariably linked with the other and is in the same direction; this uniformity is, I suspect, of the same order as many of the uniformities that form the basis of the physical sciences. And the uniformity is in more than direction. There is an extraordinary empirical stability and regularity to such magnitudes as income velocity that cannot but impress anyone who works extensively with monetary data. This very stability and regularity contributed to the downfall of the quantity theory, for it was overstated and expressed in unduly simple form; the numerical value of the velocity itself, whether income or transactions, was treated as a natural "constant." Now this it is not; and its failure to be so, first during and after World War I and then, to a lesser extent, after the crash of 1929, helped greatly to foster the reaction against the quantity theory. The studies in this volume are premised on a stability and regularity in monetary relations of a more sophisticated form than a numerically constant velocity. And they make, I believe, an important contribution toward extracting this stability and regularity, toward isolating the numerical "constants" of monetary behavior. It is by this criterion at any rate that I, and I believe also their authors, would wish them to be judged.

I began this Introduction by referring to the tradition in the field of money at Chicago and to the role of faculty members in promoting it. I think it is fitting to end the Introduction by emphasizing the part which students have played in keeping that tradition alive and vigorous. The essays that follow are one manifestation. Unpublished doctoral dissertations on money are another. In addition, I wish especially to express my own personal appreciation to the students who have participated with me in the Workshop in Money and Banking, of which this volume is the first published fruit. I owe a special debt to David I. Fand, Phillip Cagan, Gary Becker, David Meiselman, and Raymond Zelder, who have at various times helped me to conduct it.

We all of us are indebted also to the Rockefeller Foundation for financial assistance to the Workshop in Money and Banking. This assistance helped to finance some of the research reported in this book and has made possible its publication.

[11]

The Chicago Tradition,
The Quantity Theory,
And Friedman[1,2]

DON PATINKIN

I MUST BEGIN THIS PAPER with an apology for being over a decade late; for I should have written it as an immediate reaction to Milton Friedman's by now well-known 1956 essay on "The Quantity Theory of Money—A Restatement." [3] But the recent appearance of Friedman's *International Encyclopedia* article on the quantity theory[4] (though, as will be shown in Part IV below, it differs in some relevant respects from the earlier paper) provides an appropriate, if tardy, occasion to raise some basic questions—from the viewpoint of the history of monetary doctrine—about the validity of Fried-

[1] This paper was written while I was visiting at M.I.T. during 1968 under a research grant from the National Science Foundation (NSF Grant GS 1812). I am grateful to both these institutions for making this work possible. I am happy to express my deep appreciation to Mr. Stanley Fischer of M.I.T. for his invaluable assistance at all stages of the preparation of this paper—and particularly in the examination of the relevant literature. In addition, I have benefited from discussions with him and from his criticisms of earlier drafts.

I am also indebted to my Jerusalem colleagues Yosef Attiyeh, Yoram Ben-Porath, and Giora Hanoch, whose thoughtful suggestions have greatly improved the general organization of this paper, as well as the discussion of specific points. As usual, it is a pleasure to thank Miss Susanne Freund for her careful and conscientious checking of the final manuscript and its references. Needless to say, responsibility for the interpretations and views presented in this paper remain entirely my own.

[2] I would like to dedicate this paper to the memory of Miguel Sidrauski. His untimely death in August, 1968 was a great loss, not only to his family and friends, but to the economics profession in general—and particularly to the development of monetary theory. Though I do not think Miguel had a strong interest in the history of doctrine, I hope that—as a Chicago graduate—he would have been interested in reading the final product of a work whose beginnings he witnessed.

[3] In *Studies in the Quantity Theory of Money*, ed. M. Friedman [8], pp. 3–21; referred to henceforth as *Quantity Theory I*. In self-defense, I might, however, note that I have on previous occasions discussed in passing some of the points presented below, and that I have also emp. 81, n.8. See also the implicit criticism in Patinkin [29], p. 480b. See also pp. 60–61 below.

[4] Friedman [10], referred to henceforth as *Quantity Theory II*.

DON PATINKIN *is professor of economics at the Hebrew University of Jerusalem. Last year he served as visiting professor of economics at Massachusetts Institute of Technology.*

man's interpretation of the quantity theory of money, and of its Chicago version in particular.

The argument of the present paper is as follows: in both of the foregoing articles, Friedman presents what he calls a "reformulation of the quantity theory of money." In Part IV I shall show that this is a misleading designation. What Friedman has actually presented is an elegant exposition of the modern portfolio approach to the demand for money which, though it has some well-known (though largely underdeveloped) antecedents in the traditional theory, can only be seen as a continuation of the Keynesian theory of liquidity preference.

The main purpose of this paper, however, is to describe (in Parts II and III) the true nature of the Chicago monetary tradition. In this way I shall also demonstrate the invalidity of Friedman's contention (in his 1956 essay) that this tradition is represented by his "reformulation of the quantity theory." As a minimum statement let me say that though I shared with Friedman—albeit, almost a decade later—the teachers at Chicago whom he mentions (namely, Knight, Viner, Simons, and Mints), his representation of the "flavor of the oral tradition" which they were supposed to have imparted strikes no responsive chord in my memory.

Friedman offers no supporting evidence for his interpretation of the Chicago tradition. This is unfortunate. For questions about the history of economic doctrine are empirical questions. And the universe from which the relevant empirical evidence must be drawn is that of the writings and teachings of the economists in question. No operational meaning can be attached to the existence of a "tradition" which does not manifest itself in one or both of these ways.

From this it will be clear that my examination of this evidence in what follows should not be interpreted as a criticism of the individuals involved. On the contrary, I would consider it unjustified to criticize them for not having fully understood and integrated into their thinking what we have succeeded in learning only in the course of the subsequent development of Keynesian monetary theory. My quarrel is only with those who imply that such an understanding and integration existed before, or independently of, this development.

I would like finally to emphasize that my concern in this paper is with the analytical framework of the Chicago monetary tradition, and not with its policy proposals as such. Correspondingly, I shall not—except incidentally—discuss the relation between these proposals and those of Friedman. Let me, however, note that though there are, of course, basic similarities, there are also significant differences—particularly about the degree of discretion to be exercised by the monetary authorities.[5]

---

[5] Cf. note 24 below. Friedman himself discusses some of these differences explicitly in his paper on Simons referred to in note 27 below—and implicitly in his *Program for Monetary*

48 : MONEY, CREDIT, AND BANKING

I. Friedman's Chicago

Friedman begins his 1956 essay with the explanation that:

> Chicago was one of the few academic centers at which the quantity theory continued to be a central and vigorous part of the oral tradition throughout the 1930's and 1940's, where students continued to study monetary theory and to write theses on monetary problems. The quantity theory that retained this role differed sharply from the atrophied and rigid caricature that is so frequently described by the proponents of the new income-expenditure approach—and with some justice, to judge by much of the literature on policy that was spawned by quantity theorists. At Chicago, Henry Simons and Lloyd Mints directly, Frank Knight and Jacob Viner at one remove, taught and developed a more subtle and relevant version, one in which the quantity theory was connected and integrated with general price theory and became a flexible and sensitive tool for interpreting movements in aggregate economic activity and for developing relevant policy prescriptions.
>
> To the best of my knowledge, no systematic statement of this theory as developed at Chicago exists, though much can be read between the lines of Simons' and Mints' writings . . . . It was a theoretical approach that insisted that money does matter . . . .
>
> The purpose of this introduction is not to enshrine—or, should I say, inter—a definitive version of the Chicago tradition . . . . The purpose is rather to set down a particular "model" of a quantity theory in an attempt to convey the flavor of the oral tradition . . . .[6]

Friedman then goes on to present this model. Since I am interested only in the doctrinal aspects of the question, it is sufficient to cite the model's basic features. In Friedman's words:

1. The quantity theory is in the first instance a theory of the *demand* for money. It is not a theory of output, or of money income, or of the price level. Any statement about these variables requires combining the quantity theory with some specifications about the conditions of supply of money and perhaps about other variables as well.
2. To the ultimate wealth-owning units in the economy, money is one kind of asset, one way of holding wealth . . . .
3. The analysis of the demand for money on the part of the ultimate wealth-owning units in the society can be made formally identical with that of the demand for a consumption service. As in the usual theory of consumer choice, the demand for money (or any other particular asset) depends on three major sets of factors: (a) the total wealth to be held in various forms—the analogue of the budget restraint; (b) the price of and return on this form of wealth and alternative forms; and (c) the tastes and preferences of the wealth-owning units.[7]

Stability, [8a] pp. 86–90. See also M. Bronfenbrenner, "Observations on the Chicago Schools," [3a, pp. 72–73].
  Another interesting question which lies beyond the scope of the present paper is the extent to which the policy views of the Chicago school in the 1930's represented those of other quantity-theorists of the period.
  [6] *Quantity Theory I*, pp. 3–4.
  [7] *Ibid.*, p. 4.

From these and other considerations Friedman arrives at a demand function for money of the form

$$M = g(P, r_b, r_e, (1/P) (dP/dt), w, Y; u),$$ (1)

where M is the nominal quantity of money; P, the price level; r_b is the interest rate on bonds; r_e, the interest rate on equities; $(1/P) (dP/dt)$, the rate of change of prices—and hence the negative of the rate of return on money balances; w, the ratio of non-human to human wealth; Y, money income; and u, "variables that can be expected to affect tastes and preferences."[8] Friedman then makes the familiar assumption that this function is homogeneous of degree one in P and Y, and hence rewrites it as[9]

$$M/P = f(r_b, r_e, (1/P) (dP/dt), w; Y/P; u).$$ (2)

Alternatively, dividing (1) through by Y, he obtains

$$Y = v(r_b, r_e, (1/P) (dP/dt), w, Y/P; u) \cdot M.$$ (3)

"In this form the equation is in the usual quantity theory form, where v is income velocity."[10]

As an aside, I might note that at no point in the foregoing exposition does Friedman mention the name of Keynes. Indeed, one cannot escape the impression that even the term "liquidity" is being avoided.[11]

Friedman does recognize that "almost every economist will accept the general lines of the preceding analysis on a purely formal and abstract level." But Friedman defines three distinguishing features of the quantity theorist, of which the first is that the quantity theorist

accepts the empirical hypothesis that the demand for money is highly stable . . . . The quantity theorist need not, and generally does not, mean that the . . . velocity of circulation of money is to be regarded as numerically constant over time . . . . For the stability he expects is in the functional relation between the quantity of money demanded and the variables that determine it . . . .

The other two features are that the quantity theorist believes that "there are important factors affecting the supply of money that do not affect the demand for money" and that the demand for money does not become infinitely elastic (viz., absence of a "liquidity trap").[12]

There is no question that these last two features are generally found (either explicitly or implicitly) in presentations of the quantity theory. But it is equally

---

[8] *Ibid.*, pp. 4–10; the quotation is from p. 9.
[9] *Ibid.*, p. 11, equation 11.
[10] *Ibid.*, p. 11; see equation 13.
[11] Cf., e.g., *ibid.*, pp. 5, 14, and 19.
[12] *Ibid.*, pp. 15–16.

50 : MONEY, CREDIT, AND BANKING

clear to me that the first—which is crucial to Friedman's interpretation—is not. Correspondingly, one of the basic points that will be examined in the following discussion of the Chicago economists is whether they did indeed think in terms of a stable velocity in Friedman's functional sense.

II. THE OTHER CHICAGO

As against the foregoing, let me now describe a Chicago tradition of monetary theory whose approach, contents, and language can be represented by the following summary-propositions:[13]

1. The quantity theory is, first and foremost, not a theory of the demand for money, but a theory which relates the quantity of money (M) to the aggregate demand for goods and services (MV), and thence to the price level (P) and/or level of output (T): all this in accordance with Fisher's $MV = PT$.

2. V is not constant; on the contrary, a basic feature of economic life is the "danger of sharp changes on the velocity side"; or in other words, the danger "of extreme alternations of hoarding and dishoarding."[14] These "sharp changes" in turn are due to anticipations of changing price levels, as well as to the changing state of business confidence as determined by earnings.[15] Thus, if individuals expect prices to rise and earnings to be good, they will dishoard—that is, increase the velocity of circulation. But the crucial point here is that these expectations will be self-justifying: for the very act of dishoarding will cause prices to rise even further, thus leading to further dishoardings, and so on. In this way a "cumulative process" of expansion is set into operation which "feeds upon itself" and which has no "natural" limit.[16] Conversely, an indefinite "cumulative process" of hoarding, price declines and depression, and further hoarding is set into operation by the expectation that the price level will fall and/or that earnings will be poor. Thus the economic system is essentially unstable.[17]

3. Such a cumulative process might possibly take place, albeit in a much

---

[13] The following is primarily a summary of Simons' views, which were largely accepted by Mints. Knight's analysis is the same, though—quite characteristically—he seems to have had less faith than Simons and Mints in the policy proposals. For Viner, I have been able to find evidence only on the first proposition. For references to the relevant writings, see the Appendix below. Cf. also Davis [4a].

[14] Simons, "Rules versus Authorities in Monetary Policy," [33], p. 164 (this passage is cited in full in the Appendix below). That by "hoarding and dishoarding" Simons means changes in velocity is clear from p. 165. See also note 15.

[15] See Simons, "Banking and Currency Reform," as quoted in the Appendix below.

[16] Knight [18], pp. 210–11, 223–24.

[17] For supporting quotations from Simons [34], p. 222, and [35], p. 188, and Knight [18], pp. 211 and 224 see the Appendix below.

less severe form, even if the quantity of money in the economy were to remain constant.[18] In the actual world, however, the process is highly exacerbated by the "perverse" behavior of the banking system, which expands credit in booms and contracts it in depressions. As a result the quantity of money (M) and near-moneys (and hence V) increases in booms, and decreases in depressions.

4. In accordance with (2) and (3), the government has an obligation to undertake a contracyclical policy. The guiding principle of this policy is to change M so as to offset changes in V, and thus generate the full-employment level of aggregate demand MV. If prices are downwardly flexible, the operational rule which will assure the proper variation in M is that of increasing M when P falls, and decreasing it when P rises. In any event, it is "inconceivable" that a sufficiently vigorous policy of (say) expanding M in a period of depression would not ultimately affect aggregate spending in the required manner.

5. The necessary variations in M can be generated either by open-market operations or by budgetary deficits. The latter method is more efficient, and in some cases might even be necessary. Budgetary deficits, in turn, can be generated by varying either government expenditures or tax receipts. From the viewpoint of contracyclical policy, this makes no difference—for either method changes M; but from the viewpoint of the general philosophy of the proper role of government in economic life, the variation of tax receipts is definitely preferable. Hence, a tax system which depends heavily on the income tax is desirable not only from the viewpoint of distributive justice, but also from the viewpoint of automatically providing proper cyclical variations in tax receipts.

Before going on to bring out the flavor of these propositions as contrasted with that of Friedman's presentation, I would like briefly to indicate three reasons for the emphasis I have given in the foregoing to the writings of Simons. First, at the Chicago which concerns us, Simons was undoubtedly the dominant figure in discussions of monetary and fiscal policy. (In Friedman's presentation too there is more emphasis on the writings of Simons and Mints than on those of Knight and Viner.) Second, Simons' writings on these questions were the earliest by far of the writers here considered. And, third, they were sufficiently early to represent the Chicago tradition in its pristine—and pre-Keynesian—form.

The significance of this last point will become clear from our discussion of Mints at the end of this part. In connection with the first reason, I might note that Mints repeatedly makes clear his indebtedness to Simons.[19] Again, I would

---

[18] See the quotation from Simons, [33], p. 164, in the Appendix below. See also *ibid.*, p. 331, footnote 16; and Mints [25], pp. 120–22.

[19] Cf., e.g., *Monetary Policy for a Competitive Society*, [25], p. vii.

conjecture that Knight's writings referred to above also reflect Simons' influence. Similarly, in my recollections of student days at Chicago—and I think I can speak safely for my fellow students at the time—it is Simons who stands out sharply as the major source of intellectual stimulation and influence in all that regards monetary and fiscal policy. In the slang of those days, most of us were "Simonized" to some degree or other.

Let me turn now to the propositions themselves. The contrast drawn by Proposition 1 is that between the transactions approach to the quantity theory and the cash-balance approach emphasized by Friedman. Now, it is a commonplace of monetary theory that these two approaches can be made analytically equivalent. Indeed, in his general discussion of monetary influences, Fisher himself vividly shows that he was thinking in terms of a demand for money.[20] Nevertheless, if we consistently find a treatment in terms of the transactions approach, we can take this as some indication that the economists in question did not primarily approach monetary theory from the viewpoint of the demand for money. Or at least we cannot take it as an indication that they did![21]

Indeed, it is a much closer approximation to the flavor of the Chicago tradition to say that basically it was not interested in a systematic analysis of the demand for money:[22] for it believed so strongly that "the supply of money matters," that—for the policy purposes which were its main concern—the exact form of the demand function for money did not matter at all, aside from the critical (though sometimes implicit) assumption "that additional money in unlimited amounts would [not] be hoarded in its entirety." For then no matter what the demand for money—in the language of Simons and Mints: no matter what the extent of hoarding—its adverse effects could be offset by a sufficient increase in M. "Much hoarding would simply require a larger addition to the stock of money."[23] The possibility that destabilizing lags could interfere with the efficacy of such a monetary policy—a problem which has received so much attention in recent years—was either not seen (Simons) or not given much weight (Mints[24]).

It should therefore not surprise us that Simons did not present a detailed analysis of the demand for money. Indeed, despite his frequent references to "hoarding," there does not seem to be any point in his writings in which he even uses the term "demand for money." Another, and related, manifestation

---

[20] Fisher, *The Purchasing Power of Money*, [6], pp. 153–54.

[21] Actually, Friedman draws a sharper distinction on this score between the transactions and cash-balance approaches than I would; thus compare his *Quantity Theory II*, pp. 437–38 with my *Money, Interest, and Prices*, [28], pp. 166–67.

[22] It is noteworthy that the work on the empirical nature of the demand function for money that was done at Chicago during the 1940's was carried out under the inspiration not of the "Chicago oral tradition," but of the Keynesian model-builders at the Cowles Commission, which was then located at the University of Chicago. See in particular Klein [16], pp. 125 ff. and [17], pp. 95–101.

[23] The last two quotations in this paragraph are from Mints [24], p. 67; see also *ibid.*, p. 61 and [25], pp. 48–49.

[24] Mints, [25], pp. 138 ff. Mints ascribes to Milton Friedman (who by then was his colleague) the suggestion that such a destabilizing influence might occur (*ibid.*, p. 138, n. 8).

of the lack of interest in such an analysis is the fact that Simons did not spell out the details of the mechanism by which an increase in the quantity of money was supposed to increase the volume of spending on goods and services. Instead, he sufficed with the simple, sometimes implicit, and frequently mechanical statement that an increase in *M* increased aggregate demand *MV*.

Again, even the influence of the rate of interest on the demand for money was not consistently recognized by the Chicago school of the 1930's and 1940's. Thus even though Knight discussed cyclical variations in the rate of interest, he did not take account of the possible influence of such variations on the velocity of circulation.[25] Similarly, though (as indicated in Proposition 3) Simons and Mints did emphasize the influence of near-moneys on velocity, it was the *volume* of these money-substitutes to which they referred, not to the *rate of interest* upon them.

Let me turn now to the "extreme alternations" in velocity described in Proposition 2. It is not clear from the writings of the Chicago school whether it believed that the very fact that prices were, say, increasing would cause an indeterminate flight from money—so that there could exist no stable functional relationship between velocity and the anticipated rate of change of prices; or whether velocity was unstable because of the nature of the expectations function which generated a sequence of ever-increasing anticipated rates of price changes which operated through a stable demand function; or whether there were other forces in the economy (of which those described in Proposition 3 are an example) which generated such a divergent sequence—or whether it believed that a combination of some or all of these factors was at work. But in any event one point is clear: there is no place in their writings in which the aforementioned Chicago economists even hint that they were thinking in terms of Friedman's crucial assumption of a velocity which is a stable function of (among other variables) the anticipated rate of change of prices.[26, 27]

There were other respects in which the Chicago tradition lacked some of the basic ingredients of the flavor of the "model" which Friedman has presented of it. In particular, whereas (as indicated above) this tradition was primarily

---

[25] See the discussion of Knight in Appendix below.

[26] See, in this context, the statement by Knight [20], p. xlv, quoted in full in the Appendix.

[27] I might at this point note that in his recent paper on Simons, Friedman [9] cites the passage referred to in note 18 above and then concludes, "There is clearly great similarity between the views expressed by Simons and by Keynes—as to the causes of the Great Depression, the impotence of monetary policy, and the need to rely extensively on fiscal policy. Both men placed great emphasis on the state of business expectations and assigned a critical role to the desire for liquidity. Indeed, in many ways, the key novelty of Keynes' *General Theory* was the role he assigned to 'absolute' liquidity preference under conditions of deep depression" (p. 7). But Friedman gives no indication of the fact that this interpretation of Simons is hardly consistent with that of his 1956 essay, with its emphasis on the functional stability of *V* and, even more to the point, on the absence of a "liquidity trap" (see conclusion of Part I, above).

In this paper, Friedman also contends that "had Simons known the facts as we now know them [about the monetary history of the United States during the Great Depression], he would, I believe," have been less concerned with " 'the danger of sharp changes on the velocity side' " (p. 12). Without discussing the validity of this conjecture, I shall merely note that it is not relevant to the question which concerns me here, namely Simons' actual approach to the quantity theory.

concerned with the relation between the stock of money and the flow of expenditures, Friedman's primary concern is with the relation between the stock of money and the stocks of other assets. I shall return to this point in Part IV. But let me now admit that, with respect to this comment—and even more so, with respect to much of what has been said above about the lack of interest at Chicago in the demand for money—Lloyd Mints was at least a partial exception. Thus, even though it is not at all comparable in either detail or precision with Friedman's exposition, Mints's *Monetary Policy for a Competitive Society* contains a more explicit analysis of the asset-demand for money than any earlier Chicago discussion.[28] But it is highly significant that the chapter in which this analysis is presented (Chapter 3) is followed by a special appendix on Keynes's theory of liquidity preference. Similarly, as shown in Appendix II, it was in this context (and not in that of the quantity-theory of money) that Mints's lectures on the asset-demand for money were given. It is also noteworthy that the few Chicago doctoral theses of the period 1939–1950 that were concerned with the choice of money as a component of a portfolio of assets generally took Keynes as their point of departure and gave no indication that they saw this approach as stemming from the Chicago tradition (see Part III below).

Thus, the picture which emerges from all this is that by the 1940's the Chicago school itself had, quite understandably, been influenced by Keynesian monetary theory. Accordingly, not only did it begin to evince an interest in a systematic analysis of the demand for money, but it frequently did so from the Keynesian viewpoint of money as one component of an optimally chosen portfolio of assets. Indeed, it had to use this viewpoint in order to explain why it rejected some aspects of the Keynesian theory: namely, the Keynesian concentration on the choice between money and bonds, and the related interpretation of interest as a monetary phenomenon; and the emphasis on the possibility of indefinite hoarding (the "liquidity trap"), and the related Keynesian conclusion that money could not matter enough, so that only a policy of increased government expenditures could deal adequately with the problem of unemployment.[29]

III. THE ORAL TRADITION OF CHICAGO

The preceding discussion of the Chicago school has been based on its writings. It is, however, the "oral tradition of Chicago" which Friedman primarily claims to represent and to which, accordingly, I shall now turn.

A priori, it seems unlikely that scholars who had presented a consistent, and sometimes lengthy, statement of their views in print would have provided

[28] Mints [25], chap. iii; see also chap. ix, especially pp. 210–11. See also Mints [23], pp. 219–22 and [24], p. 63 *et passim*.
[29] See again the references to Mints in the preceding footnote. See also the discussion of Knight in the Appendix.

a significantly different presentation in their classroom discussions. Fortunately, there is no need to rely solely on such a priori considerations—or even on my memories of these classroom discussions as contrasted with those of Friedman. For there is concrete evidence on their nature in the form of lecture notes which I took during my graduate studies at Chicago in the period 1943–45.

Of course, these lecture notes are subject to all of the standard reservations about the accuracy with which students understand their teachers. Furthermore, they constitute only one observation on these teachings. But at the present moment this is one more than has yet been provided on the question. It should also be noted that if we accept (as I do) the fact that there was a "tradition" at Chicago, then we can also assume that there was a high degree of continuity between what was taught in my student days and what was taught before.

Mints devoted several lectures to the quantity theory at the beginning of his course on "Money." After presenting Fisher's equation of exchange (with no discussion of the determinants of V—or of the Cambridge K, to which he also referred), Mints went on to formulate the quantity theory of money in a way which has remained sharply etched in my memory—and which has always represented for me "the flavor of the Chicago tradition":

> Some attempts [have been made statistically] to verify quantity theory by showing that $MV + M'V' = PT$ is true. But quantity theory says that *P is the dependent variable*. So would have to show that exist consistent time lags. Have to establish *causal relationship*. Formula itself is a truism—doesn't need verification. Formula $\neq$ quantity theory.
>
> . . . .
>
> Mints prefers following statement of quantity theory: P is the dependent variable (in the long run) of the equation $MV = PT$. But in the short run all the variables tend to move together.[30]

For our purposes (see end of Part II), it is also most significant that Mints's discussion of the demand for money from a viewpoint which is closer to the portfolio approach did not occur in his lectures on the quantity theory, but a month later in the context of his discussion of Keynes' theory of liquidity preference. Here Mints said that there were

> . . . really four factors to be kept in equilibrium: (1) price level (2) rate of interest (3) demand for cash (liquidity preferences) and (4) quantity of money.
>   Methods of disposing of cash:
>   (1) Hold in cash
>   (2) Purchase consumer's goods
>   (3) Purchase producer's goods
>   (4) Lend on short term
>   (5) Purchase long term bonds
>   (6) Purchase corporation shares.

[30] Lecture notes from Lloyd Mints, "Money" (Economics 330), June 28 and July 3, 1944, italics in original. It is noteworthy that this distinction between the quantity theory and the identity $MV + M'V' = PT$ is also emphasized by Friedman in his encyclopedia article; see *Quantity Theory II*, pp. 434–36.

56 : MONEY, CREDIT, AND BANKING

> Keynes assumes that doubts about the future affect only (5).
> But uncertainties affect (2) and especially (3). Demand will fall off for these, prices there will fall, profits decrease, and beginning of unemployment, etc.[31]

Mints then went on to present a discussion which closely parallels that of the first part of Chapter 3 of his *Monetary Policy for a Competitive Society*.

Some other notes from Mints's lectures, as well as relevant notes from the lectures of Knight and Simons, are reproduced in the Appendix. The evidence of these notes leads unmistakably to one simple and unsurprising conclusion: the oral tradition of the Chicago school of monetary theory was entirely reflected in its written tradition; whatever was not in the latter was also not in the former.

Let me turn now to the doctoral theses written at Chicago during the period in question.[32] As we all know, students' theses reflect the interests, approach, and all too frequently even the views of their teachers. It is therefore interesting to see what we can learn about the Chicago tradition from this source. This is all the more legitimate in the present context in view of Friedman's assertion that "Chicago was one of the few academic centers at which the quantity theory continued to be a central and vigorous part of the oral tradition throughout the 1930's and 1940's, whose students continued to study monetary theory and to write theses on monetary problems."[33]

The list of relevant theses is presented in the Appendix. Even after taking account of the small number of theses which were being submitted in those days (a total of 46 for the 1930's and 52 for the 1940's), one is struck by the paucity of monetary theses written at Chicago during the 1930's. The fact that from 1931 through 1938 only one such thesis was submitted speaks for itself. The number is decidedly greater for the 1940's. Nevertheless, a casual comparison with the list of doctoral theses submitted at Harvard shows that even during the 1940's there were at least as many monetary theses being submitted at Harvard as at Chicago (though admittedly the total number of theses submitted at the former was three times as large).

Let me turn now to the far more important question as to the contents of the Chicago theses. The situation can be described quite simply: several of the theses are primarily descriptive and contain little, if any, analysis. To the extent that the theses refer to the quantity theory of money, they do so in terms of Proposition 1 above;[34] none of them do so in terms reminiscent of

---

[31] Lecture notes from Mints, "Money" (Economics 330), August 4, 1944.
[32] Without disclaiming any responsibility for what follows, I would like to express my appreciation to my assistant, Mr. Stanley Fischer, who has carefully gone through the monetary theses written at Chicago during the period 1930–1950—and on whose excellent notes I have relied heavily. I would also like to thank Professor Lester Telser of the Department of Economics at the University of Chicago and his secretary, Mrs. Hazel Bowdry, for their help in obtaining a complete list of Chicago theses and microfilms of those discussed here, as well as information about theses committees.
[33] *Quantity Theory I*, p. 3.
[34] Thus see, e.g., Benjamin F. Brooks, "A History of Banking Theory in the United States Before 1860" (1939), p. 354; Marion R. Daugherty, "The Currency School–Banking School

Friedman's "reformulation." Few theses even reflect a portfolio approach to the demand for money. Furthermore, those that do draw their primary inspiration from Keynes or his supporters.[35] Similarly, the influence of the rate of interest on the demand for money is rarely mentioned, even in appropriate contexts;[36] and when there is some mention, it is again largely inspired by Keynesian monetary theory.[37]

Of particular interest in the present context is Bach's thesis on "Price Level Stabilization: Some Theoretical and Practical Considerations" (1940). In his general analysis and policy proposals, Bach presents the position of the Chicago school as summarized in the five propositions of Part II above.[38] Furthermore, in the process of so doing he refers explicitly to an "oral tradition" at Chicago which he describes in the following terms:

> The explanation of the cycle may, for our purposes, be ultimately reduced to the existence of two basic factors, the first redivisible into two more or less separate elements. These two sub-factors in the first are (a) psychological shifts by consumers, entrepreneurs, and investors, leading to changes in the propensities to hoard, consume, and invest, and (b) perverse fluctuations in the volume of money in the system (M plus M' in the Fisherian notation). The second basic factor is the existence of "sticky" prices throughout large sectors of the economy, of which many are cost-prices, so that costs have a tendency to move more slowly than do the more flexible selling prices.*
>
> * On this reduction to essentials I am indebted to Professor Mints, although it has been in the nature of an "oral tradition" at Chicago for some time and can be found in many writers, but only more or less obscured.[39]

Controversy" (1941), p. 54; Roland N. McKean, "Fluctuations in Our Private Claim-Debt Structure and Monetary Policy" (1948), pp. 51, 98, and 103. See also the references to Bach's thesis in notes 38 and 39 below.

[35] Thus see, e.g., Martin Bronfenbrenner, "Monetary Theory and General Equilibrium" (1939), pp. iii, 43, 45, 156–57; McKean, *op. cit.*, chap. iv, and especially pp. 52 (note 5) and 57–59; and William W. Tongue, "Money, Capital and the Business Cycle" (1947), chaps. i and iii.

[36] Cf., e.g., Arthur I. Bloomfield, "International Capital Movements and the American Balance of Payments, 1929–40" (1942), pp. 578–79; see also McKean, *op. cit.*, p. 80. In all but the last chapter of his thesis (see especially chapter iv), McKean follows Simons (to whom he repeatedly refers, pp. 3, 32, 52, 68, *et passim*), in being concerned with the volume of liquid assets and debts, and not the rates of return upon them. (Cf. above, p. 53.) On the other hand, his discussion of 100 per cent money in the last chapter (see especially pp. 174–77) explicitly takes account of the effect on the demand for money (and hence velocity) of changes in the rates of interest on money substitutes.

[37] See again the references cited in note 35. See also McKean, *op. cit.*, p. 100, who, however, refers to the influence of the quantity of money on the interest rate as "the very old argument, revived in the thirties" (*ibid.*, p. 99).

It might be noted that at some points McKean's thesis also reflects the influence of Milton Friedman, who had joined the Chicago staff in 1946. Thus, see the reference to Friedman in McKean's discussion of the simultaneous influence of the interest rate on the demand for money and on savings (p. 101, n. 1). Somewhat less relevant for our present purpose are McKean's many references, in chapters i and ii and on p. 191, to Friedman's discussions of the problem of lags in monetary policy and of the proper framework for monetary and fiscal policy.

[38] See especially pp. 42–45 and 72–75 of his thesis.

[39] *Ibid.*, pp. 35–36.

It might be noted that at the time Bach wrote, the tradition was indeed largely oral: for all that then existed in print was Simons' brief discussions; the writings of Knight and Mints had yet to appear (see Appendix).

In concluding this discussion of the Chicago school, I would like to emphasize once again that its purpose has not been either to praise or to criticize—and surely not to criticize the writers of the theses—but only to convey the flavor of the Chicago tradition as it really was.

IV. THE QUANTITY THEORY, FRIEDMAN, AND KEYNESIAN ECONOMICS

As indicated in my opening remarks, the nominal occasion for the appearance of this paper is the recent publication in the *International Encyclopedia of the Social Sciences* of Friedman's article on the "Quantity Theory." From the substantive viewpoint, the "reformulation of the quantity theory" which Friedman presents on pp. 439–42 of this article is essentially the same as the one he presented in his 1956 essay (see Part I above). But from the doctrinal viewpoint which engrossed us in Parts II–III, there is a fundamental difference: for Friedman now makes no attempt to present this reformulation as a "model of the oral tradition of Chicago." Indeed, neither the Chicago school nor its individual members are even mentioned.

On the other hand, as just indicated, Friedman does continue to denote his presentation as a "reformulation of the quantity theory." The only support he adduces for this nomenclature is that "Fisher and other earlier quantity theorists explicitly recognized that velocity would be affected by, among other factors, the rate of interest and also the rate of change of prices." [40]

That such a recognition existed, there can be no doubt.[41] But, as I have indicated elsewhere,[42] the real question is the extent to which the "earlier quantity theorists" recognized the full and precise implications of these effects: the extent to which they consistently took account of these effects at the appropriate points in their discussions. For one of the fundamental facts of the history of ideas is that in general the full implications of a set of ideas are not immediately seen. Indeed, as has been frequently noted, if they were, then all mathematics would be a tautology; for its theorems are implicit in the assumptions made. The failure to see such implications is also familiar from many episodes in the history of economic doctrine: for example, from the tortuous and faltering manner in which the full implications of the marginal productivity theory were developed.[43]

Thus, there is indeed a striking passage in Fisher's *Rate of Interest* about

---

[40] *Quantity Theory II*, p. 436b.
[41] For specific references to writings of Walras, Wicksell, the much-neglected Karl Schlesinger, Fisher, and the Cambridge school (Marshall, Pigou, and especially Lavington) which discuss or at the least refer to the influence of interest on the demand for money, see Patinkin [28], pp. 372, 545, 556, and 576–80.
[42] Patinkin [29], p. 480b.
[43] See Stigler [39].

the "convenience" of money holdings which makes an individual willing to forego the interest that he could earn.[44] But the only echo of this passage in *The Purchasing Power of Money* is a passing reference to the influence of the "waste of interest" on velocity.[45] Furthermore, it is clear that Fisher did not integrate this influence into the general analysis of this book. Indeed, this influence is not mentioned at any other point in it: neither in the analysis of the effects of the higher interest rates which mark the "transition period" (Chapter iv), nor in the detailed description of the determinants of the velocity of circulation (Chapter v),[46] nor finally in the statistical investigation of the theory, with its description of how velocity varied during the periods examined (Chapters xi–xii).

I find this last omission particularly significant. For the empirical investigator is confronted with a concrete situation in which he is called upon to take account of the major theoretical variables which might explain the data (even if some of these variables will subsequently be rejected as statistically insignificant); hence this situation provides a proper and operationally meaningful test of whether the influence of a variable has been "fully recognized." It should therefore be emphasized that the failure even to mention the rate of interest as a possible explanation of the observed variations in the velocity of circulation also characterizes the writings of Carl Snyder,[47] to whose empirical work (as well as that of Fisher) Friedman refers.[48] And a similar picture obtains for the earlier studies by James W. Angell[49] and Clark Warburton,[50] to which Selden refers in his survey of empirical investigations of the income-velocity of circulation in the United States.[51] Furthermore, the fact that Angell and Warburton mention the influence of interest only in their later studies—and in explicit response to issues raised by Keynesian monetary theory[52]—reinforces my basic contention that the "early quantity theorists" did not of themselves fully recognize this influence.

p. [44] Fisher [5], p. 212. This passage is slightly elaborated upon in *The Theory of Interest* [7] an 216, where Fisher refers to the "liquidity of our cash balances [which] takes the place of y rate of interest in the ordinary sense of the term."

[45] [6], p. 152.

[46]Fisher's discussion here is in terms of the "habits of the individual," the "systems of payments in the community," and "general causes"—by which he means "density of population" and "rapidity of transportation" (*ibid.*, p. 79).

[47] Thus see Snyder [36, 37, 38].

[48] *Quantity Theory II*, p. 436b.

[49] Angell [1, 2]. Angell's detailed and systematic analysis of the velocity of circulation is almost entirely in terms of the timing and mechanics of the payment process. The passing references t o interest (on pp. 57–58 of the article, and on pp. 164–65 of the book) do not change this basic picture. Note too the discussion of "idle balances" (in [2], pp. 140 ff.) which is devoid of any reference to the interest rate.

[50] Warburton [43, 44]. Warburton's primary concern is with the secular trend in velocity, which he explains in terms of the mechanism of the payment process and a greater-than-unity income elasticity of demand for cash balances [44, pp. 443–44]. See also [46], pp. 89–90.

[51] Selden [31], pp. 184-85. Nearly half of the studies surveyed by Selden are by Angell and Warburton.

[52] Thus see Angell [3], chaps. vi and ix. Similarly, Warburton first deals with this influence in his reply to Tobin's criticism (from the viewpoint of Keynes' liquidity-preference theory) of his (Warburton's) earlier work; see Warburton [45]. It is against this background that one must also read Warburton's discussion of the rate of interest in a later article [46], pp. 89–90.

60 : MONEY, CREDIT, AND BANKING

It is true that the aforementioned empirical studies were primarily concerned with explaining the observed price level in the market, and not the
demand function for money. But to press this point too far in the present
context is to admit that these "early quantity theorists" did not really have
a major concern with the properties of this demand function. Furthermore,
even within the context of these empirical studies it is quite appropriate to
investigate the possibility that observed deviations from the hypothesized V
(whether assumed constant or secularly declining) can be explained in terms
of changes in the interest rate—provided the observed V is assumed to equal
the desired V. In fact, this is what Warburton did in his later (1949) study,
though he concluded that this possibility should be rejected.

In any event, it is significant that the first empirical study (to the best of my
knowledge) which explicitly deals with the influence of interest on the demand
for money is the 1939 Keynesian-inspired study by A. J. Brown on "Interest,
Prices, and the Demand Schedule for Idle Money." [53] I might also add that
this is the first such study which discusses a *functional relationship* between the
demand for money and "the rate at which the general price-level has lately
been changing." [54] This discussion can well be contrasted with Fisher's imprecise statement that when money "is depreciating, holders will get rid of it
as fast as possible." [55] Furthermore, Fisher sees this as an unstable process
which will cause a further rise in prices which will again increase V "and so
on." [56] In my discussion of the Chicago quantity-theorists (above, pp. 52–53),
I have already stressed the difference between this view and the stable relationship between the demand for money and rate of change of prices described by
Friedman—and by Brown.

I have dwelt at length on the treatment of the rate of interest in Friedman's
"reformulation" as compared with the actual writings of the quantity-theorists
because this difference can be well-defined and hence clearly observed in the
literature. But I attach no less significance to other, and more subtle, differences which also characterize Friedman's 1956 essay. Thus, Friedman's
presentation of the demand for money is first and foremost in terms of the
demand for an asset; for him the income variable in the demand function is
primarily "a surrogate for wealth, rather than [as in the quantity theory] a
measure of the 'work' to be done by money." [57] Correspondingly, as I have
noted elsewhere (see footnote 3 above), Friedman is primarily concerned with
the optimal relationship between the stock of money and the stocks of other
assets, whereas the quantity theorists were primarily concerned with the rela-

[53] See Brown [4].
[54] *Ibid.*, p. 34; unfortunately, Brown goes on to represent this rate by the absolute difference
$p_t - p_{t-1}$, instead of the ratio of this difference to p_t (or p_{t-1}), where p_t represents the price
level p at time t.
[55] *The Purchasing Power of Money*, [6], p. 63.
[56] *Ibid.*
[57] *Quantity Theory II*, p. 440a.

tionship between the stock of money and the flow of spending on goods and services. Furthermore, their discussions of this relationship either did not make the distinction between stocks and flows—or at least were imprecise about it Similarly, quantity theorists paid little, if any, attention to the effects on the rate of interest and other variables of shifts in tastes as to the form in which individuals wished to hold their assets.[58]

And now to our main point: all of the foregoing are precisely the differentia of Keynesian monetary theory as compared with the traditional quantity theory. They are the basic components of a theory of portfolio choice of which there are undoubtedly antecedents in the Cambridge cash-balance school and before, but whose analytical structure as it now exists stems from the publication during the 1930's of Keynes's *Treatise on Money*,[59] Hicks's "Suggestion for Simplifying the Theory of Money,"[60] and Keynes's *General Theory*.[61] Subsequent valuable contributions to this analysis were made during the 1940's and early 1950's by, among others, H. Makower and J. Marschak [21], Franco Modigliani [26], R. F. Kahn [13], Joan Robinson [30], Harry Markowitz [22], and James Tobin [40]. And in direct continuation of this intellectual line of descent, Milton Friedman provided us in 1956 with a most elegant and sophisticated statement of modern Keynesian monetary theory—misleadingly entitled "The Quantity Theory of Money—A Restatement."[62]

Actually, a careful reading of Friedman's encyclopedia article would seem to indicate that he has taken account of criticisms of his earlier exposition and that—at least in part—he himself now recognizes this intellectual indebtedness. Thus, first of all, he now describes his reformulation as one "that has been strongly influenced by the Keynesian analysis of liquidity preference."[63] Similarly, the term "liquidity," which had been avoided in the 1956 essay, is now used.[64] Second, he admits that the Keynesian analysis of the demand for money lays "greater emphasis on current interest rates" than did the "earlier quantity theorists."[65] Third, Friedman now recognizes that the "earlier quantity theory" envisaged the process of monetary adjustment in terms of the relation between the stock of money and the flow of expenditures "to the almost complete exclusion" of the Keynesian approach, which envisages it in terms of the relation between the stock of money and other assets,

[58] These differences also prevail between Friedman and the Chicago tradition; see above, pp. 53–54.

[59] Keynes [14], Vol. I, pp. 140–46.

[60] Hicks [12]. Note the reference to Lavington on p. 15, n. 2.

[61] Keynes [15], pp. 166–72, 222–29.

[62] Cf., on this intellectual genealogy, n. 3 above.

[63] *Quantity Theory II*, p. 439b. Although Friedman refers to Johnson's 1962 *American Economic Review* survey article immediately after this statement, I think that it can safely be assumed to reflect his own view as well.

[64] ". . . the services rendered by money relative to those rendered by other assets—in Keynesian terminology, . . . liquidity proper" (*Quantity Theory II*, p. 440b). Cf. *Quantity Theory I, op. cit.*, p. 14.

[65] *Quantity Theory II*, p. 438b.

particularly bonds.[66] Furthermore, Friedman himself accepts as "plausible" the Keynesian approach that "any widespread disturbance in money balances . . . will initially-be met by an attempted readjustment of assets and liabilities, through purchase and sale"—though he goes on to explain how the resulting change in prices will also "establish incentives to alter flows of receipts and expenditures."[67]

In view of all this, one can only regret that Friedman has persisted—even within the confines of an international encyclopedia—in presenting his exposition of the demand function for money as a "reformulation of the quantity theory."

APPENDIX: THE EMPIRICAL EVIDENCE

I. The Writings

The sources for the first four[67a] summary-propositions at the beginning of Part II are as follows:

HENRY C. SIMONS: *A Positive Program for Laissez Faire* [32], p. 64; "Rules versus Authorities in Monetary Policy" [33], pp. 164–66, 170–72, 326, n. 5, 331, n. 16; *Personal Income Taxation* [34], p. 222; "Hansen on Fiscal Policy" [35], p. 188. Also, "Banking and Currency Reform," p. 3 and Appendix, p. 2.[68] The last passage listed (see n. 15 above) reads:

> But any general change in business earnings will affect promptly the speculative temper of the community. Larger profits breed optimism; they stimulate investment and induce dishoarding (reduction of idle cash reserves). Producers will become more anxious to borrow for purposes of increasing inventories, expanding production, and increasing plant capacity. Lenders will have fewer misgivings about the ability of borrowers to repay. People generally will increase their

---

[66] *Ibid.*, p. 441b.

[67] *Ibid.*, pp. 441b–442a. Though he does not refer to it at this point, Friedman's discussion here essentially summarizes the analysis presented in his and Meiselman's paper on "Relative Stability of Monetary Velocity and the Investment Multiplier in the United States, 1897–1958," [11], pp. 217–22. In this analysis, Friedman and Meiselman distinguish their approach from the Keynesian one in terms of the range of assets involved in the monetary adjustment.

[67a] I have not provided specific sources for Proposition 5, which does not really bear on the issue at hand, and which has been included in the text only for the sake of completeness.

[68] "Banking and Currency Reform" is an unpublished and unsigned memorandum dated by Aaron Director as November, 1933 and ascribed by him largely to Simons. I am greatly indebted to Friedman and Director for providing me with a copy of this memorandum. See the Bibliography in *Economic Policy for a Free Society* [33], p. 313; see also Friedman 9, p. 2, n. 1. Friedman describes the Appendix to the memorandum as a "partial exception to the statement that Simons nowhere set forth a consistent statement of his theory" (*ibid.*). However, except for its explicit relating of velocity to business earnings, the theoretical presentation of this Appendix seems to me to be no more detailed or systematic than Simons' other writings.

lending and investment at the expense of their idle reserves of cash. In a word, the velocity of circulation will increase. But this change, in turn, means a larger volume of business and higher product-prices, and thus still larger earnings. The further increase of earnings, moreover, will induce further increase in the velocity of money. And so on and on, until the initially sticky prices which govern costs do finally move upward markedly and rapidly—or until some fortuitous disturbance (perhaps a mere speculative scare) happens to establish a sharp reversal of the trend in product prices. On the other hand, once earnings begin to decline, forces will be set in motion to continue and accelerate the trend— and perhaps with more striking results, for the crucial, sticky prices are peculiarly resistant to downward pressure.

The passages from Simons' writings referred to in notes 14, 17, and 18 above are as follows:

Once a deflation has gotten under way, in a large modern economy, there is no significant limit which the decline of prices and employment cannot exceed, if the central government fails to use its fiscal powers generously and deliberately to stop that decline. Only great government deficits can check the hoarding of lawful money and the destruction of money substitutes once a general movement has gotten under way. [*Personal Income Taxation, op.cit.*, p. 222.]

The bottom of an uncontrolled deflation, for all practical purposes, is non-existent—with adverse expectations causing price declines and with the actual declines aggravating expectations, etc. ["Hansen on Fiscal Policy," *op. cit.*, p. 188.]

With all its merits, however, this rule [of holding the quantity of money constant] cannot now be recommended as a basis for monetary reform. The obvious weakness of fixed quantity, as a sole rule of monetary policy, lies in the danger of sharp changes on the velocity side, for no monetary system can function effectively or survive politically in the face of extreme alternations of hoarding and dishoarding. It is easy to argue that something would be gained in any event if perverse changes were prevented merely as to quantity, but the argument is unconvincing. The fixing of the quantity of circulation media might merely serve to increase the perverse variability in the amounts of "near moneys" and in the degree of their general acceptability, just as the restrictions on the issue of bank notes presumably served to hasten the development of deposit (checking-account) banking. ["Rules versus Authorities in Monetary Policy," *op.cit.*, p. 164.]

LLOYD W. MINTS: *A History of Banking Theory* [23], pp. 218–22; "Monetary Policy" [24], esp. pp. 61, 63, and 67; *Monetary Policy for a Competitive Society* [25], chap. iii (esp. pp. 29, 32–35, 39–41, 48–49, 69–70), chap. vi (esp. pp. 120–22, 138–42), and chap. ix (esp. pp. 194, 202–203, 207, 210–11, 227).

FRANK H. KNIGHT: "Economics" [19], pp. 15, 30; "The Business Cycle, Interest, and Money: A Methodological Approach" [18], pp. 210–11, 213, 223–24; Preface to 1948 reprint of *Risk, Uncertainty, and Profit* [20], pp. xlii–xlv.

The passages from Knight referred to in footnotes 17 and 26 are as follows:

. . . in the case of money, just what does set a boundary to a movement of general prices in either direction, and especially the downward movement, becomes something of a mystery. ["The Business Cycle, Interest, and Money," *op.cit.*, p. 211.]

64 : MONEY, CREDIT, AND BANKING

> Up to a point, socialist critics have been right in regarding cycles and depressions
> as an inherent feature of "capitalism." Such a system must use money, and
> the circulation of money is not a phenomenon which naturally tends to establish
> and maintain an equilibrium level. Its equilibrium is vague and highly unstable.
> Its natural tendency is to oscillate over a fairly long period and wide range,
> between limits which are rather indeterminate. [*Ibid.*, p. 224.]

> My chief ground for disagreement with the Keynesian theory of money is the
> belief that in view of these facts, [viz., the instability of V]—some, or most, or all
> of them well recognized by Keynes as well as others—supply and demand curves
> for "liquidity" have no solid foundation and are not a sound basis for action
> but are "theoretical" in the bad and misleading sense. [*Risk, Uncertainty and
> Profit, op.cit.*, p. xlv.]

It might be noted that in his discussion of Keynes's theory of liquidity preference in his 1941 article Knight readily recognizes that the rate of interest "must
equalize the attractiveness of bonds and of money for holding" ([18], p. 221)
and earlier in this article he also describes the holding of money as an alternative to holding other assets (p. 210). But this dependence of the demand for
money on the rate of interest is not taken account of in Knight's discussion of
variations in the velocity of circulation during the course of the business cycle
—despite Knight's discussion of the cyclical changes in the rate of interest.[69]
All that is discussed in this context is the influence of price expectations.

JACOB VINER: *Studies in the Theory of International Trade* [41], pp. 40–45, 131,
et passim; "Schumpeter's *History of Economic Analysis*" [42], p. 365.

The discussion on pages 40–45 of the *Studies* show that Viner thought of the
quantity theory as specifying a causal relationship between the quantity of
money and its value. The effect of anticipations of price increases in increasing
the velocity of circulation is indicated on page 131.

The passage from Viner's review of Schumpeter is an instance in which it
would have been most appropriate for Viner to have indicated (if he had so
believed) that the quantity theory specified not the constancy of the velocity
of circulation, but the constancy of the functional relationship between this
velocity and the variables which determine it.

II. The Lectures

The only relevant passage from my notes on Simons' lectures is from his
course "Economics of Fiscal Policy." The passage reads:

> The only thing that has stopped deflationary movement is that government
> begins to get insolvent too (fears that cheap money really would set in). So we
> inevitably get a government deficit which works to stop deflation. There is no
> automatic recovery—there is nothing in the system to bring this about. This is
> Simons' theory of business cycles: deflation until governmental action. There is
> no stability in the economy—so that's why we have fluctuations to begin with.

[69] Knight [18], pp. 219–220. On p. 223, Knight does refer to high "liquidity preference"
and low interest rates in depressions; but he does not refer to a causal relationship between
these two phenomena (i.e., to a movement along a demand curve for money), and instead
presents them as parallel consequences of the same cause, namely, the depression.

Should we obtain deficits by (1) revenue changes, or by (2) spending changes? Simons is in favor of (1).[70]

My lecture notes from Mints's courses contain the following additional relevant passage, taken from his discussion of the Cambridge cash-balance approach:

> In modern theory, demand for money is said to have unitary elasticity. Assume that V and T are constant. Then P changes directly proportionate with M. The real value of total money remains the same. [A diagram of a rectangular hyperbola appears at this point.]
>
> Some have said, on a basis of post–World War I experience, that η for money $\neq 1$. E.g., the total quantity of money increased ten times, while goods that could be purchased with this [i.e., a unit of money] decreased $\frac{1}{15}$ [?]. But in this case there have been changes in V and T— contrary to our assumptions. So we assume that there has been a shift from one demand curve to another (also with $\eta = 1$) according as V and T change. [More diagrams follow here.][71]

Mints concluded his course on "Money" with a discussion of policy, in which (among other things) he stated

> If [government] stabilizes price level, it will [also] stabilize aggregate demand and thus prevent unemployment. It is inconceivable that the federal government couldn't so increase the cash balances of the public that it wouldn't want to purchase goods.[72]

Most of Mints's discussions of policy matters were, however, contained in his course entitled "Banking Theory and Monetary Policy" (Economics 331). The material presented here closely paralleled the corresponding discussions in his books *A History of Banking Theory* and *Monetary Policy for a Competitive Society* [23, 25].

There is nothing of relevance in my lecture notes from Viner's courses (on economic theory, international trade). In the notes from Knight's lectures on economic theory there is a passage which repeats the analysis of his article entitled "The Business Cycle, Interest, and Money: A Methodological Approach," [18] which had appeared a few years before. Indeed, the notes refer explicitly to this article and read:

> Keynesian economics.—The older viewpoint assumed neutral money: money only as an intermediary, so really have barter [economy]. Say's law—*loi des debouchés*. Under ideal competition [conditions?] wouldn't have any money used as medium of exchange—just as unit of account.
>
> Keynes did not do anything not adumbrated in previous writings. Instead of saying, "Every supply of goods is a demand for other goods," he said, "Every supply of goods is a demand for money." Keynes hypostatizes money under the name "liquidity preference." People want money as such—for its own sake—not as immediate purchasing power.
>
> Knight says that the demand for money is highly speculative—especially in an

[70] Lecture notes from Henry Simons, "Economics of Fiscal Policy" (Economics 361), April 20, 1945.
[71] Lecture notes from Lloyd Mints, "Money" (Economics 330), June 30, 1944.
[72] *Ibid.*, August 11, 1944.

66 : MONEY, CREDIT, AND BANKING

investors' market and even in a consumers' market. If one considers changes in prices relative to changes in interest rates—the former are much greater than the latter. Thus, if one foresees rising prices, he will borrow money to buy goods; and when he foresees lower prices he will hurry to sell now. The anticipation itself will create the price change—and this is cumulative. "Every speculation on the future value of goods is a speculation on the future value of money." The essential fact in a slump is just that. In a boom everyone begins to realize that prices are really too high—overcapitalization. All changes in the value of money tend to be cumulative—an unstable equilibrium.

In wheat futures market we have the same thing—anticipation creates changes. But there is an equilibrium there which is dependent on well-known objective facts. So have damped oscillations. But there is no definite, known equilibrium value of money. Everyone might know that money is too high—but the question is whether it will continue to rise; one doesn't know where the breaking point is.

Knight doesn't know how to stabilize the price level—or at what height to stabilize it.[73]

I cannot resist citing in addition the following typical Knightian remark, which occurred at a later point:

In medieval times men didn't look for remedies since they thought everything came from God, who was good—so everything [must be] good. Now science is the God— and we think that there must be a remedy for every disease. Maybe [there] is no answer to the business cycle: [maybe we] have to let it take its course.[74]

[73] Lecture notes from Frank Knight, "Price and Distribution Theory" (Economics 301), July 24, 1945.
[74] *Ibid.*, July 26, 1945.

THE THESES

DOCTORAL THESES ON MONETARY PROBLEMS SUBMITTED TO THE UNIVERSITY OF CHICAGO, 1930–1950

Author	Title of Thesis	Thesis Committee	Date of Submission
Ernest R. Shaw	The Investment and Secondary Reserve Policy of Commercial Banks	L. D. Edie,* S. P. Meech, L. W. Mints	1930
Francis A. Linville	Central Bank Cooperation	H. D. Gideonse (?), L. W. Mints, J. Viner	1937
Benjamin F. Brooks	A History of Banking Theory in the United States Before 1860	F. H. Knight, L. W. Mints,* J. Viner	1939
Martin Bronfenbrenner	Monetary Theory and General Equilibrium	F. H. Knight, L. W. Mints, H. Schultz,* J. Viner	1939
Joseph E. Reeve	Monetary Proposals for Curing the Depression in the United States, 1929–35	G. V. Cox, L. W. Mints,* J. Viner	1939
George L. Bach	Price Level Stabilization: Some Theoretical and Practical Considerations	L. W. Mints, H. C. Simons, J. Viner	1940
Mrs. Marion R. Daugherty	The Currency School—Banking School Controversy	G. V. Cox, L. W. Mints, J. Viner*	1941
Benjamin Caplan	The Wicksellian School—A Critical Study of the Development of Swedish Monetary Theory, 1898–1932	O. Lange, H. C. Simons, J. Viner	1942
Arthur I. Bloomfield	International Capital Movements and the American Balance of Payments, 1929–40	O. Lange, L. W. Mints, J. Viner*	1942
R. Craig McIvor	Monetary Expansion in Canadian War Finance, 1939–1945	R. Blough,* J. K. Langum, L. W. Mints	1947
Don Patinkin	On the Inconsistency of Economic Models: A Theory of Involuntary Unemployment	P. Douglas, H. G. Lewis, J. Marschak,* T. Yntema	1947
William W. Tongue	Money, Capital and the Business Cycle	O. Lange (?), H. G. Lewis, F. H. Knight, L. W. Mints*	1947
Roland N. McKean	Fluctuations in Our Private Claim-Debt Structure and Monetary Policy	A. Director, E. J. Hamilton, L. A. Metzler, L. W. Mints*	1948
Joel W. Harper	Scrip and Other Forms of Local Money	S. E. Leland,* L. W. Mints, H. C. Simons (?)	1948
Raymond H. McEvoy	The Effects of Federal Reserve Operations, 1929–1936	E. J. Hamilton, L. A. Metzler, L. W. Mints*	1950

* Where known, the committee chairman is designated by an asterisk.

68   :   MONEY, CREDIT, AND BANKING

LITERATURE CITED

1. ANGELL, JAMES W. "Money, Prices and Production: Some Fundamental Concepts," *Quarterly Journal of Economics,* 48 (November, 1933), 39–76.

2. ————. *The Behavior of Money.* New York: McGraw-Hill, 1936.

3. ————. *Investment and Business Cycles.* New York: McGraw-Hill, 1941.

3a. BRONFENBRENNER, M. "Observations on the 'Chicago School(s),'" *Journal of Political Economy,* 70 (Feb., 1962), 72–75.

4. BROWN, A. J., "Interest, Prices, and the Demand Schedule for Idle Money," *Oxford Economic Papers,* 2 (May, 1939), 46–48, as reprinted in *Oxford Studies in the Price Mechanism,* ed. T. Wilson and P. W. S. Andrews. Oxford: Oxford University Press, 1951. Pp. 31–51.

4a. DAVIS, J. R. "Chicago Economists, Deficit Budgets, and the Early 1930s," *American Economic Review,* 58 (June, 1968), 476–82.

5. FISHER, IRVING. *The Rate of Interest.* New York: 1907.

6. ————. *The Purchasing Power of Money.* 2nd revised ed., 1922; New York: Kelley and Millman, 1963 (first published in 1911).

7. ————. *The Theory of Interest.* New York: Kelley and Millman, 1930.

8. FRIEDMAN, MILTON. "The Quantity Theory of Money—A Restatement," *Studies in the Quantity Theory of Money,* ed. Milton Friedman. Chicago: University of Chicago Press, 1956. Pp. 3–21.

8a. ————. *A Program for Monetary Stability.* New York: Fordham University Press, 1960.

9. ————. "The Monetary Theory and Policy of Henry Simons," *Journal of Law and Economics,* 10 (October, 1967), 1–13.

10. ————. "Money: Quantity Theory," in *The International Encyclopedia of the Social Sciences,* ed. David L. Stills, Vol. X (1968), 432–47.

11. ————, and DAVID MEISELMAN. "The Relative Stability of Monetary Velocity and the Investment Multiplier in the United States, 1897–1958," in *Stabilization Policies,* Commission on Money and Credit. Englewood Cliffs, N.J.: Prentice-Hall, 1963.

12. HICKS, J. R. "A Suggestion for Simplifying the Theory of Money," *Economica,* 2 (February, 1935), as reprinted in *Readings in Monetary Theory,* ed. Friedrich A. Lutz and Lloyd W. Mints. Philadelphia: 1951. Pp. 13–32.

13. KAHN, R. F. "Some Notes on Liquidity Preference," *The Manchester School,* 22 (September, 1954), 229–57.

14. KEYNES, JOHN MAYNARD. *A Treatise on Money.* London: 1930.

15. ————. *The General Theory of Employment, Interest, and Money.* New York: Harcourt, Brace, 1936.

16. KLEIN, LAWRENCE R. "The Use of Econometric Models as a Guide to Economic Policy," *Econometrica,* 15 (April, 1947), 111–51.

17. ————. *Economic Fluctuations in the United States, 1921–1941,* Cowles Commission for Research in Economics Monograph No. 11. New York: Wiley, 1950.

18. KNIGHT, FRANK H. "The Business Cycle, Interest, and Money: A Methodological Approach," *Review of Economic Statistics,* 23 (May, 1941), 53–67. As reprinted in *On the History and Method of Economics.* Chicago: University of Chicago Press, 1956. Pp. 202–26.

19. ————. "Economics," *Encyclopaedia Britannica,* 1951. As reprinted in *On the*

History and Method of Economics. Chicago: University of Chicago Press, 1956. Pp. 3–33.

20. ———. *Risk, Uncertainty and Profit*. New York: Kelley and Millman, 1957.

21. MAKOWER, HELEN, and JACOB MARSCHAK. "Assets, Prices, and Monetary Theory," *Economica*, 5 (August, 1938), 261–88. As reprinted in *Readings in Price Theory*, ed. George J. Stigler and Kenneth E. Boulding. Chicago: Irwin, 1952. Pp. 283–310.

22. MARKOWITZ, HARRY. "Portfolio Selection," *Journal of Finance*, 7 (March, 1952), 77–91.

23. MINTS, LLOYD W. *A History of Banking Theory*. Chicago: University of Chicago Press, 1945.

24. ———. "Monetary Policy," *Review of Economic Statistics*, 28 (May, 1946), 60–69.

25. ———. *Monetary Policy for a Competitive Society*. New York: McGraw-Hill, 1950.

26. MODIGLIANI, FRANCO. "Liquidity Preference and the Theory of Interest and Money," *Econometrica*, 12 (January, 1944), 45–88. As reprinted in *Readings in Monetary Theory*, ed. Friedrich A. Lutz and Lloyd W. Mints. Philadelphia: 1951. Pp. 186–239.

27. PATINKIN, DON. "An Indirect-Utility Approach to the Theory of Money, Assets, and Savings," in *The Theory of Interest Rates*, ed. F. H. Hahn and F. P. R. Brechling. London, Macmillan, 1965. Pp. 52–79.

28. ———. *Money, Interest, and Prices*, 2nd ed. New York: Harper and Row, 1965.

29. ———. "Interest," in *The International Encyclopedia of the Social Sciences*, ed. David L. Sills, Vol. VII (1968), 471–85.

30. ROBINSON, JOAN. "The Rate of Interest," *Economica*, 19 (April, 1951), 92–111.

31. SELDEN, RICHARD T. "Monetary Velocity in the United States," in *Studies in Quantity Theory of Money*, ed. Milton Friedman. Chicago: University of Chicago Press, 1956. Pp. 179–257.

32. SIMONS, HENRY C. "A Positive Program for Laissez Faire" (1934). As reprinted in *Economic Policy for a Free Society*. Chicago: University of Chicago Press, 1948. Pp. 40–77.

33. ———. "Rules versus Authorities in Monetary Policy," *Journal of Political Economy*, 44 (February, 1936), 1–30. As reprinted in *Economic Policy for a Free Society*. Chicago: University of Chicago Press, 1948. Pp. 160–83.

34. ———. *Personal Income Taxation*. Chicago: University of Chicago Press, 1938.

35. ———. "Hansen on Fiscal Policy," *Journal of Political Economy*, 50 (April, 1942), 161–96. Reprinted in *Economic Policy for a Free Society*. Chicago: University of Chicago Press, 1948. Pp. 184–219.

35a. ———. "Banking and Currency Reform." Unpublished memorandum, 1933.

36. SNYDER, CARL. "New Measures in the Equation of Exchange," *American Economic Review*, 14 (December, 1924), 699–713.

37. ———. "The Influence of the Interest Rate on the Business Cycle," *American Economic Review*, 15 (December, 1925), 684–99.

38. ———. "The Problem of Monetary and Economic Stability," *Quarterly Journal of Economics*, 49 (February, 1935), 173–205.

70 : MONEY, CREDIT, AND BANKING

39. STIGLER, GEORGE J. *Production and Distribution Theories.* New York: Macmillan, 1941.

40. TOBIN, JAMES. "A Dynamic Aggregative Model," *Journal of Political Economy*, 63 (April, 1955), 103–15.

41. VINER, JACOB. *Studies in the Theory of International Trade.* New York: Harper and Brothers, 1937.

42. ————."Schumpeter's *History of Economic Analysis*," *American Economic Review*, 44 (December, 1954), 894–910. As reprinted in *The Long View and the Short.* Glencoe, Ill.: Free Press, 1958. Pp. 343–65.

43. WARBURTON, CLARK. "The Volume of Money and the Price Level Between the World Wars," *Journal of Political Economy*, 53 (June, 1945), 150–63.

44. ————. "Quantity and Frequency of Use of Money in the United States, 1919–45," *Journal of Political Economy*, 54 (October, 1946), 436–50.

45. ————. "Monetary Velocity and Monetary Policy," *Review of Economics and Statistics*, 30 (November, 1948), 304–14.

46. ————. "The Secular Trend in Monetary Velocity," *Quarterly Journal of Economics*, 63 (February, 1949), 68–91.

[12]

Money and the Stock Market

Milton Friedman

Hoover Institution

Quarterly data for the period from 1961 to 1986 suggest that the real quantity of money (defined as M2) demanded relative to income is positively related to the deflated price of equities (Standard and Poor's composite) three quarters earlier and negatively related to the contemporaneous real stock price. The positive relation appears to reflect a wealth effect; the negative, a substitution effect. The wealth effect appears stronger than the substitution effect. The volume of transactions has an appreciable effect on M1 velocity but not on M2 velocity. Annual data for a century suggest that the apparent dominance of the wealth effect is the exception, not the rule.

I. Introduction

This note had its origin in a chart covering the past quarter century prepared by a financial institution that showed a close inverse relation between the level of the Dow Jones stock market index and the velocity of the monetary aggregate now designated M2 by the Federal Reserve System.

In the extensive work on the demand for money that I and others have done, the role of the stock market in affecting velocity has been taken into account in either of two ways: first, by treating the volume of financial transactions engendered by the market as an argument in the demand function on the grounds that such transactions would "absorb" money, hence reducing income velocity;[1] second, by taking

---

I am indebted for comments on earlier drafts to Albert J. Field, Robert Hetzel, David Laidler, Allan H. Meltzer, Anna J. Schwartz, and two anonymous referees.

[1] This has been a recurring theme ever since Irving Fisher's (1911) early emphasis on the transactions approach to the quantity theory, and especially during stock market booms, from 1929 to the present. For a recent example, see "M1 Revisited" (1986) and

[*Journal of Political Economy*, 1988, vol. 96, no. 2]

the earnings or dividend yield on securities as one of the returns on an alternative to money in a portfolio (Hamburger 1966, 1977, 1983). To oversimplify, the result generally has been a finding that the direction of effect is indeed as suggested by theory but that the magnitude of effect is small.[2] In addition, there has also been considerable investigation of the reverse direction of influence, of the effect of changes in the quantity of money on stock market prices (see, e.g., Keran 1971; Sprinkel and Genetski 1977, esp. pp. 120–39).

I know, however, of no econometric attempt to relate the level of stock prices to the demand for money, except indirectly, since the value of equity stocks is included in the total of nonhuman wealth, a variable that both theory and economic evidence suggest is related to the quantity of money demanded.

The inverse relation between stock prices and monetary velocity (or direct relation between stock prices and the level of real cash balances per unit of income) can be rationalized in three different ways: (1) A rise in stock prices means an increase in nominal wealth and gener-

---

Wenninger and Radecki (1986). For an analysis of the 1920s, see Field (1984). For an analysis of post–World War II data, see Cramer (1981, 1986). In demand studies by Anna Schwartz and me, we have omitted transactions variables for the reason indicated by the following quotation:

> One variable that has traditionally been singled out in considering the demand for money on the part of business enterprises is the volume of transactions . . . per dollar of final products; and, of course, emphasis on transactions has been carried over to the ultimate wealth-owning unit as well as to the business enterprise. The idea that renders this approach attractive is that there is a mechanical link between a dollar of payments per unit time and the average stock of money required to effect it—a fixed technical coefficient of production, as it were. It is clear that this mechanical approach is very different in spirit from the one we have been following. On our approach, the average amount of money held per dollar of transactions is itself to be regarded as a resultant of an economic equilibrating process, not as a physical datum. If, for whatever reason, it becomes more expensive to hold money, then it is worth devoting resources to effecting money transactions in less expensive ways or to reducing the volume of transactions per dollar of final output. In consequence, our ultimate demand function for money in its most general form does not contain as a variable the volume of transactions or of transactions per dollar of final output; it contains rather those more basic technical and cost conditions that affect the costs of conserving money, be it by changing the average amount of money held per dollar of transactions per unit time or by changing the number of dollars of transactions per dollar of final output. This does not, of course, exclude the possibility that, for a particular problem, it may be useful to regard the transactions variables as given and not to dig beneath them and so include the volume of transactions per dollar of final output as an explicit variable in a special variant of the demand function. [Friedman 1956, pp. 12–13]

[2] The major exception is Field (1984), who concludes, on the basis of dynamic simulations, that "absent the post-1925 surge in asset exchanges . . . holdings of $M1$ would have been on average 17 percent below their actual levels" (p. 50).

ally, given the wider fluctuation in stock prices than in income, also in the ratio of wealth to income. The higher wealth to income ratio can be expected to be reflected in a higher money to income ratio or a lower velocity. (2) A rise in stock prices reflects an increase in the expected return from risky assets relative to safe assets. Such a change in relative valuation need not be accompanied by a lower degree of risk aversion or a greater risk preference. The resulting increase in risk could be offset by increasing the weight of relatively safe assets in an aggregate portfolio, for example, by reducing the weight of long-term bonds and increasing the weight of short-term fixed-income securities plus money. (3) A rise in stock prices may be taken to imply a rise in the dollar volume of financial transactions, increasing the quantity of money demanded to facilitate transactions. Offsetting these factors is (4) a substitution effect. The higher the real stock price, the more attractive are equities as a component of the portfolio. The relative strength of the inverse effect of items 1–3 and the positive effect of item 4 is an empirical question.[3]

The graph that stimulated these speculations related the nominal level of stock prices to the velocity of M2 (calculated as a ratio of personal income to M2 in order to get monthly observations). Yet the first rationalization—a wealth effect—suggested in the preceding paragraph clearly requires that the stock price be measured in real rather than nominal terms. Simple correlations using quarterly data for 1961:1–1986:4 between M2 velocity on the one hand and real and nominal stock prices on the other were consistent with this theoretical expectation since they yielded a higher correlation for real than for nominal stock prices. In addition, the highest absolute value of the correlation was attained when the real stock price was correlated with

[3] An anonymous referee wrote: "There is a fourth story . . . , as reasonable as the three offered . . . . Stock prices respond to changes in anticipations about future real activity. The market responds first because it is a rational information processor, and because the price response is close to costless. . . . Debt expands or contracts . . . , and the debt changes initially show up as changes in broad measures of 'money,' like M2. Because it is subject to larger adjustment costs, real activity is the last to move." I believe that this fourth story is not as reasonable as the three offered. It requires autonomous and predictable movements in real income, with the quantity of money responding passively to such movements. In a regime in which the monetary authority operates by manipulating an interest rate, there no doubt is some such feedback effect of changes in real income on the quantity of money. However, I believe that the bulk of the evidence contradicts a purely real theory of business fluctuations and supports the view that the predominant short-term relation between money and real income is from changes in the stock of money to changes in real income rather than from real income to (earlier) stock of money. Nonetheless, it could be worth having a more direct test of this hypothesis. However, the tests that have occurred to me would require a body of data different from those used in this paper and a research effort at least as great as that underlying this paper. Hence, I leave that task to others.

velocity three quarters later.[4] These encouraging results led me to explore further.

To incorporate the second rationalization—a rise in relative returns from risky assets—requires some measure of the relative attractiveness to portfolio holders of moderately risky versus less risky assets. As a simple measure, I took the ratio of the yield on long-term to the yield on short-term nominal securities.[5] A rise in this ratio reflects a shift in demand from long to short securities and hence toward less risky nominal assets. Simple correlations showed the log of the ratio to be correlated negatively, as implied by the hypothesis, on a synchronous basis with both the logarithm of the real stock price and the logarithm of M2 velocity. However, the absolute correlations were very low (around .25–.30) and hence somewhat ambiguous.

Adequate data for testing the third rationalization—the effect of the volume of transactions—are available for a shorter period than the remaining data: only from 1970 on. It turns out that the volume of transactions has no significant effect on M2 velocity but does on M1 velocity (see App. B).

One final introductory point: Preliminary investigations of M1 velocity and the velocity of the monetary base gave wholly negative results, which explains the concentration on M2 velocity. These results are consistent with other evidence suggesting that M1, as currently defined, is a less satisfactory aggregate for judging short-term changes in monetary holdings than either M2, as currently defined, or the base (see Friedman 1986*b*).

---

[4] The variables used were nominal stock price, Standard and Poor's composite; real stock price, nominal stock price divided by GNP deflator; and velocity, nominal GNP divided by M2 two quarters earlier as estimated and seasonally adjusted by the Federal Reserve but adjusted also from 1983:1 on to eliminate the effect of the introduction of money market mutual deposit accounts (MMDAs) (see App. A). Leading velocity was used instead of actual velocity to allow for the tendency of changes in money to precede changes in nominal income. A lead of two quarters was used on the basis of earlier studies of the length of the mean lead of money. However, in the course of the analysis for this article, it turned out that, for the past quarter century alone, a lead of three quarters gives somewhat better results. The correlations were calculated from both actual values and the logarithms of the values with essentially the same results.

[5] The yields used for the period from 1955:1 on were long-term yield, the yield on 20-year Treasury bonds, and short-term yield, the yield in the secondary market on 3-month outstanding Treasury bills (both yields were from the Board of Governors of the Federal Reserve System). I experimented also with the ratio of the yield on corporate bonds (Moody's all industries) to the yield on 3-month banker's acceptances. However, it gave poorer results, so I abandoned it, except for the period prior to 1955, to avoid the effects and aftereffects of the Federal Reserve policy of pegging the price of government securities.

II. M2 Velocity: Quarterly Data

In our earlier work, Anna Schwartz and I concluded that the major variables affecting the quantity of money demanded are (1) real per capita income; (2) the difference between the yield on other nominal assets and on money, which we approximated by the product of a short-term rate and the ratio of high-powered money to the money stock; (3) the nominal yield on real assets, which we proxied by the rate of change of nominal aggregate income; and (4) some dummy variables that are irrelevant for the post–World War II period, as well as the change in the financial sophistication of the United States prior to World War I, also irrelevant for the present purpose (see Friedman and Schwartz 1982, chap. 6, esp. pp. 259–86).

With respect to real per capita income, the use of velocity as a dependent variable along with the exclusion of real income as an independent variable is equivalent to treating the elasticity of demand for real balances with respect to real per capita income as unity—not far from the 1.14 that we had estimated for the century prior to 1975. Additional checks supported the conclusion that no violence would be done to the postwar relations by using a unit elasticity.[6]

For items 2 and 3, the differential yield on money and the proxy return on real assets, the variables that have generally been used in monetary demand studies based on quarterly data have been a yield on short-term nominal assets as a measure of the yield on an alternative to money and the rate of change of prices as a measure of the nominal yield on real assets. After experimenting with these simpler variables, I found that replacing them by the variables we had used in our *Trends* study gave decidedly better results: higher R^2's and higher t-values for the coefficients. Hence, I included R_N, the differential yield on money, and g_Y, the rate of change of nominal income, to use our earlier notation, as independent variables.[7]

---

[6] Our earlier estimate was based on averages over half-cycles. The corresponding estimate for the underlying annual data (see Sec. III below) for 1885–1985 is almost identical (1.16), for 1951–85 it is 1.03, and for 1961–85, 0.88. For quarterly data for 1961:1–1986:4, a multiple regression of the logarithm of nominal GNP on the logarithm of M2 for the current and three prior quarters yields a sum of the coefficients of M2 terms of 1.03. Interestingly, the coefficients of the M2 terms for the current and two prior quarters sum to close to zero, and the coefficient for the third prior quarter is 1.01. Including other variables in this regression yields a sum of coefficients of the monetary terms equal to 0.996. The difference between the coefficient and unity is not statistically significant from zero, at any reasonable significance level, for any of the postwar regressions.

[7] For R_N, I used the product of the yield in the secondary market on 3-month outstanding Treasury bills (RTBill) (prior to 1955, rate on 3-month banker's acceptances), expressed as a decimal (i.e., 2 percent = 0.02), multiplied by the ratio to M2 of

One final point before I present some results. In our earlier work (1982), Schwartz and I had concluded that a distinct change had occurred in the relationship between interest rates and the rate of price change around the mid-1960s. Prior to that time, there had been little relationship between the two. From the early sixties on, that relationship started to get closer and closer and after about 1965 became extremely close indeed in line with the effect that Fisher (1896, 1907) had suggested many decades earlier. It appeared likely that there would be a similar break in the relationship between monetary variables in general and stock prices. That possibility was reinforced by an examination of the relationship between velocity and stock prices. As already noted, for the period from the mid-1960s on, real stock prices seemed to lead the velocity of money with a maximum simple correlation of $-.7$ at a lead of three quarters. On the other hand, for the period prior to that date, the timing relation is reversed, with velocity leading real stock prices (maximum simple correlation equals $-.7$ at a lead of four quarters). Accordingly, I chose the period from 1965:1 to 1986:4, the latest quarter for which I had data, on which to concentrate, later expanding it to 1961:1–1986:4.

Table 1 presents the final result of experimentation with different definitions of variables and different timing relations and documents the statistically significant difference between the 1950s and the later period. Figure 1 plots, for the whole period from 1947:1 to 1986:4,

---

high-powered money (HPM), i.e., the monetary base, as estimated by the Federal Reserve without adjustment for reserve requirement changes, but with the adjustment of M2 mentioned earlier to allow for the introduction of MMDAs. For the period since the fourth quarter of 1981, the Federal Reserve has not seasonally adjusted the base without adjustment for reserve requirements. Accordingly, I use throughout the ratio of the nonseasonally adjusted HPM to nonseasonally adjusted M2. For the period before 1959, I did not have quarterly data on HPM, so I interpolated HPM from annual data. For g_Y, I used a four-quarter difference between the logarithms of nominal GNP, i.e., the logarithm of nominal GNP in one quarter minus the corresponding logarithm of nominal GNP four quarters earlier. The use of R_N raises a problem of possible spurious correlation because the money multiplier (M2/HPM) enters into both M2 velocity (M2/GNP = [M2/HPM] × [HPM/GNP]) and R_N (R_N = RTBill × [HPM/M2]). This spurious correlation is mitigated by three factors: (1) The money multiplier enters velocity for a period two quarters earlier than it enters R_N, which was found to give best results on a synchronous basis. However, the effect of using a lagged value is minor since the serial correlation of the money multiplier with a lag of two quarters is .9925. A more important point is that the money multiplier enters primarily as a trend effect, having little effect on quarter-to-quarter movements. (2) The dependent variable is the logarithm of velocity; R_N is the original value, not its logarithm. (3) The variance of R_N is dominated by the variance of RTBill. In a decomposition of the variance of log R_N, the variance of log RTBill is .207621, that of log(HPM/M2) is .0260255, and the cross-correlation term is $-.116284$. A more detailed analysis of this statistical problem is contained in Friedman and Schwartz (1982, p. 270, n. 46), where it is concluded that the spurious statistical effects are not serious for our phase-average relations.

TABLE 1

Regression of Logarithm of Leading Velocity of M2 on Other Variables for 1951:1–1986:4 and Two Subperiods
(No Correction for Serial Correlation)

Independent Variable*	1951:1–1986:4		1951:1–1960:4		1961:1–1986:4	
	Coefficient	Absolute t-Value	Coefficient	Absolute t-Value	Coefficient	Absolute t-Value
Constant	.5157	42.9	.5070	12.1	.4551	31.9
Logarithm of real stock price	-.0475	7.5	-.0170	1.4	-.0255	3.3
Logarithm of long-short yield ratio	.0155	1.3	.0040	.1	.0780	5.8
Differential yield (R_N)	7.33	7.7	9.35	1.6	11.34	11.0
Proxy yield on real assets (g_Y)	.0849	2.0	.1708	2.8	.1415	2.9
Adjusted R^2	.674		.481		.825	
Standard error of estimate	.0159		.0136		.0126	
Standard deviation of dependent variable	.0279		.0189		.0302	
Durbin-Watson statistic	.382		.604		.545	
Number of observations	144		40		104	

Analysis of Variance of Difference between Periods†

Period	Number of Observations	Number of Degrees of Freedom	Sum of Squares	Mean Square
1951:1–1960:4	40	35	.006460	.000185
1961:1–1986:4	104	99	.015787	.000159
Total:				
Within	144	134	.022247	.000166
Between		5	.012984	.002597
Total	144	139	.035231	

* The logarithm of real stock prices leads by three quarters; other independent variables are synchronous with the dependent variable.
† F-value is 15.6. The .001 value of F for 5 and 134 degrees of freedom is 4.4. A similar analysis of variance between regressions for 1961:1–1964:4 and 1965:1–1986:4 gives an F-value of 2.5 compared to a .05 value for 5 and 94 degrees of freedom of 2.3.

FIG. 1.—Log leading velocity of M2: actual and predicted, 1947:1–1986:4. Velocity is predicted from the logarithm of the real stock price three quarters earlier and concurrently, the logarithm of the ratio of the long-term to short-term interest rate, the differential yield on M2, and the four-quarter change in log GNP, all concurrently.

the observed logarithm of the velocity of M2 and the values predicted by the equation for 1961:1–1986:4 in table 1. It provides perhaps the best bird's-eye summary of the overall results.

One striking feature is the initial rise in observed velocity until it reaches the level predicted from the regression based on much later data. The two lines cross between the second and third quarters of 1951, which, by no coincidence, is two quarters after the famous accord was reached between the Federal Reserve and the Treasury ending the Federal Reserve's pegging of interest rates.[8] Prior to that accord, rates on short-term highly liquid assets had been kept artificially low and stable by Federal Reserve policy, greatly reducing their attractiveness as an alternative to holding cash balances. From then on, there was something much closer to a free credit market, though of course the Fed intervened frequently. The timing of the accord explains why I start the detailed regression analysis with data for that quarter.

A second notable feature of figure 1 is the consistency of the relationship between the observed and predicted velocities throughout the period as a whole, even for the period prior to that for which the regression was calculated. As noted, there is a statistically significant difference between the two periods, yet they are sufficiently similar that from 1951 to 1961 observed velocity moves up and down around predicted velocity and displays occasional parallelism. The major discrepancies are (1) decidedly higher actual than predicted velocity in 1951, 1952, and 1953, almost surely attributable to the effect of the Korean War on anticipations of inflation;[9] (2) a reaction during the next 2 years; and, then again, (3) decidedly higher actual than predicted velocity in 1955, 1956, and 1957, a discrepancy for which I have no ready explanation.

A third striking feature is that there is no period in which there is a major break in the relationship. In particular, despite all the talk about how the relation between money and other variables has shifted drastically in recent years, there is no sign of that in the figure. That remark should be qualified, however, in one respect. The values for M2 used in these calculations do make an adjustment, as described in Appendix A, for the introduction of MMDA's in 1983.

---

[8] "Two quarters after" because the denominator for leading velocity for 1951:3 is M2 for 1951:1.

[9] The Korean War period is the only major inflationary episode that I know of that was not preceded by more rapid monetary growth and hence can be regarded as the result, initially at least, of an autonomous increase in velocity.

A.   *Wealth and Substitution Effects of the Real Stock
     Price*

To return to table 1, the key result, for our purposes, is that the
coefficient of the logarithm of real stock prices is negative in all the
equations and statistically significant for both the period as a whole
and 1961–86. That was equally true in the many minor variations of
these equations that I calculated in the course of settling on the final
variables and timing relations to be used. This is the sign implied by
the three rationalizations of an inverse relationship offered earlier: a
wealth effect, a risk-spreading effect, and a transactions effect. However, the situation is different for the long-short yield ratio. The risk-
spreading relationship implies that this variable should have a negative coefficient. Indeed, in calculations in which the variable is entered
with a three-quarter lead, the coefficient is generally negative. However, it either is not statistically significant or is on the margin of
significance, and it consistently performs better if entered synchronously. However, on a synchronous basis, the coefficient is positive.
This result is puzzling. A rise in the yield ratio implies that short-term
interest rates are expected to rise, which might be a reason for a later
reduction in the ratio of cash balances to income, that is, a rise in
velocity, but not for the current effect that the positive coefficient
implies.[10] Similarly, a rise in the yield ratio is a reflection of a fear of
future inflation, but any such effect should be allowed for by our
proxy for the nominal yield on physical assets.

The low values of the Durbin-Watson statistic for the three equations in table 1 led two referees of an earlier version of this paper to
question whether the results would remain valid if allowance were
made for the indicated strong serial correlation of residuals. Such
serial correlation does not bias the estimated coefficients but does
suggest that the effective number of degrees of freedom is less than
what a mere count of observations would indicate and hence may bias
the *t*-values, altering the apparent statistical significance of the results.[11] To check this possibility, table 2 compares the table 1 equation

---

[10] Note that the "reduction" referred to is not in nominal monetary balances. They
refer to the second prior quarter and are thus predetermined. However, current
spending is not predetermined, so what is implied by the correlation is that a rise in the
yield ratio encourages holders of cash balances to increase spending by a greater
amount than they would otherwise regard as appropriate, given their prior cash balances.

[11] I have mixed reactions to the current widespread tendency to regard serial correlation of residuals as a pure nuisance, if not the original sin, in analyzing time series.
Serial correlation of residuals does have the effects indicated in the text and, hence,
does deserve attention. However, some of the means used to attain serially uncorrelated residuals may lead analysts to throw out the baby with the bath. It is often useful
to regard time series as a combination of transitory stochastic and more permanent

TABLE 2

COMPARISON OF REGRESSIONS TO JUDGE EFFECT OF SERIAL CORRELATION OF RESIDUALS ON REGRESSION IN TABLE 1 FOR 1961:1–1986:4

	REGRESSION IN TABLE 1						
	Initial		Plus Lagged Dependent Variable			Plus Cochrane-Orcutt Correction for Serial Correlation‡	
INDEPENDENT VARIABLE*	Coefficient	Absolute t-Value	Coefficient	Long-Run Estimate†	Absolute t-Value	Coefficient	Absolute t-Value
Constant	.46	31.9	.16	.46	5.0	.50	84.4
Logarithm of real stock price	−.026	3.3	−.012	−.034	2.1	−.050	4.2
Logarithm of long-short yield ratio	.078	5.8	.016	.049	1.5	.042	2.9
Differential yield (R_N)	11.3	11.0	3.3	9.9	3.1	5.86	4.4
Proxy yield on real assets (g_Y)	.14	2.9	.12	.35	3.4	.38	6.3
Lagged dependent variable	...	...	.66	...	10.1	...	...
Serial correlation (ρ)	...	...	...	...	...	.80	16.1
Adjusted R^2	.825		.914			.937	
Standard error of estimate	.0126		.0089			.0078	
Durbin-Watson statistic	.54		1.47			1.85	

NOTE.—Standard deviation of the dependent variable is .0302. Number of observations is 104.

* Logarithm of real stock prices leads by three quarters; other independent variables are synchronous with the dependent variable.
† Coefficients in the preceding column are divided by unity minus the coefficient of the lagged dependent variable.
‡ Computed using TSP computer program.

for 1961–86 with two others designed to reduce serial correlation of residuals: one that adds the lagged value of the dependent variable, the other that uses the Cochrane-Orcutt correction for first-order serial correlation. The first device reduces the serial correlation appreciably but does not eliminate it; the second goes much farther in that direction. For our purposes, however, the main result is that neither alternative regression is inconsistent with the basic conclusions suggested by the initial regression. While the coefficients differ somewhat in size among the three regressions, they are all in the same ballpark and, with one exception (the coefficient of the long-short ratio in the regression containing the lagged dependent variable), all retain significance.[12]

If the wealth effect and the substitution effect operate with the same reaction speed, there is no way to isolate their separate effects. However, it is plausible that the substitution effect operates more rapidly than the wealth effect. To test this possibility, I expanded the multiple regression for 1961:1–1986:4 in table 1 by including the real stock price with a zero lead. The two equations are compared in table 3, which also contains additional regressions to check the effect of serial correlation of residuals.

The inclusion of the synchronous real stock price raises the correlation and reduces the standard error, though only modestly, for both equations B and C. More important, the constant aside, every common coefficient and its *t*-value in these equations is increased in absolute value, and the coefficient of the synchronous real stock price

---

underlying components and to regard the two components as reflecting two different sets of forces; e.g., purely random measurement errors may have a far larger impact on the transitory component than on the permanent component. The process of obtaining serially uncorrelated residuals may in effect simply eliminate the permanent components, leaving the analyst to study the relation among the stochastic components of his series, which may be pure noise, when what is of economic interest is the relation between the permanent components he has discarded in the process of seeking to satisfy mechanical statistical tests. For this reason, plus the problem of interpreting statistical tests of significance for a regression that has been chosen from among many trials because it yields the "best" result, I have long been skeptical of placing major emphasis on purely statistical tests, whether *t*-values, Durbin-Watson statistics, or any others. They are no doubt useful in guiding research, but they cannot be the major basis for judging the economic significance or reliability of the results and cannot be a substitute for a thorough examination of the quality of the data used. Personally, I prefer to put more emphasis on the consilience of evidence from a number of different sources or periods—as, in this paper, the annual as well as quarterly data. And I would regard the testing of my conclusions by examining, for example, similar data for other countries as more rewarding than a more intensive statistical mining of the quarterly series I have used.

[12] Cochrane-Orcutt corrections were also applied to the two other regressions in table 1, with similar results, and to the regression in table 2 that includes the lagged dependent variable, with the result of rendering the coefficient of the lagged dependent value not significantly different from zero.

TABLE 3

COMPARISON OF REGRESSIONS DESIGNED TO SEPARATE WEALTH AND SUBSTITUTION EFFECTS OF REAL STOCK PRICE: 1961:1–1986:4, WITH AND WITHOUT CORRECTION FOR SERIAL CORRELATION

INDEPENDENT VARIABLE	EQUATION A		EQUATION B		EQUATION C			EQUATION D	
	Coefficient	Absolute t-Value	Coefficient	Absolute t-Value	Coefficient	Long-Run Coefficient	Absolute t-Value	Coefficient	Absolute t-Value
Constant	.46	31.9	.43	28.7	.16	.42	5.1	.49	80.2
Logarithm of real stock price (lead = 3 quarters)	-.026	3.3	-.048	4.7	-.026	-.071	3.4	-.049	4.1
Logarithm of long-short yield ratio	.078	5.8	.087	6.6	.025	.067	2.2	.042	2.8
Differential yield (R_N)	11.3	11.0	12.8	11.8	4.58	12.4	4.0	5.72	4.0
Proxy yield on real assets (g_r)	.14	2.9	.16	3.4	.13	.36	3.9	.38	6.2
Logarithm of real stock price (lead = 0 quarters)	...	...	.035	3.2	.021	.057	2.6	-.0025	0.2
Lagged dependent variable	...	...	...	...		.63	9.8		
Serial correlation (ρ)	...	...	...	...	...	...	...	.87	17.7
Adjusted R^2	.825		.840			.919		.933	
Standard error of estimate	.0126		.0121			.0086		.0087	
Durbin-Watson statistic	.54		.62			1.45		1.85	

NOTE.—Standard deviation of the dependent variable is .0302. Number of observations is 104.

is positive, as the substitution effect would imply, and statistically significant. Hence, these regressions suggest that there is both a wealth effect and a substitution effect, with the wealth effect the stronger. However, equation D, with the Cochrane-Orcutt correction for serial correlation, gives a very different result: the coefficient of the contemporaneous stock price is negative and statistically insignificant, and the other coefficients and t-values are unchanged. This clearly raises some questions about the strength of the evidence for a positive substitution effect. However, it may also be that correction of the real stock price for serial correlation leaves largely a random series—white noise—and eliminates the more permanent component of the real stock price that alone would be expected to produce a substitution effect. This possibility is reinforced by the results based on annual data presented in Section III below. However, the question remains why the wealth effect is not also erased by the correction for serial correlation. There remains, therefore, a puzzle.

Though the coefficient of the leading real stock price is statistically significant and is of the expected sign in both tables 1 and 2, its economic significance is less clear. If the coefficient is regarded as a wealth effect, it would represent (with sign changed) the elasticity of real cash balances with respect to the total value of the assets whose prices can be regarded as represented by the real stock price. So interpreted, the results for 1961–86 would mean that a 1 percent increase in the real value of such assets would lead to roughly a one-fortieth or one-twentieth of 1 percent increase in the real value of M2 cash balances, according to tables 1 and 2, respectively.

To judge whether a response of this size can plausibly be regarded as a wealth effect requires comparing the magnitudes of such assets, on the one hand, and M2 balances, on the other, with total nonhuman wealth or, perhaps more broadly, with total wealth of all kinds, human as well as nonhuman. If the assets regarded as represented by the real stock price are taken to correspond to those traded on major U.S. markets, their total value is of the same order of magnitude as M2. Total nonhuman wealth is something like five or more times the value of market equities, and total wealth, of course, is an even larger multiple. In addition, an increase in the value of market assets is likely to reflect a heightened preference for such assets relative to other assets and, hence, to be offset at least in part by a reduction in the value of other assets. It follows that a 1 percent increase in the value of market assets means something less, and perhaps considerably less, than a one-fifth of 1 percent increase in the value of total nonhuman wealth, and an even smaller increase in the value of total wealth. The same percentage increase in cash balances would be required to keep its share of total wealth unchanged. The estimated one-fortieth or

one-twentieth of 1 percent increase in cash balances is only one-eighth
or one-quarter the size of the maximum estimated increase in nonhuman wealth. However, given the uncertainty of that estimate, an elasticity of .025 or .05 is certainly within the ballpark of the range of
values that could be regarded as plausible for a wealth effect, especially when it may reflect an offsetting substitution effect not fully
allowed for by the inclusion of the synchronous real stock price.

The most plausible alternative interpretation of the coefficient of
the leading real stock price is that the real stock price is proxying for
the volume of financial transactions. Data to test this explanation are
available only for the period from 1970 on. The data are monthly
estimates of current account, capital account, and total transactions
debits compiled by Paul Spindt at the Board of Governors of the
Federal Reserve System.[13] For the period from 1970:1 to 1986:4, I
recalculated the multiple correlations A and B in table 3, adding as an
additional variable the logarithm of current, capital, or total transactions, or of the ratio of current, capital, or total transactions to GNP,
in order to get transactions per unit of GNP. I included the transactions variables both synchronously and with a one-quarter lead. The
coefficient of the transactions term was in no case close to statistical
significance. In addition, most of the coefficients had the wrong sign.

I conclude that the negative coefficient of the leading real stock
price cannot be interpreted as a response of M2 velocity to the volume
of transactions but is more plausibly interpreted as reflecting a wealth
effect.

This result is not surprising. Insofar as the volume of transactions
tends to influence monetary holdings, its major influence would presumably be on a narrower aggregate than M2, one corresponding
more closely to a medium-of-exchange role of money. And, indeed,
in the course of exploring the role of transactions, I did find a significant relation with M1 velocity. Some of the results of my explorations
are reported in Appendix B.

B. Effects of Yields

There remain two variables in the regressions reported in tables 1 and
3 that have not yet been discussed. These variables, R_N and g_Y, are the
same as the variables that Schwartz and I used in our long-term analysis in *Monetary Trends*. It is interesting to compare the coefficients. Our

[13] I am grateful to Richard D. Porter for making the Fed's unpublished estimates
available to me. The estimates are by type of account (currency plus traveler's checks,
demand deposit accounts, other checkable deposits, money market mutual funds, telephone transfers, and money market deposit assets). I have used only the totals, aggregated by quarters.

final equation, combining data for the United States and the United Kingdom for the century 1870–1970, yielded a coefficient of -9.3 for R_N and -0.47 for g_Y, with the qualification that these were single-valued estimates within fairly broad limits (Friedman and Schwartz 1982, pp. 284–85). That equation was for the quantity of money demanded, whereas the equations dealt with here are for velocity. A rise in the quantity of money demanded means a decline in velocity. Hence, in comparisons of these coefficients with those in tables 1, 2, and 3, the signs should be reversed. If we do so, the coefficients are remarkably close for R_N for the 1961–86 equations that do not use the Cochrane-Orcutt correction for serial correlation. They range from 9.9 to 12.8, compared with the longer-run estimate of 9.3.[14] The Cochrane-Orcutt correction yields lower coefficients, ranging from 5.7 to 6.6, presumably because the effect of the correction is to eliminate at least part of the longer-term effect of a change in R_N. For g_Y the situation is different. The coefficient is decidedly smaller in magnitude though of the correct sign, ranging from 0.14 to 0.38, compared with the longer-term estimate of 0.47. An obvious explanation is that the year-to-year percentage change in quarterly nominal income is a less accurate proxy for the nominal yield on physical assets for quarterly data than the phase-average rate of change of nominal income is for phase-average data. The effect of the greater "noise" in this proxy would be to lower the numerical size of the coefficient so that this result cannot be regarded as inconsistent with our earlier results.

III. Tests from Annual Data

The similarity of these results from post–World War II quarterly data with our results for the longer period suggests using the annual data as an additional source of information on the effect of the real stock price. The data used in *Monetary Trends* ended in 1975. In connection with work that I have been doing on the cyclical pattern of money demand, I have extended the data forward to 1985 and calculated an identical regression using annual rather than phase-average data.[15]

The dependent variable in the demand function for money was the logarithm of real money balances per capita ($\log m$); the independent variables were the logarithm of real income per capita ($\log y$), the

---

[14] For this comparison, I have used the long-run coefficients as estimated in the equations with lagged dependent variables.

[15] When identical data were not available for the later period, I extrapolated the earlier data using the correlation between later and earlier data for an overlapping period. This was necessary primarily for the money and income series because of subsequent revisions in definitions and statistical estimates.

TABLE 4

COEFFICIENT AND ABSOLUTE t-VALUE OF PRIOR YEAR'S LOGARITHM OF REAL STOCK
PRICE IN MULTIPLE REGRESSIONS OF REAL PER CAPITA MONEY ON OTHER VARIABLES;
STANDARD ERRORS OF ESTIMATE OF REGRESSIONS INCLUDING AND EXCLUDING STOCK
PRICE; ANNUAL DATA, 1886–1985, AND VARIOUS SUBPERIODS

| | | LOGARITHM OF PRIOR YEAR'S REAL STOCK PRICE | | STANDARD ERROR OF ESTIMATE OF REGRESSION | |
PERIOD	NUMBER OF OBSERVATIONS	Coefficient	Absolute t-Value	Excluding Stock Price	Including Stock Price
1886–1985	100	−.0089	.5	.056	.056
1886–1939	54	−.105	3.3	.056	.051
1940–85	46	−.0485	2.0	.038	.037
1886–1914	29	−.0647	.8	.029	.029
1919–39	21	.0002	.003	.041	.042
1951–85	35	−.0598	4.5	.023	.018
1961–85	25	−.0047	.4	.012	.012
1951–73	23	−.1550	8.9	.023	.010
1974–85	12	.0483	1.7	.014	.012

NOTE.—All equations contain as other independent variables the logarithm of real per capita income, the differential yield on money, and the proxy yield on real assets. In addition, some equations include a postwar adjustment dummy and a shift adjustment dummy.

difference between the nominal yield on money and other nominal assets (R_N), the rate of change of money income as a proxy for the nominal yield on physical assets (g_Y), two dummy variables to allow for postwar adjustments (W) and a significant liquidity shift from 1929 to 1954 (S), and an adjustment for changing financial sophistication in the United States prior to World War I. As is to be expected, an equation calculated from annual data agrees very closely with the equation calculated on the basis of phase-average data.[16]

Table 4 summarizes the results of adding the logarithm of the real stock price as an independent variable to multiple correlations based on the annual data for various periods during the century from 1886 to 1985. Since the dependent variable is real per capita income rather than velocity, the wealth effect, risk-spreading effect, and transactions effect would all tend to produce a positive coefficient on the real stock

[16] The two equations are: annual data for 1886–1985:

$$\log m = -1.55 + 1.16 \log y - 11.9 R_N - .51 g_Y + .023 W + .138 S,$$
$$\quad\;\;(19.6)\quad(99.3)\qquad\quad(6.4)\quad\;(7.9)\quad(5.6)\qquad(7.1)$$
$$\text{SEE} = 5.6 \text{ percent};$$

phase-average data for United States for 1873–1975:

$$\log m = -1.53 + 1.15 \log y - 8.82 R_N - .59 g_Y + .025 W + .17 S,$$
$$\quad\;\;(9.4)\quad(50.7)\qquad\quad(4.4)\quad\;(3.5)\quad(3.8)\qquad(6.9)$$
$$\text{SEE} = 5.1 \text{ percent}.$$

price, the substitution effect a negative coefficient. With annual data, we cannot separate the two effects, given that any difference in timing is apparently measured in quarters, not years. Accordingly, we can only estimate the net effect, and even that only crudely.

The fascinating feature of table 4 is that the coefficients are predominantly negative, suggesting that the substitution effect has been dominant. Moreover, the only coefficients statistically significant at a .05 level or lower are negative—for 1886–1939, 1940–85, 1951–85, and, most strongly, 1951–73. The positive coefficient for 1919–39 is trivial. The only positive coefficient that approaches statistical significance is the one for 1974–85, the final 12 years of the period covered by our earlier analysis of quarterly data.

IV. Reconciliation of Results from Annual and Quarterly Data

These results for the annual data do not contradict our earlier conclusions for the quarterly data, but they do put them in a different light. They suggest that the recent period has been atypical, that for most of our history substitution effects have dominated wealth effects, and that the opposite has prevailed only for the past several decades. The important—and unanswered—question is whether this is a temporary reversal or a permanent one.

The reversal is linked in time at least to the emergence of the Fisher effect as a dominant element in the movement of interest rates. And both are linked—not only in time but also as possible cause and effect—to the changed monetary regime in the world. As I have emphasized elsewhere, the world's monetary regime since 1971 has no historical precedent (Friedman 1986*a*). It is the first time that every major currency in the world has severed all links to a commodity and is on a strictly inconvertible paper or fiat standard, and is so, not as a temporary expedient in time of crisis, but as a system intended to be permanent. The transition was of course not discontinuous, even though its final formal inception can be precisely dated as occurring when President Nixon closed the gold window on August 15, 1971. It was a gradual transition that doubtless had its effects long before the final step.

Why should this transition have had the suggested effects? For interest rates, the answer is clear: the end of a commodity link, however tenuous, meant the end of a long-term anchor to the price level and hence ushered in a period of increased long-term uncertainty about future nominal values. The effect of anticipated inflation or deflation stressed by Fisher became potentially more important, and experience of accelerating inflation in the 1960s and 1970s, and disinflation in the 1980s, converted the potentiality into a clear and present actuality. Witness the explosion of financial futures markets after 1971.

For real stock prices, the answer is less clear. The changed monetary regime enhanced the importance in portfolio choice and, in the valuing of portfolios, of real versus nominal assets. However, that would seem to strengthen both the substitution and the wealth effect, and, indeed, the 1951–73 period shows the strongest net substitution effect of any of the subperiods for the annual data. But why, then, would the annual data show a wealth effect in the final 12 years, and why should that effect have been dominant for the final 25 years of the quarterly data? I have no persuasive answers to these questions raised by the comparison of the quarterly and the annual data.

V. Conclusion

The purpose of this paper has been to explore the role of the real stock price as a variable in the demand function for money. The results are suggestive but not conclusive. Quarterly data for the period since 1961 suggest that the real quantity of money (defined as M2) demanded relative to income is positively related to the real stock price, three quarters earlier, and negatively related to the contemporaneous real stock price. The positive relation appears to reflect a wealth effect, the negative a substitution effect. The wealth effect appears stronger and is supported better by the data than the substitution effect. The data contradict any effect on M2 velocity of the volume of total, current, or financial transactions, though, as indicated in Appendix B, there is such an effect on M1 velocity.

Annual data for a longer period suggest that the apparent dominance of the wealth effect is the exception, not the rule. For all but the final 12 years of the century analyzed, the substitution effect appears to dominate any wealth effect. These results raise some puzzles that I have not been able to resolve.

Appendix A

Explanation of Peak in M2 Rate of Change in Second and Third Quarters of 1983

1. The introduction of money market mutual deposit accounts (MMDA) led to a shift of deposits out of savings deposits (SD), time deposits (TD), and money market mutual funds (MMMF), which would cancel in total M2. In addition, it led to noncanceling transfers from non-M2 funds. The following tables estimate the size of the shift.

	REPORTED LEVELS IN INDICATED MONTHS				
	M2	MMDA	SD	TD	MMMF
12/82	1,952.6	43.2	357.9	852.8	185.2
1/83	2,007.1	191.0	333.0	794.7	168.2
2/83	2,044.7	281.3	321.6	755.8	160.6
3/83	2,061.5	323.1	318.6	736.5	154.8

	CHANGE FROM PRIOR MONTH					EXCESS MMDA	CUMULATIVE EXCESS
	M2	MMDA	SD	TD	MMMF		
1/83	54.5	147.8	−24.9	−58.1	−17.0	47.8	47.8
2/83	37.6	90.3	−11.4	−38.9	−7.6	32.4	80.2
3/83	16.8	41.8	−3.0	−19.3	−5.8	13.7	93.9

	ADJUSTED M2 (Reported M2 Minus Cumulative Excess)			ANNUAL RATE OF CHANGE	
	M2	Cumulative Excess	Adjusted M2	Original	Adjusted
12/82	1,952.6	...	1,952.6	...	...
1/83	2,007.1	47.8	1,959.3	39.15	4.20
2/83	2,044.7	80.2	1,964.5	24.95	3.23
3/83	2,061.5	93.9	1,967.6	10.32	1.91
4/83	2,078.2	93.9	1,984.3	10.17	10.67

2. Quarterly estimates using adjusted M2:

			ANNUAL RATE OF CHANGE	
	REPORTED M2	ADJUSTED M2	Original	Adjusted
1982:4	1,938.0	1,938.0	...	...
1983:1	2,037.8	1,963.8	22.25	5.43
1983:2	2,093.6	1,999.7	11.41	7.52
1983:3	2,130.8	2,036.9	7.30	7.65

3. To get consistent series, I multiplied all later M2's by the ratio of adjusted to reported M2 for 1983:3 (.95593).

4. This adjustment probably overstates the effect of the introduction of MMDAs since it implicitly assumes that there would have been no increase at all in SD + TD + MMMF if MMDAs had not been introduced. However, I suspect the error is minor, given that the adjustment started earlier and continued later.

5. These calculations were made in May 1986 on the basis of the then-current data.

Appendix B

M1 Velocity and the Volume of Transactions

In the course of exploring the effect of the volume of transactions on the velocity of M2, I also made some calculations for M1 velocity. Since M1 comes closer than M2 to approximating a medium-of-exchange concept of money, there is reason to expect that the demand for M1 would be affected more by the volume of transactions than the demand for M2, and that has turned out to be the case.

I have not made a detailed analysis for M1 velocity, but I report here some calculations based on quarterly data for 1970:1–1986:2 that are suggestive.[17]

The first conclusion, not recorded in the tables that follow, is that neither the differential yield on M1 (computed like R_N except using M1 instead of M2 in the ratio of high-powered money to the stock of money) nor g_Y seems to be a significant variable in the demand for M1; these returns on nominal and real assets are understandably far more significant for the broader concept of money than for M1. On the other hand, the 3-month T-bill rate is a significant variable and so, clearly, is a time trend.

At first impression, equation A in table B1 suggests that total transactions relative to GNP are an important variable. However, examination of charts of the basic data suggests that the first impression is misleading. As is well known, the upward trend in M1 velocity came to a sharp halt in 1980 and was replaced by a declining trend. It so happens that total transactions accelerated sharply after 1980 thanks largely to an explosion in stock market activity and capital transactions. The negative coefficient attached to this acceleration in transactions offsets the positive coefficient of time. So the transactions variable is really contributing only one observation. Equation B tests this conjecture by replacing time by a combination of time to 1979:4 and a constant thereafter. The result is a statistically insignificant coefficient of the transactions variable and a lower standard error of estimate. Equation C shows that replacing total transactions by current transactions improves the correlation. The coefficient of the current transactions variable is highly significant statistically and the standard error is lower.[18]

Equation D, which includes capital and current transactions, gives an even lower standard error of estimate, with the coefficients of both being negative and statistically significant, though the coefficient of the current transactions variable both is larger and has a higher t-value.

As far as these regressions go, they give a somewhat mixed message. They support what I take to be the received view on current transactions, that their ratio to GNP has a sizable positive effect on the demand for the medium of exchange. However, with respect to capital transactions, regression D suggests that they too have a significant, if much smaller, effect, whereas I take the received view to be that financial transactions are so highly money-

---

[17] For the text of this paper, I have updated through 1986:4 the data used in my initial explorations. For this appendix, I have not done so.

[18] In a correlation such as eq. A with a straight time variable, the logarithm of the ratio of current transactions to GNP has a positive rather than negative coefficient (of 1.09) with a t-value of 3.6. However, the standard error of estimate is more than double that of eq. A.

TABLE B1

REGRESSIONS OF LOGARITHM OF LEADING VELOCITY OF M1 ON TRANSACTIONS AND OTHER VARIABLES FOR 1970:1–1986:2 ($N = 66$)

VARIABLE	EQUATION A		EQUATION B		EQUATION C		EQUATION D	
	Coefficient	Absolute t-Value	Coefficient	Absolute t-Value	Coefficient	Absolute t-Value	Coefficient	Absolute t-Value
Constant	2.00	72.1	1.52	129.0	1.33	35.0	1.26	29.7
Logarithm of ratio to GNP of:								
Total transactions	−.47	16.7	.011	1.0	−.58	5.3	−.82	6.2
Current transactions	...	...	...	...	...	...	...	...
Capital transactions	...	...	...	...	...	...	−.03	2.9
Interest rate on 3-month T-bill	.0082	8.7	.0043	4.6	.0066	7.3	.0073	8.2
Time	.015	26.5	...	...	...	...	...	...
Time and dummy*	...	...	.0094	28.2	.0097	57.4	.010	32.4
R^2	.983		.985		.9897		.991	
Standard error of estimate	.0176		.0167		.0139		.0132	

NOTE.—Leading velocity is GNP divided by M1 two quarters earlier.
* Variable equals quarters elapsed from 1969:4 to 1979:4, 40 thereafter.

TABLE B2

Regressions for Subperiods of Logarithm of Leading Velocity of M1 on Transactions and Other Variables

Variable	1970:1–1986:2		1980:1–1986:2				1970:1–1979:4					
	Equation A		Equation E		Equation F		Equation G		Equation H		Equation I	
	Coefficient	Absolute t-Value	Coefficient	Absolute t-Value	Coefficient	Absolute t-Value	Coefficient	Absolute t-Value	Coefficient	Absolute t-Value	Coefficient	Absolute t-Value
Constant	2.00	72.1	1.86	28.6	1.91	33.9	1.24	21.3	1.77	53.5	1.64	12.1
Logarithm of ratio to GNP of:												
Total transactions	−.47	16.7	−.059	.6	−.36	6.4	−.85	5.3				
Current transactions									−.30	6.7	−.24	1.0
Capital transactions									.001	1.2	−.24	3.2
Interest rate on 3-month T-bill	.0082	8.7	.0077	4.21	.0017	1.6	.0052	3.5			.0024	1.5
Time	.015	26.5	.0025	.94	.0138	21.0	.010	49.3	.014	21.2	.013	13.8
R^2	.983		.466		.992		.980		.992		.992	
Standard error of estimate	.0176		.0154		.0104		.0114		.0102		.0102	
Number of observations	66		26		40		40		40		40	

efficient that they do not absorb any appreciable quantity of media of exchange and have little if any effect on velocity.[19]

As a further check on the effect of the shift from accelerating inflation to disinflation, table B2 repeats regression A of table B1, adds similar regressions for two subperiods, 1970:1–1979:4 and 1980:1–1986:2, and adds additional regressions for the first period.

Regressions E and F confirm the conclusion from table B1 about the role played by the transactions variable for the period as a whole. For 1980:1–1986:2, neither total transactions nor time is statistically significant. However, the regressions for the earlier period do not confirm what I called the received view about the relative importance of capital and current transactions. According to these regressions, while the current transactions ratio alone does yield a statistically significant coefficient (t-value of 5.3), the t-value for the capital transactions ratio alone is even higher, and if the two ratios are included separately, the capital transactions ratio is dominant. There is essentially nothing to choose among equations F, H, and I. According to equation F, the elasticity of M1 velocity with respect to the ratio of total transactions to GNP is -0.36, and, according to equation I, with respect to the ratio of either current or capital transactions alone, -0.24.

Disentangling the somewhat conflicting conclusions suggested by the regressions for the period as a whole and for the first subperiod will require additional evidence. The Federal Reserve may provide some such evidence if Paul Spindt is able to extend his estimates of the volume of transactions to the period prior to 1970.

References

Cramer, J. S. "The Volume of Transactions and of Payments in the United Kingdom, 1968–1977." *Oxford Econ. Papers*, n.s., 33 (July 1981): 234–55.

———. "The Volume of Transactions and the Circulation of Money in the United States, 1950–1979." *J. Bus. and Econ. Statis.* 4 (April 1986): 225–32.

Field, Alexander J. "Asset Exchanges and the Transactions Demand for Money, 1919–29." *A.E.R.* 74 (March 1984): 43–59.

Fisher, Irving. *Appreciation and Interest.* New York: Macmillan (for American Econ. Assoc.), 1896.

———. *The Rate of Interest.* New York: Macmillan, 1907.

———. *The Purchasing Power of Money.* New York: Macmillan, 1911; 2d ed., 1913.

Friedman, Milton. "The Quantity Theory of Money—a Restatement." In *Studies in the Quantity Theory of Money,* edited by Milton Friedman. Chicago: Univ. Chicago Press, 1956.

———. "Monetary Policy in a Fiat World." *Contemporary Policy Issues* 4 (January 1986): 1–9. (*a*)

———. "M1's Hot Streak Gave Keynesians a Bad Idea." *Wall Street J.* (September 18, 1986). (*b*)

Friedman, Milton, and Schwartz, Anna J. *Monetary Trends in the United States*

[19] This is the conclusion reached by Wenninger and Radecki (1986). In an unpublished paper, Kretzmer and Porter (n.d.) are more uncertain, suggesting that total transactions measures may improve "the explanation of demand deposits." But they are exceedingly tentative about this conclusion.

*and the United Kingdom: Their Relation to Income, Prices, and Interest Rates,
1867–1975.* Chicago: Univ. Chicago Press (for NBER), 1982.

Hamburger, Michael J. "The Demand for Money by Households, Money
Substitutes, and Monetary Policy." *J.P.E.* 74 (December 1966): 600–623.

———. "The Behavior of the Money Stock: Is There a Puzzle?" *J. Monetary
Econ.* 3 (July 1977): 265–88.

———. "Recent Velocity Behavior, the Demand for Money and Monetary
Policy." In *Proceedings of the Conference on Monetary Targeting and Velocity.*
San Francisco: Fed. Reserve Bank San Francisco, 1983.

Keran, Michael W. "Expectations, Money, and the Stock Market." *Fed. Reserve
Bank St. Louis Rev.* 53 (January 1971): 16–32.

Kretzmer, Peter E., and Porter, Richard D. "Total Transactions Measures
and M1 Growth." Manuscript. Washington: Bd. Governors, Fed. Reserve
System, n.d.

"M1 Revisited: Financial Transactions and Money Growth." *Morgan Econ. Q.*
(September 1986), pp. 7–9.

Sprinkel, Beryl W., and Genetski, Robert J. *Winning with Money: A Guide for
Your Future.* Homewood, Ill.: Dow Jones–Irwin, 1977.

Wenninger, John, and Radecki, Lawrence J. "Financial Transactions and the
Demand for M1." *Fed. Reserve Bank New York Q. Rev.* 11 (Summer 1986):
24–29.

[13]

2

On the Demand for Money and the Real Balance Effect

1. THE LONG- AND SHORT-RUN DEMAND FOR MONEY

No proposition in macroeconomics has received more attention than that there exists, at the level of the aggregate economy, a stable demand for money function. When we say that the demand for money function is stable we mean at the very least that money holdings, as observed in the real world, can be explained, to conventionally acceptable levels of statistical significance, by functional relationships which include a relatively small number of arguments. We also mean, or should mean, that the same equation is capable of being fitted to samples of data drawn from different times and places, without it being necessary to change the arguments of the relationship in order to achieve satisfactory results, and also without the estimated quantitative values of the parameters changing too much.

Now of course a cavalier treatment of the requirements that the number of parameters be 'relatively small', and that parameter values not change 'too much' when the data are changed, could permit claims to be made on behalf of the stability of almost any relationship, but, in this case, there is no need to abuse the English language. In practice a 'small' number of arguments has meant three or four – typically including a scale variable such as income,

40   MONETARIST PERSPECTIVES

permanent income or wealth, an opportunity cost variable such as a nominal interest rate or some measure of the expected inflation rate, and, if nominal balances have been the dependent variable, the general price level. The requirement that parameters not change 'too much' has meant not only that they have been expected to take their theoretically predicted sign, but also to stay within reasonable quantitative ranges as well, in the region of 0.5–1.0 or a little greater for the real income elasticity of demand for money, somewhere around $-0.1--0.5$ or less for the interest elasticity depending upon the interest rate, not to mention the definition of money, utilised, and since economic theory predicts that the demand for money is a demand for 'real' balances, a price level elasticity of demand for nominal balances of close to 1.0.

I have surveyed empirical work on the demand for money elsewhere (Laidler 1977, 1980), and there is no need to go into detail about these matters again here. It will suffice to note that, although not every test on every set of data has proved satisfactory, the demand for money has turned out to be 'stable' in the sense in which I have used the word above quite often enough to convince the majority of monetary economists, some of whom twenty years ago were quite sceptical (see e.g. Modigliani 1978), of the importance of the relationship for our understanding of macroeconomic phenomena. One characteristic of the results generated by empirical work on the demand for money which seems to be rather general is that, unless one is dealing with data which are highly aggregated over time – business cycle phase averages for example (see Friedman 1959) – or which cover such a long period of time – fifty years or more, say – that the variation in the data used is dominated by secular changes, it has proved necessary to distinguish between the 'long-run' and the 'short-run' demand for money in order to achieve satisfactory results.

The long-run aggregate demand for money function may be thought of as being generated by the outcome of the following thought experiment: consider an economy in which, given the values of the various arguments in the function, the aggregate of agents desire to hold a certain quantity of money and are able to do so; then ask how much money they would be observed to hold in various *alternative* circumstances in which the variables that determine money holding took different values. If the tastes of agents *vis à vis* money holding did not change over time, and if there were no barriers to their moving instantaneously from holding one amount of money to another, the outcome of this experiment would be the same as that generated by varying the values of the arguments of the demand for money function over time and then observing the changes in cash balances associated with those variations. However, if agents face any costs of adjusting their money holdings, so the argument goes, they will not move immediately to a new point on their long-run demand for money function when one of its arguments changes. They will begin to move towards that point, but the speed of the approach will be determined by their response to the adjustment costs involved in getting there.

It will help with the clarity of the argument to put all this into a familiar algebraic form at this point. It is convenient to work with a log linear (constant elasticity) form of the demand for money function, and to divide time up into discrete periods, Hicksian 'weeks' say. Thus, with X a vector of factors determining the demand for real balances, p the log of the general price level, m^* the log of the quantity of money demanded as determined by the long-run function, we write

$$m^* = f(X) + p \qquad (1)$$

which is the long-run aggregate demand for money function.

Following practices which I shall in due course criticise, we may also write, with the subscript -1 denoting a one-period time lag and with m the log of nominal money demanded,

$$m - m_{-1} = b(m^* - m_{-1}) \qquad 0 < b \leqslant 1 \qquad (2)$$

which tells us how much of the gap between actual and ultimately desired money holdings will be closed during one period. Together these equations yield the short-run demand for money function

$$m = b\{f(X) + p\} + (1 - b)m_{-1} \qquad (3)$$

An equation such as (3), or something very like it, has been used in an enormous number of studies of the demand for money, and the lagged dependent variable has almost invariably proved an important addition as far as increasing the relationship's explanatory power is concerned. The addition in question has usually been regarded as quite innocuous, because the kind of adjustment cost argument which I have just sketched out has been widely applied, not just to the demand for money, but to the consumption function as well, not to mention the demand for various durable goods (see Harberger 1960). Indeed, one well-known, and still frequently cited, article on this particular aspect of the demand for money (Chow 1966) was explicitly an application to money of techniques which its author had used when working on the demand for automobiles, techniques which, in essence, give econometric content to the Marshallian distinction between the long-run and short-run response of quantity demanded of some good to a change in some argument of its demand function, a distinction which seems at first sight to be universally applicable.

The bulk of this essay will be devoted to elaborating upon the proposition that, notwithstanding the widespread practice of adding a lagged dependent variable to the demand for money function, the belief implicit in this practice that the demand for money *in the aggregate economy* can be modelled in the long and short runs 'as if' money was a consumer durable good, is fallacious. It will also examine some of the implications of this proposition for what we do and do not know about the aggregate demand for money. The phrase 'in the aggregate economy' is italicised, because the problem to be discussed arises at the level of what Patinkin (1956) called the market experiment, and not at the level of the individual experiment at all. It will nevertheless be helpful to begin the argument with an examination of the relevant individual experiment.

2. THE INDIVIDUAL EXPERIMENT AND THE REAL BALANCE EFFECT

Though it was a controversial matter at one time, it is by now as near to universally accepted as anything in economics ever is that once the relevant object of choice is recognised to be 'real balances' (money holdings measured in constant purchasing power terms), and once their durability is taken account of, the individual agent's demand for money can, and indeed should, be analysed along with his demand for everything else. The amount of real balances which he will hold will be the outcome of the interaction of his utility function with his budget constraint, just like the quantity of anything else he will demand. It was at one time widely questioned whether it made sense to argue that money yielded 'utility' to the individual in the same way as other goods, but it is by now well established that, from the point of view of the individual experiment, the 'story' which one tells about this matter makes no critical difference.

One may argue that, by holding real balances, the individual agent is able to avoid the embarrassment of being unable to pay up promptly when unexpectedly called upon to meet his obligations in cash (Patinkin 1965, Ch. 5); one may argue that he is enabled to cut down on the transactions costs involved in liquidating income earning assets when cash is required (Baumol 1952, Tobin 1956); one may argue that the agent can avoid the uncertainties about future command over resources inherent in holding variable capital value assets such as bonds (Keynes 1936, Ch. 15, Tobin 1958); and so on. What is postulated here turns out to make no difference to our ability to integrate the analysis of the demand for money with that of other aspects of the agent's choices, any more than the motives we attribute to the owners of automobiles make any difference to our ability to apply choice theory to analysing the demand for that durable good.

What is important, as Patinkin (1965, Chs 5–7) showed quite clearly, is that agents *do* desire to hold real balances, and not *why*. This is not to deny that if we formulate some precise hypothesis about the nature and source of the 'utility' which money holding yields the individual, we might thereby put ourselves in a position also to formulate more precise hypotheses about the quantitative nature of the agent's demand for money function than generalised choice theory would yield. After all, the Baumol–Tobin 'square root rule' is an example of just this possibility working out in practice. However, if the qualitative predictions yielded by the basic theory of choice are sufficient for any particular purpose, then there is no need to ask why cash balances yield utility before applying that theory to analysing the demand for money. This is *not* to say that, when we engage in economic analysis, we never need to pay attention to those special characteristics of money as a social institution which facilitate the processes of exchange; but it is to say that, when considering the money holding behaviour of an individual agent acting alone, it will suffice to treat real money balances 'as if' they are a service-yielding consumer durable.

Using the same symbols as before, but attaching to them, where appropriate, the subscript i to indicate that we are indeed dealing

44   MONETARIST PERSPECTIVES

with an individual, we may write the individual agent's long-run demand for money function, where 'long run' is defined in a manner analogous to that already used above, as

$$m_i^* = f_i(X)_i + p \tag{4}$$

Here, it is as well to note explicitly that m_i^* refers to the quantity of nominal balances the individual will plan to end up holding at the end of the current period, given the price level and the values of the variables included in X that rule during the period, if he faces no costs of adjusting his money holdings. If we are willing to entertain the possibility of our agent being off his long-run demand for money function over a time span longer than one period, and we should be, if only because Archibald and Lipsey (1958) established one set of mechanisms that make this a reasonable postulate, we might also argue that he moves back towards it slowly according to

$$(m_i - m_{i-1}) = b(m_i^* - m_{i-1}) \tag{5}$$

Once again then, we can derive a short-run demand for money function of the conventional form

$$m_i = b\{f_i(X)_i + p\} + (1-b)m_{i-1} \tag{6}$$

Here m_i is the amount of money the agent *actually* plans to hold at the end of the current period, and m_{i-1} is the amount of money with which he *begins* the current period; as we shall see in a moment, m_{i-1} may or may not be the amount of money he *chose* to hold in period -1. Be that as it may, the adjustment parameter b is easily enough motivated in the individual experiment. If, by the end of the period for which he is choosing his cash holdings, our agent is not on his long-run demand for money function, he obviously enjoys less utility, or incurs greater costs somewhere or other, than he otherwise would. Suppose, however, that in moving back towards that long-run relationship over the period in question he also incurs transactions costs of some sort. Call the first cost K_1 and the second K_2, and let them be determined in the following way:

$$K_1 = \alpha_1(m_i^* - m_i)^2 \tag{7}$$

$$K_2 = \alpha_2(m_i - m_{i-1})^2 \tag{8}$$

The agent seeking to minimise the sum of these costs will adjust his cash balances over time according to equation (5) where

$$b \equiv \alpha_1/(\alpha_1+\alpha_2) \qquad\qquad (9)$$

The above cost functions are undoubtedly arbitrary; their quadratic form has much more to do with the fact that this enables us to derive a linear, and therefore easy to handle, adjustment process, than with any well thought through microeconomic analysis; also, the existence of an adjustment cost function such as (8) for the individual is not easily reconciled with the lump sum adjustment costs which are sometimes used in deriving the long-run demand for money function (when, for example, the Baumol–Tobin inventory approach is used), but such criticisms are not of any great importance for present purposes. Nothing fundamental in the arguments which follow depends upon the linearity of the adjustment process, but the simplicity of the argument is enhanced if we make the arbitrary assumptions which have to be made in order to keep the individual's short-run demand for money function in the form given by (6), not least because that is the form which is usually thought of as underlying the similar relationship used in empirical work on aggregate data.

Equation (6) tells us that the amount of nominal money we will observe our individual holding at the end of any time period will depend upon the general price level at which trade takes place during the period, whatever factors we might put in X – let us say, real income and a representative nominal interest rate over the period – and the quantity of nominal money he held at the beginning of that period. Such an equation makes perfectly good economic (and econometric) sense. The price level and nominal interest rates are quite beyond the individual's control, as is real income – unless we go into a model in which the labour–leisure choice is endogenous; and if we did that we ought to put the real wage, and some endowment of labour power, into the relationship instead. Beginning of period money is also exogenous from the point of view of current period behaviour, however it may be determined. The only endogenous variable in the equation is indeed the one which appears on its left-hand side.

Equation (6) is a meaningful, if rather trivial, expression, which can form the basis for a series of equally meaningful, and equally trivial, individual experiments. We can start our individual out on his long-run demand for money function, face him with changes in

46   MONETARIST PERSPECTIVES

his real income, the interest rate, or the price level, and use equation (6) to generate the resulting time path of his nominal money holdings. In this case, note that m_{-1}, beginning of period money holdings, will be given by the value taken by the dependent variable of equation (6) in period -1. We can also present our individual with a windfall gain in nominal money holdings (perhaps as a result of the passage of a helicopter, cf. Friedman 1969), hold interest rates, prices and his income constant, and once again use equation (6) to tell us about his reaction. In this case, of course, beginning period money will not be equal to the individual's money holdings at the end of period -1.

We do not usually come across this latter experiment in the discussions of the demand for money, finding it instead in discussions of the 'real balance effect' where the influence of money on expenditure flows is at the centre of attention. However, it is a point too often taken for granted, and perhaps for that reason not fully enough appreciated, that, in the individual experiment, whenever there arises a discrepancy between desired long-run money holdings and actual money holdings, for no matter what reason, there must be accompanying effects on expenditure flows, either on current consumption goods and/or on the acquisition of other assets. The change in money holdings on the left-hand side of equation (5) must have its counterpart in the agent's expenditure if his budget constraint is to be satisfied. That is to say, when we talk of the adjustment over time of the agent's money holdings towards their long-run equilibrium, we are also talking about what is, to all intents and purposes, a real balance effect, or as Chick (1973, pp. 76–77 following Mishan 1958) called it, a 'cash balance effect'. This is true whether the experiment we are describing is set in motion by a variation in the arguments of the agent's long-run demand for money function, or by a change in his endowment of nominal money.

I am here using the phrase 'real balance effect' in a rather broader sense than did Patinkin (1956), because he reserved the term to characterise only wealth effects. He used the phrase 'substitution effect' to describe the consequences of those disturbances to the individual which required him to change only the composition of his assets. Here I am bringing both types of reaction under the one heading as Patinkin himself tended to do (1967). Moreover, this analysis of the dynamics whereby desired long-run money holdings are reached, presented above, is different from the account offered by Archibald and Lipsey (1958) to which I have already alluded, in their extension to the multi-period case of Patinkin's (1956) analysis of the operation of the real balance effect in the individual experiment. However, these differences reflect the fact that the foregoing analysis has started from the literature on the Demand for Money, rather than that which deals with the integration of Monetary Theory and General Equilibrium Theory. They do not imply that the conclusions which have been stated above about the relationship between monetary adjustments and expenditure flows are in any way misplaced. Thus, we may use the insights yielded by Patinkin's and Archibald and Lipsey's work to illuminate the connection between the individual and market experiments in the analysis of the role of adjustment costs in the demand for money function. This is a matter of considerable importance because, as Patinkin showed, the operation of the real balance effect in the market experiment is very different from its operation in the individual experiment. I now turn to a discussion of these issues.

3. THE MARKET EXPERIMENT WITH EXOGENOUS NOMINAL MONEY

The way in which a market experiment having to do with the demand for money, the real balance effect, and so on, works out must obviously depend on the nature of the market in which it is performed. It is convenient to begin here with the kind of economy analysed by Patinkin (1965, Chs 10 and 11): that is, one in which perfect competition reigns throughout, prices are perfectly flexible, tastes, technology and resource endowments are given and held constant over time, the money supply consists of tokens whose nominal quantity is exogenously given at the beginning of each period, and individual agents face no portfolio adjustment costs. In such a case, one conceivable source of disturbance would be a change in the nominal money supply: given perfect price flexibility (and setting aside distribution effects), the outcome of the operation of the real balance effect in the market experiment would be an *instantaneous* change in the price level. Its effect as far as the demand for money is concerned would be to keep the economy on its *long-run* function.

48   MONETARIST PERSPECTIVES

This does not imply that in empirical work it would be appropriate to substitute the logarithm of actual money supply for m^* on the left-hand side of equation (1), and estimate that relationship as a demand for money function, because, with the money supply exogenous and the price level endogenous, these two variables ought to change places. However, because the price level is endogenous in this economy, so are real balances and it would be appropriate to re-write the long-run demand for money function as

$$m^* - p = f(X) \tag{10}$$

Then, provided there was some exogenous variation over time in the factors included in X, a long-run demand for real balances function could be estimated in this form if m_s was substituted for m^*.

All this is somewhat academic, since we have noted already that the kind of quarterly and annual data which we use in our empirical work on the demand for money will not permit us successfully to estimate such a long-run relationship. We have also noted that it is usual to deal with this problem by adding a lagged dependent variable to the demand function, and that this practice is often defended by referring to the existence of adjustment costs. Suppose that we attempted to introduce these costs into the kind of economy we have briefly described above. Could we account for the presence of a lagged dependent variable in our aggregate demand for money function in these terms? We could not, as I shall now argue. To begin with, recall that equation (3) pictures nominal balances adjusting slowly over time in response to a change in some argument or another of the demand for money function, and note that in the economy I have just described it is the nominal money supply which changes to disturb agents' money holdings, and exogenously at that. In such an economy, where prices are perfectly flexible, individual adjustment costs would have no observable consequences for aggregate behaviour in the face of an exogenous change in the nominal money supply.

The latter assertion seems to fly in the face of certain conclusions which have a well established place in the existing literature of monetary economics. As long ago as 1966 Donald Tucker embedded an aggregate demand for money function, essentially the same as equation (3), in an IS–LM model, and showed that the presence of such an equation in a model of that type implies that at least one of the arguments of the demand for money function overshoots its long-run equilibrium value as an instantaneous response to a change in the money supply. This result is *mathematically* coherent, but it is *logically* incompatible with the existence of the individual adjustment costs on which the presence of a lagged dependent variable in the demand for money function is usually supposed to be based.

To see why, consider how Tucker's result would apply to an economy in which all the arguments of the demand for real balances (X) are held constant (at their 'full employment' levels, perhaps) and in which, therefore, only the price level can adjust to absorb a change in the quantity of money. In such an economy, let the nominal money supply be increased by a certain amount. If there is no lagged dependent variable in the demand for money function, that change in the quantity of money will lead to an equi-proportional change in the price level as a result of the pressure of demand exerted on goods markets as all agents try to restore their cash balances. The algebra here is trivial: from (1), if we postulate that the demand and supply of money are to be in equilibrium, we have

$$m_s = m^* = f(X) + p \qquad (11)$$

and

$$p = m_s - f(X) \qquad (12)$$

so that

$$\partial p / \partial m_s = 1 \qquad (13)$$

Now suppose that we maintain the 'supply and demand for money are in equilibrium' assumption, but add a lagged dependent variable to the demand for money function. When the nominal money supply changes, a *greater than proportional* change in the price level *seems* to be required. From (3) we have

$$p = \frac{1}{b} m_s - f(X) - \frac{1-b}{b} m_{-1} \qquad (14)$$

from which it *seems* to follow that

$$\frac{\partial p}{\partial m_s} = \frac{1}{b} > 1 \qquad (15)$$

This is a very strange result indeed. Faced with portfolio

adjustment costs, the individual experiment tells us that the typical agent in the economy is prepared to take time about getting back to equilibrium, and that he therefore changes his demand for goods by less than he would in the absence of such costs when he receives an addition to his holdings of money. Yet we are asked to believe that the aggregate effect of this *smaller* increase in demand, this *weaker* real balance effect, is to cause the price level to change by a *greater* amount than it otherwise would. The conclusion is obvious nonsense.

The problem here has arisen because we have given the wrong interpretation to the variable m_{-1} in the aggregate demand for money function. The individual experiment which must underlie the market experiment we are discussing here is one in which the typical agent receives a windfall gain in money holdings and sets in motion expenditure which enables him to adjust his money holdings towards their long-run equilibrium level. As we have seen, in this individual experiment it is crucial to distinguish the cash balances the individual agent chose to end up holding at the end of period -1 on the one hand, and those with which he begins the current period on the other, because these two amounts are not the same when the individual's holdings of nominal money are exogenously disturbed. If he faces portfolio adjustment costs, the individual attempts to move his holdings of nominal money part of the way from where they are at the *beginning* of the period to the value given by his long-run demand for money. That is the meaning of equation (6). The individual can always do this, but when the nominal money supply is exogenous, the whole economy can not. In the aggregate, the money which is available to be held must be held.

But does not equation (15) tell us by how much the price level must change in order for the increased stock of nominal money to be held willingly? It does not, and the reason why it does not may be seen by considering equation (6), the individual short-run demand for money function. The aggregate demand for money is, of course, obtained by adding up the latter expression over all individuals in the economy. However, in the experiment we are considering we must substitute the individual's beginning of period money holding for the variable m_{i-1} on the right-hand side of (6). Therefore, the *current period's money supply* rather than the *previous period's aggregate demand for nominal money* ought to be substituted for the variable labelled m_{-1} on the right-hand side of equation (3). If we do this, equation (14) becomes

$$p = \frac{1}{b} m_s - f(X) - \frac{1-b}{b} m_s \qquad (16)$$

which of course reduces to the long-run equation

$$p = m_s - f(X) \qquad (12)$$

so that we have

$$\partial p / \partial m_s = 1 \qquad (13)$$

Thus, the 'overshoot' effect is non-existent, and the economy is always on its long-run demand for money function even in the presence of portfolio adjustment costs.

A similar argument can be mounted against Tucker's (1966) analysis, where output and interest rates, rather than prices, respond to the change in the money supply, and indeed William White (1978, 1981) essentially does just that. I shall return to this point below, but for the moment let it be clear that what is at stake here is not whether Tucker's results follow from the model which he writes down, because they do, but whether the experiments he carried out with his model are compatible with the underlying adjustment lag assumptions used to justify the presence of a lagged dependent variable in the aggregate demand for money function. An alternative motivation for lags in the demand for money function, for example one based upon sluggishness on the part of expectations to respond to experience, in a world in which the demand for money depends upon the expected rather than actual values of the arguments in the function, would be quite consistent with Tucker's market experiment. His results retain their interest even if we quarrel with one set of premises from which they might be derived. The results are in fact very similar (though not identical) to those discussed in Laidler (1968) where the existence of lags in the demand for money function, and elsewhere, is justified, following Friedman (1959), along expectational lines.

The above qualification is of some importance, because a good deal of work on the demand for money function has been devoted to investigating whether or not expectation lags are, in fact, a better explanation of the need to distinguish between a short-run and a long-run demand for money function in our empirical work than are

52   MONETARIST PERSPECTIVES

adjustment lags. Specifically, it is well known that, if we substitute the logarithm of real permanent income y^*, and the logarithm of some interest rate r, for X in equation (1), and generate permanent income according to the log–linear error learning formula

$$y^* - y^*_{-1} = q(y - y^*_{-1}) \qquad (17)$$

then, with the δs being the parameter of the long-run demand for money function, the short-run demand for money function is given by

$$m = q\delta_0 + q\delta_1 y + q\delta_2 r + qp + \\ (1-q)m_{-1} - (1-q)\delta_2 r_{-1} - (1-q)p_{-1} \qquad (18)$$

If this were the true short-run demand for money relationship, we would need to posit no adjustment lags in the individual experiment; agents could always be thought of as holding just the quantity of money they desired, and the long-run–short-run distinction, upon which successful empirical work seems to depend, would hinge upon discrepancies between current and permanent income.

However, it does not seem possible to defend the proposition that (18) is the true form of the demand for money function in the face of available empirical evidence, even though Feige's (1967) seminal paper on this subject seemed to show that it was. To begin with, Feige used annual data and did not rule out the possibility that quarterly data might reveal a role for adjustment lags. Subsequent work with quarterly data does seem to show that they have a role to play even in the presence of expectation lags, or at least Laidler and Parkin (1970) claimed that this was the case for the United Kingdom. Stephen Goldfeld (1973) went further and concluded that a lag structure of the type captured in equation (3) left nothing for expectations lags to explain in the context of recent United States quarterly data. Furthermore, with similar data, also for the United States, Laidler (1980) found that equation (18) systematically performed worse than an adjustment lag formulation of the function (though not of quite the same form as Goldfeld's, as we shall see in a moment). He found that this result held up with annual data too. Moreover, none of this is to mention that recent work on the notion of Rational Expectations must imply that equation (17) is a very dubious formulation of the relationship between permanent income and current income.

In short, appealing though the expectations lag hypothesis is as a solution to the problem of linking individual and market experiments

ON THE DEMAND FOR MONEY   53

while maintaining the distinction between the short- and long-run demand for money functions, the empirical evidence in favour of this solution is weak. Equations like (3) do fit the data rather well, but if that was because they were really good approximations to equation (18), then the latter would fit even better; and it does not do so on any systematic basis. However, this does not alter the fact that, in an exogenous money supply world, portfolio adjustment costs cannot be used to motivate the long-run–short-run demand for money distinction.

There is yet a third explanation of the presence of the lagged dependent variable in the aggregate demand for money relationship to be found in the literature on the demand for money. The explanation involves the 'real' (as opposed to 'nominal') adjustment model of the short-run demand for money. The model is usually written in the following way:

$$m-p = bf(X)+(1-b)(m_{-1}-p_{-1}) \qquad (19)$$

It is then estimated on the assumption that $m_s = m$. By way of comparison, consider equation (3) once more and substract from both sides of it the logarithm of the current value of the general price level. This yields an expression which differs from equation (19) only in the timing of the value of the price level observation by which lagged nominal balances are deflated.

$$m-p = bf(X)+(1-b)(m_{-1}-p) \qquad (20)$$

With this equation too, for empirical purposes the money supply is substituted for the quantity of money demanded. Clearly, if one of these expressions fits a particular data set well, so will the other, unless the price level series is extremely erratic; but in practice the series is highly autocorrelated. It was this real adjustment form of the function which Laidler (1980) found to fit better than that derived from an expectations lag, and in this study it also turned out that the real adjustment form performed better than its nominal counterpart, in the sense of providing an estimate of $(1-b)$ that was less than unity. Benjamin Friedman (1977) also obtained this result.

At the level of the individual experiment, the 'real' adjustment notion is, to say the least, decidedly odd. To apply it to the individual experiment is to argue that, if the general price level varies, the typical agent will instantaneously adjust his nominal balances in order to keep his real money holdings constant, but that

54   MONETARIST PERSPECTIVES

a change in any other argument of the long-run function will meet
with a lagged response. The price level is quite as exogenous as any
other variable in the individual experiment, and any adjustment of
real balances must involve the agent acquiring or running down
nominal balances. It is therefore hard to see why this should be the
case. However, when it comes to the market experiment, equation
(19) perhaps makes more sense, because it tells us that real
balances, rather than exogenous nominal balances, adjust slowly to
any disturbance. As we have already noted, real balances are
endogenous at the level of the market experiment even when
nominal balances are not, and Alan Walters suggested as long ago
as 1965 that an equation like (19) might be interpreted as a price
level adjustment equation in an economy where nominal balances
are exogenous.

In fact equation (19) is not quite accurately specified as a price
level adjustment equation, as I shall now show. If we have, as our
aggregate demand for money function,

$$m^* = f(X) + p \qquad (1)$$

then with an exogenously given money supply, the equilibrium
value for the price level p^* is given by

$$p^* = m_s - f(X) \qquad (21)$$

Suppose that, for some reason, the structure of the economy was
such that the price level moves slowly over time towards equilibrium according to

$$p - p_{-1} = b(p^* - p_{-1}) \qquad (22)$$

Then, substitution of (22) into (21), and the addition of m_s to both
sides of the equation, yields, with a little rearrangement,

$$m_s - p = bf(X) + (1 - b)(m_s - p_{-1}) \qquad (23)$$

This expression is very like both (19) and (20), and if it was in fact
the true relationship describing the way in which the money supply
and the arguments of the demand for money function interact over
time, one would expect that the other two relationships would
display considerable explanatory power as well. Indeed, economet-
rically speaking, if the 'true' relationship was

$$m_s - p = bf(X) + (1 - b)(m_s - p_{-1}) + \varepsilon \qquad (24)$$

then this would imply, for the 'real' adjustment model when m_s is substituted for m,

$$m_s - p = bf(X) + (1-b)(m_{s_{-1}} - p_{-1}) + u \tag{25}$$

where

$$u = \varepsilon + (1-b)\Delta m_s \tag{26}$$

and for the 'nominal' adjustment model

$$m_s - p = bf(X) + (1-b)(m_{s_{-1}} - p) + \eta \tag{27}$$

where

$$\eta = \varepsilon + (1-b)\Delta(m_s - p) \tag{28}$$

The importance of the presence of lagged dependent variables in empirical work on the aggregate demand for money function can then be explained in terms of price level stickiness, and this seems to me to be the best available explanation. The portfolio adjustment cost explanation is logically invalid, as we have seen, and the expectations lag explanation does not consistently stand up to empirical testing. However, if this conclusion is accepted, other problems immediately arise, problems which imply that attempts to bring empirical evidence to bear on this issue simply by attempting to fit equations (24), (25) and (27) to data would be unsatisfactory.

If the price level is sticky, then macroeconomics tells us that such variables as interest rates and real income will tend to change as the money market attempts to clear itself, but these are exactly the variables that one might expect to find in the vector (X). This in turn means that the use of single equation econometric techniques to estimate relationships such as (19), (20) or (23) in an economy where the nominal money supply is believed to be exogenous, is at the very least open to criticism for ignoring simultaneity problems. Jonson (1967a) has much to say about this matter in arguing that the demand for money function is best estimated as part of a complete macro system, rather than in isolation, and Cooley and Leroy (1981) have recently raised related issues in discussing the identifiability of the demand for money function.

Econometric questions are undoubtedly important, and it is not my intention to belittle them in any way when I say that, nevertheless, they are not central to the issues which I am attempting to tackle in this paper. The latter are economic in nature. I have shown in the last few pages that adjustment costs at the level of the individual demand for money experiment will produce no observable consequences at the level of the market experiment in an economy in which the nominal money supply is exogenous to the arguments of the demand for money function. It follows from this conclusion that there is something badly wrong with our habit of motivating the long-run–short-run demand for money distinction in terms of the existence of such adjustment costs. Nevertheless, we seem to need this distinction if we are to deal with a wide variety of real-world data on the determinants of money holding in a more or less satisfactory way.

I have argued that the best way out of this impasse is to interpret the typical short-run demand for money function as a slightly mis-specified price level adjustment equation. If this suggestion is accepted, it follows that the equation which we call a 'short-run demand for money function' is not a structural relationship at all, but a mixture of structural relationship (the long-run demand for money function whose parameters may or may not be being properly estimated if we use single equation techniques) and some reduced form of the whole economy. In particular, the adjustment parameter b must be interpreted as encapsulating the workings of those mechanisms whereby the price level moves slowly towards equilibrium after a monetary disturbance.

The fact that the adjustment speeds which are typically discovered in studies of the aggregate demand for money are very slow – it is not uncommon for money holdings to appear to move less than half way towards their long-run value within a year – has often puzzled monetary economists; but in the light of the above arguments, this fact would appear to tell us that sluggish price adjustment is an important fact of real-world economic life. This in turn means that the real balance effect is not just a factor which causes prices to change in some 'meta-time' when markets are clearing along Walrasian lines, but is an important empirical phenomenon underlying the generation of real-world data.

This conclusion might at first sight seem implausible, because it implies that the supply and demand for money can remain out of equilibrium for rather long periods of time, while the notion that the money market clears quickly is a commonplace of elementary macroeconomics. It is one thing to argue, however, that it is easy for the individual agent to rid himself of (or to acquire) cash, and quite another thing to argue that the economy as a whole can do so. In the latter case, as I have already pointed out, if the nominal money supply is exogenous, then any adjustment to the stock of real balances requires a price level change.

More to the point, even though, in the presence of price level stickiness, it is *possible* that the rate of interest can move to equate the supply and demand for money, it does not follow that this will in fact happen. In the standard classroom exposition of what Chick (1973, Ch. 3) has so aptly called the 'pseudodynamics of IS–LM', it is true that a change in the quantity of money is portrayed as causing a change in the rate of interest sufficiently large to keep the supply and demand for money in equilibrium, with changes in income and prices coming later. Nevertheless, there is no empirical basis for the proposition that in the real world the interest rate change in question is sufficient to establish money market equilibrium. All that is required to get the so-called 'transmission mechanism' to start working is that a change in the quantity of money move the interest rate away from a value which equates saving and investment at the current level of income, and not that the interest rate should attain a value which will equate the supply and demand for money. In any event, as White (1978, 1981) argues, interest rate changes are every bit as exogenous to money holders as price level changes. If the real world did indeed work as the above-mentioned 'pseudodynamics' suggest, we would never observe anything but a 'long-run' demand for money function. Hence this particular piece of analysis seems to be incompatible with the facts. However, this conclusion holds only for an economy in which the nominal money supply is determined independently of the demand for nominal money. As we shall now see, matters are more complex if the money supply is endogenous.

4. A DIGRESSION CONCERNING ENDOGENOUS NOMINAL MONEY

The arguments developed in the last few pages apply to an economy in which the nominal money supply is exogenous to the variables which determine the demand for it. It is sometimes suggested that, in many economies, not least in the United States and the United Kingdom, the actual conduct of policy in recent years has been such

58   MONETARIST PERSPECTIVES

as to make it appropriate to think of the nominal money supply as responding passively to demand side factors in a manner which is reasonably captured by a nominal adjustment version of the short-run demand for money function similar to equation (3) or (20). That view is defended in the following way. Whatever changes there may or may not have been in the targets and indicators of monetary policy in the post-war period, its instruments have consistently been interest rates. The monetary authority has attempted to achieve whatever may have been its ends by standing ready to buy and sell securities at a price which, although not necessarily constant over time, is exogenously given at any moment. If over any reasonably short period – say a quarter – real income and prices may be regarded as predetermined, and if the monetary authority, and hence the banking system, stands ready to buy and sell securities at a given price, then there is no obstacle in the way of the economy as a whole adjusting its nominal money holdings towards a desired level at a pace of its own choosing. Given this view of the money supply process, equation (3) is sometimes defended as an appropriate and correctly specified tool for investigating the demand for money.

The argument just presented seems to me to be fallacious, or at least too simple. It rests upon a version of what Brunner and Meltzer (e.g. 1976) have termed the 'money market hypothesis' of the generation of the money supply, adapted to a situation in which the interest rate is the policy instrument; and they have argued that this hypothesis, though widely accepted, is crucially deficient. What Brunner and Meltzer term the 'credit market' hypothesis differs from it in correctly insisting that the non-bank public's supply of securities to the banking system is not simply the mirror image of its demand for the liabilities of that system. This is because the non-bank public also holds income-earning assets of a type distinct from those which it supplies to the banks when it borrows from them. It is convenient (but not logically necessary) to think of this third asset as reproducible physical capital. To see the significance of this characteristic of the credit market hypothesis for the issues under discussion here, it is helpful to begin with a situation of full portfolio equilibrium on the part of the banking system and the non-bank public, and then ask what happens, according to the two hypotheses, when the monetary authorities raise the price at which they are willing to buy securities.

ON THE DEMAND FOR MONEY   59

The 'money market' hypothesis implies that the public will want to hold more cash balances, and will attempt to acquire them by offering securities to the banking system. It also tells us that any influence on output and prices will come later as a consequence of the effect of the lower interest rate on the level of aggregate demand for goods and services; and that, as output and price level changes materialise, more money will be forthcoming from the banking system as the public demands it. In short, the nominal stock of money will passively adjust to changes in the arguments of the demand function. If the money market hypothesis is true, nominal money will be just as much an endogenous variable in the market experiment as in the individual experiment, and equation (3) might indeed be an appropriate formulation.

The 'credit market' hypothesis leads one to tell a different story. Certainly a rise in security prices will lead the public to attempt to increase money holdings, but it will also, according to this hypothesis, lead agents to attempt to substitute physical capital for securities. In the market experiment, the whole of the non-bank public will try to make such a substitution, and the trick can only be accomplished by selling securities to the banks and taking the proceeds to buy physical capital – but of course the proceeds of such a sale of securities take the form of money, newly created, not because the non-bank public as a whole wants to hold it, but because each individual member of that public wants to use money to offer in exchange for capital. Once created, that money must be held, but its creation will coincide with, or even precede, the setting in motion of streams of expenditure which in turn will have consequences for the other arguments of the demand for money function, namely output and prices.

Eventually, the economy will end up with new long-run levels of income, prices, money holdings and so on, which may differ little from those which would be predicted by a model which ignored the distinction between securities and physical capital. However, we are here concerned with short-run adjustment, with the *process* whereby this equilibrium is approached, and that is critically different. It involves excess money operating upon expenditure flows which tend to force the arguments of the demand for money function to move towards new values; that is to say, it involves real balance effects. This is not to deny that money will also be created and extinguished in such a world in response to changes in the arguments of the demand for money function and in that sense be endogenous, but it is to argue that cause and effect will not run in the simple one-way manner from other variables to money which would be implied by the money market hypothesis, and which would justify equation (3) as a basis for empirical work.

The foregoing arguments fail to touch on yet another reason for not treating the nominal money supply as merely passively responding to the behaviour of the arguments of the demand for money function, even when the monetary authorities treat the interest rate as their principal policy instrument, namely that it is not only the extension of credit to the private sector, but also to the fiscal authorities, which leads to the creation of money. Even if, at a particular rate of interest, the values of income, prices, the rate of return on capital and so on are such as to render the supply of money and bank credit compatible with portfolio equilibrium on the part of the banking system and the non-bank public, that in no way guarantees either that the fiscal authorities' budget is in balance, or that, if it is not, the private sector will be willing to absorb just the right number of new government bonds to finance whatever deficit is being incurred. A fiscal deficit can therefore become an independent source of monetary expansion when the monetary authorities are treating the interest rate as their policy instrument. Once again, cause and effect will run from money creation to variations in the arguments of the demand for money function as well as *vice versa*, and real balance effects will be at work in influencing the outcome of any market experiment.

Closely related to the matters which I have just discussed are considerations having to do with the linkages between the balance of payments and the nominal money supply in an open economy operating a fixed exchange rate. It is true that the balance of payments can provide a channel whereby the nominal money supply will passively adjust to exogenous changes in the arguments in the demand for money function, and that, in a sample of data in which the only, or to put it more practically the major, source of money market disturbance lies in exogenous changes in those arguments, an equation such as (3) might be found to fit the data. In such a case, the parameter b would not be capturing the effects of adjustment costs which face individual agents attempting to re-arrange their portfolios; rather it would be summarising, in one statistic, the structure of the economy's balance of payments mechanism, and in particular the influence of real balance effects on that mechanism. This, however, is only part of the point. In a fixed exchange rate open economy, domestic monetary policy can obviously be an independent source of short-run disturbance to the domestic money market, while any shocks originating in the world economy which have balance of payments side effects can also lead to changes in the money supply which are exogenous to the arguments of the demand function. To say that, in such an economy, the nominal money supply is endogenous, is to say that variation in the nominal money supply is one equilibrating factor at work in the system. To this extent, the monetary behaviour of a fixed exchange rate open economy is different from that of the textbook closed-economy-with-an-exogenous-money-supply model, which we considered in the previous section of this essay; but the fact of long-run endogeneity of the nominal money supply stops far short of establishing the general validity of modelling the short-run demand for money along the conventional partial stock adjustment lines embodied in equation (3).

As to the flexible exchange rate case, here we are back to a system which is similar to the closed economy model, at least as far as the relationship between the factors governing the supply of money and the arguments of the demand for money function are concerned. Though the transmission mechanism for the effects of monetary changes to the price level may differ in this case from that to be found in a closed economy (see Essay 4, pp. 148–9, below), it is nevertheless that transmission mechanism, and not simply the portfolio adjustment costs facing individual agents, which must underlie any short-run deviation of actual money holdings and those predicted by the long-run demand for money function.

5. CONCLUSIONS

The arguments presented in this essay have been rather taxonomic, but it is nevertheless possible to draw certain general conclusions from them, conclusions which in their turn yield important implications about our empirical knowledge of the properties of the demand for money function in particular and of the macroeconomy in general. The basic purpose of this essay has been to argue that the simple portfolio adjustment cost model, on which the distinction between the short-run and long-run demand for money hinges in the individual experiment, will not do to motivate that same distinction at the level of the economy as a whole. In an economy in which the nominal money supply is exogenous, it is possible for the individual agent to change his holdings of real balances by adjusting his holdings of nominal money; but the whole economy can only accomplish this by changing the general price level. If such an economy is kept 'off' its long-run demand for money function by adjustment costs, and the data seem to tell us that this is a pervasive phenomenon, then I have argued that the relevant costs are those of changing prices, not those involved in portfolio adjustment.

I have nevertheless argued that, for an economy in which it is believed that the nominal money supply is exogenous to the variables determining the demand for money, various widely used forms of the 'short-run' demand for money function *might* deal adequately with the data. They will do so if the complex transmission mechanism, which lies between money and prices, happens to be such that its dynamics can be captured in that single parameter b; if the simultaneity problems, which must arise here in principle, turn out to be unimportant in practice; and if the money supply and the price level are sufficiently highly autocorrelated that the mis-specifications involved in using the 'wrong' lagged dependent variable (cf. equations (19), (20) and (23)) are also unimportant.

In the case of economies in which the nominal money supply might reasonably be thought of as sometimes adjusting to the arguments of the demand for money function, rather than *vice versa*, either because of the way in which monetary policy is conducted, or because of the exchange rate regime, the above argument cannot be made as a general proposition. In such economies, whether nominal money does in fact predominantly adjust to demand side factors, or *vice versa*, depends upon the nature of the shocks to which the economy is being subjected. Even here though, where the shocks in question are such that the nominal money supply is a passively adjusting variable, any slowness on the part of the economy to get back 'on' its long-run demand for money function, after being driven 'off' it, will not simply be a matter of the adjustment costs facing individual money holders. Instead, it will involve the operations of the financial system, and perhaps of the balance of payments mechanism as well.

All this implies that the adjustment parameter b, which in empirical work on the aggregate demand for money plays such an important role in enabling us to get 'satisfactory' econometric results, must in general be thought of as summarising the dynamics of a good part of the economic system, and not merely the structural dynamics of the demand for money function itself. In the market experiment, a demand for money function which contains a lagged dependent variable can only be interpreted as being a structural relationship in and of itself if the presence of that variable is justified in terms of expectations lags; and as I have argued, such a justification is hard to sustain as the whole story – though it may be an important component of the story – in the face of available empirical evidence.

The question must arise as to what we are to make of all the empirical evidence which we have on the demand for money function in the light of the foregoing arguments. First, it must not be forgotten that there have been studies of the aggregate demand for money, using long time period samples, and/or data with a high degree of time aggregation, which have not invoked the 'short-run–long-run' distinction, and which have generated more or less satisfactory results (e.g. Friedman 1959, Meltzer 1963, Laidler 1966). Second, and this is important, the vast majority of studies of the 'short-run' demand for money *have* produced implicit estimates of the parameters of the 'long-run' relationship which are reasonably consistent with those derived from the studies just cited. On this basis, I am inclined to argue that, although the interpretation of short-run dynamics which has usually accompanied studies of the short-run demand for money is inappropriate and misleading, nevertheless, for most of the data which have been used, the practice of adding a lagged dependent variable to the function, crude and arbitrary though it is, has turned out to be an adequate way of allowing for the fact that the economy is not always in long-run equilibrium when we observe it.

The above argument presents a conjecture, not a well established truth, and it should not lead anyone to conclude that all is well with our empirical knowledge of the demand for money function. In order to find out whether the argument is true, we would have to construct explicit macroeconomic models, which permit the economy in general and the money market in particular, to deviate from long-run equilibrium; and then explicitly investigate the relationship between the structure of those models and the functional forms which typically have been fitted in studies of the short-run demand for money. The parameter b, it has been argued above, is a 'black box' parameter which summarises what we may loosely refer to as the dynamics of the real balance effect, and we do not currently know just what is buried in it.

A number of writers, notably Jonson (1967a) and Mervyn Lewis (1978) have noted that those samples of data that seem to give us the most trouble, as far as finding a stable demand for money function is concerned, are drawn from times and places where the monetary system has been subjected to particularly large shocks, for example the United Kingdom or the United States in the 1970s. They have speculated that the difficulties involved here have stemmed from inadequacy in our modelling of the dynamics of the monetary system. That too is a conjecture, but it is one which follows naturally from the arguments advanced in this paper, and it too could be investigated by carrying out the type of experiment suggested above. The work of Jonson and his associates, which builds upon that of Bergstrom and Wymer (1974), has involved the construction of complete econometric models in which expenditure flows of various sorts are explicitly modelled as responding to real balance effects (see e.g. Jonson 1976b, Jonson, Moses and Wymer 1976, Jonson and Trevor 1980) and could provide a framework in terms of which such an investigation could be carried out.

Be that as it may, the arguments which I have advanced imply a severe criticism of much econometric modelling of the conventional post-Keynesian sort. For example, in the FMP model of the United States economy as described by Modigliani and Ando (1976), a demand for money function complete with lagged dependent variable is estimated independently of the rest of the system, and is treated as a structural relationship to be included in the model, which is then put through all manner of simulation exercises. If the coefficient of the lagged dependent variable of that demand for money function is in fact capturing, in some approximate and unspecified fashion, aspects of the dynamic behaviour of the economy as a whole, then to treat the relevant function as if it were a structural relationship, and to use it in complete model simulation exercises, is inappropriate. When this is done, the economy's structure is being utilised twice, once in 'black box' form in the coefficient of the lagged dependent variable in the demand for money function, and once explicitly in terms of the rest of the model. This criticism, which of course applies to far more pieces of work than the FMP model, is in fact a variation on the argument advanced above when we commented on the incompatibility of Tucker's (1966) model with the adjustment lag hypothesis so often used to motivate its structure. There is no need, therefore, to repeat it here in any detail; enough has already been said to make the seriousness of its implications for much of our econometric work quite obvious.

The basic conclusion to be drawn from the arguments of this essay is very simple. In treating money as if it were just another durable good in our empirical work on the aggregate demand for money, we have overlooked the critical distinction between the individual and market experiments which Patinkin made so clearly in his theoretical work on the real balance effect. In doing so, we have used reasoning which should only be applied to the individual experiment when dealing with the market experiment. As a result, much of our empirical work on the demand for money, particularly on the 'short-run' relationship, has no proper theoretical basis in terms of which it can be interpreted, and our knowledge of that relationship is therefore much less robust than we might have thought. We do, already, have the basic tools with which we can set about remedying this state of affairs in the shape of those pioneering macro models which explicitly try to get to grips with the dynamics of real balance effects, but the work of developing those models and applying them to the issues raised here has only just begun.

[14]

Excerpt from B. Friedman (1988), 'Lessons on Monetary Policy from the 1980s', *Journal of Economic Perspectives*, **2** (3), Summer, 57–64

Collapse of the Money-Income and Money-Price Relationships

What makes this unusual record of monetary policy actions look so successful in retrospect is that the bizarre behavior of money growth in no way corresponded to the behavior of income or prices. The familiar relationships that had characterized prior experience simply disappeared.

Instabilities in the money-income relationship—or, in more sophisticated forms, the money demand function—had actually begun to become more pronounced as early as the mid-1970s, and their appearance had already spawned a substantial new body of empirical literature even before the new monetary policy experiment commenced in October 1979.[7] By 1980 the Federal Reserve System had already adopted a whole new set of definitions of the monetary aggregates, designed in part to overcome just such difficulties. A survey paper bearing the suggestive title "The Search for a Stable Money Demand Function: A Survey of the Post-1973 Literature," and including more than eighty references, was already in print in the *Journal of Economic Literature* before Paul Volcker acknowledged in October 1982 that the Federal Reserve was suspending its $M1$ growth target (Judd and Scadding, 1982.)

As Figure 2 makes clear, however, the instability that generated so much concern and research in the pre-1982 period was small stuff in comparison to what followed.

---

[7]The standard reference to state first is the contrast between the findings in Goldfeld (1973) and Goldfeld (1976). The most widely read studies done at the time by the Federal Reserve's own staff include Enzler *et al.* (1976), Porter *et al.* (1979), and Simpson and Porter (1980).

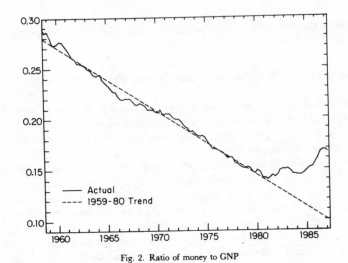

Fig. 2. Ratio of money to GNP

Note: The series plotted is the ratio of $M1$, as a quarterly average of monthly data (source: Board of Governors of the Federal Reserve System) to quarterly GNP at annual rates (source: U.S. Department of Commerce). Both series are seasonally adjusted.

The figure plots the ratio of the $M1$ money stock to GNP for each quarter since the start of the redefined $M1$ series in 1959:$Q1$. Through the end of 1980, the $M1$-to-GNP ratio displayed the familiar downward trend of roughly 3 percent per annum that most students of the money-income relationship had come to see as inevitable in the post-war period, with a standard deviation around this trend of only .0044 (in comparison to a 1980:$Q4$ value of .1466). After 1980 the $M1$-to-GNP ratio not only experienced wider fluctuations but even reversed course. A simple extrapolation of the 1959-80 trend implies a ratio of .1007 by 1987:$Q2$ (the last quarter plotted). The actual value in 1987:$Q2$ was .1686, different from the trend extrapolation by more than 15 times the 1959-80 standard deviation.

Discussion of this phenomenon at the popular level has typically offered as an explanation the fact that "velocity" has declined. Because the so-called income velocity of money is nothing other than the ratio of GNP to money (the reciprocal of the ratio plotted in Figure 2), however, such explanations are completely empty of content. Given the definition of "velocity" in this context, the fact that velocity declined is simply identical to the fact that money grew rapidly while income did not. Saying that money growth outpaced income growth because velocity declined is like saying that the sun rose because it was morning.[8]

[8]I owe the analogy to William Bennett.

The mere fact of instability in the simple money-income ratio need not, of course, imply instability in more fully specified behavioral representations of the money-income relationship. The impression that stands out on a first glance at Figure 2 is representative of the results that researchers employing a variety of statistical strategies have found, however. A standard Goldfeld-type money demand function, estimated for quarterly data spanning 1952:$Q$3–1979:$Q$3, indicates a standard error of .42 percent. Extending the sample to 1986:$Q$4 raises the standard error to .61 percent. Deleting the earlier data, so that the sample is 1974:$Q$2–1986:$Q$4, further raises the standard error to .84 percent. Dynamic out-of-sample simulations of such equations deliver cumulative errors with root mean squares in the range of 4-8 percent for different parts of the post-1982 period, in comparison with 0.5–1.5 percent for different parts of the pre-1974 period. Attempts to do better with alternative specifications have met at best only very limited success.[9]

The story is approximately the same for efforts to investigate the money-income relationship from the perspective of determining income rather than money. A "St. Louis" type equation relating nominal GNP to four-quarter lags on both $M$1 and high-employment government expenditures, estimated in logarithmic differences for quarterly data spanning 1960:$Q$1–1979:$Q$3, indicates an adjusted coefficient of determination ($\bar{R}^2$) of .32. Extending the sample to 1986:$Q$4 reduces the $\bar{R}^2$ to .11. Deleting the earlier data, so that the sample is 1970:$Q$3-1986:$Q$4, further reduces the $\bar{R}^2$ to just .02. More sophisticated autoregression methods testing for a significant role of money in "causing" either nominal or real income, in the sense of accounting for income fluctuations not already accounted for by prior fluctuations in income itself, have produced results that are sufficiently varied to generate more skepticism than confidence in any strong conclusion on the subject, either positive or negative.[10]

Finally, in considering the money-*price* relationship it is even necessary to be on guard against results that are strongly statistically significant but with the wrong sign to make any sense in economic terms. The double-digit average growth rate maintained for five years following mid-1982 represents the most rapid sustained money growth the United States has experienced since World War II, yet these same years also saw the strongest sustained deceleration of prices in the postwar period (see again Figure 1). Price inflation as measured by the GNP deflator peaked at 9.7 percent in 1981 and declined in each of the next five years, reaching 2.6 percent in 1986. The rate of increase of consumer prices peaked at 13.3 percent in 1979 and declined in all but one of the next seven years, reaching 1.1 percent in 1986. Given the role that high-variance observations play in dominating results based on the least-squares methodology, as of the late 1980s it is necessary to take care not to find results indicating that *faster* money growth implies *slower* inflation.

[9] The specific results cited here are from Goldfeld and Sichel (forthcoming), which also provides an extensive survey. Roley (1985) also showed the results of experimenting with a wide variety of alternative specifications.

[10] See, for example, the differing results reported in Friedman (1986), Eichenbaum and Singleton (1986), and Stock and Watson (1987).

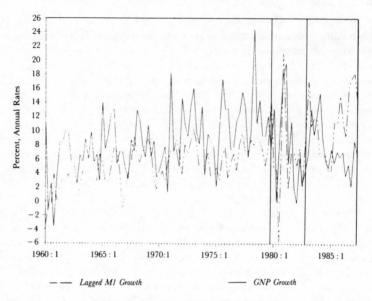

Fig. 3. Growth rates of GNP and lagged money

Two examples, both drawn from the same paper, readily illustrate the pitfalls that confronted anyone who continued to rely closely on straightforward money-income and money-price relationships during this period. First, Figure 3 is an expansion, both backward in time and forward, of a figure included in a paper by Milton Friedman (1984) in the *American Economic Review*. The figure plots the respective annualized quarter-to-quarter growth rates of GNP and, with a one-quarter lag, $M1$. The figure covers 1960:$Q1$–1987:$Q2$ and distinguishes three time intervals. The middle one, 1979:$Q4$–1983:$Q4$, is identical to that plotted by Friedman. It spans the period from the October 1979 inception of the new monetary policy experiment through what was presumably the most recent observation available as of his time of writing.

After pointing out that the correlation between these two series during 1979:$Q4$–1983:$Q4$ was .46, or .71 after eliminating the two quarters affected by the credit control episode, Friedman wrote, "Two things are notable about the relation between money and income in these years: first, the lag is both shorter on the average and less variable than in earlier years, second, the relation is unusually close. I believe that both are a consequence of the exceptionally large fluctuations in $M1$ growth. The effect was to enhance the importance of the monetary changes relative to the numerous other factors affecting nominal income and thereby to speed up and render more consistent the reaction."

Table 1 summarizes the record of the GNP-to-lagged-$M1$ growth correlation and the variability of $M1$ growth for the three intervals shown in Figure 3. Money growth on a quarter-to-quarter basis (as used by Friedman in his paper) was certainly more

Table 1

Money growth volatility and the GNP-to-lagged-M1 correlation, 1960–1987

Sample	Standard deviation of M1 growth	Correlation between GNP growth and lagged M1 growth
1960:$Q$1–1979:$Q$3	2.87%	.47
1979:$Q$4–1983:$Q$4	6.16	.45
1979:$Q$4–1980:$Q$1, 1980:$Q$4–1983:$Q$4	4.18	.47
1984:$Q$1–1987:$Q$2	4.80	– .10

Data are seasonally adjusted at annual rates. Money data are quarterly averages.

variable during 1979:$Q$4–1983:$Q$4 than it had been during the prior two decades. The GNP-to-lagged-$M$1 correlation was not "unusually close" during 1979:$Q$4– 1983:$Q$4 compared to the past, however. The correlation of .45 computed over these eleven quarters (Friedman reported .46) is essentially identical to that for the previous 79 quarters. Excluding 1980:$Q$2 and 1980:$Q$3 reduces the variability of money growth, but does not materially affect the GNP-to-lagged money correlation. (Subsequent data revisions have reduced the .71 correlation reported by Friedman to .47 as shown in Table 1—identical to the correlation for the earlier period.)

More importantly, what stands out in both Table 1 and Figure 3 is the changes that occurred after 1983. Although the variability of money growth remained high, the positive GNP-to-lagged-$M$1 correlation disappeared entirely. In its place is a small *negative* correlation.

Table 2, focusing on the money-price relationship, is simply an updated version of a table that Friedman presented in the same 1984 paper. The horizontal line in each column indicates entries not included in the original version. In describing the data shown above the two lines, Friedman wrote, "The long-period evidence suggests that inflation has much inertia and that the lag between money and inflation is of the order of two years. Table [2] shows that this relation has held in recent years as well. There is a one-to-one relation between movements in monetary growth, and in the GNP deflator two years later over successive two-year periods since 1971... The increased rate of monetary growth in the 1981-83 biennium suggests that we have passed the trough in inflation and that inflation will be decidedly higher from 1983 to 1985 than it was from 1981 to 1983."[11]

[11]Friedman made the some prediction more forcefully in writings directed at broader audiences. In a column in the September 26, 1983 issue of *Newsweek*, for example, Friedman wrote, "Inflation has not yet accelerated. That will come next year, since it generally takes about two years for monetary acceleration to work its way through to inflation...The monetary explosion from July 1982 to July 1983 leaves no satisfactory way out of our present situation...The result is bound to be renewed stagflation—recession accompanied by *rising* inflation and high interest rates." A lengthy interview in the March 19, 1984, issue of *Fortune* indicated that Friedman "...also sees a strong possibility that by the end of [1984] inflation could reach an annual rate as high as 9%."

Table 2
Rates of change in money and in inflation eight quarters later

| Period for money | Annual rate of change over eight quarters | | Period for deflator |
	$M1$	Deflator eight quarters later	
1971:$Q$3–1973:$Q$3	6.9%	9.5%	1973:$Q$3–1975:$Q$3
1973:$Q$3–1975:$Q$3	5.2	6.3	1975:$Q$3–1977:$Q$3
1975:$Q$3–1977:$Q$3	6.4	8.3	1977:$Q$3–1979:$Q$3
1977:$Q$3–1979:$Q$3	8.6	9.4	1979:$Q$3–1981:$Q$3
1979:$Q$3–1981:$Q$3	6.1	4.8	1981:$Q$3–1983:$Q$3
1981:$Q$3–1983:$Q$3	9.2	3.3	1983:$Q$3–1985:$Q$3
1983:$Q$3–1985:$Q$3	8.1	2.8	1985:$Q$3–1987:$Q$3

Data are seasonally adjusted.
Source: Friedman (1984), updated. (The entries above the lines differ from Friedman's because of subsequent data revisions, but the differences are slight.)

As the below-the-line entries in Table 2 show, quite the opposite happened. Growth of $M1$ during 1981:$Q$3–1983:$Q$3 was the fastest for any of the six biennia in Friedman's sample, but inflation in 1983:$Q$3–1985:$Q$3 turned out to be the lowest. Rapid money growth continued in 1983:$Q$3–1985:$Q$3, but inflation slowed still further in 1985:$Q$3–1987:$Q$3. The simple correlation between the two time series shown, calculated for the first five observations only, is .70. Calculated for all seven observations, the correlation is *minus* .23.

Other Money and Credit Aggregates

The breakdown of long-standing relationships to income and prices has not been confined to the $M1$ money measure. Neither $M2$ nor $M3$, nor the monetary base, nor the total debt of domestic nonfinancial borrowers has displayed a consistent relationship to nominal income growth or to inflation during this period. On a quarter-to-quarter basis, standard relationships like Goldfeld-type equations fitting movements in these aggregates to movements of income and interest rates, or St. Louis-type equations fitting movements of nominal income to movements of an aggregate and a measure of fiscal policy, showed pronounced deterioration for each of these aggregates. (The *largest* $\bar{R}^2$ for any of these St. Louis equations, estimated for quarterly data spanning 1970:$Q$3–1986:$Q$4, is .09.) On a longer-term basis, the average growth rate for each of these aggregates during the half-decade from mid-1982 to mid-1987 was in excess of any prior postwar experience; yet inflation lessened substantially, and the average growth of nominal income was hardly extraordinary. By mid-1987 the ratio of each aggregate to nominal GNP was above the level implied by an extrapolation of the corresponding pre-1980 trend by an amount ranging from three standard deviations (for $M2$) to twenty-three (for the credit aggregate), based on the pre-1980 variability. It is difficult to imagine how anyone could have successfully predicted the behavior of either income or prices during this period on the basis of foreknowledge of the path of any—or, for that matter, all—of these aggregates.

The manifest failure of the credit aggregate to perform satisfactorily in this context perhaps merits a special comment. I had earlier advocated the use of a broad credit aggregate in conjunction with one or more monetary aggregates in formulating U.S. monetary policy, precisely on the ground that credit might provide some safeguard against false signals given by the monetary aggregates under conditions of instability affecting the public's demand for money (see, for example, Friedman, 1982, 1983). Because credit is a measure of activity on the liability side of the public's balance sheet, while the monetary aggregates are various measures of the non-bank public's assets, it seemed (and to me still seems) reasonable to think that expanding the information base explicitly underlying the monetary policy process to encompass both money and credit measures would provide potentially useful diversification in the context of portfolio behavior that is at best imperfectly understood, and inevitably subject to a multiplicity of shocks. In addition, empirical investigations relying on a variety of statistical methods indicated little basis for concluding that the total debt of all domestic nonfinancial borrowers was any less (or any more) closely related to movements of income or prices than was any of the standard monetary aggregates.[12]

In any event, the movement of credit during the post-1982 period bore no more relation to income or prices than did that of any of the monetary aggregates. Worse still, the false signals provided by the growth of credit were in the same direction as those provided by the growth of money. Figure 4 plots the credit-to-GNP ratio for the same sample for which Figure 2 shows the $M1$-to-GNP ratio. After decades of trendless stability, the credit ratio began an unprecedented climb in 1982 which has not stopped as of the time of writing. Moreover, disaggregated data show that essentially all categories of domestic nonfinancial borrowers—including the federal government, state and local governments, individuals, and businesses—have played major roles in this extraordinary surge of indebtedness.[13] Anyone who had relied on prior credit-based relationships to predict the behavior of income or prices during this period would have made forecasts just as incorrect as those derived from money-based relationships. Anyone who had derived additional confidence in such predictions

---

[12] There are several obvious problems with attempting to measure the relevant concept of credit in this way. One is simply that the available data measure long-term debts at par value rather than at market prices (or some equivalent for nonmarketable debts). Another is that, although the category of "nonfinancial" borrowers excludes any entity explicitly set up as a financial intermediary, there is inevitably some degree of double-counting due to what amounts to financial intermediation carried out by ordinary businesses and even individuals. Whether this problem is more or less severe than comparable problems affecting the monetary aggregates—for example, the apparently widespread use of U.S. currency in black markets around the world, or even in the United States for a variety of purposes not related to familiar theories of demand for money—is an empirical question.

[13] The one exception is the farm sector.

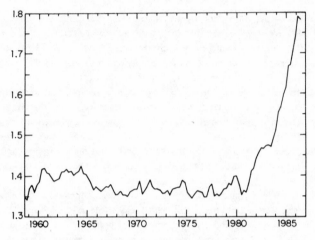

Fig. 4. Ratio of credit to GNP

Note: The data are analogous to those in Figure 2 except that the numerator is end of quarter outstanding debt of domestic nonfinancial borrowers (*Source*: Board of Governors of the Federal Reserve System.)

because the respective signals given by both money and credit confirmed one another would have found that confidence misplaced.

I have speculated elsewhere on the causes of the breakdown of the relationship between credit and income in the 1980s (Friedman, 1987). For purposes of the monetary policy issues under discussion here, it is sufficient to say that attempts to "fix up" this relationship in any simple way are likely to be no more successful than such efforts directed at parallel relationships for the monetary aggregates have been.

A Relationship That Did Hold Up

In sharp contrast to the collapse of relationships connecting the ultimate objectives of monetary policy to standard quantity measures of policy actions, the long-standing relationship between the two most prominent macroeconomic policy objectives—inflation and unemployment—remained intact during this period. The point is of some interest because one of the principal supposed merits widely claimed in favor of the use of publicly announced money growth targets for monetary policy was a potential lessening of the real costs of disinflation. The idea was that public knowledge of such targets would affect expectations in such a way as to minimize (according to some models, to eliminate altogether) the usual negative impact of disinflationary monetary policy on employment, output, incomes, and profits.

Part IV
Money and Interest Rates

[15]

Anticipated Inflation and Interest Rates: Further Interpretation of Findings on the Fisher Equation

By Maurice D. Levi and John H. Makin*

This paper extends the approach first taken by Robert Mundell of employing a general equilibrium model to question the Fisher hypothesis that the real rate of interest is invariant with respect to changes in anticipated inflation. The extension involves the inclusion of a labor sector which rationalizes short-run Phillips curves of positive or negative slope and the incorporation of the effect of taxes on nominal interest as discussed by Michael Darby.

A labor market is introduced which clears when money wages demanded by labor suppliers are equal to money wages offered by labor demanders. This implies the existence of income and employment effects arising from changes in anticipated inflation whenever the elasticity of money wages demanded by labor suppliers with respect to actual inflation differs from unity.[1] For values of such an elasticity below unity, the implied positive impact upon real income arising from a rise in anticipated inflation adds to the impact upon saving arising from real balance effects and thereby increases the effect of a change in anticipated inflation upon the real rate of interest. Taxes on nominal interest earnings produce

an additional effect. Our aim is to present a framework within which to consider all of these effects simultaneously.[2]

The assumption that money wages are rigid downward along with employment of the Correspondence Principle allows us to place limits upon the range of values of the elasticity of money wage demands with respect to inflation. Allowing this parameter to vary over such a range produces, along with other parameter values, comparative static results which are consistent with observable magnitudes. In particular, results are obtained describing the impact of a change in expected inflation on nominal interest and an implied impact on real interest which are consistent with the measured impact discovered by empirical researchers. However, contrary to the assumption of empirical investigators (including William Gibson; Eugene Fama; Kajal Lahiri; and John Carr, James Pesando, and Lawrence B. Smith), our results are also consistent with the hypothesis that neither the real rate of interest nor the after-tax real rate (discussed below), is independent of the expected rate of inflation.

The paper consists of three sections. Section I briefly reviews the theoretical literature questioning the independence of the real rate from the level of anticipated inflation implied by the Fisher hypothesis. We present our model and describe its implications for the relationship between nominal and real after-tax interest rates and

*Associate professor, faculty of commerce, University of British Columbia, and professor, department of economics, University of Washington, respectively. The U.S. Treasury Department and the Federal Reserve Bank of San Francisco provided financial support. We owe thanks for comments and stimulation to Charles R. Nelson, John Murray, A. L. Annanthanarayanan, and to the managing editor of this *Review*. All views expressed and any remaining errors are ours alone.

[1] The key role played in the massive contemporary literature on the Phillips curve by the elasticity of money wages demanded with respect to prices and/or anticipated prices has been ably surveyed by John Rutledge.

[2] We note that our model is consistent with a changing relationship between unemployment and inflation hypothesized by Irving Fisher (1926). This same model also produces results consistent with Fisher's *findings* on the impact of anticipated inflation upon nominal interest rates.

802   THE AMERICAN ECONOMIC REVIEW   DECEMBER 1978

anticipated inflation. Section II discusses the implications of results obtained with our model for the interpretation of the estimates obtained in a number of empirical investigations of the Fisher hypothesis. Section III presents some concluding remarks.

I. A General Equilibrium Framework for Investigating the Effects of Anticipated Inflation

This investigation is by no means the first attempt to find a theoretical rationale to reconcile Fisher's hypothesis with empirical findings. Mundell showed, in a full employment world with real balance effects, that the real interest rate is dependent upon the level of anticipated inflation. Implicit in Mundell's model (since his *LM* schedule was not vertical) was a nonzero interest elasticity of money demand, a condition necessary for the link between real interest and anticipated inflation within his formulation. This requirement was made explicit by Thomas Sargent who used a model not requiring full employment, where all behavior is dependent upon distributed-lag representations of variables affecting the money and commodity markets. Sargent showed that the initial impact of a change in anticipated inflation on nominal interest is less than unity, but the full impact over long periods of time is equal to unity. Under his formulation this means that changes in anticipated inflation have only a transitory effect on the real interest rate. Ignazio Visco, with a model identical to Sargent's save for the inclusion of a real balance effect upon expenditure, showed that even in Sargent's dynamic model, after full adjustment, Mundell's comparative static real balance effect is preserved, whereby a change in anticipated inflation permanently affects the real interest rate.

The proposition is advanced in this paper that the Fisher equation ought to be viewed as a reduced-form relationship derivable from a simple general equilibrium model. This model should allow for the impact of a number of factors which affect the influence of a change in anticipated inflation upon

the nominal rate of interest. These factors include taxes on interest earnings; induced changes in income and employment which may accompany a change in anticipated inflation; real balance effects; and the size of the interest elasticity of the demand for money. To account for these factors we introduce a macro-economic model which determines the impact of changes in expected inflation upon the nominal interest rate. The closed economy model will consist of equilibrium conditions in commodity, money, and labor markets with the bond market eliminated by Walras' Law. The money market is expressed in stock equilibrium terms.[3]

We shall entertain the Darby modification of the Fisher hypothesis which states in effect that the after-tax real rate of interest is independent of the level of anticipated inflation. The relationship between

[3] In a recent paper Lewis Johnson derived a result that the real rate is dependent upon the level of anticipated inflation. As in earlier studies, this requires both a real balance effect and a nonzero interest elasticity of money demand. Johnson also introduced a flow equilibrium condition in the money market, "momentary equilibrium," which results in a solution for the relationship between the level of anticipated inflation and the nominal and/or real interest rate dependent upon the speed at which individuals adjust money demand in response to money market (stock) disequilibria. Such a model permits accommodation of the "anticipation effect" whereby individuals anticipating inflation and desiring to cut holdings of real money balances will also realize that their desires will be to some extent satisfied, given no action at all, insofar as anticipated inflation does materialize. Of course it must be assumed that the rate of growth of the nominal money supply is known as well. While Johnson's model is both innovative and promising, it does require explicit knowledge about the speed with which money markets adjust. He in fact concluded that his model assumes "implausible" dynamics whereby portfolio adjustment takes time while goods markets adjust instantaneously. In order to keep a model in a form which involves only parameters for which estimates are readily available, we shall retain the stock equilibrium formulation in the money market. This formulation is equivalent to the flow formulation, as Johnson notes, if it is assumed that instantaneous stock adjustment always keeps flow demand at zero. Later we shall show that the model we propose is stable despite the assumption of instantaneous adjustment in the money market.

the Fisher hypothesis and the Darby hypothesis and their implications can be seen clearly from the following. Let i be the nominal interest rate, r the real interest rate, and π the expected rate of inflation. Let r^* be the after-tax real interest rate, and τ be the marginal tax rate on interest income. The Fisher hypothesis begins with the relationship

$$(1) \qquad i = r + \pi$$

and states that $di/d\pi = 1.0$, given $dr/d\pi = 0$. The Darby hypothesis begins with the relationship

$$(2) \qquad r^* = i(1 - \tau) - \pi$$

or, alternatively,

$$(3) \qquad i = \frac{r^* + \pi}{(1 - \tau)}$$

and states that $di/d\pi = 1/(1 - \tau)$ given $dr^*/d\pi = 0$.[4] We shall incorporate equation (3) into the general equilibrium model to be developed below.

Equilibrium conditions for our model are stated as follows (with i expressed by equation (3)):[5]

----

[4] Here we follow Darby and ignore the effect of possible taxes on capital gains which could materialize if commodity prices actually rise at the expected rate. The effect suggested by Darby will follow as long as the marginal tax rate on income lies above that on capital gains. For example, setting $\tau = 0.5$ and the tax rate on capital gains $\tau_K = 0.25$ would imply rewriting (3) as

$$(3') \qquad i = \frac{r^*}{1 - \tau} + \frac{1}{1 - \tau_c} \pi$$

where $\tau_c = (\tau - \tau_K)/(1 - \tau_K) = .33$.

[5] The commodity market is cleared by employing the simplest possible formulations of investment and savings behavior. The term r^* could be included in the savings function with the effect that changes in r^* produce larger changes in excess demand or supply in the commodity markets. The same impact can be introduced by varying the sensitivity of investment with respect to r^*. The impact of such variation is investigated in the Appendix. Note that in (4), it is assumed that tax proceeds are employed to retire government debt. Explicit government expenditure is omitted from the commodity market equation for simplicity. Its inclusion would not affect our major conclusions below.

$$(4) \qquad I(r^*) - S(Y(N), M/P) = 0$$
$$L(Y(N), i, P) - M = 0$$
$$PY'(N) - W(P, N^s) = 0$$

The first equation sets real investment I, expressed as a function of the real after-tax rate of return, equal to real savings which is determined by real income and the level of real money balances M/P. Real income, equal to real output, is determined by the quantity of labor employed and is written as $Y(N)$. The second equation sets nominal money demand, $L(Y(N), i, P)$, equal to nominal money supply M. The third equation sets the money wage offered, or the value of the marginal product of labor, $PY'(N)$, equal to the money wage demanded, expressed as a function of the price level P, and the quantity of labor supplied N^s. Thus N^s is set equal to N, the quantity of labor demanded. Employment and output rise when the money wage offered to labor exceeds the current money wage demanded and conversely. The level of anticipated inflation and the money supply are exogenous variables. The first two equations set quantities equal with price adjustments implicitly assumed to clear markets while the labor market equation sets nominal wages demanded equal to nominal wages offered, with adjustments in the quantity of labor implicitly assumed to clear that market. The dynamics of this system will be given explicit consideration in the Appendix.

The system of equations in (4) is differentiated and the coefficients expressed in elasticity form. This permits the use of "ball park" parameter values. Some numerical analysis is necessary since a priori proximity of $di/d\pi$ to $1/(1 - \tau)$ is an important issue here. Letting Σ_{xy} be defined as "the elasticity of x with respect to y" we summarize signs and ball park figures (in parentheses) for the relevant parameters:[6]

----

[6] Our results are unaffected if we allow money demand to depend upon after-tax nominal interest, $i^* = i(1 - \tau)$. There of course exist many estimates of the parameter values employed here. Some will prefer to insert values which they consider more likely. This

804

THE AMERICAN ECONOMIC REVIEW   *DECEMBER 1978*

TABLE 1—COMPARATIVE STATIC PROPERTIES OF A SIMPLE MACRO MODEL

	$\beta = (1 - \Sigma_{WP}) > 0$	$\beta < 0$	$\beta = 0$
$\dfrac{M}{P}\dfrac{dP}{dM}$	+	+	+ (1.0)
$\dfrac{\pi}{P}\dfrac{dP}{d\pi}$	+	+	+
$\dfrac{di}{d\pi}$	less than $1/(1-\tau)$	$\lesseqgtr 1/(1-\tau)$ as $\beta \gtreqless \Sigma_{Sm}$	less than $1/(1-\tau)$
$\dfrac{M}{i}\dfrac{di}{dM}$	−	+	0
$\dfrac{M}{N}\dfrac{dN}{dM}\left(=\dfrac{M}{Y}\dfrac{dY}{dM}\right)$	+	−	0
$\dfrac{\pi}{N}\dfrac{dN}{d\pi}\left(=\dfrac{\pi}{Y}\dfrac{dY}{d\pi}\right)$	+	−	0

investment: $\Sigma_{Ir^*} < 0 \quad (-0.4)$

savings: $\Sigma_{SY} > 0 \quad (1.0)$

  $\Sigma_{Sm} < 0 \quad (-0.2)$

  $m = M/P$

money demand: $\Sigma_{LY} > 0 \quad (1.0)$

  $\Sigma_{Li} < 0 \quad (-0.5)$

  $\Sigma_{LP} > 0 \quad (1.0)$

output:[7] $\Sigma_{YN} > 0 \quad (1.0)$

  $\Sigma_{Y'(N)N} = 0$

wage demand: $(0 \leq \Sigma_{WP} \leq 1.69)$

  $\Sigma_{WN} > 0 \quad (1.0)$

The parameter of most interest here is the elasticity of money wages demanded with respect to price Σ_{WP}, upon which we have placed a range estimate running from 0 to 1.69. Neither number is arbitrary. The lower limit reflects downward rigidity of money wages. The upper limit represents the maximum value of Σ_{WP}, given other parameter values already specified, that is consistent with dynamic stability (discussed in the Appendix) of the system described

by (4). The term Σ_{WP} is not expected to be constant. During the initial stages of a rise in the rate of inflation, institutional rigidities associated with wage contracts or slowness in identifying the true process describing the behavior of prices lead us to expect $\Sigma_{WP} < 1$.[8] For the same reasons, during the initial stages of a fall in the rate of inflation or during the period when (previously reduced) real wages are being restored, we expect $\Sigma_{WP} > 1$. During steady inflation as the true process describing the behavior of prices comes to be correctly perceived we expect Σ_{WP} to approach unity. As a matter of fact, estimates of Σ_{WP} reported in the survey of the Phillips curve literature by Rutledge vary widely over time and location, with values reported ranging from about 0.2 to unity. We shall investigate the significance of changes in Σ_{WP} for our results once the comparative static properties of (4) have been determined.

[8]These factors are emphasized by William Poole in a discussion of phenomena which may lead to observation of events such as business cycles or real effects of nominal disturbances which are inconsistent with fully rational expectations. In addition, as noted by Milton Friedman, higher rates of inflation tend also to be more volatile. Therefore prices in the future become more difficult to predict from prices now and *ex post* values of Σ_{WP} will be more likely to differ from unity when rates of inflation are high and volatile.

can easily be done, but it will be discovered that the nature of our findings is not largely altered by changes to other parameter values which lie within the range frequently estimated. (See the Appendix.)

[7]We assume constant returns to scale.

Differentiating (4) and converting into elasticity form gives results summarized in Table 1. The sign of the relationship between percentage changes in exogenous M and π, and the percentage change in each of the endogenous variables P, i, and N is given to acquaint the reader with the general properties of the model under alternative values of β, defined equal to $1 - \Sigma_{WP}$. The impact of anticipated inflation on interest is given simply as $di/d\pi$ for comparison with the value obtained for this derivative under the Darby hypothesis. An explicit expression for $di/d\pi$ implied by our model is given below in (5). Recall that given percent changes of M and π will produce percent changes of N identical to those of Y since $\Sigma_{YN} = 1.0$.

Our primary interest is in $di/d\pi$. The other results will be given some further consideration below. First, it can readily be seen from Table 1 that values of $di/d\pi$ smaller than that anticipated by the Darby hypothesis will arise for nearly all possible values of $\beta = (1 - \Sigma_{WP})$. Further, an elasticity of money wages demanded with respect to inflation of greater than unity implies a reduction in real output and employment when the money stock is increased.[9]

Taking Σ_{YN}, Σ_{SY}, and Σ_{WN}, all equal to unity, we may write:[10]

[9]Some other results given in Table 1 are worth noting. When $\beta = 0$ the natural rate hypothesis is satisfied by the classical result: the rate of increase in the price level is identical to the rate of increase in the money supply (the "1" under $\beta = 0$), while output and employment are independent of monetary growth. The Fisher/Darby hypothesis is contradicted even in the classical case where $\beta = 0$ due to the real balance effect, as was noted by Mundell. The result whereby $(\pi/N)(dN/d\pi) > 0$ is exactly that hypothesized and measured by Fisher (1926) in his "discovery" of the Phillips curve whereby employment too is termed a "dance of the dollar." Of course Fisher is appropriately skeptical about the ultimate impact of rising inflation upon employment, noting that, after a rise in inflation, "Employment is then stimulated—for a time at least" (p. 498).

[10]The labor market-clearing equation in (4) has money wages demanded dependent upon the price level and the quantity of labor supplied. Thus our assumption $\Sigma_{WN} = 1.0$ is equivalent to an assumption of unitary elasticity of labor supply with respect to money wages at a given price level or $1/\Sigma_{WN} = \Sigma_{NW} = 1.0$.

$$(5) \quad \frac{di}{d\pi} = \frac{1}{(1 - \tau) + \dfrac{\Sigma_{Li}(\beta - \Sigma_{Sm})}{(i/r^*)\Sigma_{Ir^*}(\beta + 1)}}$$

Equation (5) gives the Mundell–Sargent–Visco result since, given $\tau = 0$, $di/d\pi = 1.0$ requires setting Σ_{Li} equal to zero.[11] Thus $\beta = 0$ is equivalent to a full employment assumption in a model where real wages are constant and equal to the marginal product of a given (full employment) quantity of labor. Mundell did fail to note, however, that his result whereby $di/d\pi < 0$ given the real balance effect also required $\Sigma_{Li} < 0$, though this condition was implicit, as we have noted, in the negatively sloped LM curve appearing in his Metzler-type diagram. His result gives $di/d\tau = 0$ if $\Sigma_{Ir^*} = 0$.

Crude as they may be, the ball park parameter values permit us to suggest some limits for values of $di/d\pi$ under different assumptions about i/r^* and β as well as τ. One thing which characterizes empirical estimates of $di/d\pi$ is variety, and some investigators like Gibson and Lahiri report evidence of structural changes or breaks in estimated values of $di/d\pi$, particularly around 1960. First we note that, given Σ_{WN}, Σ_{YN}, $\Sigma_{SY} = 1.0$, if $\beta > \Sigma_{Sm} > -1$:

$$(6) \quad \frac{d}{d\beta}[di/d\pi] = \frac{(-i/r^*)\Sigma_{Ir^*}\Sigma_{Li}[1 + \Sigma_{Sm}]}{|A|^2} < 0$$

$$(7) \quad \frac{d}{d(i/r^*)}(di/d\pi) = \frac{\Sigma_{Li}\Sigma_{Ir^*}(\beta - \Sigma_{Sm})(\beta + 1)}{|A|^2} > 0$$

where $|A| \equiv [(i/r^*)\Sigma_{Ir^*}(1 - \tau)(\beta + 1) + \Sigma_{Li}(\beta - \Sigma_{Sm})] < 0$

Such an assumption, which amounts to unitary elasticity of labor supply with respect to real wages, seems reasonable enough and serves to reduce the complexity of comparative static solutions to the model.

[11]The only other possibility would have a negative β equal in absolute value to Σ_{Sm} given Σ_{WN}, Σ_{SY}, and $\Sigma_{YN} = 1.0$.

806 THE AMERICAN ECONOMIC REVIEW DECEMBER 1978

Now, as expected inflation rises we expect Σ_{WP} to rise thereby lowering β and, given (6), in turn raising $di/d\pi$. At the same time, a rise in π raises $i/r^* = (1/(1 - \tau))(1 + \pi/r^*)$ as long as π increases faster than r^*. This in turn adds to the positive impact upon $di/d\pi$ arising from an increase in Σ_{WP} since (7) carries a positive sign.

To place a lower limit on $di/d\pi$, set $\Sigma_{WP} = 0$ ($\beta = 1.0$). If initially $\pi = 0$, $i/r^* = 1/(1 - \tau)$. We set $\tau = 0.33$ consistent with the marginal tax rate on nominal interest suggested by Darby to be consistent with observed differentials between taxable and tax-free returns on bonds. These parameter values along with those already given imply $di/d\pi = 0.857$.

Alternatively, suppose $r^* = \pi = 4.0$ percent and $\Sigma_{WP} = 1.0$ ($\beta = 0$). Given these assumptions, $di/d\pi = 1.333$. It is also clear from (5) that as β approaches Σ_{Sm}, in this case -0.2, $di/d\pi$ approaches $1/(1 - \tau)$. Finally, it is easy to account for estimates of $di/d\pi$ close to unity by selecting values between the extremes already mentioned. Given $i/r^* = 2.0$ and $\tau = 0.33$, a value of $\beta = 0.695$ ($\Sigma_{WP} = 0.305$) gives a value of $di/d\pi = 1.0$ since these values satisfy

$$(8) \qquad \tau = \frac{\Sigma_{Li}(\beta - \Sigma_{Sm})}{i/r^* \Sigma_{Ir^*}(\beta + 1)}$$

which, given equation (5), is a necessary and sufficient condition for $di/d\pi = 1.0$.

As simple as our model is and as crude as our parameter estimates may be, it is by now evident that it is an easy matter to employ both to account, first, for most of the estimated values of $di/d\pi$ and, second, for changes in the value of $di/d\pi$ over time, given changes over time in the value of Σ_{WP}. Finally we can show that the existence of estimates of $di/d\pi$ close to unity do not confirm the Fisher hypothesis in any general sense and in particular do not imply after-tax real returns that are independent of the level of anticipated inflation.

Returning to Table 1, it is worthwhile to consider the general economic situations which could be expected to accompany changing values of $di/d\pi$. Lower values of $di/d\pi$ would be expected to arise when Σ_{WP}

is relatively low (less than one so that $\beta > 0$) due say to a recent rise in the rate of inflation. Given such circumstances an exogenous increase in π will raise prices, real output, employment, and nominal interest rates. If π continues to rise, given that wages begin to respond more promptly to increases in actual inflation, β will fall while i/r^* rises and if β becomes negative, there may arise a period of rising inflation and falling real output and employment, accompanied by rising nominal interest rates. In fact β describes the ratio of the impact upon real output (employment) and prices arising from monetary expansion or a rise in anticipated inflation based on the model given by (4). The implied mix in the relative response of real output (employment) and inflation to monetary growth or a rise in anticipated inflation goes from a maximum value of 1.0 ($\beta = 1.0$, $\Sigma_{WP} = 0$) downward to a minimum value of -0.69 ($\Sigma_{WP} = 1.69$).[12] The case where $\beta = 0$ ($\Sigma_{WP} = 1.0$) is consistent with the natural rate hypothesis (a vertical Phillips curve) which in turn reflects the absence of money illusion implicit in a value of $\Sigma_{WP} = 1.0$. In addition where β is falling for reasons cited above, $di/d\pi$ can be expected to rise, suggesting that real effects follow from changes in nominal M or π, when the inflation rate forecast is wrong. Such real effects vary with the degree of inaccuracy of inflation forecasts. Under the assumption however that inflation forecasts are correct in the long run, the steady-state value of Σ_{WP} is unity and $\beta = 0$. Our results are then consistent with the notion that an unemployment inflation tradeoff is a short-run phenomenon.

The economics behind the results just discussed are straightforward. The rise in expected inflation produces an excess demand for commodities as investment rises due to an initially depressed real rate of interest. Simultaneously there occurs an excess supply of money in the face of antici-

---

[12]Based on the requirement that β lie above -0.69 for the model in (4) to be stable. This result is derived in the Appendix.

pated depreciation of money in terms of goods, caused by the rise in π and the initial rise in the nominal interest rate. In short, anticipated inflation leads to a desire to convert financial to real assets. In a full employment model with no real balance effects the new equilibrium in the commodity sector requires a restoration of the original after-tax real rate which in turn requires $di/d\pi = 1/(1 - \tau)$. With real balance effects, the higher price level resulting from excess commodity demand lowers real balances, thereby shifting out the savings schedule and requiring a lower after-tax interest rate to reequilibrate the commodity sector. Of course, if the interest elasticity of money demand is zero, no excess supply condition ever arises in the monetary sector. Even with a real balance effect there is no impact upon the after-tax real interest rate since no reduction in money demand is available to increase commodity demand. The price level remains constant and i simply rises by $\pi/(1 - \tau)$.

Once the assumption of fixed output is dropped and attention is paid to the impact of price level changes upon real wages, employment, and output, the potential for an impact of changes in expected inflation upon the real rate of interest is further enhanced. If $\Sigma_{WP} < 1$ ($\beta > 0$), then the changes described above are accompanied by a rise in real income (output). As a result savings are increased and the new equilibrium real interest rate can be still lower in response to a rise in π. The condition $\Sigma_{WP} = 1.0$ freezes real income which simply returns us to the full employment case of Mundell, while $\Sigma_{WP} > 1$ means that real income falls given a rise in π. This in turn means that $dr^*/d\pi$ will be $\lessgtr 0$ ($di/d\pi \lessgtr 1/(1 - \tau)$) depending on whether the fall in real balances results in an increase in savings that is greater than, equal to, or less than the decrease in savings caused by a fall in real income.

Finally, it is interesting to note that the results presented in Table 1 rationalize the Gibson Paradox, whereby a higher price *level* is associated with higher nominal interest rates, in cases were Σ_{WP} exceeds

unity. In such cases monetary expansion will result in inflation and higher nominal interest which will in turn cause high levels of prices and interest rates to appear simultaneously.

II. Measurement of the Impact of Anticipated Inflation on Nominal Interest

Ever since Fisher uneasily concluded in 1930 that "when prices are rising, the (nominal) rate of interest tends to be high *but not so high as it should be to compensate for the rise*" (p. 43, emphasis added), empirical investigations into the effect upon nominal interest rates of changes in anticipated inflation rates have generally ended with some *ad hoc* theorizing, either on why it is that nominal interest rates do not rise by the full amount of an increase in anticipated inflation, or why it is that the measured impact of changes in inflationary expectations upon nominal interest rates is not constant over time.[13]

Frequently the problem is found to be one of properly modeling and measuring just how it is that people form their expectations about future rates of inflation. The implication of the Fisher legacy is a search for measures of anticipated inflation that can predict nominal interest rates with a regression coefficient of unity. As a consequence we find studies like that of Lahiri employing "weighted," "adaptive," "extrapolative," and "regressive" expectations to model the formulation of expected inflation rates along with one-, two- or three-stage least squares estimates of the impact of such weights upon nominal interest rates. Even with all of these variants the results do not support the hypothesized impact upon nominal interest rates arising from changes in expected rates of inflation, however measured, and there appears to be a structural break in the data around 1960. It is our contention here that neither of these results is at all surprising and that the prior beliefs

[13]See articles surveyed by Richard Roll, and more recently, articles by Gibson; Lahiri; Carr, Pesando, and Smith.

generated by the Fisher hypothesis can and have in some cases seriously misled empirical investigators.

Despite the rather extensive efforts of theorists investigating the Fisher hypothesis, empirical researchers have in some cases found theorists easy to ignore, particularly on the question of constancy of the real rate. Gibson, citing Reuben Kessel and Armen Alchian and Mundell, simply assumes $dr/d\pi = 0$ because "There is as yet no theoretical consensus on the relationship between the real rate and the expected rate of inflation" (p. 855). This might be ignored if he did not conclude later on that his results "...lend support to the hypothesis that the real rate of interest is not affected by price expectations over a six month period..." (p. 863).[14]

Lahiri appears to recall late in his article the significance of his initial assumption that the real rate is independent of anticipated inflation when he writes somewhat cryptically: "Though some effects of price expectations on [the] real rate can never be overemphasized, I did not pursue that point in this paper" (p. 130).

The Fisher legacy has been carried a step further by Fama. Based on the joint hypothesis that expectations are rational and that the real rate of interest is constant, Fama concludes that one cannot reject the hypothesis that "all variation through time in one- to six-month nominal rates of interest mirrors variation in correctly assessed one- to six-month expected rates of change in purchasing power" (p. 282). Fama in effect requires that the Fisher *hypothesis*, which predicts a unit impact upon nominal interest rates of changes in expected inflation, be empirically verified if we are to

conclude first, that expectations are rational and second, that the real rate is constant in general and, in particular, is independent of changes in the expected rate of inflation.[15]

Fama's innovative empirical approach which requires that both market efficiency (in the sense of rational expectations) and a constant real rate be included in the null hypothesis, carries with it the danger that the hypothesis of market efficiency may erroneously be rejected if one clings to the validity of the hypothesis that real rates are constant. In a paper modifying Fama's conclusions, Charles Nelson and G. William Schwert (N–S) argue that Fama's test could not have been expected to produce rejection of his joint hypothesis. More powerful tests performed by N–S do result in rejection of that hypothesis. They choose to conclude, based upon copious evidence of market efficiency, much of it produced by Fama himself, that their results suggest rather that the real interest rate is not constant. We have argued that if the after-tax real rate of interest depends upon the level of anticipated inflation, efficient markets imply that the Fisher hypothesis *cannot* be fulfilled but that one may, given the validity of the Darby hypothesis, erroneously infer that the Fisher hypothesis holds.

The prior belief that $di/d\pi = 1.0$ implies independence of the real rate from anticipated inflation really involves a compound error, given a general equilibrium model coupled with the Darby hypothesis of independence of the real after-tax rate from anticipated inflation. To see this consider first the implication of the general equilibrium model for the value of $di/d\pi$ given only the Fisher hypothesis and investment determined by the real rate unadjusted for taxes, r. In this case

---

[14]To be fair it should be noted that Gibson is here commenting on a finding that for some of his results $di/d\pi$ lies close to unity which, ignoring tax effects, *could* imply $dr/d\pi$ close to zero. But many of his results do not show $di/d\pi$ close to unity and as Gibson himself notes $di/d\pi = 1$, while consistent with $dr/d\pi = 0$, is also consistent with a world in which "positive (negative) effects on the real rate are exactly matched by underadjustment (overadjustment) of nominal rates" (p. 855).

[15]It is important to distinguish clearly between the Fisher *hypothesis* stated here and the Fisher *finding* that indeed the nominal interest rate does *not* appear to change by the full amount of a change in the expected rate of inflation which is measured in turn by a distributed lag on past and current observed rates of inflation.

$$(5') \quad \frac{di}{d\pi} = \frac{1}{1 + \dfrac{\Sigma_{Li}(\beta - \Sigma_{Sm})}{(i/r)\Sigma_{Ir}(\beta + 1)}}$$

which becomes unity under conditions identical to those which make (5) equal to $1/(1 - \tau)$. Given (5') we are not surprised to find estimates of the impact of changes in π upon i lying below unity. However, note that if $\beta = \Sigma_{Sm}$, and negative effects of falling income on saving arising from a rise in real wages (given $\Sigma_{WP} > 1.0$ and $\beta < 0$) cancel positive effects of lower real balances on saving, the real rate may be unaffected. But this is a rather special case, likely to appear only in a period of rapidly decelerating inflation and/or past reductions in real wages. In any case, should the estimated impact of a rise in anticipated inflation upon the nominal interest rate be unity, we could, given (5'), correctly infer under the Fisher hypothesis, a constant real rate.

The real difficulty associated with the prior belief that $di/d\pi = 1.0$ implies independence of the real rate from anticipated inflation arises under the Darby hypothesis, given that we take investment to depend upon the after-tax real rate. If one looks back at our equation (5), it is seen that its right-hand side exceeds the r.h.s. of (5') when $\tau > 0$ and $\Sigma_{Ir^*} = \Sigma_{Ir}$.[16] As we have already noted, the r.h.s. of (5) can assume a value of unity, given our parameter values when $\Sigma_{WP} = .30$. Should this result coincide with the prior beliefs associated with the Fisher hypothesis, one would wrongly conclude, given the Darby hypothesis and $I = I(r^*)$, that the real rate is unaffected by anticipated inflation when in fact such a result implies that neither the after-tax real rate nor the real rate displays such independence.[17] Thus Fama's estimate of 0.98 for the impact of anticipated inflation on nominal interest supports neither independence of the real rate nor of the after-tax real rate from anticipated inflation.

Tests of the Darby hypothesis conducted on Canadian data by Carr, Pesando, and Smith which were termed "inconclusive" by their authors in fact produced results quite consistent with those predicted by our equation (5). A wide variety of formulations to represent expected inflation produced statistically significant estimates of $di/d\pi$ running from 0.86 to 1.34 with a mean value of 1.03 and a standard deviation of 0.12 employing interest rates on instruments with a range of maturities from ninety days to ten years.[18]

Carr, Pesando, and Smith given a prior belief based on the Darby hypothesis of an after-tax *real* rate independent of anticipated inflation that $di/d\pi = 1/(1 - \tau)$ were led to the "inconclusive" view of their results. We would argue simply that they entertained an incorrect prior belief.

III. Concluding Remarks

It is our view that empirical investigators of the effects of anticipated inflation have not been well served by prior beliefs based either on the Fisher hypothesis or the Darby hypothesis. The Fisher hypothesis has tended to serve as a criterion for the validity of measures of anticipated inflation for those investigators who search for the measure which results in an estimate of $di/d\pi$ close to unity. Some investigators like Fama have estimated values of $di/d\pi$ that are in fact close to unity and, we contend, have wrongly inferred independence of the real rate from anticipated inflation. In-

---

[16]Note that i/r^* will exceed i/r since $r - r^* = i\tau$.

[17]This follows since independence of the after-tax rate requires $di/d\pi = 1/(1 - \tau)$ (the Darby hypothesis). Also, when the r.h.s. of (5) equals unity, and we ignore the $i\tau$ term for $r - r^*$, it implies the r.h.s. of (5') equal to $1/(1 + \tau)$ which contradicts the Fisher hypothesis.

[18]Based on data running from 1959–71, there were thirty such estimates deemed acceptable by Carr, Pesando, and Smith with ten others rejected due to some wrong or insignificant signs on estimated coefficients. Since the authors admit to being unable to reconcile all the different estimates of $di/d\pi$, the rather crude expedient of characterizing their results by simply calculating a mean and standard deviation for all estimates obtained does not seem an inappropriate way to characterize the state of such estimates. Implications for results of Carr, Pesando, and Smith arising from the openness of the Canadian economy from which data were drawn are considered in Makin.

vestigators like Carr, Pesando, and Smith, who have employed the Darby hypothesis as a basis for their prior beliefs about $di/d\pi$, have been misled to view their results as inconclusive when in fact they are quite consistent with results predicted by a general equilibrium approach to the effects of changes in anticipated inflation.

More generally, it is our view that, like the Philips curve, neither the Fisher hypothesis nor the Darby hypothesis represents an isolated phenomenon, but rather should be viewed as a reduced-form relationship derivable from a set of structural equations which compose a reasonably comprehensive macro-economic model. Viewed in this way the results obtained by empirical investigations of both hypotheses are at once consistent with expectations based upon theory and inconsistent with the notion that the real rate of interest, before or after taxes, is independent of the level of anticipated inflation. Insofar as instruments of monetary and fiscal policy have, under rational expectations, a direct effect on the rate of anticipated inflation, then the conclusion implied by our results also implies that real variables are directly affected by such instruments.

Finally, our results suggest that the role played by income effects, as opposed to that played by real balance effects, in affecting the impact of anticipated inflation upon nominal interest may vary over time due to changes in the elasticity of money wages demanded with respect to prices. A shift in that parameter may help to explain the discovery by Lahiri, Gibson, and William Yohe and Denis Karnosky, of a break occurring about 1960 in the measured impact of anticipated inflation on nominal interest. More generally, these and other empirical investigators of the Fisher hypothesis, and recently, of the Darby hypothesis, may be obtaining a wide range of estimates of the impact of changes in anticipated inflation upon nominal interest, not because of any wide variation in the adequacy of different proxies employed to measure anticipated inflation, but rather because of the simple fact that they are attempting to measure a coefficient which varies randomly over time.

APPENDIX A: CONSTRAINING Σ_{WP} WITH THE CORRESPONDENCE PRINCIPLE

Here we explore the dynamic properties of the model given in (4) as a means to place some lower limit on values of β by employing Samuelson's Correspondence Principle. It will also be of interest to consider the behavior of a system in which two markets (commodities and money) are assumed to adjust via price adjustments while a third (labor) is assumed to adjust via quantity adjustments. We have:

$$(A1) \quad dP/dt = K_1[I(r^*) - S(Y(N), M/P)]$$
$$di/dt = K_2[L(Y(N), i, P) - M]$$
$$dN/dt = K_3[PY'(N) - W(P, N)]$$

The characteristic equation which determines the solution of the above system of linear differential equations in the neighborhood of equilibrium is (letting $K_i = 1.0$ $i = 1, 2, 3$):

(A2)

$$\begin{vmatrix} \Sigma_{Sm} - \lambda & (1 - \tau)(i/r^*)\Sigma_{Ir^*} & -1.0 \\ 1.0 & \Sigma_{Li} - \lambda & 1.0 \\ \beta & 0 & -1.0 \\ & & -\lambda \end{vmatrix} = 0$$

Local stability requires that the roots of (A2) be negative. Equation (A2) may be written out as a cubic equation:

$$(A3) \quad a_0\lambda^3 + a_1\lambda^2 + a_2\lambda + a_3 = 0$$

where

$a_0 = 1$

$a_1 = (-\Sigma_{Sm} - \Sigma_{Li} + 1) > 0$

$a_2 = -\Sigma_{Li} + \Sigma_{Sm}(\Sigma_{Li} - 1)$
$\quad - (1 - \tau)(i/r^*)\Sigma_{Ir^*} + \beta \gtrless 0$
$\quad$ as $\beta \gtrless -1.6$

$a_3 = -|A| \gtrless 0$ as $\beta \gtrless -0.69$

The roots of equation (A3) will be negative

TABLE 2—SENSITIVITY OF $di/d\pi$ TO PARAMETER CHANGES

Parameter Range	Range of $di/d\pi$					
	$\beta = 1.0$		$i/r^* = 1.5$	$\beta = 0$		$i/r^* = 3.0$
$\Sigma_{Sm} = -0.1$ to -0.3	0.889	to	0.827	1.411	to	1.262
$\Sigma_{Li} = -0.2$ to -0.8	1.153	to	0.682	1.428	to	1.249
$\Sigma_{Ir^*} = -0.1$ to -0.7	0.375	to	1.050	1.00	to	1.400

if $a_1 > 0$; $a_2 > 0$; $a_3 > 0$; $a_1 a_2 - a_0 a_3 > 0$. A sufficient condition to satisfy all four conditions given the ball park parameters employed above (given $\tau = 0.33$ and $i/r^* = 3.0$) is $\beta > -0.69$ or $\Sigma_{WP} < 1.69$.

If the money market is assumed to adjust instantaneously so that stock equilibrium and flow equilibrium conditions are identical, the characteristic equation for the system becomes a quadratic equation which has the same sufficient condition for negative roots (stability) as the cubic equation.

APPENDIX B: IMPACT OF CHANGES IN PARAMETER VALUES ON $di/d\pi$

As already noted in footnote 6, the results obtained for $di/d\pi$, while not radically altered, will be affected by changes in parameter values. Assuming parameters employed in the text except as noted otherwise, range estimates are given for $di/d\pi$ in Table 2. The results suggest first, that lower estimates of $di/d\pi$ obtained by Gibson are consistent with either a higher interest elasticity of money demand with respect to nominal interest or a lower elasticity of investment with respect to after-tax real interest. Second, adjustments of Σ_{Ir^*} and Σ_{Li} in the same direction would tend to offset each other. Third, the general impression obtained from Table 2 is one of relative stability for estimated values of $di/d\pi$ with sensitivity to changes in Σ_{Ir^*} being the greatest. Finally, sensitivity of $di/d\pi$ to changes in Σ_{Li} and Σ_{Ir^*} falls as the rate of anticipated inflation and Σ_{WP} rise (β falls). In view of the persistent actual and therefore, anticipated inflation in most countries over recent years, the ranges associated with $\beta = 0$ are probably more typical and of course will be likely to hold in the long run given constancy of real wages.

APPENDIX C: IMPACT OF CAPITAL GAINS TAXES ON $di/d\pi$

If $\tau \neq \tau_K$ we obtain the result:

$$(5'') \quad \frac{di}{d\pi} = \cfrac{1}{\cfrac{1-\tau}{1-\tau_K} + \cfrac{\Sigma_{Li}(\beta - \Sigma_{Sm})}{(1 - \tau_K)(i/r^*)\Sigma_{Ir^*}(\beta + 1)}}$$

Given parameters associated with $\beta = 1.0$ (see text) and values of $\tau = 0.5$ and $\tau_K = 0.25$, $di/d\pi = 0.750$. If $\beta = 0$, the comparable value for $di/d\pi$ becomes 1.285. As is obvious from $(5'')$ implied values of $di/d\pi$ fall as the difference between τ and τ_K rises.

REFERENCES

J. Carr, J. E. Pesando, and L. B. Smith, "Tax Effects, Price Expectations and the Nominal Rate of Interest," *Econ. Inquiry*, June 1976, *14*, 259–69.

M. R. Darby, "The Financial and Tax Effects of Monetary Policy on Interest Rates," *Econ. Inquiry*, June 1975, *13*, 266–76.

E. Fama, "Short-Term Interest Rates as Predictors of Inflation," *Amer. Econ. Rev.*, June 1975, *65*, 269–82.

Irving Fisher, "A Statistical Relation Between Unemployment and Price Changes," *Int. Labour Rev.*, June 1926, *13*, 785–92; reprinted as "I Discovered the Phillips Curve," *J. Polit. Econ.*, Mar./Apr. 1973,

81, 496–502.

———, *The Theory of Interest*, New York 1930.

M. **Friedman,** "Nobel Lecture: Inflation and Unemployment," *J. Polit. Econ.*, June 1977, *85*, 451–72.

W. E. **Gibson,** "Interest Rates and Inflationary Expectations," *Amer. Econ. Rev.*, Dec. 1972, *62*, 854–65.

L. **Johnson,** "Inflationary Expectations and Momentary Equilibrium," *Amer. Econ. Rev.*, June 1976, *66*, 395–400.

R. A. **Kessel and A. A. Alchian,** "Effects of Inflation," *J. Polit. Econ.*, Dec. 1962, *70*, 521–37.

K. **Lahiri,** "Inflationary Expectations: Their Formation and Interest Rate Effects," *Amer. Econ. Rev.*, Mar. 1976, *66*, 124–31.

J. H. **Makin,** "Anticipated Inflation and Interest Rates in an Open Economy," paper no. 77-1, Instit. Econ. Res., Univ. Washington, Jan. 1977.

R. A. **Mundell,** "Inflation and Real Interest," *J. Polit. Econ.*, June 1963, *71*, 280–83.

C. R. **Nelson and G. W. Schwert,** "On Testing the Hypothesis that the Real Rate of Interest is Constant," *Amer. Econ. Rev.*, June 1977, *67*, 478–86.

W. **Poole,** "Rational Expectations in the Macro Model," *Brookings Papers*, Washington 1976, *2*, 463–505.

R. **Roll,** "Interest Rates on Monetary Assets and Commodity Price Index Changes," *J. Finance*, May 1972, *27*, 251–78.

J. **Rutledge,** "The Unemployment Inflation Tradeoff: A Review Article," *Claremont Econ. Papers*, No. 141, July 1975.

T. J. **Sargent,** "Anticipated Inflation and Nominal Interest," *Quart. J. Econ.*, May 1972, *86*, 212–25.

I. **Visco,** "Inflation and the Rate of Interest," *Quart. J. Econ.*, May 1975, *89*, 303–10.

W. P. **Yohe and D. S. Karnosky,** "Interest Rates and Price Level Changes," *Fed. Reserve Bank St. Louis Rev.*, Dec. 1969, *51*, 19–36.

[16]

Monetary Policy Regimes and the Reduced Form for Interest Rates

JOE PEEK

JAMES A. WILCOX

"Just as everybody talks about the weather, every economist talks about endogenous stabilization policy, but nobody ever does anything about it."

(Goldfeld and Blinder 1972)

1. INTRODUCTION

TWO NOTABLE FEATURES OF ESTIMATED REDUCED FORMS for interest rates are their inability to account for the level and volatility of rates in the 1980s and their intertemporal coefficient instability. Clarida and Friedman (1983, 1984) have demonstrated that, relative to the predictions of either a structural or an astructural model, interest rates in the early 1980s were "too high." Peek and Wilcox (1983) conclude that, although their model passes standard

We would like to thank, without indicating the approval of, Robert McDonald, Richard Meese, Robert Murphy, Mark Toma, Janet Yellen and seminar participants at the Federal Reserve Banks of Dallas and San Francisco, the NBER Summer Institute, the Board of Governors of the Federal Reserve System, Miami (O.) University, Michigan State University, the University of California, San Diego, the University of California, Davis, and two diligent, anonymous referees. Financial support was provided by a Boston College Research Expense Grant, the Berkeley Center for Real Estate and Urban Economics, and the Institute for Business and Economic Research at Berkeley. The views expressed here are those of the authors and do not necessarily reflect those of the Federal Reserve Bank of Boston or the Board of Governors of the Federal Reserve System.

JOE PEEK *is associate professor, Boston College, and visiting economist, Federal Reserve Bank of Boston.* JAMES A. WILCOX *is associate professor, University of California, Berkeley, and faculty research fellow, National Bureau of Economic Research.*

Journal of Money, Credit, and Banking, Vol. 19, No. 3 (August 1987)
Copyright © 1987 by the Ohio State University Press

coefficient stability tests, the evidence suggests that specification and resulting stability issues remain. Here we investigate whether, apart from effects operating through expectation-formation parameters, the reduced form for interest rates has responded to monetary policy regime changes and whether such changes can account for the otherwise puzzling recent behavior of interest rates.

Whether reduced-form coefficients have changed or are likely to change by meaningful amounts in response to policy regime shifts has been hotly debated for a decade. Lucas (1976) suggested that conventional reduced-form coefficients may vary appreciably over time due to the dependence of private sector expectation-formation parameters on government policy parameters. Sims (1982) has countered that this objection should be regarded as no more than a "cautionary footnote" (p. 108) since policy rules "have not changed frequently or by large amounts" (p. 138). He argues that in fact there has been little drift in (final form) parameter estimates through time. We hypothesize that significant and quantifiable changes in monetary policy parameters took place when the chairmanship of the Federal Reserve changed. We test whether these regime changes appreciably altered the parameters of the money supply function and correspondingly those of the reduced form for interest rates.[1]

The next section presents the simple macromodel our estimates are based on. Sections 3 and 4 describe our measurement and estimation methodology. The latter section also contains the estimation results and a comparison of the in-sample and out-of-sample performance of the conventional and the changing-regime models. Section 5 summarizes the results and draws implications.

2. THE REDUCED FORM FOR INTEREST RATES

This section presents a macromodel consisting of IS, LM, wage, and aggregate supply relations. It differs from convention in that it also includes a money supply function that embodies a time-varying monetary authority policy rule. These relations can be expressed in linearized form as

$$Y - Y^N = a_0 - a_1 r^* + a_2 \Delta Y_{-1} + a_3(G - Y^N) - a_4(T - Y^N)$$
$$- a_5 SS, \tag{1}$$

$$M - P - Y^N = b_0 + b_1(Y - Y^N) - b_2 i^* + b_3 SD, \tag{2}$$

$$W = c_0 + P^e - c_1 SS, \tag{3}$$

$$P = d_0 + W + d_1(Y - Y^N) + d_2 SS, \tag{4}$$

---

[1]This agenda ignores technological changes such as improvements in information processing and data transmission. Though these even "deeper" parameters of technology may vary over time, such shifts are less readily quantified and are outside the range of this study.

and

$$M - P^e - Y^N = M_x + e_1(i-\bar{i}) ,$$
(5)

where the coefficients of all the variables are assumed to be positive and

Y = the logarithm of actual real output,
Y^N = the logarithm of natural real output,
ΔY_{-1} = the percentage change in real output lagged one period,
G = the logarithm of real government purchases,
T = the logarithm of full-employment real government taxes net of transfers,
M = the logarithm of the nominal money stock,
M_x = the logarithm of the non-interest-rate-reactive component of the real money stock,
P = the logarithm of the actual price level,
P^e = the logarithm of the expected price level,
W = the logarithm of the nominal wage,
SS = the supply shock variable,
SD = the standard deviation of the after-tax nominal interest rate,
r^* = the after-tax real interest rate,
i^* = the after-tax nominal interest rate, and
$\bar{i}$ = the recent average nominal interest rate.

The two after-tax interest rates are related to the nominal interest rate i by (6) and (7):

$$i^* \equiv i(1 - t) ;$$
(6)

$$r^* \equiv i^* - \pi^e$$
(7)

where t is the marginal tax rate on interest income and π^e is the anticipated inflation rate.

Real expenditures depend on the real after-tax interest rate, an investment accelerator term, exogenous real government purchases, exogenous full-employment real net taxes, and real shocks emanating from the supply side. Money demand is hypothesized to depend on output and on the after-tax nominal interest rate, which represents the opportunity cost of holding money when interest income is taxed. The third argument in the money demand function SD represents a measure of the capital-value risk associated with holding bonds as alternatives to money in wealth portfolios (see Slovin and Sushka [1983] for discussion and empirical evidence in favor of this hypothesis). The wage and price equations embody the natural rate hypothesis.

Equation (5) posits a monetary authority policy rule whereby the Fed predetermines an exogenous portion of the money stock M_x.[2] In addition, the Fed attenuates movements in nominal interest rates (to the extent it chooses e_1 to be positive) by having part of the money stock be endogenous. The Fed is assumed to set both components of the money stock relative to the price level expected to prevail over the coming period and to the level of real natural output. The endogenous component of the money stock rises and falls with the deviation of the current interest rate from its recent average value. This makes the total money stock endogenous with respect to interest rates and therefore an inappropriate variable in a reduced form for interest rates.

This focus on the Fed's accommodation of interest rate movements reflects a common assessment of Fed policy over the past three decades, especially by those who have worked for the Fed. To wit: "Even a casual look at post-accord Federal Reserve policy would confirm the view that, for better or worse, the System was pursuing the money market strategy . . ."(Lombra and Torto 1973). Guttentag (1966) observes that "under the money market strategy, the principal open market target is the condition of the money market" by which "is meant the interest rate on short-term claims . . ." Keran and Babb (1969) conclude that shifts in the monetary base supply function in the 1950s and 1960s were primarily driven by movements of nominal interest rates away from their "normal" levels.[3]

Shifts in the slope parameter, e_1, in (5) can be seen to capture some of the shifts in basic Federal Reserve policy, or regime, during the postwar period. The reduced pegging of interest rates after the 1951 Treasury Accord, the increased emphasis on monetary aggregates in the 1970s, and the October 1979 shift to reserves targeting can be represented by successive declines in e_1. The Fed almost certainly has reacted to other factors as well: cyclical unemployment, inflation, international forces, and the preferences of individual policymakers. Here, since only the systematic response of the money stock to interest rates is taken to be endogenous, reactions to all other factors are impounded in M_x. To the extent any one Fed chairman reduced the money supply (relative to P^e and Y^N), for example to reduce inflation, he would be choosing lower values of M_x.

Equations $(1-7)$ can be combined to yield the reduced-form equation for the nominal interest rate:

$$i = \beta_0 + \beta_1 \pi^e + \beta_2 \Delta Y_{-1} + \beta_3 G' + \beta_4 T' + \beta_5 M_x + \beta_6 SS$$
$$\quad (+) \qquad (+) \qquad (+) \qquad (-) \qquad (-) \qquad (?)$$

$$+ \ \beta_7 SD + \beta_8 \bar{\iota}$$
$$\quad (+) \qquad (+) \tag{8}$$

[2] It is natural to specify (5) in levels, rather than growth rates for example, since real output and interest rates in the short run are driven by the level of the money supply in $(1)-(4)$. Given the prior level of money, (5) may also be interpreted as describing the implied money growth rate.

[3] In addition, the money stock may be endogenous with respect to nominal interest rates due to the behavior of the private sector. To the extent that excess reserves, discount window borrowings, and movements of deposits across accounts with different reserve requirements respond to changes in nominal interest rates relative to their recent levels, the parameter e_1 reflects private sector as well as Federal Reserve responses.

where $G' = (G - Y^N)$, $T' = (T - Y^N)$ and

$$\beta_0 = \frac{a_0(b_1 + d_1) + b_0 + c_0 + d_0}{D} = \frac{\alpha_0}{D}, \tag{9}$$

$$\beta_1 = \frac{a_1(b_1 + d_1)}{D} = \frac{\alpha_1}{D}, \tag{10}$$

$$\beta_2 = \frac{a_2(b_1 + d_1)}{D} = \frac{\alpha_2}{D}, \tag{11}$$

$$\beta_3 = \frac{a_3(b_1 + d_1)}{D} = \frac{\alpha_3}{D}, \tag{12}$$

$$\beta_4 = \frac{-a_4(b_1 + d_1)}{D} = \frac{\alpha_4}{D}, \tag{13}$$

$$\beta_5 = \frac{-1}{D} = \frac{\alpha_5}{D}, \tag{14}$$

$$\beta_6 = \frac{(d_2 - c_1) - a_4(b_1 + d_1)}{D} = \frac{\alpha_6}{D}, \tag{15}$$

$$\beta_7 = \frac{b_3}{D} = \frac{\alpha_7}{D}, \tag{16}$$

$$\beta_8 = \frac{e_1}{D}, \text{ and} \tag{17}$$

$$D = (1-t)[a_1(b_1 + d_1) + b_2] + e_1 = (1-t)\alpha_8 + e_1. \tag{18}$$

If the model is taken literally, $\alpha_5 = -1$. However, this simplified model ignores other considerations that might cause α_5 to deviate from minus one (e.g., the existence of a real balance effect). So that we can obtain a measure of the marginal significance for the M_x coefficient, we have chosen not to impose the constraint that $\alpha_5 = -1$. The sign of β_6 is indeterminate a priori. An adverse supply shock reduces investment and real wages and thus the interest rate, while at the same time increasing input costs which, operating through the aggregate supply equation, raise the interest rate. The investment-real wage effect might be expected to dominate, suggesting a negative value for β_6. The results presented in Peek and Wilcox (1983) and Wilcox (1983a, 1983b) support this interpretation.

To the extent that e_1 varies over time, the reduced-form coefficients change. A decrease in the response of the money supply to the deviation of i from $\bar{\imath}$ will raise all of the β's (except β_8) by the same proportion through its effect on D. Since e_1

also appears in the numerator of β_x, the interest rate response to $\bar{i}$ is affected differently; it falls as e_1 declines.

3. METHODOLOGY

Equations (9)–(18) illustrate the relationship between the monetary policy parameter and the reduced-form coefficients. Our hypothesis is that failure to allow for movements over time in this policy parameter has contributed to poor interest rate predictions, even ex post, and to observed reduced-form estimate instability. We rectify this shortcoming by including values of the time series of the proxy for the monetary policy parameter, e_1. This allows us to test whether monetary policy regime changes contributed to these problems.

To obtain a time series for e_1, we specify the monetary policy rule (5) as

$$M - P^e - Y^N = h_0 + h_1 AFB + h_2 GWM + h_3 PAV + h_4 DI$$

$$+ h_5 AFBDI + h_6 GWMDI + h_7 PAVDI +$$

$$h_8 TIME .   \qquad (19)$$

AFB, GWM, and *PAV* are dummy variables that are assigned a value of one during the terms of the Fed Chairmen who followed Martin: Burns, Miller, and Volcker, respectively. Fed Chairman Martin's regime is represented by the constant term, h_0. The same variables with the suffix *DI* are those dummies multiplied by the deviation of the nominal interest rate from its recent average value, $DI = i - \bar{i}$. *TIME* is a time trend that allows for gradual, exogenous change in velocity (e.g., due to technological innovations).

This specification permits e_1, the reaction of the money supply to changes in nominal interest rates, to vary across the regimes of the different Fed chairmen, but restricts it to be constant within each regime. The three intercept dummies are included to lessen the likelihood that variations in the overall stringency of monetary policy across regimes be mistakenly attributed to variations in the systematic-response coefficient, i.e., to avoid empirically confusing intercept and slope shifts in the money supply function. These intercept dummies can be interpreted as reflecting differences among regimes in reacting to non-interest rate variables (e.g., reflecting the anti-inflation stance of each regime).

The (step function) time series for the money supply reaction coefficient can be read directly from (19). Since the three regime coefficients reflect effects relative to the Martin regime, the values for e_1 are h_4, (h_4+h_5), (h_4+h_6), and (h_4+h_7) for 1952:06–1970:06, 1970:12–1977:12, 1978:06–1979:06, and 1979:12–1984:12, respectively. Similarly, h_0, (h_0+h_1), (h_0+h_2), and (h_0+h_3) reflect the average relative degree of monetary stringency for the four Fed Chairman regimes. M_x is also based on (19). Movements in M_x, $M - P^e - Y^N$ minus the four reaction elements and the time trend component, consist of all movements in money other than those due to the Fed's reaction to the variation in interest rates and trend-like changes in transactions technology.

4. EMPIRICAL RESULTS

Estimates Based on No Federal Reserve Policy Reaction

This section presents the results of estimating (8) subject to (9)–(18). When e_1 is taken to be zero through time, constant-coefficient, ordinary least squares (OLS) suffices. These restrictions imply that the entire money stock is exogenous $(M_x = M - P^e - Y^N)$, that $\bar{i}$ no longer appears as an explanatory variable, and that the denominator (D) is proportional to $(1-t)$. As a result, (8) can be expressed as

$$i = \beta_0 + \beta_1 \pi^e + \beta_2 \Delta Y_{-1} + \beta_3 G' + \beta_4 T' + \beta_5 MDTR$$
$$+ \beta_6 SS + \beta_7 SD \tag{20}$$

where $MDTR = (M - P^e - Y^N)$ less its own time trend, and in (9)–(16),

$$D = (1-t)[a_1(b_1 + d_1) + b_2] = (1-t)\alpha_8 . \tag{21}$$

From (21), it can be seen that the time series for $(1-t)$ can be factored out of the coefficient of each explanatory variable. We can express (20) with constant reduced-form coefficients when we divide each of the right-hand-side variables (including the constant term) by $(1-t)$.[4] Now, $1/(1-t)$ is included in the explanatory variables rather than in their coefficients, and we obtain estimates of α_i / α_8 in (9)–(16) rather than the β_i's. The implied reduced-form coefficients in (20) at any time are then the estimated constant coefficients multiplied by the value of $1/(1-t)$ for that period. To do this we require time series data for the marginal tax rate of the marginal investor, t. If a tax-exempt institution is the marginal investor, the marginal tax rate is zero. If individuals are the marginal investors, the appropriate tax rate is the marginal personal income tax rate.[5] The progressivity of the personal income tax rate makes measuring that rate problematic. As our measure of t, we use the average marginal tax rate on interest income constructed from data contained in annual editions of *Statistics of Income, Individual Income Tax Returns* (see Peek 1982). The tax rate is calculated as a weighted average of the marginal personal income tax rate for each adjusted gross income

---

[4]Peek and Wilcox (1984) estimate a specification similar to (20)–(21) with $(1-t)$ replaced by $(1-\theta t)$, where θ reflects the degree of (lack of) fiscal illusion. Using nonlinear least squares, the estimate of θ closely approximates one, indicating no fiscal illusion. Therefore, we here restrict θ to unity, implying complete adjustment to changes in tax rate policies.

[5]Peek and Wilcox (1986) present evidence that the effective marginal investors in the Treasury bill market are households rather than corporations or tax-exempt institutions.

class. The weight for each class is equal to its share of the total interest received by all income classes.[6]

June and December averages of the secondary market yield (on a bond equivalent basis) on one-year U.S. Treasury bills are used as the dependent variable.[7] π^e is the Livingston survey one-year expected inflation rate, recorded in June and December. This measure of expected inflation has the advantages of being truly ex ante and of embodying whatever sophistication agents actually use to form their expectations.[8] The Lucas proposition is likely to apply to expectations generating mechanisms with particular force. The measure used here is the output of that presumably varying mechanism and therefore is not subject to that critique. The remaining variables are measured with second and fourth quarter data (except SD and $\bar{\imath}$). We use the sum of currency and demand deposits as our measure of the nominal money stock.[9] P^e is the price level expected six months ahead, again from the Livingston survey. Y^N, natural real output, is based on the potential real GNP series from the Council of Economic Advisors (1977, p. 54).[10] In this specification, $(M - P^e - Y^N)$ has been detrended by regressing it on a linear time trend and using the residual as $MDTR$. G' is the logarithm of the ratio of real government purchases to real natural output. T' is the logarithm of the ratio of full-employment real taxes net of transfers to real natural output. The full-employment net tax measure is calculated from the Bureau of Economic Analysis measures of cyclically adjusted federal receipts and expenditures for 1955–84 (see DeLeeuw and Holloway 1983). The 1952–54 observations are based on the Federal Reserve Bank of St. Louis's high-employment federal government receipts and expenditures series. ΔY_{-1} is the four-quarter growth rate of real GNP up to the preceding quarter. SS is the ratio of the import deflator to the GNP deflator, adjusted for exchange rate changes. SD is the 18-month moving standard deviation of the after-tax nominal interest rate, lagged one month. $\bar{\imath}$ is the average of the one-year U.S. Treasury bill yield for the previous twelve

[6]This tax series serves as an index of the marginal tax rate of the marginal individual, moving with that rate but perhaps not measuring its level exactly.

[7]Before December 1959, when one-year Treasury bills were introduced, the interest rate measure is based on the yield on Treasury bills with 9- to 12-month maturities.

[8]In Peek and Wilcox (1984), we found that substituting an expected inflation measure based on prior interest rates did not affect our qualitative findings.

[9]This measure of the money stock removes NOW, Super-NOW, and ATS balances, credit union share draft balances, traveler's checks, and demand deposits at thrifts from $M1$. These "other checkable deposits" apparently behave much more like savings balances than the transaction balances measure we seek. The 1984 turnover rate for ATS and NOW accounts was 16. This compares to turnover rates for demand deposits and savings deposits of 434 and 5, respectively.

Some econometric evidence also suggests our $M1A$-type measure bears a more stable relation to the economy than $M1$ does. Based on his money-demand estimates, Gordon (1984) argues "that a substantial part of the 1981–1983 velocity puzzle is attributable to the consequences of financial deregulation, which increased the fraction of $M1$ consisting of new types of deposits with a relatively low transactions turnover." Hafer (1984) finds than an $M1A$-type measure outperforms $M1$ in a reduced-form GNP equation. Furthermore, the reduced-form GNP equation fit based on that $M1A$-type measure does not deteriorate when the 1980s are added to the sample, whereas the fit of the $M1$-based equation deteriorates badly.

[10]The 1979, 1980, and 1981 Council Reports update this series. Potential real GNP is assumed to have grown at a steady 2.9 percent annual rate from 1980 until 1984.

TABLE 1

OLS ESTIMATES OF ONE-YEAR TREASURY BILL YIELD EQUATIONS: SEMIANNUAL OBSERVATIONS

Sample Period	Constant	π^e	ΔY_{-1}	G'	T'	MDTR	SS	SD	D79S4	R^2	D-W	SEE
1. 1952:06–1979:06	13.4 (5.93)	0.813 (8.63)	7.96 (2.54)	2.43 (2.57)	1.20 (1.61)	0.15 (0.06)	-3.03 (3.39)	0.38 (0.88)	—	0.8932	1.49	0.80
2. 1952:06–1984:12	13.1 (5.00)	0.838 (9.64)	7.78 (2.04)	3.20 (2.74)	-1.26 (2.17)	-12.28 (6.22)	-5.62 (5.31)	0.04 (0.08)	—	0.9088	1.45	1.12
3. 1952:06–1984:12	10.8 (4.28)	0.690 (7.56)	6.80 (1.93)	1.76 (1.52)	-0.01 (0.09)	-4.18 (1.39)	-3.92 (3.57)	-0.02 (0.04)	3.72 (3.36)	0.9241	1.53	1.03

Note: Absolute values of t-statistics in parentheses.

Monetary Theory

months. *D7984* is a dummy variable that takes the value one starting with the December 1979 observation. Throughout, the June 1980 observation has been omitted due to the presence of credit controls; otherwise, the full sample is 1952:06–1984:12.

Table 1 presents the results of estimating (20). The estimates in row 1 imply that rises in expected inflation, government purchases, full-employment real net taxes and real money balances, faster real growth, and more volatile interest rates raise rates while positive supply shocks lower them. Net taxes, money and interest rate volatility have statistically insignificant effects. After 1979 interest rates were both surprisingly high and volatile. Row 2 shows that when the post-1979 period (omitting the 1980:06 credit controls observation) is added to the sample, the standard error of estimate rises by 40 percent and both net taxes and money now have significant, negative effects (as predicted). There is no evidence that increased interest rate volatility raised the level of interest rates. With the exception of *T'* and *MDTR*, adding the post-1979 period seems to change the estimated coefficients relatively little. The sharp jump in the money coefficient and decline in the tax coefficient reflect econometric attribution of the unusually high real interest rates in recent years to the major tax reduction and unusually restrictive monetary policy. While most of the coefficient estimates appear stable, a formal stability test paints a different picture. The hypothesis of stability for this specification over a mid-1979 sample split is soundly rejected (F-statistic $(8,49) = 6.53$; critical value $F(8,50) = 2.13$). This sample split corresponds to the beginning of the Volcker regime. If, instead, we test for stability across the Martin and Burns regimes (1952:06–1977:12, split after 1970:06), we cannot reject coefficient stability at the five percent level of significance (F-statistic $(8,36) = 2.01$; critical value $F(8,40) = 2.18$).

Including *D7984* in row 3, however, reduces the estimated coefficients on *G'*, *T'* and *MDTR* to insignificance. The coefficient of 3.72 on *D7984* in row 3 indicates that the surprises were large and primarily on the upside. However, even allowing for this nonexplained upward shift, the standard error of the estimate is much larger than that for the pre-1980 sample period.

Estimates Based on Changing Monetary Policy Rules

When e_1 is nonzero, nonlinear least squares can be used to estimate equation (8) while imposing the coefficient restrictions described in (9)–(18). Incorporating the definition of e_1 implicit in (19), we can rewrite (8) as

$$i = \frac{\alpha_0}{D} + \frac{\alpha_1}{D} \pi^e + \frac{\alpha_2}{D} \Delta Y_{-1} + \frac{\alpha_3}{D} G' + \frac{\alpha_4}{D} T'$$

$$+ \frac{\alpha_5}{D} M_x + \frac{\alpha_6}{D} SS + \frac{\alpha_7}{D} SD + \frac{e_1}{D} \bar{i} \tag{22}$$

where

$$D = (1 - t)\alpha_8 + e_1 \tag{23}$$

and

$$e_1 = h_4 + h_5 AFB + h_6 GWM + h_7 PAV . \tag{24}$$

While (22) is a reduced-form equation, we cannot estimate it [even incorporating (23) and (24)] in isolation. We must also estimate (19) to obtain a measure of M_x. The two equations could be estimated sequentially or jointly. A two-step procedure would ignore the uncertainty in the estimates of both M_x and e_1 and would ignore M_x being partly composed of some predicted values from the money supply rule (the Chairman dummies times their coefficients). Thus, to allow for cross-equation error correlation, to obtain efficient estimates, and to make valid inferences, joint estimation of (19) and (22) is employed (see Pagan 1984). Using maximum likelihood we estimate the system composed of (19) and (22), with D and e_1 defined as in (23) and (24).

We anticipate positive values for $\alpha_1, \alpha_2, \alpha_3, \alpha_7$ and α_8, and negative values for $\alpha_4, \alpha_5,$ and α_6. The following are estimates for the 1952:06–1984:12 sample, again omitting the 1980:06 credit controls period (absolute values of t-statistics in parentheses):

$$M - P^e - Y^N = - 1.287 + 0.0511AFB - 0.125GWM - 0.278PAV$$
$$(118.67) \quad (3.47) \qquad (4.68) \qquad (12.67)$$

$$+ 0.080DI - 0.0143AFBDI - 0.00297GWMDI$$
$$(13.95) \qquad (1.67) \qquad (0.19)$$

$$- 0.0412PAVDI + 0.0161TIME + \hat{\mu}_M , \tag{25}$$
$$(5.75) \qquad (37.77)$$

$$R^2 = 0.977; \quad SEE = 0.0577; \quad D\text{-}W = 1.71;$$

$$i = (0.0675 + 0.0317\pi^e + 0.158\Delta Y_{-1} + 0.149G' + 0.0229T'$$
$$(0.92) \quad (11.37) \qquad (1.52) \qquad (4.44) \qquad (1.25)$$

$$- 0.678M_x - 0.355SS - 0.0555SD + e_1\bar{i})/(0.0328(1-t)$$
$$(12.99) \qquad (13.12) \qquad (5.76) \qquad (7.97)$$

$$+ e_1) + \mu_i , \tag{26}$$

$$R^2 = 0.982; \quad SEE = 0.467; \quad D\text{-}W = 1.56;$$

where

$$e_1 = 0.0797 - 0.0143AFB - 0.00297GWM - 0.0412PAV \tag{27}$$
$$(13.95) \qquad (1.67) \qquad (0.19) \qquad (5.75)$$

and

$$M_x = M - P^e - Y^N - \underset{(13.95)}{0.0797 DI} + \underset{(1.67)}{0.0143 AFBDI}$$

$$+ \underset{(0.19)}{0.00297 GWMDI} + \underset{(5.75)}{0.0412 PAVDI} + \underset{(37.77)}{0.161 TIME}$$

$$= \underset{(118.67)}{- 1.287} + \underset{(3.47)}{0.0511 AFB} - \underset{(4.68)}{0.125 GWM} - \underset{(12.67)}{0.278 PAV}$$

$$+ \mu_M . \tag{28}$$

It should be emphasized that we estimated a two-equation (not a four-equation) system composed of (25) and (26). To simplify the presentation of (26), we chose to substitute the symbols e_1 and M_x for the more complicated expressions appearing in (27)–(28). Within-equation (as well as across-equation) coefficient restrictions were imposed in (26). Furthermore, as can be seen from a comparison of (25) and (27)–(28), there are also across-equation restrictions imposed on the coefficients determining the time series for the Fed reaction parameter (e_1).

With the exception of the T' and SD coefficients, the general pattern of signs and significance of the coefficients in (26) mirrors the OLS results in row 2 of Table 1. We now obtain an insignificant positive coefficient on T' and a significant negative response of interest rates to interest rate volatility. To the extent that the higher degree of volatility occurs in long-term interest rates as well, a negative response of our short-term interest rate would be consistent with a flight of funds from long-term securities to relatively less risky (in terms of capital-value) short-term instruments. That is, the term structure curve would steepen. There would be an unambiguous rise in long-term rates, while very short-term rates would certainly rise by less and might even fall if there were a sufficient increase in the demand for very short-term maturities. Our results are consistent with this latter case.

Another interesting feature of (26) compared to our Table 1 results is the increased significance of the money coefficient. While the $MDTR$ coefficient is significant in row 2 of Table 1, it is insignificant in rows 1 and 3 and it is positive in the shorter sample. In previous studies (both ours and those of others), there similarly has been a tendency for the money stock coefficient to be insignificant and, at times, to be positive. This could be attributed to offsetting liquidity and real balance effects. However, while real balance effects have played an important role in theoretical debates, it is unlikely that they are the source of positive estimated money effects on interest rates.

A more likely explanation is the presence of an endogenous component in $MDTR$ arising from the Federal Reserve's attempts to mitigate movements in interest rates. Increases in the money supply in response to (or in anticipation of) an increase in the interest rate would tend to camouflage the true relationship between exogenous money and interest rates. This policy-induced simultaneous-equations bias is analogous to that pointed out by Goldfeld and Blinder (1972).

Our two equation system estimates the Federal Reserve feedback component in the total money stock and eliminates it from $M - P^e - Y^N$ to form our exogenous money measure, M_x. This exogenized measure of money has a strong, negative estimated impact on interest rates, the absence of which has perplexed many previous investigators.

Though the $MDTR$ and M_x series deliver very different estimated coefficients, they are highly correlated; only a small portion of the movement of the total money stock measure, $M - P^e - Y^N$, is attributed to its endogenous component. Regressions of M_x and of the purely endogenous component of money, $(M - P^e - Y^N) - M_x$, on the total money stock produce coefficients of 0.87 and 0.13, respectively.[11] Thus, only about one-eighth of the movements of money are estimated on average to have been endogenous.

We have written (25) in such a way that we can easily compare the relative degree of (interest rate) accommodation across regimes using the Martin years as a benchmark. From (27) we can compute the estimated (step-function) time series for the Fed response parameter, e_1. Those values are 0.0797, 0.0654, 0.0767 and 0.0385 for the Martin, Burns, Miller, and Volcker regimes, respectively. This suggests that the Volcker regime accommodated interest rate changes least while the Martin and Miller years saw the most accommodation. The Burns regime appears to have been only slightly less accommodative than the Martin and Miller regimes. The statistically significant coefficient on $PAVDI$ indicates that Volcker was significantly less accommodative than Martin. While the point estimates indicate that both Burns and Miller were slightly less accommodative than Martin, the differences are not statistically significant. When the system was re-estimated with a constant (non-zero) degree of accommodation over the entire sample period ($h_5 = h_6 = h_7 = 0$), we could easily reject that restriction (chi-square statistic = 17.2; critical value for the 1 percent level = 11.3).

Similarly, the intercept dummy estimates can be used to assess the average tightness of the exogenous portion of the money stock for each of the four Fed chairman regimes. These estimates imply that exogenous monetary policy was easiest during the Burns years, and tightest under Volcker. Both differed significantly from the benchmark Martin regime. The primary difference between the Martin regime and the Burns and Miller regimes appears to be in the relative tightness of exogenous monetary policy rather than in the degree of interest rate accommodation. Not surprisingly, the estimates portray the Volcker regime as being least accommodative of interest rate movements and as having exercised the greatest degree of exogenous monetary stringency.

Using (26) and (27) and the income tax rate series, t, we can calculate the time series for the reduced-form coefficient for π^e, β_1. Within each regime, only tax rate movements cause β_1 to change.[12] The average values within each of the four

---

[11] The estimated trend factor from (25) was removed from total money so that each series was trendless.

[12] The implied coefficient exhibits a slight downward drift until the mid-1960s, due to a small decline in the effective tax rate series. Tax schedule reductions in 1954 and 1964–65 and a slight

regimes are: 0.306, 0.358, 0.321, and 0.524. These values are much lower than most other estimates because, in this model, β_1 represents the net effect on nominal rates of the usual upward shift in the IS curve coupled with the endogenous downward shift in the LM curve produced by the Fed's reaction function. The estimated effect on nominal rates of a rise in expected inflation, apart from any endogenous reaction of the money stock can be seen by setting e_1 to zero. In this case, β_1 reduces to $(\alpha_1/\alpha_8) (1/(1-t))$. Based on our estimates, β_1 is (0.97) $(1/(1-t))$.

The closeness of the estimates of β_1 to $1/(1-t)$ implies that the estimated interest elasticity of money demand is very close to zero. Indeed, the interest semielasticity of money demand, $\alpha_8 - \alpha_1 = b_2$, is estimated to be $0.0328 - 0.0317 = 0.0011$ ($t = 0.37$). Even at an after-tax nominal interest rate as large as 10 percent, the estimated elasticity is only 0.011. The small and insignificantly negative estimated response of money demand suggests that, apart from the endogenous reaction of the money supply, the LM curve is all but vertical. Nonetheless, the estimates indicate that the LM curve is not vertical. The source of the less than infinite LM slope is the larger and significantly positive estimated response of the money supply to nominal interest rates.

Including $D7984$ as an additional explanatory variable in the interest rate equation (not shown) permits us to test whether the reduced-form coefficient movement that we ascribe to policy shifts remains when a dummy variable for the later part of the sample is included. Given the significant differences found for the Volcker regime responses, one might suspect that the differential response attributed to Volcker would be eliminated by the inclusion of the 1979–84 dummy variable. However, this is not the case. The response coefficients on DI, $AFBDI$, $GWMDI$, and $PAVDI$ are 0.088, -0.016, 0.00007, and -0.047 with t-statistics of the same magnitude as without $D7984$ (e.g., the t-statistic for the $PAVDI$ coefficient is -5.95). The coefficients and associated t-statistics on the constant term and regime dummy variables are very similar to those in (25).

In addition, the estimated $D7984$ coefficient indicates that our model does not seriously underpredict the interest rate during the 1979–84 period, contrary to the linear specification in Table 1. Allowing for policy parameter change reduces the estimated coefficient on $D7984$ by over four hundred basis points (from $+3.72$ (t = 3.36) to -0.72 ($t = -2.03$)). Consequently, our results not only suggest a significant role for changing policy parameters, but also help explain the systematic underprediction of interest rates in the early 1980s. Furthermore, unlike the Table 1 results, the money coefficient retains its significance (-0.779, $t = -15.86$) when $D7984$ is included as an explanatory variable.

Because some of the estimates (especially the $MDTR$ coefficient) in the first

---

response to economic slack in the late 1950s and early 1960s combine to reduce effective tax rates. After 1965, strong nominal income growth lifted the effective tax rate and, hence, β_1. This slow upward drift occurs in the Burns and Miller regimes as well. During the Volcker regime, β_1 rises initially and then begins to decline as the multistage tax rate reductions become effective through the early 1980s.

two rows of Table 1 are very sensitive to the sample period selected, we have re-estimated our two-equation system over the pre-Volcker, 1952:06–1979:06 period. The results [(29)–(31)] are very similar to those obtained for the longer sample:

$$M - P^e - Y^x = -1.288 + 0.0651 AFB - 0.149 GWM$$
$$ (91.10) \quad (3.65) \qquad (5.02)$$

$$+ 0.101 DI - 0.0179 AFBDI + 0.0121 GWMDI$$
$$(14.16) \qquad (1.77) \qquad\quad (0.69)$$

$$- 0.0163 TIME + \mu_M , \tag{29}$$
$$(29.25)$$

$$R^2 = 0.919; \quad SEE = 0.0702; \quad D\text{-}W = 1.80;$$

$$i = (-0.143 + 0.0175\pi^e + 0.0293\Delta Y_{-1} + 0.108 G' + 0.0315 T'$$
$$ (1.39) \quad (3.30) \qquad (2.72) \qquad (3.51) \qquad (1.23)$$

$$- 0.622 M_x - 0.246 SS - 0.0094 SD + e_1\bar{i}\,)/(0.00926(1-t)$$
$$(14.82) \qquad (8.46) \qquad (0.69) \qquad\qquad (1.58)$$

$$+ e_1) + \mu_i \tag{30}$$

where

$$e_1 = 0.101 - 0.0179 AFB + 0.0121 GWM . \tag{31}$$
$$(14.16) \quad (1.77) \qquad (0.69)$$

The primary differences are that the SD coefficient and the coefficient on $(1-t)$ in the denominator are no longer significant while that on ΔY_{-1} is now significant. The t-statistic for the expected inflation rate coefficient drops substantially, but the coefficient retains its significance. The M_x coefficient does not lose its statistical significance when the sample period is shortened as was the case in Table 1. In fact, the implied β's in (26) and (30) are very similar. Further, (25) and (29) tell the same story regarding the relative interest rate accommodation and average exogenous restrictiveness of the Martin, Burns, and Miller regimes.

Table 2 lists the actual values of interest rates and the values predicted in- and out-of-sample using the no-reaction (linear), constant policy reaction ($h_5 = h_6 = h_7 = 0$) and variable policy reaction specifications. As always, the 1980:06 credit control observation is omitted. The summary measures in Table 2 show that, out-of-sample or in, the variable reaction equations outperform those from Table 1 over the most recent period. The relative improvement is particularly striking in the out-of-sample forecasts. In the in-sample case, the mean error is virtually eliminated, the mean absolute error is reduced by $(1.10 - 0.51 =\,)$ 59 basis points (54 percent), and the root-mean-squared error (RMSE) is reduced

Monetary Theory

TABLE 2

INTEREST RATE PREDICTIONS OF ALTERNATIVE POLICY REGIME MODELS:
SEMIANNUAL OBSERVATIONS 1979:12 – 1984:12

Date	Actual (1)	In-Sample			Out-of-Sample		
		No Reaction (2)	Constant Regime (3)	Variable Regime (4)	No Reaction (5)	Constant Regime (6)	Variable Regime (7)
1979:12	12.26	13.81	12.59	12.91	11.42	12.40	12.43
1980:12	15.25	15.59	14.70	14.97	12.34	14.91	14.98
1981:06	15.23	14.09	14.49	14.43	10.13	15.27	15.36
1981:12	13.08	14.09	14.36	14.10	9.02	15.19	15.17
1982:06	14.38	10.75	14.03	14.23	5.62	15.48	15.43
1982:12	8.97	9.75	10.12	9.92	4.31	11.17	11.07
1983:06	9.73	9.24	9.64	9.48	4.70	10.58	10.60
1983:12	10.18	10.36	9.83	9.92	4.66	10.57	10.62
1984:06	12.27	10.69	11.37	11.57	5.15	12.25	12.32
1984:12	9.41	9.16	9.52	9.46	3.43	10.51	10.50
Mean error		0.32	0.01	−0.02	5.00	−0.76	−0.77
Mean absolute error		1.10	0.58	0.51	5.00	0.83	0.82
Root-mean-squared error		1.46	0.71	0.61	5.41	1.13	1.10

by nearly 60 percent. The column 3 information answers the question: How well could we explain interest rates over the 1979:12–1984:12 period, allowing only for a non-zero but constant policy reaction coefficient, e_1? The evidence is that incorporating even a constant policy reaction improves the fit substantially. Even when h_5, h_6, and h_7 are restricted to be zero, both the mean absolute error and the RMSE fall by approximately 50 percent.

For the 1979:12–1984:12 period, allowing regime-specific reactions provides only a slight further improvement. While in this particular in-sample subperiod the constant regime specification does about as well as the variable regime specification, the latter formulation dominates on average. Over the full sample period, the constant regime specification has a 16 percent larger SEE (0.544 compared to 0.467). Using a likelihood ratio test, we are able to soundly reject the restriction that $h_5 = h_6 = h_7 = 0$ (chi-squared statistic = 17.22; 1 percent critical value = 11.3).

Because an estimate of h_7 (the relative degree of accommodation during the Volcker regime) is required, we could not perform standard out-of-sample predictions for the variable reaction specification. To obtain our variable regime out-of-sample predictions (column 7), we allowed differences in the degree of accommodation among the Martin, Burns, and Miller regimes. The out-of-sample predictions were based on the assumption that Volcker would continue the accommodation policy pursued by Miller (the estimated h_6 value was 0.01207). When we compare the summary measures that appear at the bottom of Table 2, we see that the variable regime specification again substantially outperforms the no-reaction specification. Both the mean error and mean absolute error are reduced by approximately 85 percent. The RMSE is reduced by 80 percent. Column 6 indicates that allowing for some (even constant) degree of accommodation is the major source of the improvement for this subperiod. As was the case with the in-sample prediction, allowing for different degrees of accommodation across regimes produces only a slight improvement over the constant reaction specification.

The variable regime out-of-sample predictions in Table 2 are inconsistent with the original hypothesis of this project. We have argued that the monetary policy response to interest rate fluctuations has differed across Federal Reserve Chairman regimes. Yet we constructed the out-of-sample (Volcker regime) predictions assuming that the value of e_1 during the Volcker regime was identical to that in the Miller regime. To obtain an estimate of h_7 to be used in the out-of-sample predictions, we must include at least a part of the Volcker regime in our initial estimation period.

Table 3 presents the results from such an experiment. We have estimated the equations through the first half of the Volcker regime and include only the last half of that regime in the out-of-sample forecast period. The first four columns in Table 3 are identical to those in Table 2. Their summary statistics tell a similar story, although the differences between the no-reaction and variable regime specifications are not quite as dramatic. The out-of-sample predictions indicate that specifications which allow for constant policy response substantially outperform the no-response predictions (the RMSEs are reduced by approximately 50 percent). The RMSEs of the constant and variable regimes are quite similar indicating there is no gain in predicting interest rates for the 1982:12–1984:12 period achieved by allowing e_1 to vary across regimes. In fact, the constant regime RMSE is slightly lower. While that holds for this particular subperiod, the variable regime specification outperforms the constant regime specification over the full sample period (as noted above).

TABLE 3

INTEREST RATE PREDICTIONS OF ALTERNATIVE POLICY REGIME MODELS:
SEMIANNUAL OBSERVATIONS 1982:12 – 1984:12

		In-Sample			Out-of-Sample		
Date	Actual (1)	No Reaction (2)	Constant Regime (3)	Variable Regime (4)	No Reaction (5)	Constant Regime (6)	Variable Regime (7)
1982:12	8.97	9.75	10.12	9.92	8.99	10.24	9.84
1983:06	9.73	9.24	9.64	9.48	8.63	9.61	9.28
1983:12	10.18	10.36	9.83	9.92	9.15	9.63	9.35
1984:06	12.27	10.69	11.37	11.57	9.39	11.22	10.98
1984:12	9.41	9.16	9.52	9.46	7.65	9.47	8.97
Mean error		0.27	0.02	0.04	1.35	0.08	0.43
Mean absolute error		0.65	0.52	0.44	1.36	0.61	0.78
Root-mean-squared error		0.83	0.68	0.55	1.65	0.78	0.84

290   :   MONEY, CREDIT, AND BANKING

5. CONCLUDING REMARKS

There is considerable intertemporal instability in previous interest rate equation estimates. We hypothesized that monetary policy parameter shifts have been important sources of that instability. We incorporate Federal-Reserve-Chairman-specific values of this policy parameter (the Fed response to interest rate changes) in our model and estimate deeper, presumably more stable parameters. The estimates generate reduced-form coefficients that move by sizeable amounts in response to policy parameter change. Statistical tests imply that allowing for a varying monetary policy reaction parameter provides a significantly better explanation of interest rates. Our model explains not only statistically significant movement of the reduced-form coefficients, but economically meaningful changes as well. Both in-sample and out-of-sample forecasts from the proposed model outperform the more traditional specification, which ignores monetary policy reaction. Furthermore, the model that accounts for varying monetary policy regimes is able to explain the heretofore puzzling high real interest rates in the early 1980s.

LITERATURE CITED

Clarida, Richard H., and Benjamin M. Friedman. "Why Have Short-Term Interest Rates Been So High?" *Brookings Papers on Economic Activity*, No. 2 (1983), 553–78.

———. "The Behavior of U.S. Short-Term Interest Rates Since October, 1979." *Journal of Finance* 39 (July 1984), 671–82.

Council of Economic Advisors. "Annual Report." In *Economic Report of the President.* Washington, D.C.: U.S. Government Printing Office, 1977.

deLeeuw, Frank, and Thomas Holloway. "Cyclical Adjustment of the Federal Budget and Federal Debt." *Survey of Current Business* (and the May 1985 update) 63 (December 1983), 25–40.

Goldfeld, Stephen M., and Alan S. Blinder. "Some Implications of Endogenous Stabilization Policy." *Brookings Papers on Economic Activity*, No. 3 (1972), 585–640.

Gordon, Robert J. "The Short-Run Demand for Money: A Reconsideration." *Journal of Money, Credit, and Banking* 16 (November 1984, Part 1), 403–34.

Guttentag, Jack. "The Strategy of Open Market Operations." *Quarterly Journal of Economics* 80 (February 1966), 1–30.

Hafer, R. W. "The Money-GNP Link: Assessing Alternative Transactions Measures." Federal Reserve Bank of St. Louis *Review* 66 (March 1984), 19–27.

Keran, Michael W., and Christopher T. Babb. "An Explanation of Federal Reserve Actions (1933–68)." Federal Reserve Bank of St. Louis *Review* 51 (July 1969), 7–18.

Lombra, Raymond E., and Raymond G. Torto. "Federal Reserve 'Defensive' Behavior and the Reverse Causation Argument." *Southern Economic Journal* 40 (July 1973), 47–55.

Lucas, Robert E., Jr. "Econometric Policy Evaluation: A Critique." In *The Phillips Curve and Labor Markets*, edited by Karl Brunner and Allan H. Meltzer, pp. 19–46. Amsterdam: North-Holland, 1976.

Pagan, Adrian. "Econometric Issues in the Analysis of Regressions with Generated Regressors." *International Economic Review* 25 (February 1984), 221–47.

Peek, Joe. "Interest Rates, Income Taxes, and Anticipated Inflation." *American Economic Review* 72 (December 1982), 980–91.

Peek, Joe, and James A. Wilcox. "The Postwar Stability of the Fisher Effect." *Journal of Finance* 38 (September 1983), 1111–24.

_____. "The Degree of Fiscal Illusion in Interest Rates: Some Direct Estimates." *American Economic Review* 74 (December 1984), 1061–66.

_____. "Tax Rate Effects on Interest Rates." *Economics Letters* 20 (February 1986), 183–86.

Sims, Christopher. "Policy Analysis with Econometric Models." *Brookings Papers on Economic Activity,* No. 1 (1982), 107–52.

Slovin, Myron B., and Marie Elizabeth Sushka. "Money, Interest Rates, and Risk." *Journal of Monetary Economics* 12 (September 1983), 475–82.

Wilcox, James A. "The Effects of Inflation Uncertainty and Supply Shocks on Real Interest Rates." *Economics Letters* 12 (1983), 163–67 (a).

_____. "Why Real Interest Rates Were So Low in the 1970s." *American Economic Review* 73 (March 1983), 44–53 (b).

U.S. Internal Revenue Service. *Statistics of Income, Individual Income Tax Returns.* Washington, D.C.: U.S. Government Printing Office, 1947–79.

Part V
Alternative View of Monetary Theory

[17]

Money, Credit, and Prices in a Real Business Cycle

By Robert G. King and Charles I. Plosser[*]

An important recent strain of macroeconomic theory views business cycles as arising from variations in the real opportunities of the private economy, which may include shifts in government purchases or tax rates as well as technical and environmental conditions.[1] These models are often viewed as incomplete or wrong because they do not generate the widely emphasized, but not easily explained, correlation between the quantity of money and real activity.

This paper integrates money and banking into real business cycle theory. The result is a class of models that can account for the correlation between money and business cycles in terms that most economists would label reverse causation.[2] The main focus of

*Department of Economics and Graduate School of Management, respectively, University of Rochester, Rochester, NY 14627. A preliminary version of this paper was presented at the Seminar on Monetary Theory and Monetary Policy, Konstanz, West Germany, June 1981. We have benefited from the comments of Robert Barro, Herschel Grossman, John Long, Bennett McCallum, anonymous referees, and participants at seminars at the universities of Rochester, Chicago, Pennsylvania, Harvard, and Princeton. The National Science Foundation and the Center for Research in Government Policy and Business of the University of Rochester have supported this research. The above individuals and institutions should not be regarded as necessarily endorsing the views expressed in this paper.

[1] Robert Lucas (1980) provides an overview of the general equilibrium approach to business cycles. Recent work by Fynn Kydland and Edward Prescott (1982) and by John Long and Plosser (1983) illustrate how these models can mimic key elements of business cycles, including complex patterns of persistence and comovement in economic time-series.

[2] The idea that monetary quantities are endogenous is an old one, but has received little recent emphasis. We find it useful to categorize earlier stories into two broad classes: (*i*) banking system explanations such as ours; and (*ii*) explanations that stress central bank policy response. For example, James Tobin (1970) provides an analysis of a model with endogenous money that emphasizes central bank policy response. Tobin's deterministic treatment involves the Keynesian idea that money and real activity respond to the same causal influence—aggregate demand. In Fischer Black's (1972) analysis, external money passively responds to all varia-

the analysis is on the banking system, building on the earlier work of James Tobin (1963) and Eugene Fama (1980). In our real business cycle model, monetary services are privately produced intermediate goods whose quantities rise and fall with real economic developments.

In the absence of central bank policy response, the model predicts that movements in external money measures should be uncorrelated with real activity. Some preliminary empirical analysis (using annual data from 1953 to 1978) provides general support for our focus on the banking system since the correlation between monetary measures and real activity is primarily with inside money.

Our proposed explanation of the correlation between money and business fluctuations stands in sharp contrast to traditional theories that stress market failure as the key to understanding the relation and interpret monetary movements as a primary source of impulses to real activity. Given the controversies surrounding the main contending hypotheses concerning money and business cycles—the incomplete information framework of Robert Lucas (1973) and Keynesian sticky wage models as revitalized by Stanley Fischer (1977)—it seems worthwhile to consider alternative hypotheses.[3]

tions in money demand including those arising from fluctuations in real activity.

[3] In our view, there are good reasons for dissatisfaction with existing macroeconomic theories. Keynesian models typically rely on implausible wage or price rigidities, from the textbook reliance on exogenous values to the recent more sophisticated effort of Fischer (1977) that relies on existing nominal contracts. As Robert Barro (1977) points out, a key feature of the Fischer model is that agents select contracts that do not fully exploit potential gains from trade. In addition, Costas Azariadis' (1978) micro-based model of wage-employment contracts implies that perceived monetary disturbances do not alter output.

Recent analyses of monetary nonneutrality that stress expectation errors based on "imperfect information" (Lucas, 1977, provides a summary of this viewpoint)

The organization of the paper is as follows. In Section I we describe a simple model that is capable of generating real business cycles. The model is used to discuss correlations between an internal monetary quantity and real activity. In Section II, with fiat money included in the model, we analyze the relation between monetary quantities, output, and the price level in both an unregulated and regulated banking environment. In Section III we discuss some of the empirical implications of the theory and provide a preliminary analysis of the postwar U.S. experience.

I. The Real Economy

In this section we describe a simple model economy in which business cycles arise as a consequence of the intertemporal optimizing behavior of economic agents. Our model has two productive sectors with one intermediate and one final good. The output of the final goods industry is stochastic and serves as either a consumption good or as an input into future production. The output of the financial industry is an intermediate good called transaction services that is used by firms in the final goods industry and by households. The demand for transaction services arises because these services economize on time and other resources required to accomplish the exchange of goods.

Recent real general equilibrium theories of the business cycle (such as Finn Kydland and Edward Prescott; John Long and Plosser) stress produced inputs and interrelations between sectors as central to understanding the persistence and comovement of macroeconomic time-series. The simple model economy that we study has only one final product and thus does not possess such a rich set of dynamics or sectoral interactions. Nevertheless, the framework embodies our view that

the output of the financial-banking industry is an input into production and purchase of final goods. This view is consistent with the general focus on produced inputs and sectoral interactions that is the hallmark of real business cycle models.

A. Final Goods Industry

The single final product (y) is produced by a constant returns to scale production process that uses labor (n), capital (k), and transaction services (d) as inputs. The production technology is summarized by

$$(1) \qquad y_{t+1} = f(k_{yt}, n_{yt}, d_{yt}) \phi_t \xi_{t+1},$$

where k_{yt} is the amount of capital, n_{yt} is the amount of labor services, and d_{yt} is the amount of transaction services used in the final goods industry. Capital services are measured in commodity units allocated to production at time t, labor services are hours worked, and transaction services can be viewed as the number of bookkeeping entries made (described more fully below). We also make the standard assumptions of positive and diminishing marginal products to each factor. The production process is subject to two random shocks, ϕ_t and ξ_{t+1}, that are dated by the time of their realization.

Transaction services in (1) are viewed as an intermediate good purchased by final good producers from the financial industry (to be described below). Although not involved directly in the production of output in the same sense as labor and capital, transaction services are part of a cost-reducing activity similar to other organizational and control inputs.

The sequences $\{\phi_t\}$ and $\{\xi_t\}$ are assumed to be strictly positive stationary stochastic processes that are mutually and serially independent with $E(\phi_t) = E(\xi_t) = 1$. The roles played by the two shocks are quite different. At this point it is sufficient to note that ϕ_t alters *expected* time $t+1$ output and affects time t input decisions by altering intertemporal opportunities. On the other hand, ξ_{t+1} represents the basic uncertainty of the production process by altering output in an *unexpected* manner. The multiplicative na-

similarly rely on an apparent failure in the market for information. For example, information on monetary statistics is cheap and readily available. King (1981) demonstrates that in Lucas' (1973) model, real output should be uncorrelated with contemporaneously available monetary information. John Boschen and Herschel Grossman (1982) empirically investigate this proposition and find that it is rejected by the data.

ture of the randomness in total production implies a technological neutrality of the shocks with respect to individual factors of production. Alternatively, different stochastic elements could be associated with particular factors.

Production is assumed to be under supervision of identical competitive firms. Firms operate by selling claims against the future output and using the proceeds to purchase factors of production. Labor, capital, and transaction services are rented at rental prices w_t, q_t, and ρ_t, respectively. Each firm is assumed to sell one unit of claim for each unit of expected output as determined by $f(k_{yt}, n_{yt}, d_{yt})$, which amounts to defining a "share" in the firm. If the market price of claims is v_t, the firm faces a static maximization problem involving the choice of inputs that maximizes profits, $v_t f(k_{yt}, n_{yt}, d_{yt}) - w_t n_{yt} - q_t k_{yt} - \rho_t d_{yt}$. The assumption of constant returns to scale implies that the firm has a supply of claims that is horizontal at the price v_t^*, corresponding to minimum unit cost at prices q_t, w_t, and ρ_t.

B. Financial Industry

The financial industry provides accounting services that facilitate the exchange of goods by reducing the amount of time and other resources that otherwise would be devoted to market transactions. The production of this intermediate good, which we call transaction services, is summarized by the production function (2) in which n_{dt} and k_{dt} are the amounts of labor and capital allocated to the financial sector:

$$(2) \qquad d_t = h(n_{dt}, k_{dt})\lambda_t.$$

This instantaneous production structure embodies the hypothesis that production of transaction services requires less time than production of the consumption-capital good. Technological innovation in this industry is captured by λ_t, which is assumed to be a strictly positive stochastic process with a mean of one. Finally, we assume (2) represents a constant returns to scale structure so that, at given factor prices w_t and q_t, the

financial industry has a supply curve that is horizontal at a particular rental price, ρ_t^*.

Although at this stage of our analysis we focus on the flow of transaction services, the transaction (banking) industry typically (but not necessarily) provides these services in conjunction with portfolio management or intermediary services. It is convenient to imagine, therefore, that the financial industry holds claims (shares) on the probability distribution of output and issues other claims (deposits). In the process of market exchange, the claims that individuals and firms hold on the bank's portfolio (deposits) are altered through simple bookkeeping entries. Banks pass on to depositors the return to the portfolio of assets less a fee for transaction services.

The structure of the financial industry implies that the direct cost of bookkeeping services, ρ_t, does not depend on the character or composition of the bank's portfolio. As discussed by Fama (1980), it follows that there is no reason to expect homogeneous deposits in an unregulated financial industry. More generally, this conclusion holds so long as the respective portfolio costs and transaction services are borne by portfolio holders and transaction users.

C. Households

The individual households in the model are consumers, suppliers of labor services and capital goods, purchasers of transaction services, and ultimate wealth holders. The representative individual is assumed to be infinite lived and possess the intertemporal utility function,

$$(3) \qquad U_t \equiv \sum_{j=0}^{\infty} \beta^j u(x_{t+j}, \bar{n} - n_{t+j}),$$

where β is a fixed utility discount factor and $u(\cdot)$ is a single period utility function that depends on consumption (x_{t+j}) and leisure ($\bar{n} - n_{t+j}$) with $\bar{n}$ indicating the total hours available in each period. The utility maximand is the expected utility measure $E_t U_t$, where E_t denotes the conditional (rational) expectation based on all information available at time t.

The representative agent arrives at date t with total wealth equal to the sum of current realized output (y_t) and the depreciated value of the previous period's capital stock ($k_{t-1} - \delta k_{t-1}$). The agent's current decisions involve the selection of the levels of consumption (x_t) and of total effort (n_t) as well as allocation of effort to market and nonmarket activities. These decisions imply a level of saving that then must be efficiently allocated, along with current wealth, to purchases of investment goods (i_t) and financial assets (for example, real bonds, shares, etc.).

Households are assumed to combine time and transactions services to accomplish purchases of consumption and investment goods. In particular, the time required for this nonmarket activity is

$$(4) \quad n_{\tau t} = \tau(d_{ht}/(x_t + i_t))(x_t + i_t),$$

where $\tau' < 0$, $\tau'' < 0$. Our individual selects an amount of transactions services d_{ht} so as to minimize the total transactions cost, $w_t n_{\tau t} + \rho_t d_{ht}$. So long as hours are freely variable, w_t is the opportunity cost of effort, and this minimization problem can be treated separately from the household's general allocations. (However, efficiently selected transactions patterns will have wealth and substitution effects on desirable household allocations.)

Minimizing the total cost of transactions activities implies a derived demand for purchases of transaction services of the form $d_{ht}^* = g(\rho_t/w_t)(x_t + i_t)$, where $g' = (\tau'')^{-1} < 0$. Similarly, hours allocated to transactions activities are proportional to expenditures, taking the form $n_{\tau t}^* = \tau(g(\rho_t/w_t))(x_t + i_t)$.

The presence of transaction costs for the purchase of consumption and investment goods implies that the total cost of a unit of consumption or investment goods in terms of a unit of output is greater than unity (i.e., $1 + [w_t \tau(g(\rho_t/w_t)) + \rho_t g(\rho_t/w_t)]$). Selection of an optimal pattern of consumption (x_t), total effort ($n_t = n_{yt} + n_{dt} + n_{\tau t}$), and portfolio allocations involves the usual sort of intertemporal efficiency conditions with the exception of this modification. Fischer (1982) provides an interpretation of the altered efficiency conditions in a similar context.

D. Equilibrium Prices and Quantities

Analysis of dynamic, stochastic general equilibrium models is a difficult task. One strategy for characterizing equilibrium prices and quantities is to study the planning problem for a representative agent (see Lucas, 1978, or Long and Plosser). This procedure is valid so long as the competitive equilibrium is Pareto optimal. The planning problem can also be used to generate specific equilibria if explicit functional forms for preferences and technologies are assumed.

We do not pursue this strategy in detail as our objective is more modest. Instead, we make a number of simplifying assumptions regarding the general framework proposed above that allow us to highlight the conditions necessary to obtain certain business cycle comovements in general equilibrium.

The state of the economy at date t is summarized by the values of four variables; y_t, $(1 - \delta)k_{t-1}$, ϕ_t, and λ_t. The first is a measure of national income, the second is the current stock of depreciated capital, ϕ_t is a technical factor affecting current opportunities to transfer resources intertemporally, and λ_t is a technical factor influencing the production of transaction services. The agent's vector of decisions variables is (n_{yt}, n_{dt}, $n_{\tau t}$, d_{ht}, d_{yt}, k_{yt}, k_{dt}).

In order to simplify the problem, we make three assumptions that are sufficient to reduce the state vector to two elements and the decision vector to two elements while preserving the essential features of the model. First, we assume a depreciation rate of 100 percent, eliminating $(1 - \delta)k_{t-1}$ as a state variable. Second, we assume that transaction services are produced deterministically ($\lambda_t = 1$, for all t) and depend only on labor input ($d_t = h_0 n_{dt}$). Deterministic production of transaction services eliminates λ_t as a state variable and the simplified production technology implies that the competitive price is $\rho_t^* = w_t h_0$. This implies that households (and firms below) use time and purchased transaction services in fixed proportions.

The third assumption is to restrict the final goods production function to employ financial services in a manner that is symmetric to households. This means that firms (like households) purchase transaction services, d_{yt}, and allocate labor services to transaction activities in fixed proportions where the scale variable corresponds to total payments to factors of production and thus is closely related to next period's output (for households the scale variable is $x_t + i_t$). The second and third assumptions eliminate n_{dt}, $n_{\tau t}$, d_{ht}, d_{yt}, and k_{dt} from the vector of decision variables.

There is a discounted dynamic programming problem whose solution corresponds to the competitive equilibrium of this simplified model economy. The decision rules for the problem are stationary functions of the state variables y_t and ϕ_t. Rather than solve this problem for an explicit specification of preferences and technologies, the essential features of the interactions between the final goods industry and the financial industry can be analyzed by employing the following restrictions on the decision rules; $0 < \partial k_{yt}/\partial y_t < 1$, $\partial k_{yt}/\partial \phi_t \cong 0$, $\partial n_{yt}/\partial y_t > 0$, and $\partial n_{yt}/\partial \phi_t > 0$.

These restrictions follow from assumptions about preferences and production opportunities. For example, an increase in the amount of the initial stock, y_t, involves additional wealth so that the consumption of final product and leisure are expected to rise. Agents, however, choose to spread some portion of this wealth increment over time and do so by increasing the amount of commodity allocated to capital services so that $0 < \partial k_{yt}/\partial y_t < 1$. The other conditions on the decision rules require stronger restrictions on preferences and production possibilities. For example, an increase in y_t raises the marginal product of labor if capital and labor are complements in production. If the wealth effect on labor supplied, which arises from the increased output of final goods next period, is outweighed by the increase in the real wage (marginal product of labor) then hours worked rises.[4]

Analogously, an increase in ϕ_t involves both wealth and substitution effects. Given

current inputs, future production is higher and the current returns to additional units of factors of production are higher. These offsetting effects are analogous to the income and substitution effects of a real interest rate change. Essentially, the small impact of a shift in ϕ_t on the amount of output allocated to capital accumulation ($\partial k_{yt}/\partial \phi_t \cong 0$) reflects the idea that the income and substitution effects on consumption are roughly offsetting. On the other hand, the substitution effect of such shifts on labor supply is presumed to dominate so that $\partial n_{yt}/\partial \phi_t > 0$, which generates procyclical work effort.

Once quantity behavior is determined, equilibrium factor prices, interest rates, and share prices are straightforward to construct. In particular, competitive prices correspond to marginal rates of substitution at optimal planned quantities. For example, there is a riskless commodity interest rate r_t that we discuss below. We also can construct the expected return to shares, $E_t(r_{yt}) = E_t[\phi_t \xi_{t+1} - v_t)/v_t] = (\phi_t - v_t)/v_t$. In our setup, this expected return exceeds the riskless rate, $E_t(r_{yt}) > r_t$, since the holders of these shares must be compensated for bearing production risk.

E. Inside Money, Credit, and the Real Business Cycle

In our real business cycle model, a positive correlation (comovement) of real production, credit, and transaction services arises from the general equilibrium of production and consumption decisions by firms and households. The timing patterns among these variables, however, depends on the source of the variation in real output.

Unexpected output events (ξ_t) operate by altering the initial conditions pertinent for economic agents' plans for consumption, investment, and hours of work. As discussed above, an unexpected wealth increment ($\xi_t > 1$) leads to higher net investment than would otherwise have been the case. Furthermore, hours worked also rises so that real output increases and exhibits positive serial correlation. During the course of such an economic expansion, the volume of credit (shares) is also high as firms finance relatively large

---

[4] This result also requires that the amount of time allocated to transaction activities by firms and household is small relative to total time allocated to market activity or production.

amounts of goods in process. This positive correlation between the total volume of credit and real activity is potentially an important prediction of our framework, especially since evidence presented by Benjamin Friedman (1981) suggests that there is a tighter relation be:ween total credit and output than between the individual components of credit and real activity.

The movements in final goods production induces a higher volume of transaction services demanded by firms and households. Thus, our model generates the positive comovement of output with measures of bank clearings, long noted by empirical researchers in the business cycle area (for example, Wesley Mitchell, 1930, pp. 116–51). Finally, real rates of return move in a countercyclical direction as agents' opportunities to spread wealth over time are subject to diminishing returns (i.e., total time is in fixed supply).

The predictions of our model focus on the flow of transaction services. It is important to provide a link between these flows and the stock of deposits that has been the more traditional focus of monetary analysis. It is convenient to assume that the stock of deposits is proportional to the flow of transaction services and can be represented by γd_t.[5] Under this assumption, our model implies that the volume of inside money (deposits) is positively correlated with output with a rough coincidence in timing. More generally, this may reflect the role of deposits as a store of wealth or a temporary element of the credit process.

At least some cycle episodes, however, are commonly viewed as involving a different timing pattern. For example, traditional business cycle analysts (Arthur Burns and Mitchell, 1946), modern time-series macro-

econometricians (Christopher Sims, 1972; 1980),[6] and monetary historians (Milton Friedman and Anna Schwartz, 1963) view monetary variables as "leading" measures of real activity.[7]

One way of generating a different timing pattern is through shifts in the intertemporal opportunities of the economy as a whole. Real events of this type, respresented by ϕ_t, alter agents' allocations of leisure and consumption between the present and the future for a given level of national wealth. A higher than average shock ($\phi_t > 1$), under the assumptions outlined above, expands hours worked with little accompanying change in consumption or capital. The fact that financial services are an intermediate product— which can be produced more rapidly than the final product—leads to an expansion of the quantity of such services and of bank deposits. Consequently, movements in hours worked, interest rates, and security prices, deposits-financial services, and trade credit all occur prior to the expansion of output.[8] The subsequent increment to time $t+1$ wealth (stemming from the joint impact of the exogenous shift, ϕ_t, and agents' responses to that shift) works much like the above discussion of unexpected output events. Typically, we suspect the initial phases of business fluctuations incorporate a combination of both types of shocks (i.e., shifts in current and expected future production possibilities).

II. Currency, Deposits, and Prices

In order to investigate the relation between nominal aggregates and the real business cycle it is necessary to augment the

---

[5]It is sufficient for our purposes that deposits be related to transaction services by any monotonic increasing function. Although this assumption is a conventional assumption with physical capital, it is nevertheless an *ad hoc* element that is troubling. For example, transaction services do not, in principle, require any specific asset position, as is clear from checking accounts that have overdraft privileges or carry a zero balance at the end of the day. In addition, there are important secular and cyclical variations in the volume of debits relative to the stock of deposits.

[6]Sims (1980) discusses reverse causation of money and output working through central bank operating policies. The present setup is a first step toward the type of small-scale general equilibrium model that is necessary to evaluate the reverse causation argument.

[7]We deliberately employ the idea of a "leading variable" in a loose manner so as to capture the common elements of these alternative discussions.

[8]It is commonly stressed that asset prices and returns incorporate information about predictable components of future output (i.e., ϕ_t). In general equilibrium models such as ours, however, such information is also incorporated into all quantity decisions such as effort, consumption, and investment.

hypothetical economy developed above. In this section, a non-interest-bearing government-supplied fiat currency (dollars) is introduced and the factors affecting its value are analyzed.

In order for currency to be a well-defined economic good, and thus to have a determinate price in terms of a unit of output $(1/P)$, there must be a demand function for currency that reflects the economic value assigned to the services of currency by economic agents. For simplicity, we assume that households are the principal demanders of currency. To generate a stable demand for currency, real currency is viewed as a substitute—but not a perfect one—for transactions services purchased from the financial sector. In particular, currency yields a real service flow in that there are some transactions (either of magnitude or character) that are more efficiently carried out using currency than the accounting system of exchange. We revise the household's time spent in transactions activities, equation (4), to reflect these expanded opportunities:

$$(5) \qquad n_{\tau t} = \tau(d_{ht}/y_t, c_t/y_t)y_t,$$

where y_t is the total market transactions of our household, c_t is the stock of currency purchasing power, and d_{ht} is the flow of financial services purchased from the financial industry.[9]

Thus, a household minimizing its cost of transaction activities will select amounts of $n_{\tau t}$, d_{ht}, and c_t in a manner that is analogous to our earlier discussion. The demands for each input will be a function of the rental price of real currency, $R_t/(1 + R_t)$, the effective cost of financial services $\bar{\rho}_t$ and the opportunity cost of time, w_t.

In forming these rental prices, two important assumptions are made. First, there is a market for one-period nominal bonds that bear interest rate R_t. This nominal rate is the sum of the real component, r_t, and an expected rate of inflation, $E(\pi_t)$. Second, if banks are required to hold non-interest-bearing reserves, the returns earned by depositors may not match market rates. Given the pro-

portional link between financial services (d_t) and deposits (γd_t), the effective cost of a unit of deposit services, $\bar{\rho}$, is influenced by this reserve regulation. In the absence of regulations $\bar{\rho}_t = \rho_t$, where ρ_t is the rental price of deposit services in the competitive environment of Section I.

Transactions cost minimization by households implies real demands for currency and financial services of the following forms,

$$(6a) \qquad c_t = l(\underset{-}{R_t/(1 + R_t)}, \underset{+}{\bar{\rho}_t}, \underset{+}{w_t})y_t,$$

$$(6b) \qquad d_{ht} = \delta(\underset{+}{R_t/(1 + R_t)}, \underset{-}{\bar{\rho}_t}, \underset{-}{w_t})y_t.$$

The signs below the arguments denote the signs of the partial derivative (for example, $\partial c_t/\partial \bar{\rho}_t > 0$). These signs are insured if $\tau(\cdot)$ is such that currency purchasing power and financial services are substitutes.

The structure of the markets for currency and financial services is analogous to Fama (1980). As he points out, determinacy of the price level is insured if the government fixes the nominal quantity of currency—direct or indirect regulation of financial sector quantities and/or characteristics is not necessary. Nevertheless, regulations can be important for two reasons. First, regulations produce a differentiated class of suppliers of financial services (banks) whose deposits are sometimes described as inside money. Second, regulations can influence the price level by altering the effective rental price of financial services.

The analysis below focuses on the implications of alternative banking structures for the behavior of currency, deposits, and prices. For clarity, the bulk of the discussion is conducted under the assumption that the treasury-central bank maintains a policy of controlling the issue of nominal currency so that the stock of currency $(C_t = P_t c_t)$ is an exogenous random variable. This assumption means that the behavior of the price level can be analyzed by investigating equilibrium in the currency market. Other models of central bank behavior are discussed in Part B below. In all of our discussions, however, the price level is best viewed as being set in the

[9] We assume that $\tau_1 < 0$, $\tau_2 < 0$, $\tau_{11} < 0$, $\tau_{22} < 0$, and $\tau_{12} < 0$.

market for that nominal asset whose quantity the central bank seeks to control.

A. *Money and Prices — Unregulated Banking*

In an unregulated banking environment we assume that the deposit industry would hold virtually no currency. Consequently, the determination of the price level involves the requirement that the real supply of currency (C_t/P_t) be equal to the real demand for currency given by (6a) above. The equilibrium price level is then

$$(7) \qquad P_t = C_t / l(\,\cdot\,),$$

where $l(\,\cdot\,)$ is the demand function for real currency. Using the arguments of $l(\,\cdot\,)$ we can rewrite this condition as

$$(8) \qquad P_t = P(C_t, y_t, R_t, \bar{\rho}_t, w_t).$$
$$\qquad\qquad\quad +\ \ -\ \ +\ \ -\ \ -$$

The signs of the respective derivatives in (8) are straightforward and warrant little explanation.

An important feature of (8) is the absence of nominal demand deposits. Thus, as stressed by Fama (1980), there is no need for government control of banking or the supply of deposits to insure a determinate price level. Banks, in a competitive, unregulated environment, simply pass portfolio returns on to their depositors less a fee charged for the provision of transactions services, so that $\bar{\rho}_t = \rho_t$. The only way in which developments in the banking sector are relevant to price level determination is through variations in the cost of financial services (ρ_t).

This view of price level determination implies that once and for all changes in the quantity of currency are completely neutral. The volume of transaction services (d_t) and deposits (γd_t) are determined solely by variations in the real economy as discussed in Section I. Nevertheless, the *nominal* quantity of deposits $(P_t \gamma d_t)$ is likely to be positively correlated with real activity if currency is determined exogenously and prices are not excessively countercyclical (see Part C below).

On the other hand, sustained increases in the growth of currency may have real effects.

The resulting increased inflation leads to a rise in the nominal interest rate, R, which implies a fall in the demand for real currency and a rise in real transaction services and time allocated to transaction activities. Since an increase in real transaction services involves the use of real resources, the economy is made worse off by sustained inflation. We assume, however, that this increase in the size of the financial sector has no important implications for the real general equilibrium.[10] It is not obvious that this is a good assumption from an empirical point of view. Nevertheless, it does serve to bring into sharp focus the distinction between inside and outside money, particularly with respect to the neutrality and super-neutrality of government currency issue.

B. *Money and Prices — Regulated Banking*

In an unregulated environment the price level is determined in the currency market and deposits play no essential role. There are, however, a number of regulations that serve to distinguish banks from other financial intermediaries and thereby inside money from credit. Here we discuss the extent to which these regulations alter the nature of price level determination. As it turns out, the impact of regulations depends on (i) the interaction of banking regulation with the external money supply policy of the central bank-treasury, and (ii) the extent to which government mandates can be offset by countervailing private substitutions.

1. *Portfolio Regulations and Reserve Requirements.* It is useful to start by discussing a set of regulations that do not have any important consequences for the price level.

---

[10] In other words, we assume that our model is approximately "super-neutral" in the language of monetary growth theory. It is worthwhile pointing out that this literature does not provide a clearcut guide to the nature of departures from super-neutrality. For example, Tobin (1965), has argued that an increase in inflation will lower real rates of return and raise capital formation, by lowering the real value of money and, consequently, raising saving. By contrast, Alan Stockman (1981) argues that inflation acts as a tax on the saving process (in which money is an input) and, hence, depresses capital formation.

Suppose that the government specifies the "risk composition" of the underlying assets against which deposits are claims. As long as agents can offset this restriction by rebalancing the contents of their portfolios (i.e., the distribution of total wealth between the banking sector and other portfolio managers), then this regulation will have no impact on any real variables or the price level. However, such restrictions may serve to distinguish inside money for other forms of credit.

On the other hand, restrictions specifying that banks must hold some fraction, say θ, of their nominal asset portfolio in the form of non-interest-bearing reserves issued by the central bank may have important effects. For example, the central bank could specify that reserve accounts are deposits of securities with nominal interest accruing to the central bank. This mechanism is one way of imposing a deposit tax with the consequence that the cost of deposit services would be $\bar{\rho}_t > \rho_t$. Such a deposit tax results in a reduction in the size of the banking sector and an increase in the real demand for currency. The impact of this reserve requirement on price-level determination depends on the central bank policy. For example, if the treasury-central bank makes currency in the hands of the public an exogenous quantity, unresponsive to developments in the banking sector, then the price level continues to be determined by the requirement that the real stock of currency outstanding (C_t/P_t) be equal to the real demand. In these circumstances, the behavior of deposits and deposit services would be similar to that in an unregulated banking system.

2. *Alternative Central Bank Policies.* The currency market determines the price level if the central bank is assumed to make currency an exogenously controlled quantity. There are, however, other control methods available to the central bank. For example, if the central bank combines a reserve requirement with a policy of controlling the sum of currency and nominal bank reserves (high-powered money), then the price level can be viewed as being determined in the market for high-powered money.

Let $B_t = \theta(P_t\gamma d_t)$ be the nominal stock of bank reserves and $H_t = B_t + C_t$ be the exogenous total of bank reserves and currency. Under this regime, the price level may be viewed as arising from the requirement that the total private demand for fiat money equals the supply. That is, $H_t = P_t\{c_t + \theta\gamma d_t\} = P_t\{c_t + B_t/P_t\}$. The equilibrium price level can be expressed as

$$(9) \qquad P_t = H_t/(l(\cdot) + (B_t/P_t)),$$

or using the arguments of $l(\cdot)$,

$$(10) \qquad P_t = P(H_t, y_t, R_t, \bar{\rho}_t, w_t, (B_t/P_t)).$$
$$\qquad\qquad\quad + \quad - \quad + \quad - \quad - \qquad -$$

Once again the signs of the partial derivatives are straightforward. Note, in particular, that an increase in the demand for real reserves (B_t/P_t) holding high-powered money fixed necessitates a fall in the price level.

A central bank policy of controlling high-powered money, therefore, implies that the equilibrium price level is determined in the market for this exogenously controlled nominal quantity. Consequently, real activity (including real deposit services and real deposits) is neutral with respect to changes in high-powered money and, as in the case of currency, we assume that high-powered money is approximately super-neutral under this regime.

As discussed in Fama (1980, pp. 52–53), there are other central bank policies that could be used to make the price level determinate. In particular, the central bank could choose to make nominal bank reserves an exogenous quantity and supply currency on demand. In this case (which some argue are the current policies of the Federal Reserve), the price level can be viewed as being determined in the market for reserves. The equilibrium price level would be determined by the exogenous supply of nominal reserves (B_t) and the total real demand for deposit services.[11]

----

[11]We have not yet analyzed price-level determination when the central bank attempts to control the interest rate. However, this may be important to an appropriate empirical investigation of some time periods.

C. *The Price Level and the Real Business Cycle*

Price-level movements in response to the two shocks (ϕ_t and ξ_t) involve two important factors. First, there is the impact of movements in real output on the demand for outside money. Second, there is the impact of nominal interest rates on the demand for outside money. Since variation in the price level also depends on central bank policy, we focus on the case of a regulated banking system with the central bank assumed to make the quantity of high-powered money exogenous.

It is convenient to summarize household and bank behavior in the following demand function for outside money:[12]

$$h_t^d = p_t + \lambda y_t - \psi R_t, \qquad \lambda > 0, \; \psi > 0,$$

where h_t is the logarithm of high-powered money, y_t is the logarithm of real output, p_t is the logarithm of the price level, and R_t is the nominal interest rate. Using the fact that $R_t = r_t + (E_t p_{t+1} - p_t)$ and the monetary equilibrium condition that $h_t = h_t^d$, it follows that a rational expectations solution for the price level along the lines of Thomas Sargent and Neil Wallace (1975) can be written as

$$p_t = (1+\psi)^{-1} \left\{ \sum_{j=0}^{\infty} (\psi/(1+\psi))^j \right.$$
$$\left. \cdot E_t \big[h_{t+j} + \psi r_{t+j} - \lambda y_{t+j} \big] \right\}.$$

Unexpected wealth increments ($\xi_t > 1$) lead to a business cycle where output is high and the real rate of return is low. Consequently, a wealth increment leads to lower prices due to both lower real returns and higher real income.

In Section I we describe how a better than average opportunity to transfer resources intertemporally ($\phi_t > 1$) leads to an increase in r_t. In addition, the increase in wealth that is brought about by such a shift leads to lower

future returns and higher future outputs. Thus, the overall impact on the price level is ambiguous, involving the positive influence of the higher current real return and the negative influence of the lower expected future returns and higher expected future outputs.

The above two examples suggest that the model produces a price level that is likely to be countercyclical. For some macroeconomists, the procyclical character of the general price level is such a well established empirical regularity that this feature alone is sufficient to reject real business cycle theory (for example, Lucas, 1977, p. 20).[13] If it is indeed necessary to generate procyclical price movements, then there appear to be two principle channels. First, an alternative structure that involves a more permanent, capital-augmenting form of technological change could heighten the real return effects discussed above. Combining this structure with a sufficiently interest-sensitive demand for money could lead to procyclical prices. Second, policy response to real activity also could generate procyclical price movements. For example, a positive response of outside money creation to output could lead to a positive correlation between prices and output.

III. Empirical Analysis

The preceding sections describe a simple model economy with business cycles that are completely real in origin. Nevertheless, correlations between real activity and monetary measures arise from the operation of the banking system and central bank policy responses. Here we discuss some of the predictions that our model makes concerning the joint time-series behavior of output, monetary aggregates, rates of return, and the price level. In addition, we discuss U.S. business cycle experience during the post-World

---

[12] For simplicity, we ignore movements in the cost of deposit services and real wage as important factors affecting the price level.

[13] Recent work using post-World War II data (for example, Robert Hodrick and Prescott, 1980, and Fama, 1982) suggests that the positive correlation between output and price level movements may be not as robust as sometimes thought.

War II period, providing some preliminary empirical evidence that bears on the potential relevance of our theoretical stories.

Before proceeding, it is useful to consider briefly general strategies for investigating the empirical importance of real business cycle theories, and to discuss how the present analysis of money and the price level could be related to such investigations.

One empirical strategy is to isolate a group of observable real disturbances that provide an explanation of much of a particular nation's business cycle experience, in the sense of delivering a good fit. Candidates for such real shocks include government purchase, tax, and regulatory actions; changes in technological and environment conditions, and movements in relative prices that are determined in a world market. The goal is to provide a direct substitute for the high explanatory power of monetary variables found in other business cycles studies (for example, Friedman and Schwartz, and Barro, 1981a). The natural extension would be to study the explanatory power of such real factors for monetary variables and the price level. In our framework, many of these real variables would be restricted to influence monetary quantities (particularly, inside money) through their influence on output and a small set of relative prices. In this sense, aspects of the present type of monetary theory do provide meaningful restrictions on the data.

Another approach is to treat the fundamental real shocks as unobservable and to focus on the interactions between sectors that arise during business cycles; a strategy that is the empirical analogue of the theoretical analysis of Long and Plosser. Since a particular real business cycle theory restricts own- and cross-serial correlation properties of industry output and relative prices, this route can provide valuable information about the regular aspects of business cycles even though the sources of shocks are not identified. Again, the principal testable restrictions of theorizing along these lines would arise from the restricted fashion that variations in production in other sectors were allowed to influence developments in the monetary sector.

Unfortunately, analysis of monetary phenomena using either of these strategies is not feasible given the state of real business cycle models. Consequently, the present empirical investigation is limited to providing some admittedly crude correlations among the variables suggested by the theory.

A. *Summary Statistics*

Summary measures of the series to be discussed below are presented in Table 1. The data are annual (generally yearly averages) for the period 1953–78. We focus on the 1953–78 interval primarily to avoid the period when the Federal Reserve maintained a policy of pegging the yields on U.S. government securities. The implications of such a policy may be very different from those described in the previous section where the central bank controls some nominal quantity.

The most noticeable feature in Table 1 is the different behavior of nominal and real variables. Typically, the growth rates of real variables display much less serial correlation than the growth rates of nominal variables. For example, the growth of real demand deposits is much less autocorrelated than the growth rate of nominal demand deposits. Indeed, as previously noted by Charles Nelson and Plosser (1982), as well as other authors, many real variables are close to random walks in logarithmic form. The most noticeable exceptions to this random walk behavior are real currency (C_t/P_t) and real service charges (ρ_t), both of which display significant positive and persistent serial dependences in growth rates.

B. *Real Factors and Aggregate Output*

This paper is not the appropriate place for an empirical investigation of the role of real factors as impulses to business fluctuations. Barro (1981b), however, provides some results that are pertinent. Specifically, he finds that temporary increases in government purchases have a significant expansionary impact on real output. These results are suggestive and one could investigate the impact of other governmental tax and expendi-

TABLE 1—SUMMARY STATISTICS, ANNUAL DATA: 1953–78

Series	Mean	Standard Deviation	ρ_1	ρ_2	ρ_3	ρ_4
A. Real Variables						
Growth Rate of Real						
GNP (y_t)	.0327	.0249	−.01	−.24	−.12	.29
Wages (w_t)	.0177	.0324	.59	−.00	−.02	.14
Deposits (γd_t)	−.0002	.0226	.36	−.22	−.19	.20
Currency (C_t/P_t)	.0101	.0209	.65	.39	.26	.25
High-Powered Money (H_t/P_t)	.0027	.0253	.40	.33	.08	.19
Reserves (B_t/P_t)	−.0110	.0449	.32	−.01	−.05	−.02
Service Charges (ρ_t)	−.0252	.0601	.81	.69	.66	.56
B. Nominal Variables						
Growth Rate of						
Price Level (P_t)	.0371	.0233	.84	.64	.66	.84
Deposits ($P_t\gamma d_t$)	.0373	.0211	.58	.35	.43	.58
Currency (C_t)	.0481	.0329	.93	.88	.85	.82
High-Powered Money (H_t)	.0398	.0338	.71	.76	.59	.68
Reserves (B_t)	.0260	.0455	.37	.03	.09	.32
Change in the Short-Term Interest Rate (R_t)	.2177	1.4710	.03	−.71	−.29	.68

Note: ρ_i is the sample autocorrelation coefficient at lag i, for $i = 1, \ldots, 4$. The large sample standard error is .20.
Sources: Real GNP and the GNP deflator are taken from The National Income and Product Accounts of the United States, 1929–1941 and various issues of the Survey of Current Business. Currency in the hands of the public, demand deposits, and bank reserves are from Business Statistics, 1979. High-powered money is the sum of currency in the hands of the public and bank reserves. The interest rate is the 4- to 6-month prime commercial paper rate taken from Banking and Monetary Statistics 1941–1970 and various issues of the Annual Statistical Digest. The real wage is average hourly earnings divided by the producer price index, from Business Statistics, 1979. Finally, the service charge variable is the ratio of total service charges on demand deposits accrued by Federal Reserve member banks to total check clearings by the Federal Reserve. Both series are taken from Banking and Monetary Statistics, 1941–1970, and various issues of the Annual Statistical Digest.

ture measures on real activity. More recently, David Lilien (1982) documents the importance of a measure of the dispersion of sectoral shifts in understanding the movements in aggregate unemployment during the postwar period. James Hamilton (1983) presents evidence on the relation between oil price changes and postwar recessions.

Additional evidence on the importance of real disturbances in output fluctuations is offered in Nelson and Plosser. Using an unobserved components model of output and the observed autocovariance structure of real GNP, Nelson and Plosser infer that real (nonmonetary) disturbances are the primary source of variance in real activity. This result is based on the commonly held view that monetary disturbances should have no permanent effects on real output, and thus disturbances that are of a permanent nature must be associated with real rather than monetary sources.

C. *Money-Output Correlations*

The theoretical model stresses that real internal monetary balances should be positively correlated with real activity since transaction services are a produced input. Further, the model predicts that autonomous external nominal money creation/destruction is neutral with respect to output growth. These two ideas suggest the value of analyzing money-output correlations in two forms: real vs. nominal balances and internal vs. external monetary measures.

Table 2 presents information on the contemporaneous relations between output growth and growth rates of alternative monetary measures. Equation (i) shows the strong positive contemporaneous correlation that exists between real demand deposits and economic activity. This strong contemporaneous correlation is shared by real external balances measured as currency or as high-

TABLE 2—CONTEMPORANEOUS MONEY-OUTPUT REGRESSIONS

$$\Delta \ln y_t = \alpha_0 + \alpha_1 \Delta \ln M_t + \varepsilon_t$$

Equation	$\hat{\alpha}_0$	Independent Variables (M_t)						R^2	$SE(\hat{\varepsilon})$	ρ_1
		Real Monetary Measures			Nominal Monetary Measures					
		γd_t	H_t/P_t	C_t/P_t	$P_t\gamma d_t$	H_t	C_t			
(i)	.033[b] (.004)	.740[b] (.167)						.450	.0188	−.08
(ii)	.031[b] (.004)		.510[b] (.103)					.337	.0206	−.18
(iii)	.025[b] (.005)			.664[b] (.202)				.311	.0211	−.01
(iv)	.015 (.009)				.465[b] (.222)			.155	.0233	.10
(v)	.026[b] (.007)					.171 (.146)		.054	.0247	.00
(vi)	.027[b] (.009)						.111 (.153)	.022	.0251	.01
(vii)	.025[b] (.006)	.742[b] (.161)				.176[a] (.108)		.507	.0182	−.11
(viii)	.023[b] (.006)	.784[b] (.162)					.194[a] (.111)	.514	.0181	−.08
(ix)	.017[a] (.010)				.558[a] (.326)	−.080 (.203)		.161	.0238	.10
(x)	.015 (.010)				.661[b] (.307)		.181 (.197)	.185	.0234	.07

Notes: See Table 1; $\Delta \ln(\cdot)$ indicates the change in the log of the variable; R^2 is the coefficient of determination; $SE(\hat{\varepsilon})$ is the standard error of the regression; ρ_1 is the estimated first-order autocorrelation coefficient of the residuals, which has a large sample standard error of .20. Standard errors of the coefficients are shown in parentheses.

[a] Indicates significance at the 10 percent level.

[b] Indicates significance at the 5 percent level.

powered money (equations (ii) and (iii)). In nominal balance form, equations (iv), (v), and (vi) show demand deposits are more strongly correlated with real activity than either of the nominal external money measures. Finally, (vii) and (viii) indicate that nominal high-powered money and currency growth have a weak positive partial correlation with output given real demand deposits.

From the standpoint of our theoretical discussion, the key aspects of these correlations are as follows. First, the fact that much of the correlation with real activity is with internal monetary measures is consistent with our general view of the relation between money and real activity. Second, the fact that currency or high-powered money may be positively correlated with real activity is at odds with our model so long as the monetary authority makes such nominal monetary measures evolve in an autonomous manner.

Table 3 reports some additional regression results that incorporate lags of the alternative monetary measures. Equation (i) shows the results of adding two years of lagged real deposits to the output regression. The F-statistic pertinent for evaluating the marginal contribution of these lags is 2.48, which is well below the 95 percent critical value of 3.49, so that there is no strong evidence that these lags are important. Equations (ii) and (iii) show analogous results for nominal money growth measures.

Equations (iv) and (v) investigate the extent to which nominal money growth is correlated with real activity after accounting for real deposit growth. The contemporaneous and second lag of high-powered money and currency in the hands of the public are not important explanatory variables (the 95 percent critical value for $F(3,17)$ is 3.20 and the F-statistics for the lags of high-powered

TABLE 3—MONEY GROWTH AND OUTPUT GROWTH REGRESSIONS

$$\Delta \ln y_t = \alpha_0 + \sum_{i=0}^{2} \beta_i \Delta \ln \gamma d_{t-i} + \sum_{i=0}^{2} \gamma_i \Delta \ln H_{t-i} + \sum_{i=0}^{2} \delta_i \Delta \ln C_{t-i} + \varepsilon_t$$

		Independent Variables											
		Real Deposits (γd_t)			High-Powered Money (H_t)			Currency (C_t)					
Equation	$\hat{\alpha}_0$	$\hat{\beta}_0$	$\hat{\beta}_1$	$\hat{\beta}_2$	$\hat{\gamma}_0$	$\hat{\gamma}_1$	$\hat{\gamma}_2$	$\hat{\delta}_0$	$\hat{\delta}_1$	$\hat{\delta}_2$	R^2	$SE(\hat{\varepsilon})$	ρ_1
(i)	.034[b]	.644[b]	.135	−.352[b]							.651	.0152	.01
	(.003)	(.159)	(.166)	(.159)									
(ii)	.035[b]				.489[b]	−.399[a]	−.175				.236	.0225	.05
	(.008)				(.239)	(.210)	(.243)						
(iii)	.032[b]							.342	−.577	.262	.068	.0249	.18
	(.010)							(.487)	(.493)	(.360)			
(iv)	.034[b]	.607[b]	.066	−.296[a]	.263	−.229	−.059				.713	.0150	.00
	(.006)	(.160)	(.189)	(.162)	(.182)	(.145)	(.185)						
(v)	.031[b]	.644[b]	.119	−.333[a]				.302	−.313	.017	.674	.0160	.00
	(.006)	(.173)	(.178)	(.171)				(.317)	(.321)	(.238)			
(vi)	.033	.605[b]	.091	−.305[a]	.233[a]	−.233[a]					.710	.0142	.02
	(.003)	(.150)	(.157)	(.151)	(.118)	(.118)							
(vii)	.033	.642[b]	.114	−.343[b]				.297	−.297		.670	.0152	.00
	(.003)	(.158)	(.167)	(.159)				(.280)	(.280)				

Note: See Table 2. Equations (vi) and (vii) are the results of the regressions that constrains $\gamma_0 = -\gamma_1$ and $\delta_0 = -\delta_1$.
[a,b] See Table 2.

money and currency terms are 1.22 and .40, respectively). However, the estimated coefficient on current and lagged high-powered money are opposite in sign and nearly identical in magnitude, so that the change in high-powered money growth appears to be positively correlated with real activity (see equation (vi)).

Overall, our interpretation is that the correlations reported in Tables 1 and 3 indicate that much of the relation between money and real activity is apparently one with inside money, which is comforting given the key role that the banking system plays in our theoretical story.[14] Nevertheless, somewhat weaker correlations between real activity and nominal outside money may exist, suggesting it may be necessary to analyze policy re-

sponse in greater detail for the 1953–78 period, or to relax our maintained assumption of super-neutrality.

D. *Money-Inflation Correlations*

The theoretical model predicts that variations in external money, real activity, the nominal interest rate, and a measure of the cost of banking services should be important in explaining movements in the price level. Table 4 provides estimates of the price-level equations (8) and (10) of Section III under the assumption that a log-linear functional form is appropriate. Although the nominal interest rate is endogenous and the above discussion indicates that high-powered money and/or currency may be endogenous due to policy response, ordinary least squares methods are employed. Since there is a substantial empirical literature on price-level/money demand equations, our discussion focuses principally on new aspects that are raised by the theoretical discussion above.

First, the theory suggests that a measure of external money, such as currency or high-powered money, is the relevant nominal ag-

[14]Although we confine our empirical analysis to a comparison of inside and outside money correlations with output, broader measures of financial assets (or credit) should behave similarly to inside money. Friedman presents additional empirical support for this view. He finds that broader measures of money (or credit) exhibit a higher correlation with real output than more narrowly constructed measures.

TABLE 4—INFLATION REGRESSIONS

$$\Delta \ln P_t = \alpha_0 + \alpha_1 \Delta \ln M_t + \alpha_2 \Delta \ln y_t + \alpha_3 \Delta R_t + \alpha_4 \Delta \ln w_t + \alpha_5 \Delta \ln \rho_t + \alpha_6 \Delta \ln(B_t/P_t) + \varepsilon_t$$

Equation	$\hat{\alpha}_0$	$\hat{\alpha}_1$	$\hat{\alpha}_2$	$\hat{\alpha}_3$	$\hat{\alpha}_4$	$\hat{\alpha}_5$	$\hat{\alpha}_6$	R^2	$SE(\hat{\varepsilon})$	ρ_1
A. Currency as External Money										
(i)	.027[b]	.474[b]	−.276[b]	−.000	−.224[b]	−.014		.842	.0103	.32
	(.005)	(.098)	(.115)	(.002)	(.097)	(.056)				
(ii)	.025[b]	.457[b]	−.246[b]	.001	−.201[b]	−.029	−.091	.862	.0099	.33
	(.005)	(.094)	(.112)	(.002)	(.094)	(.054)	(.055)			
(iii)	.008	1.00	−.397[b]	.001	−.134	.178[b]		.519	.0158	.39
	(.005)		(.173)	(.003)	(.145)	(.065)				
(iv)	.007	1.00	−.381[b]	.002	−.118	.712[b]	−.058	.521	.0161	.38
	(.006)		(.177)	(.003)	(.150)	(.067)	(.088)			
B. High-Powered Money as External Money										
(i)	.035[b]	.334[b]	−.240	−.002	−.255[b]	−.070		.753	.0130 ·	.29
	(.005)	(.119)	(.144)	(.002)	(.120)	(.068)				
(ii)	.023[b]	.498[b]	−.208[a]	.001	−.165[a]	−.035	−.240[b]	.870	.0096	−.06
	(.005)	(.097)	(.107)	(.002)	(.092)	(.051)	(.058)			
(iii)	.017[b]	1.00	−.386[a]	−.004	−.157	.163[a]		.464	.0202	.07
	(.007)		(.221)	(.003)	(.186)	(.084)				
(iv)	.007	1.00	−.285[a]	.001	−.057	.129[b]	−.362[b]	.735	.0146	−.32
	(.005)		(.161)	(.003)	(.135)	(.061)	(.080)			

Note: See Table 2.
[a,b]See Table 2

gregate for price level determination (Fama, 1982, also advances this hypothesis and provides relevant evidence). Table 4 presents empirical results for both currency and high-powered money.

Second, in the regulated banking environment described in Section II, the relevant cost of deposit services (denoted $\bar{\rho}_t$) involves both the direct cost of providing an accounting system of exchange (denoted ρ_t) and the interest that the bank-depositor must forego due to reserve requirements. The empirical counterpart to the nominal unit cost of deposit services that we have constructed is the ratio of total service charges on demand deposits accrued by Federal Reserve member banks to total check clearings by the Federal Reserve. Deflating this measure by the price level leads to a measure of the real costs of deposit services, entered in Table 4 as ρ_t. However, during some portions of the period under study, banks faced apparently binding constraints on the level of interest payments that could be paid on demand deposits. It is frequently argued that explicit service charges would be reduced as a means of avoiding the interest rate constraint. As a result, we are not completely comfortable with our interpretation of this variable.

Third, our model of transaction costs implies that the real wage is also a pertinent relative price variable for agents in determining the mix of currency and transaction service purchases. As the real wage rises, individuals substitute toward the use of currency and purchased transaction services in market exchange.

Finally, when reserve requirements are present and the central bank is controlling the quantity of high-powered money the theory predicts that the volume of real reserves should negatively influence the price level given the stock of high-powered money. On the other hand, when currency is the controlled external quantity, real reserves should not be relevant.

In Panel A of Table 4, equations (ii) and (iv) report the results of estimating the price level (inverse money demand) equation over the sample period 1953–78, with currency as the measure of external money. The main features of these equations are broadly consistent with other studies: a negative impact of real activity, positive impact of nominal money growth, and minor or negligible impact of the short-term interest rate (4- to 6-month commercial paper rate). Although not included in many other studies, the real wage enters these equations in a manner that is consistent with our theory. If currency is the appropriate measure of external money the theory predicts a zero coefficient on real reserves. In equation (ii) this coefficient is negative but insignificant by the usual criteria. The tendency of our service charge measure to switch sign with the imposition of the unit constraint on currency (iv) is troubling, casting some doubt on the appropriateness of this relative price measure. There also appears to be marginally significant residual autocorrelation in these equations.

In Panel B of Table 4, equations (ii) and (iv) report analogous results for high-powered money as the measure of external money with general features that are again broadly consistent with other studies. Under our theory, real bank reserves should enter negatively in such price level equations if high-powered money is the controlled measure of external money. This is borne out by significant negative coefficients in both the unconstrained equation (ii) and constrained equation (iv). As before, the service charge variable has a tendency to change sign when the unit constraint on high powered money is imposed.

Overall, the results of Table 4 are broadly consistent with the theoretical stories told in the sections above. The negative influence of real reserves on the price level potentially is important, both in terms of explaining postwar price-level behavior and in explaining the apparently anomalous behavior of the price level during the interwar period. Finally, additional work needs to be done in producing measures of the market prices of bank services.

IV. Conclusions

This paper describes a class of real business cycle models that is capable of accounting for the relation between money, inflation, and economic activity, providing a coherent alternative framework to the monetary theories of the business cycle advanced by Lucas (1973) and Fischer (1977). Although the empirical work presented is simplistic, we draw two main lessons from it. First, much of the contemporaneous correlation of economic activity and money is apparently with inside money, with inflation principally resulting from changes in the stock of fiat (or outside) money and variations in real activity. This empirical observation implies that care should be taken in empirical studies to distinguish inside from outside money. Second, future work along these lines may have to consider policy responses that are broad enough to produce variations in outside money that are correlated with real activity.

A main direction of our future work in this area will be to develop the implications of the analysis for security returns so that the general equilibrium predictions for these variables can be exploited in tests of the model. This topic is especially important because Sims (1980) and Fama (1981) have provided some hints about the interrelationship of money, asset returns, and real activity.

In conclusion, it seems worthwhile to discuss two recurrent comments on this line of research that we have received. First, there has been a surprising willingness on the part of many individuals to simultaneously argue that our model (a real business cycle model with an explicit banking sector and central bank) is probably observationally equivalent to many existing monetary theories *and* that a "common sense" view leads one to prefer alternative models as descriptions of reality.[15] This line of argument puzzles us, since it was presumably on empirical grounds (not common sense) that the profession rejected pre-Keynesian "equilibrium theories" of the business cycle that stressed real causes of economic fluctuations.

Second, some individuals have argued that market failure is central to both the understanding of cyclical fluctuations and the primary reason for economists to study these phenomena. Our view is that widespread market failure need not be a necessary component of a theory of business fluctuations, and that real equilibrium business cycle theory promises to make important contributions to positive economics. This perspective, however, is not inconsistent with the view

---

[15] Grossman (1982) makes an explicit statement of this view.

that the accumulation of scientific knowledge may lead to the design of more desirable government policies toward business fluctuations (such as tax and expenditure policies) or toward the regulation of the financial sector.

REFERENCES

Azariadis, Costas, "Escalator Clauses and the Allocation of Cyclical Risks," *Journal of Economic Theory*, June 1978, *18*, 119–55.

Barro, Robert, (1981a) "Unanticipated Money Growth and Economic Activity in the U.S.," *Money, Expectations, and Business Cycles*, New York: Academic Press, 1981, ch. 5.

_____, (1981b) "Output Effects of Government Purchases," *Journal of Political Economy*, December 1981, *89*, 1086–121.

_____, "Long-Term Contracting, Sticky Prices and Monetary Policy," *Journal of Monetary Economics*, July 1977, *3*, 305–16.

Black, Fischer, "Active and Passive Monetary Policy in a Neo-Classical Model," *Journal of Finance*, September 1972, *27*, 801–14.

Boschen, John and Grossman, Herschel, "Tests of Equilibrium Macroeconomics Using Contemporaneous Monetary Information," *Journal of Monetary Economics*, November 1982, *10*, 309–34.

Burns, Arthur A. and Mitchell, Wesley, *Measuring Business Cycles*, New York: National Bureau of Economic Research, 1946.

Fama, Eugene, "Banking in the Theory of Finance," *Journal of Monetary Economics*, January 1980, *6*, 39–57.

_____, "Stock Returns, Real Activity, Inflation and Money," *American Economic Review*, September 1981, *71*, 545–65.

_____, "Inflation, Output and Money," *Journal of Business*, April 1982, *55*, 201–31.

Fischer, Stanley, "Long-Term Contracts, Rational Expectations, and the Optimal Money Supply Role," *Journal of Political Economy*, February 1977, *85*, 191–205.

_____, "A Framework for Monetary and Banking Analysis," Working Paper, Massachusetts Institute of Technology, July 1982.

Friedman, Benjamin, "The Relative Stability of Money and Credit Velocities in the United States: An Overview of the Evidence," Working Paper, Harvard University, November 1981.

Friedman, Milton and Schwartz, Anna, *A Monetary History of the United States*, Princeton: National Bureau of Economic Research, Princeton University Press, 1963.

Grossman, Herschel, Review of James Tobin's *Asset Accumulation and Economic Activity*, in *Journal of Monetary Economics*, July 1982, *10*, 134–38.

Hamilton, James, "Oil and the Macroeconomy Since World War II," *Journal of Political Economy*, April 1983, *91*, 228–48.

Hodrick, Robert and Prescott, Edward, "Post-War U.S. Business Cycles: An Empirical Investigation," Working Paper, Carnegie-Mellon University, November 1980.

King, Robert, "Monetary Information and Monetary Neutrality," *Journal of Monetary Economics*, March 1981, *7*, 195–206.

Kydland, Fynn and Prescott, Edward, "Time to Build and Aggregate Fluctuations," *Econometrica*, November 1982, *50*, 1345–70.

Lilien, David, "Sectoral Shifts and Cyclical Unemployment," *Journal of Political Economy*, August 1982, *90*, 777–93.

Long, John and Plosser, Charles, "Real Business Cycles," *Journal of Political Economy*, February 1983, *91*, 39–69.

Lucas, Robert, "Some International Evidence on Output-Inflation Tradeoffs," *American Economic Review*, June 1973, *63*, 326–34.

_____, "Understanding Business Cycles," in K. Brunner and A. Meltzer, eds., *Stabilization of the Domestic and International Economy*, Vol. 5, Carnegie-Rochester Series on Public Policy, *Journal of Monetary Economics*, Suppl. 1977, 7–29.

_____, "Asset Prices in an Exchange Economy," *Econometrica*, December 1978, *46*, 1429–48.

_____, "Methods and Problems in Business Cycle Theory," *Journal of Money, Credit and Banking*, November 1980, *12*, 696–715.

Mitchell, Wesley, *Business Cycles: The Problem and Its Setting*, New York: National Bureau of Economic Research, 1930.

Nelson, Charles and Plosser, Charles, "Trends and Random Walks in Macroeconomic Time Series: Some Evidence and Implications," *Journal of Monetary Economics,* September 1982, *10,* 139–62.

Sargent, Thomas and Wallace, Neil, "Rational Expectations, the Optimal Monetary Instrument and the Optimal Money Supply Rule," *Journal of Political Economy,* April 1975, *83,* 241–54.

Sims, Christopher, "Money, Income, and Causality," *American Economic Review,* September 1972, *62,* 540–52.

_____, "Comparison of Interwar and Postwar Business Cycles: Monetarism Reconsidered," *American Economic Review Proceedings,* May 1980, *70,* 250–57.

Stockman, Alan, "Anticipated Inflation and the Capital Stock in a Cash-in-Advance Economy," *Journal of Monetary Economics,* November 1981, *8,* 387–94.

Tobin, James, "Commercial Banks as Creators of 'Money'," 1963; reprinted in *Essays in Economics,* Vol. 1: *Macroeconomics,* North-Holland: Amsterdam, 1971, ch. 16.

_____, "Money and Economic Growth," 1965; reprinted in *Essays in Economics,* Vol. 1: *Macroeconomics,* North-Holland: Amsterdam, 1971, ch. 9.

_____, "Money and Income: Post Hoc Ergo Propter Hoc?," 1970; reprinted in *Essays in Economics,* Vol. 1: *Macroeconomics,* North-Holland: Amsterdam, 1971, ch. 24.

Board of Governors of the Federal Reserve System, *Annual Statistical Digest,* Washington, various issues.

_____, *Banking and Monetary Statistics, 1941–1970,* Washington, 1976.

U.S. Department of Commerce, *Business Statistics, 1979,* Washington, 1979.

_____, *National Income and Product Accounts of the United States, 1929–1974,* Washington.

[18]

Journal of Monetary Economics 6 (1980) 39–57. © North-Holland Publishing Company

BANKING IN THE THEORY OF FINANCE

Eugene F. FAMA*

University of Chicago, Chicago, IL 60637, USA

Banks are financial intermediaries that issue deposits and use the proceeds to purchase securities. This paper argues that when banking is competitive, these portfolio management activities in principle fall under the Modigliani–Miller theorem on the irrelevance of pure financing decisions. It follows that there is no need to control the deposit creation or security purchasing activities of banks to obtain a stable general equilibrium with respect to prices and real activity. In practice, however, banks are forcibly involved in the process by which a pure nominal commodity or unit of account is made to play the role of numeraire in a monetary system. The paper examines the nature of such a nominal commodity and how, through reserve requirements, banks get involved in making it a real economic good.

1. Introduction

This paper studies commercial banking from the viewpoint of the theory of finance. We take the main function of banks in the transactions industry to be the maintenance of a system of accounts in which transfers of wealth are carried out with bookkeeping entries. Banks also provide the service of exchanging deposits and other forms of wealth for currency, but in modern banking this is less important than the accounting system of exchange. Moreover, although both can be used to carry out transactions, one of our main points is that currency and an accounting system are entirely different methods for exchanging wealth. Currency is a physical medium which can be characterized as money. An accounting system works through bookkeeping entries, debits and credits, which do not require any physical medium or the concept of money.

In principle, providing an accounting system of exchange does not require that banks hold the wealth being exchanged. In practice, the costs of operating the system – replenishment costs for depositors and costs to banks and transactors of determining when transactions are feasible – are probably smaller when this is the case. Thus, banks assume a second major function,

*Theodore O. Yntema, Professor of Finance, Graduate School of Business, the University of Chicago. This research is supported by a grant from the National Science Foundation. The comments of F. Black, A. Drazen, N. Gonedes, M. Jensen, R. Lucas, D. Patinkin, and M. Scholes, and the insightful prodding of M.H. Miller are gratefully acknowledged.

portfolio management. They issue deposits and use the proceeds to purchase securities. A basic point of this paper is that when banking is competitive, the portfolio management activities of banks are the type of pure financing decisions covered by the Modigliani–Miller (1958) theorem. From this result we can infer that there is no need to control either the deposit creation or the security purchasing activities of banks for the purpose of obtaining a stable general equilibrium with respect to prices and real activity.

In examining the nature of banking, it is helpful to start with the assumption that banks are unregulated. This case provides the clearest view of the characteristics of an accounting system of exchange and of the fact that the concept of money plays no essential role in such a system. The unregulated case also provides the clearest application of the Modigliani–Miller theorem to the deposit creation and asset management decisions of banks. Having analyzed unregulated banking, we then study the effects of two main forms of bank regulation, reserve requirements and the limitation of direct interest payments on deposits.

Finally, much of the analysis centers on the argument that in principle the banking industry has no special role in the determination of prices. In practice, however, banks are forcibly involved in the process by which a pure nominal commodity or unit of account is made to play the role of numeraire in a real world monetary system. Our last task is to examine the nature of such a pure nominal commodity and how banks get involved in making it a real economic good.

2. An unregulated banking system

To get an understanding of the microeconomic structure of an unregulated banking industry, let us, for the moment, take the economy's pricing process as given. For concreteness, let us assume there is a numeraire, some real good, in terms of which prices are stated, leaving the issues connected with the pricing process for later. Finally, to focus on the issues of immediate interest, let us also assume, temporarily, that currency does not exist.

With unregulated banking, we might expect to observe a competitive banking system like that described by Johnson (1968) or Black (1970). In brief, banks pay competitive returns on deposits, that is, they pay the returns that would be earned by depositors on securities or portfolios that have risk equivalent to that of the deposits, less a competitively determined management fee; and banks charge for the transactions services they provide, again according to the competitively determined prices of these services. It is fruitful, however, to examine more closely both the transactions mechanism and the likely nature of unregulated deposits.

2.1. Bank deposits as portfolio assets

In the unregulated environment described by Black and Johnson, there is nothing special about bank deposits as portfolio assets since deposits pay the same returns as other managed portfolios with the same risk. Although Black and Johnson presume that bank deposits would be low risk portfolio assets, Tobin's (1963) conjecture seems more valid; that is, in an unregulated environment there is unlikely to be a clear distinction between banks and other portfolio managers. Although banks may be more interested in supplying transactions services, competition will induce them to provide different types of portfolios against which their depositors can hold claims. Although other financial institutions, like mutual funds, may be more interested in managing portfolios, competition will induce them to provide the transactions services normally associated with banks. In the end, one will observe financial institutions, all of which can be called banks, that provide accounts with different degrees of risk and allow individuals to carry out exchanges of wealth through their accounts.

In cases where individuals choose to hold deposits against risky portfolios, the value of an account fluctuates because of withdrawals and deposits and because of fluctuations in the market values of the portfolio assets on which the account has claim. For example, some banks may offer deposits which are nothing more than claims against an open end mutual fund. Such funds now issue and redeem shares on demand at the current market value of the portfolio. In a more open environment, they would allow the same thing to be done by check or any other mechanism coincident with the tastes of 'depositors' and whose costs the depositors are willing to bear.

One might also expect to observe banks that provide personalized portfolios of assets for the deposits of individual investors. The 'general accounts' maintained by New York Stock Exchange brokers for their customers could easily be transformed into such personalized bank accounts. As currently operated, an investor can borrow on demand, usually with a phone call to the broker, against a general account. When the broker's check is received, it can be endorsed over to an arbitrary third party. It is a short step from this to allowing investors to write checks against their accounts, with the checks covered, according to the choice of the investor, either with an automatic loan against the account or by the sale of specified assets from the account. There are similar simple mechanisms whereby the recipient of the check can instruct his broker–banker to use the addition to his account either to purchase new portfolio assets or draw down existing loans.

There will also be riskless deposits, that is, deposits not subject to capital gains or losses, where the value of the deposit varies only because of transactions executed and the accumulation of interest. Such riskless deposits might be direct claims against a portfolio of short-term riskless securities, in effect, a riskless mutual fund. Or a bank may issue both riskfree and risky deposits against a given portfolio of assets, with any capital gains or losses in the portfolio absorbed by those holding the risky deposits. The latter scenario would look more familiar if we assumed instead that the risk in the portfolio is borne by stockholders. However, our risky deposits are common stock with the additional benefits provided by access to the bank's transactions services.

2.2. An accounting system of exchange

Consider a transaction in which wealth is to be transferred from one economic unit to another. In a complicated world where there are many types of portfolio assets and a spectrum of consumption goods and services, the form of wealth one economic unit chooses to give up in a transaction does not generally correspond to the form of wealth that the other eventually chooses to hold. Thus, one transaction generally gives rise to a set of transactions involving transfers of portfolio assets or consumption goods among many economic units. In a currency type system, each transaction in this resettling of wealth involves the intervention of a physical medium of exchange which serves as a temporary abode of purchasing power, but which is soon given up for consumption goods or new holdings of portfolio assets. In contrast, in a pure accounting system of exchange, the notion of a physical medium or temporary abode of purchasing power disappears. Its role in the transactions sequence is replaced by bookkeeping entries, that is, debits and credits to the deposits of the economic units involved.

Thus, when one economic unit wishes to transfer a given amount of wealth to another, he signals his broker–banker with a check or some more modern way of accessing the bank's bookkeeping system. The broker–banker debits the sending account and the same or another broker–banker credits the receiving account for the amount of the transaction. The debit to the sending account generates a sale of securities from the portfolio against which the sending depositor has claim while the credit to the receiving account generates a purchase of securities for the portfolio against which the receiving depositor has claim. All prices, including prices of securities, are stated in terms of a numeraire, which we have assumed is one of the economy's real goods, but the numeraire never appears physically in the process of exchange described above. The essence of an accounting system of exchange is that it operates through debits and credits, which do not require any physical medium.

Of course, the existing checking system is not as free as the unregulated one we have described. There are regulations concerning what types of securities can be held in the bank portfolios against which deposits represent claims; there are regulations limiting the returns that can be paid on deposits; and for banks in the Federal Reserve system, there are regulations concerning how the bookkeeping entries generated by transactions move through the accounts that individual banks must keep with Federal Reserve banks. Nevertheless, the checking mechanism still operates through debits and credits that generate sales and purchases of securities from the portfolios against which the deposits involved have claims. Both in our unrestricted environment and in the real world's regulated environment, the accounting system of exchange provided by banks operates without the intervention of a physical medium of exchange or temporary abode of purchasing power.

2.3. Deposits, prices, and real activity

Although an accounting system of exchange involves no physical medium, like any system of exchange its efficiency is improved when all prices are stated in units of a common numeraire. For the purposes of a pure accounting system, the numeraire need not be portable or storable. It could well be tons of fresh cut beef or barrels of crude oil. However, in the type of unregulated banking system we have described, there is no meaningful way in which deposits can be the numeraire since deposits can be tailored to have the characteristics of any form of marketable wealth. Unregulated banks provide an accounting system in which organized markets and bookkeeping entries are used to allow economic units to exchange one form of wealth for another. But the deposits of the system are not a homogeneous good in which prices of all goods and securities might be stated.

The point is more than semantic. For example, after an insightful analysis of the social optimality of an unregulated banking system, Johnson (1968, p. 976) concludes that such a system would produce an upward spiralling price level:

'The analysis thus far has been concerned with the efficiency of the banking system, considered as an industry like any other industry. The banking system cannot, however, in strict logic, be so treated, because of the special characteristics that distinguish its product – money, the means of payment – from the products of other private enterprises – real goods and services . . . Less abstractly, a competitive banking system would be under constant incentive to expand the nominal money supply and thereby initiate price inflation.

Stability in the trend of prices (a special case of which is price stability) and in the trend of expectations about the future course of prices – which are generally agreed to be important to the social welfare – requires social control over the total quantity of money supplied by the banking system.'

Johnson is bothered by the fact that the deposits of an unregulated banking system involve no opportunity cost. There is no reason for investors to limit their holdings of deposits, and the supply of deposits is limited only by the economy's total invested wealth. However, the appropriate conclusion is not that prices measured in units of deposits will tend upward without limit, but rather that it makes no sense to try to force deposits to be numeraire in a system where 'deposits' is a rubric for all the different forms of portfolio wealth that have access to the accounting system of exchange provided by banks. Moreover, in a system where deposits can take on the characteristics of any form of invested wealth, deposits are a means of payment only in the sense that all forms of wealth are a means of payment, and the banking system is best understood without the mischief introduced by the concept of money.

The point in quoting from Johnson (1968) is not to single him out for special criticism. Other treatments of unregulated banking agree that determination of the price level is a special problem in such systems. Like Johnson, Pesek and Saving (1967) conclude that with unregulated banking, the price level will tend to spiral upward, while Gurley and Shaw (1960) and Patinkin (1961) argue that the price level is indeterminate. In all of these analyses, the problem of price level determinacy arises from treating unregulated deposits as 'money' and then trying to force this money to be the numeraire.

Since the economy in which we have embedded our competitive unregulated banking system is basically non-monetary, with some real good serving as numeraire, price level determinacy reduces to a standard problem concerning the existence of a stable general equilibrium in a non-monetary system. We examine now the role of banks in a general equilibrium, that is, in the determination of prices, real activity and the way that activity is financed.

In the world we are examining, banks have two functions. They provide transactions services, allowing depositors to carry out exchanges of wealth through their accounts, and they provide portfolio management services. The transactions services of banks allow economic units to exchange wealth more efficiently than if such services were not available, and in this way they are a real factor in a general equilibrium. However, there is no reason to suppose that these services are subject to special supply and demand conditions which would make them troublesome to price. Rather, the concern with banks in macroeconomics centers on their role as portfolio managers, whereby they purchase securities from individuals and firms (and a loan is, after all, just a purchase of securities) which they then offer as portfolio holdings (deposits) to other individuals and firms. Thus, banks are in the center of the process by which the economy chooses its real activities and the way those activities are financed.

In spite of their apparently strategic position, from the viewpoint of the theory of finance the portfolio management decisions of banks are the type of pure financing decisions that can be subject to the Modigliani–Miller (1958) theorem. The theorem has a strong form and a weak form, and we consider below how each can be applied to the portfolio management activities of banks. But the common message in both forms of the theorem is that as portfolio managers, banks are financial intermediaries with no special control over the details of a general equilibrium.[1]

Suppose that in purchasing securities from investors or firms and in issuing portfolios that represent claims against these securities, banks have no special privileges or comparative advantages vis à vis investors, firms or other financial intermediaries. Given such equal access to the capital market on the part of all economic units, the standard proof of the Modigliani–Miller theorem implies that the portfolios offered to depositors by banks can be refinanced by the depositors or their intermediaries so as to allow the depositors to achieve portfolio holdings that conform best to their tastes. In short, in an equal access market, a strong form of the Modigliani–Miller theorem holds. The basic constraints on portfolio opportunities are defined by the real production–investment decisions of firms. The way firms finance these decisions, or the way they are refinanced by intermediaries, including banks, neither expands nor contracts the set of portfolio opportunities available to investors. In this world, banks hold portfolios on behalf of their depositors because this probably allows them to provide transactions services (the accounting system of exchange) more efficiently, but the portfolio management activities of banks affect nothing, including prices and real activity.

Under the equal access assumption, the portfolio management decisions of the entire banking sector are of no consequence. However, the equal access assumption is stronger than is necessary for the weaker conclusions that each and every bank is subject to the Modigliani–Miller theorem (its portfolio decisions are of no consequence to investors) and that the banking sector is at most a passive force in the determination of prices and real activity. Thus, suppose access to the capital market for individuals is more limited than for banks, but among banks access to the market is competitive in the sense that an individual bank cannot offer to purchase securities and provide deposits which cannot also be purchased and offered by other banks. In other words, there are always actual or potential perfect substitutes for the portfolio management activities of any bank. As pointed out by Tobin (1963), if a bank is to survive, it must attract depositors, which means providing portfolios against which depositors are willing to hold claims. Moreover, competitive banks

---

[1] A discussion of the Modigliani–Miller theorem, covering both the 'equal access' and 'perfect substitutes' approaches used in what follows, is in Fama (1978).

simply turn over the returns on their portfolios to their depositors, less a competitively determined management fee. Banks are concerned with the fees they earn rather than with the types of portfolios they provide, so in a competitive equilibrium they provide, in aggregate, portfolios to the point where each different type produces management fees at the same rate.

Suppose now that, for whatever reason, one bank perturbs the equilibrium by arbitrarily providing more deposits of a given type and less of another. If other banks do not respond, deposits of different types no longer produce management fees at the same rate. Thus, other banks respond by exactly offsetting the changes in the portfolio management decisions of the perturbing bank and in this way restore the original general equilibrium. It follows that the portfolio management decisions of individual banks are of no consequence to investors, that is, no bank can by itself alter the portfolio opportunities available to investors, and individual banks are subject to the Modigliani–Miller theorem.

The essence of the story is that even when they have comparative advantages in the capital market vis à vis individual investors, competitive unregulated banks end up simply bringing together demanders and suppliers of portfolio assets and then acting as repositories for the securities that are thereby created. If all or most portfolio wealth is managed by banks, this means that banks succeed, under the impetus of competition, in eliciting securities from individuals and firms and in transforming these securities into portfolio holdings that conform to the opportunities and tastes of the ultimate suppliers and demanders of securities. Since banks just respond to the tastes and opportunities of demanders and suppliers of portfolio assets, banks are simple intermediaries, and the role of a competitive banking sector in a general equilibrium is passive. The controlling forces in the economic activity that takes place, the way that activity is financed, and the prices of securities and goods are the tastes and endowments of individual economic units and the state of the economy's technology.

Finally, a rigorous development of the Modigliani–Miller theorem [see, for example, Fama (1978)] would require, among other assumptions, that there are no transactions costs in purchasing and selling securities. In the strong form of the theorem, which is based on equal access to the capital market on the part of both individuals and firms, the optimizing portfolio rearrangements undertaken by individuals must be costless. In the weak form of the theorem, which in our analysis is based on the assumption that there are perfect substitutes among banks for the portfolio management activities of any individual bank, the offsetting portfolio rearrangements that take place among banks to return the system to a general equilibrium in response to a perturbation must be costless.

However, the rigorous application of perfect competition to any industry always involves a similar assumption about frictionless reallocations of resources. The standard scientific hope is that the major conclusions drawn from simplified scenarios are robust in the face of real world complications. For our purposes, the complications introduced by transactions costs in trading securities are not likely to overturn the general conclusions that a competitive banking sector is largely a passive participant in the determination of a general equilibrium, with no special control over prices or real activity, which in turn means that there is nothing in the economics of this sector that makes it a special candidate for government control.

3. A regulated banking system

Understanding unregulated banking makes analysis of the major forms of bank regulation straightforward. We consider first a reserve requirement and then a limitation on direct payments of returns to deposits. For the moment, we maintain the assumption that the numeraire is one of the economy's real goods and that there is no currency. The role of banks in defining a pure nominal commodity or unit of account which serves as numeraire is taken up subsequently.

3.1. Reserve requirements

Suppose banks, that is, intermediaries that offer deposits that provide access to an accounting system of exchange, are required to keep a minimum fraction of their assets 'on reserve' at the government's central bank, with the return on these reserves passing to the central bank. Such a reserve requirement is a direct tax on deposit returns since it lowers the return on deposits by the fraction of deposits that must be held as reserves. Deposits now involve opportunity costs, that is, lower returns than non-deposit assets with the same risk. Investors and firms are induced to economize their holdings of deposits and so to incur replenishment and other costs that would be unnecessary in the absence of a reserve requirement. Moreover, the reserve requirement causes some intermediaries to choose not to provide access to the accounting system of exchange, so the reserve requirement has the effect of differentiating banks from other intermediaries.

However, there are important conclusions on which a reserve requirement has no effect. It is still true that the payments mechanism provided by banks is a pure accounting system of exchange wherein transfers of wealth take place via debits and credits that give rise to sales and purchases of securities in the portfolios against which the sending and receiving accounts have claim. The reserve requirement simply means that there must also be a resettling of the reserve accounts that the banks involved must keep with the central bank.

Moreover, aside from the fact that they are taxed, there is still nothing special about deposits as portfolio assets. In the absence of further restrictions, deposits can represent claims against any form of invested wealth. If banks are competitive, deposits pay returns just like comparable non-deposit portfolios, less, of course, the tax imposed by the reserve requirement. Thus, deposits are still not a homogeneous good and they are not an appropriate candidate for numeraire.

Most important, if banking is competitive, banks remain passive intermediaries, with no control over any of the details of a general equilibrium. With respect to these issues, the 'perfect substitutes' analysis of unregulated banking can be applied intact. In brief, because they are concerned with management fees and not with the types of portfolios they manage, in their portfolio management decisions, banks simply cater to the tastes and opportunities of suppliers of securities and demanders of deposits. Thus, the real activity that takes place, the way it is financed, and the prices of securities and goods are not controlled either by individual banks or by the banking sector.

3.2. Limitation of interest payments on deposits

Suppose that in addition to a reserve requirement, there is a complete restriction on the payment of explicit returns on deposits. The restriction is complete in the sense that capital gains and losses on deposits as well as interest payments are not allowed and the value of a deposit is fixed, at least in units of whatever the system uses as numeraire. Since deposits must now be riskfree, a bank either limits its asset portfolio to riskfree securities or it has stockholders that absorb any variation in the market value of its portfolio. In short, except for the units in which they are denominated, deposits now look much like those of real world commercial banks.

If banks remain competitive, the restriction of interest payments on deposits does not yield them monopoly profits. One thing that is likely to happen, and which we in fact observe, is that banks charge less than cost for the transactions services they provide. In general, banks will now compete in finding ways to pass back returns on portfolio assets in the form of services to depositors. This special task of transforming ordinary interest bearing securities into securities (deposits) that pay returns in kind further differentiates banks from other financial intermediaries. However, if banks are competitive, the services they provide to depositors use up returns equivalent to those on non-deposit riskfree portfolio assets.[2]

---

[2]If the limitation of interest payments on deposits does not generate either profits for competitive banks or taxes for the government, one can wonder why sufficient political pressure has not been generated to cause this restriction to be eliminated. One possibility is that the

Because they pay returns in kind, deposits are not perfect substitutes for non-deposit portfolio assets with the same risk. Thus, the size of the banking sector is limited on the demand side by the incentives of investors to restrict their holdings of deposits. On the supply side, there is nothing special about the actions of any individual bank in transforming returns earned on portfolio assets into returns paid to depositors as services, so that this activity is likely to be characterized by constant returns to scale, at least at the industry level. Thus, the 'perfect substitutes' approach to the Modigliani–Miller theorem again holds. Perturbations to the overall equilibrium of the banking sector by any individual bank are offset by other banks, making the activities of any individual bank of no consequence. The banking sector as a whole just passively responds to the demands of investors for its particular type of financial intermediation.

In short, the limitation of direct payment of returns on deposits differentiates the portfolio management activities of banks from those of other financial intermediaries. Banks get into the business of transforming ordinary securities into special securities, deposits, that pay returns in the form of services. Nevertheless, as in the earlier cases, competitive banks end up as passive intermediaries fully subject to the Modigliani–Miller theorem, which means that there is no need to control their activities for the purpose of obtaining a stable general equilibrium with respect to prices and real activity.

4. Banking when the numeraire is a pure nominal or unit of account

In large part, the analysis of banking presented above can be viewed as a development of Tobin's (1963) insight that banking is just another industry whose equilibrium is subject to standard economic analysis. Elaborating this point has been simplified by the fact that we have so far treated banking in a non-monetary economy, which also allows us to give content to Tobin's conjecture that the special characteristics of banks as financial intermediaries derive more from regulations, for example, restrictions on returns paid on deposits, than from any role played by banks with respect to money.

On the other hand, we have so carefully kept anything resembling money out of banking that our analysis so far has nothing to say about how banks get involved in the process by which a pure nominal commodity or unit of account is made to play the role of numeraire in a real world monetary

---

limitation has tax advantages. For individuals, interest received from banks would be taxable but payments for transactions services, like other expenses involved in generating consumption, would not be tax deductible. Thus, when banks transform interest payments into 'free' transactions services, they are in effect allowing individuals to realize tax-free returns on their deposits. Note that this form of tax avoidance tends to offset the implicit taxes that the government collects from the banking sector through the imposition of a reserve requirement.

system. We turn now to this issue. First we consider the case where the unit of account is introduced through a fiat currency. We then consider how a reserve requirement can be used to force on deposits the problem of transforming a unit of account into a well-defined economic good.

4.1. Currency

Suppose that for some transactions a hand-to-hand medium of exchange is more efficient than an accounting system. Let us jump right to a system where the physical medium is a non-interest-bearing fiat currency produced monopolistically by the government. Assume also that the government chooses to supply currency to the private sector via banks; it supplies currency to banks in exchange for securities or deposits. Banks, in turn, inventory currency on behalf of their depositors; they provide the currency convertibility service, allowing depositors to 'turn in' deposits for currency and vice versa.

Having described how currency gets into an economic system and how banks get involved in its distribution, the problem now is to give economic content to the pure nominal unit of account (say, a dollar) in which currency is measured, that is, to make this unit of account a good that can serve as numeraire. Applying the analysis of Patinkin (1961), the problem is to ensure that the nominal commodity, currency in the present case, is subject to sufficiently well-defined demand and supply functions to give the unit in which it is measured determinate prices in terms of other goods.[3]

Since currency produces real services in allowing some exchanges to be carried out with lower transactions costs, currency has a demand function. For example, one might hypothesize that there is an aggregate demand for real currency which depends on (i) the opportunity cost of currency, the interest rate on a short-term bond whose promised pay-off in the nominal unit (say dollars) in which currency is measured is certain, (ii) some measure of real transactions activity of the type in which currency has a comparative advantage, and (iii) the minimum real costs of executing these transactions through methods other than currency.

As the wording suggests, in most models the demand for currency is expressed in real terms, units of goods and services, rather than in the nominal unit of account in which currency is denominated. To get a well-defined equilibrium in the currency market, that is, a price for the unit of account in terms of goods and services, the supply function for currency

---

[3]Since our goal is just to examine how banks get involved in introducing a pure nominal unit of account into the economy, we mean to bypass the type of price level determinacy issue, discussed by Brock (1974) and others, which arises when currency is treated as an asset with an infinite life. Let us just assume that the currency in our model will be expropriated and destroyed at some distant future date.

must be stated in terms of the unit of account. One possibility is that the government fixes the supply of nominal currency in terms of units of account, and then lets the public's demand function for the services of real currency determine the price level or the real value of a unit of account.

When the currency market is used to transform the unit of account into a real economic good, there is no need for government control of banking. Thus, suppose the unit in which currency is measured is the economy's numeraire, and currency exists side-by-side with an accounting system of exchange. Suppose the government monopolizes the production of currency but the banking sector is uncontrolled and competitive in the sense of section 2: Banks pass the returns they earn on portfolio assets over to depositors, they charge depositors for portfolio management and transactions services according to competitively determined fees, they allow deposits to be claims against portfolios with any degree of risk desired by depositors, and they allow depositors to participate in two kinds of transactions services, the currency convertibility privilege and access to an accounting system of exchange.

Since the nominal unit (say, a dollar) in which currency is measured is assumed to be the numeraire, the value of deposits like the value of all securities and goods, is expressed in this same nominal unit. However, in the present scenario, transforming the unit of account into a real economic good takes place in the currency market, via well-specified demand and supply functions for currency. For deposits, the analysis of section 2 holds intact. The portfolio management decisions of banks, that is, their decisions to issue deposits and purchase securities, are subject to the Modigliani–Miller theorem, which means that there is no reason to control these financing decisions of competitive banks for the purpose of obtaining equilibrium with respect to prices and real activity.

4.2. A reserve requirement

Although currency alone could be used to define a nominal unit of account as a separate good in an economic system, this function can also be imposed on deposits. One possible device is a reserve requirement. When an abstract nominal unit (a dollar) is numeraire, a regulation which says that a minimum fraction of the portfolio against which deposits represent claims must be non-interest bearing reserves issued by a central bank in effect requires that a minimum fraction of the value of the portfolio must be held in pure nominal units of account 'issued' by the central bank.

As in the case of currency, if the unit of account is to be defined through reserves, reserves must have demand and supply functions. The demand for currency arises from the direct transactions services that it provides as a physical medium of exchange. In contrast, the demand for required reserves arises because of the reserve requirement: By making non-interest bearing reserves a required part of an accounting system of exchange which yields valuable transactions services, the government creates a demand for non-interest bearing central bank reserves which would not exist in the absence of the reserve requirement.

The point bears emphasis. Even in a competitive unregulated system, there may be securities that can be exchanged among banks at lower transactions costs than other portfolio assets. Such securities might be convenient for resettling accounts within and among banks. As a consequence, depositors may generally choose to have some amount of such low transactions cost assets in the portfolios against which their deposits have claim in order to reduce the charges they must bear when transactions through deposits require purchases or sales of assets. Thus, such low transactions cost assets may come to play the role of 'reserves'. However, these 'reserves' of an unregulated competitive system would be interest bearing since they would be ordinary securities for which competitive trading involved low transactions costs.[4]

Currency and the accounting system of exchange maintained by banks are substitutes but not perfect substitutes as methods of executing transactions. Thus, currency and reserves have separate demand functions. It follows that by controlling the nominal supply of currency alone, the government could continue to use currency alone to render the real value of the unit of account (the price level) determinate. The government could follow a passive policy with respect to reserves, allowing banks to exchange securities (but not currency) for reserves on demand. In this situation, the earlier analysis of the reserve requirement would apply: The reserve requirement is simply a tax on deposit returns which does not imply a need to control the level of either reserves or deposits.

Alternatively, since currency and reserves have separate demand functions, the government could choose to define the unit of account through reserves alone, controlling the nominal quantity of reserves, but following a passive policy with respect to currency, that is, allowing banks to exchange currency for ordinary securities (but not reserves) on demand. Finally, the government could choose to follow a passive policy with respect to the mix of currency and reserves, allowing banks to exchange currency for reserves on demand. In this case, there is no separate supply function for either currency or reserves, but determinacy of the real value of the unit of account can be

---

[4]There would be no particular problem in the arrangement of competitive interest payments on reserves, even though they may be continuously shifting among banks. For example, the federal funds market now provides an efficient mechanism whereby banks can earn competitive interest on a day-to-day basis on any reserves they may happen to have in excess of the legal minimum. In earlier times, banks paid interest on the deposits kept with them by other banks to resettle accounts in response to transactions among their depositors.

obtained by controlling the sum of currency and reserves. This last possibility seems to correspond best to the stated policy of the central bank in the U.S.

4.3. Patinkin and the price level

The preceding draws heavily on the analysis of Patinkin (1961), who in turn builds on the work of Gurley and Shaw (1960, ch. 7). However, Patinkin and Gurley and Shaw always tie control of the supply of units of account to control of bank reserves or deposits, in which case determinacy of the price level implies controlled banking. It is clear from the analysis above that currency alone could be used to define the unit of account and so obtain a determinate price level. The government could leave reserves uncontrolled or the reserve requirement could be dropped; that is, the assets (if any) that banks choose to hold as reserves to resettle accounts in response to transactions executed through their accounting system of exchange could be left unregulated, and all other aspects of banking could also be left unregulated.

Patinkin, at least, does not seem to be misled on this matter. At the end of his review of the Gurley and Shaw (1960) book, he states (1961, p. 116):

'The general conclusion that we can draw from all this is that, in the absence of distribution effects, the necessary conditions for rendering a monetary system determinate are that there be an exogenous fixing of (1) some nominal quantity and (2) some rate of return. It follows that if we were to extend the argument to an economy with both inside and outside money (something G–S do not do) it would suffice to fix the quantity of outside money and its rate of return (say, at zero). In such an economy the price level would be determinate even if the central bank were to fix nothing, . . . subject to the restriction that the quantity of outside money is fixed.'

If the term 'outside money' is interpreted as currency, and 'inside money' is taken to mean unregulated deposits, then the contention of Patinkin's statement is exactly our conclusion that controlling the supply of currency alone is sufficient to render the price level (the real value of the unit of account) determinate.[5]

---

[5]We might note that when he applies his results to reserves, Patinkin's analysis is incomplete. He concludes that the real value of the unit of account becomes determinate when the government fixes the supply of reserves and the interest rate paid on them, leaving the fraction of deposits held as reserves to the discretion of the banks. In other words, he concludes that there is no need for a reserve requirement. However, since his analysis implies that the interest rate fixed for reserves must be below what a free market would pay, the optimal strategy for banks is to hold no central bank reserves. When reserves pay less than a competitive return banks must be forced

The fact that Patinkin may not be misled does not mean that the implications of his analysis about the feasibility of uncontrolled banking are clear. We saw in the earlier quote from Johnson (1968) that he felt that a determinate price level requires government control over the total quantity of money, including the fully interest-bearing deposits of competitive banks, and Johnson explicitly considered a system where non-interest bearing, government-produced currency exists side-by-side with the deposits issued by competitive banks. Moreover, in a later comment on the Pesek and Saving (1967) book, Johnson (1969) re-iterates his position and indicates that he sees it to be consistent with Patinkin's:

> 'This analysis shows that reduction of the alternative opportunity cost of holding money to zero and reduction of the purchasing power of money to zero are two extremely different things involving different policies. The confusion between them has probably been fostered by an ambiguity in the concept of 'competition' among banks as providers of the money supply. If deposits cost nothing to create and yet the assets held against them yield a positive return, banks subject to no restraint on the nominal quantity of money they can create in the aggregate will be under competitive pressure to expand the nominal money supply until its purchasing power is reduced to zero. At best the money supply so determined will be in neutral equilibrium.
>
> On the other hand, if banks are competitive but subject either to a quantitative restraint on the aggregate money supply they can create or to a policy of stabilization of the aggregate price level mediated through control of the aggregate money supply, competition among them will force them to pay interest to their depositors and so optimize the supply of real balances without reducing the real value of money to zero . . .
>
> In conclusion, it may be noted that Figure 4.4 can be used to establish in a simple way the proposition, which emerged from Patinkin's critique of Gurley and Shaw's work that the monetary authority needs to control both a nominal magnitude and an interest rate to control the price level.'

The confusion in Johnson's interpretation of Patinkin probably arises in part from the fact that Patinkin, like everyone but Black (1970), treats unregulated competitively produced deposits as money. Even though he distinguishes between this 'inside money' and 'outside money', like currency, which is produced exogenously, and even though he is clear on the point that controlling only the quantity of outside money (and the interest paid on

---

to hold them. This is the function of a reserve requirement. Alternatively, a demand for reserves can be created by making central bank reserves the only eligible security for settling accounts among banks in response to transactions among customers. However, such a regulation would probably be more difficult to enforce than a reserve requirement.

it) can render the price level determinate, the temptation is there for others to treat all things called money alike, and, like Johnson, to conclude that price level determinacy requires that competitive banks are 'subject either to a quantitative restraint on the aggregate money supply they can create or to a policy of stabilization of the aggregate price level mediated through control of the aggregate money supply.

Perhaps a more important source of confusion is that Patinkin consistently uses phrases like 'the necessary conditions for *rendering a monetary system determinate* are that there be an exogenous fixing of (1) some nominal quantity and (2) some rate of return' [Patinkin (1961, p. 116), italics mine]. The precise problem is not rendering a monetary system determinate, but rather giving content to a pure nominal unit of account (a dollar) as a separate, well-defined economic good. It turns out, of course, that the unit of account is generally defined through parts of what is usually referred to as the monetary system, and, more specifically, through currency and the non-interest bearing reserves that member banks are required to hold with central banks. Nevertheless, when the price level determinacy problem is focused directly on the unit of account, one is less likely to fall into the error of concluding that price level determinacy requires control over all parts of the monetary system. One might even be tempted to conclude that the price level determinacy problem could be solved and the efficiency of the transactions and portfolio management industries could be improved if the government got out of the banking business, that is, if the activities of banks in managing portfolios (issuing deposits and purchasing securities) and in providing an accounting system of exchange were deregulated, and if the problem of defining a unit of account were focused solely on the currency end of the transactions industry.

5. A concluding parable

Finally, let us consider a scenario in which it is clear that, at least in principle, the problem of defining a nominal unit of account is not coincident with the problem of rendering a monetary system determinate. Suppose we have a completely unregulated banking system in the sense of section 2, and an advanced society in which it is economic to carry out all transactions through the accounting system of exchange provided by banks. The system finds no need for currency or other physical mediums of exchange, and its numeraire has long been a real good, say steel ingots. The society is so advanced that terms like money, medium of exchange, means of payment, and temporary abode of purchasing power have long ago fallen from its vocabulary, and all written accounts of the ancient 'monetary age' were long ago recycled as part of an ecology movement.

Suppose now that, for whatever reason, the government of this society decides that it would be more aesthetic to replace steel ingots as numeraire with a pure nominal commodity which will be called a 'unit' but which has no physical representation. Although monetary theory has long since passed away, value theory has strengthened with time, and the government's economists realize that the 'unit' cannot be established as numeraire by simple decree. It must be a well-defined economic good, that is, the 'unit' needs demand and supply functions which can determine its equilibrium value in terms of other goods.

Controlling the supply of 'units' is no problem, but creating a demand for them is another matter since they have no intrinsic usefulness. The solution hit upon by the authorities is to use a reserve requirement to forcibly join the holding of 'units' with something that does provide valuable services. In the monetary age the appropriate industry to burden with the reserve requirement would have been clear, but in the new more enlightened age it is evident that there are many potential candidates. In the end, the government imposes the reserve requirement on spaceship owners. Every spaceship owner has to keep a reserve of X 'units' with the central 'unit' authority. Since most citizens of the society desire the transportation services of private spaceships, the reserve requirement creates a real demand for 'units'. The government then renders the price of the 'unit' determinate by fixing the interest rate paid on 'units', perhaps at zero, and controlling the supply of 'unit' reserves.

The reserve requirement, of course, has a depressing effect on the spaceship industry. Because X 'units' must be purchased along with every spaceship, people economize more on their holdings of spaceships, existing spaceships are used more intensively, and alternative forms of transportation services are substituted to some extent for spaceships. On the other hand, sales of 'units' by the government can substitute for other forms of taxation. Indeed, most of the citizens of this enlightened society feel this new form of taxation is the major reason for the government's interest in replacing the ingot as numeraire with the 'unit'.

References

Black, Fischer, 1970, Banking and interest rates in a world without money, Journal of Bank Research, Autumn, 9–20.

Brock, William A., 1974, Money and growth: The case of long-run perfect foresight, International Economic Review 15, Oct., 750–777.

Fama, Eugene F., 1978, The effects of a firm's investment and financing decisions on the welfare of its securityholders, American Economic Review 68, June, 272–284.

Gurley, John G. and Edward S. Shaw, 1960, Money in a theory of finance (The Brookings Institution, Washington, DC); chapter 7 of the book is most relevant for the purposes of this paper.

Johnson, Harry G., 1968, Problems of efficiency in monetary management, Journal of Political Economy 76, Sept./Oct., 971–990.

Johnson, H.G., 1969, A comment on Pesek and Saving's theory of money and wealth, Journal of Money, Credit and Banking 1, Aug., 535–537.

Modigliani, Franco and Merton H. Miller, 1958, The cost of capital, corporation finance, and the theory of investment, American Economic Review 48, June, 261–297.

Patinkin, Don, 1961, Financial intermediaries and the logical structure of monetary theory, American Economic Review 51, March, 95–116.

Pesek, Boris and Thomas R. Saving, 1967, Money, wealth and economic theory (Macmillan, New York).

Tobin, James, 1963, Commercial banks as creators of 'money', in: Dean Carson, ed., Banking and monetary studies (Irwin, Homewood, IL) 408–419.

[19]

LONGER WAVES IN FINANCIAL RELATIONS: FINANCIAL FACTORS IN THE MORE SEVERE DEPRESSIONS

By HYMAN P. MINSKY
University of California, Berkeley

I. *Introduction*

In his 1959 testimony before the Joint Economic Committee Professor Abramowitz stated that "it is not yet known whether they (the long swings) are the result of some stable mechanism inherent in the structure of the U. S. economy, or whether they are set in motion by the episodic occurrence of wars, financial panics or unsystematic disturbances."[1] Quite casually financial panics were identified as exogenous, episodic rather than as endogenous, systemic events. T heargument in this paper is that the stable mechanism which has generated the long swings centers around the cumulative changes in financial variables that take place over the long-swing expansions and contractions.

The long swings reach a climax in a deep depression business cycle. Friedman and Schwartz's chronology of deep depression cycles coincides with Abramowitz's chronology of severe contractions that occur at the end of the long waves. Although the evidence for the monetary explanation of mild depression cycles is admitted to be tenuous by Friedman and Schwartz,[2] the evidence that money is a significant part of the mechanism generating a deep depression is strong. The long-wave hypothesis cannot be distinguished from the hypothesis that there are two types of business cycles, mild and deep depression, and that the conditions which must be satisfied if a deep depression cycle is to take place are generated over a number of mild depression cycles.

During the expansion phase of a long swing, or alternatively over a period in which only mild recessions occur, systematic changes in the financial structure occur. These reflect the financial aspects of high

---

[1] United States 86th Cong. Joint Economic Committee, *Employment and Growth and Price Levels, Hearings Part 2 Historical and Comparative Rates of Production, Productivity and Prices*, p. 12.

[2] M. Friedman and S. J. Schwartz, "Money and Business Cycles," *Rev. of Econ. and Statis. Sup.*, Feb., 1963, p. 55. "The case for a monetary explanation is not nearly so strong for the minor U.S. economic fluctuations. . . ." Friedman and Schwartz make a case for a monetary explanation of mild depression cycles by arguing that: "Is not a common explanation for both more appealing than separate explanations, especially when there is no well-tested alternative separate explanation?" (P. 55.)

rates of growth by leading sectors, revaluation of assets to allow for growth expectations and the growing financial layering at the same time as ultimate liquidity[3] grows slowly if at all.

The exact nature of the changes that take place in financial variables during long-swing expansions and the significance of these changes are sensitive to institutional arrangements. Financial institutions and usages evolve, both in response to market forces and as a result of administrative processes and legislation. Thus the exact course of financial variables over the phase of the longer waves differs greatly among the various observed cycles. This makes it quite useless to engage in sophisticated statistical analysis, if the object is to determine the significance of financial factors in the cyclical behavior of the economy, for the fitted relations need not give us the reaction path of the economy at any time.

The present set of financial institutions and arrangements are quite different from those that ruled during the most recent financial panic-deep depression combination, that of 1929–33. Thus the question must be raised whether a financial panic of the sort that occurred in the past can now occur.

The hypothesis is that the financial panic which is present during deep depressions and absent during mild depressions is not a random exogenous affair; rather it is endogenous to the economy. The financial panic is made possible by the changes in the financial structure that take place during the long-swing expansion. As a result, the triggering event for a deep depression need not be specially severe, even though at an earlier date in the expansion a similar event could not trigger a deep depression.

Once a financial panic occurs, the decline in asset values, the forced changes in portfolios, and the revaluation of prospects combine to lower both consumption and investment demand, thus depressing income further than in a mild depression. We will not discuss the further ramifications of such a deflationary spiral; our attention will be upon the initiating event and the preparation of the environment for this event. However, it is worth noting that during the liquidation phases of a deep depression the financial "stage" is set for a long-wave expansion as debts are reduced, equity assets decline in value, and the stock of ultimate liquidity increases.

The view presented here is that the strictly defined money supply is a proxy for deeper, more significant financial variables; and that the observed relations between changes in the money supply and economic activity really reflect the impact of the evolving financial structure upon

[3] Ultimate liquidity can also be labeled outside money. It consists of government liabilities to the public (including the monetary system) and the gold stock.

economic activity. The central role of the money supply in past deep depressions is due to the institutional accident that commercial banks were the dominant financial intermediary. Under alternative institutional arrangements, where much greater weight is attached to non-bank financial institutions, a financial panic could occur even though the money supply does not fall. What changes do occur in the money supply may very well be induced by the behavior of the economy and the financial structure, witness the "excess reserves" of commercial banks in the 1930's.

Before we proceed, the financial structure of an economy should be defined. The financial structure of an economy consists of the set of financial assets and liabilities and the network of payment commitments among units. The financial structure includes the assets owned and the liabilities emitted by ultimate units, financial intermediaries, and governments. The "specialized" central bank guarantees, by organizations such as the FDC and the FHA, are a part of the financial structure. As a result of the existence of these organizations, it is now certain that in a crisis period certain losses will be absorbed by government and that an increase in the government debt and the money supply owned by the public will take place.

One view is that the institutional arrangements are now such that a financial panic cannot occur. Once again, it is maintained that we have entered a "new era." If the long swings are to persist and if the evolving financial structure is part of the generating mechanism for these swings, then the financial changes that accumulate over the expansion phase must be such as to constrain the sectors that would otherwise lead the continued expansion even in the absence of a dramatic financial panic.

The major task of this paper is to examine the implications of the cumulative changes in the financial structure that take place over a long-swing expansion for the stability of the financial system.

II. *Financial Instability*

A. *The Determinants of Financial Instability*. Mild and deep depression cycles are, to a point, the result of a common cycle generating mechanism. However, in a deep depression cycle an initial downturn of income or a random decrease in particular asset values, triggers a general decline in asset values. In a mild depression cycle no such financial reaction takes place. Which type of cycle occurs at any time depends upon the stability properties of the existing financial system.

For the hypothesis central to this paper to be true, the changes in the structure of financial assets and liabilities that occur during a period in which only mild depression cycles take place must be such as to make the financial system less stable. Three dimensions of the financial systems will be emphasized here: (1) the rise of debts relative to income for the income producing sectors, (2) the rise in price of stock market and real estate assets, and (3) the decrease in the relative size of ultimate liquidity.

The financial system is stable with respect to a change in income per period of a particular size or a given level of defaults per period on debts (or some combination of the two) if a change of this magnitude will not lead to a sharp fall in asset prices. Whether or not a financial system is stable with respect to changes of a given magnitude depends not only on the asset price, payments process, and ultimate liquidity factor mentioned above but also upon the extent to which government and central bank agencies absorb risk and maintain prices in various financial markets. Many of the government interventions in financial markets are of the form that will lead to an automatic improvement in the ultimate liquidity of the system and tend to stabilize the payments process once a financial panic is set off; there are automatic financial as well as income stabilizers.

Simple diagrams can be used to illustrate the stability properties of a financial structure. Let us assume that the initiating changes are declines in income and defaults in financial contracts, both as a rate per period. Given the existing financial structure there is a set of maximal shortfalls of income-financial defaults (both per period) combinations which cannot lead to a financial crisis; there also exists a set of minimal shortfalls of income-financial defaults per period which must lead to a financial crisis. Between these two border sets there is a set of income declines—financial defaults which may or may not lead to a financial panic. That is, for every financial structure the shortfalls of income-financial default plane is divided into regions in which the financial system is stable, unstable, and quasi-stable (illustrated in Chart I).

As the financial structure changes, the borders between the stable, quasi-stable, and unstable regions of the plane shift. The borders of the regions shift towards the origin as a long-swing expansion matures; that is, stable and quasi-stable regions become smaller parts of the plane.

Assume that the normal unamplified recession decline in income is in the range $\Delta Y_1 - \Delta Y_2$ and the usual value of defaults per period, when no financial crisis is underway and income is falling by $\Delta Y_1 - \Delta Y_2$, lies between f_1 and f_2. Two dimensions of the financial structure that change over the long swings will be used to illustrate the argument: the debt income ratios of households and business firms. For an initial change of the designated size the financial system will be stable, quasi-stable, or unstable depending upon the size of household and business debt income ratios; the higher the debt income ratio the less stable the financial structure (illustrated in Chart II).

In the light of the above, the hypothesis that the financial system evolves from being stable to being unstable over the long-swing expan-

CHART I

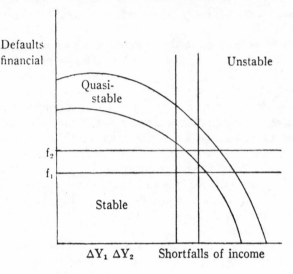

sion takes the form that business and household debt-income ratios increase during such a period. However debt-income ratios, or the payments relations they reflect, are but one aspect of the financial system relevant to its stability; two other aspects are the market value of assets and the relative size of the stock of ultimate liquidity. We will now proceed to investigate how all three of these determinants of stability evolve over a long-swing expansion.

B. *Payments.* The current fashion in monetary theory is to emphasize "money at rest," to look at money as one among many assets that are included in portfolios because it yields valuable returns. To examine the relation between money and financial instability it is necessary to look at "money on the wing."

CHART II

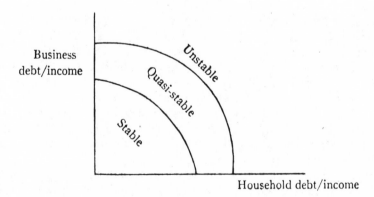

The money on the wing perspective is not irrelevant for the current portfolio balance view of monetary theory. Money holdings yield services in kind in the form of protection against specific repercussions of various contingencies. The repercussions of not having enough money on hand are those which follow from not being able to meet payment commitments. Money is held at rest because of the conditions facing the owning unit which will lead to its taking wing. The size of the stock of money held relative to payment commitments depends upon the various arrangements available which generate assets that are "as good as money" for the satisfaction of precautionary motives, as well as the return from not holding money.

One aspect of the evolution of the financial system from being stable to being unstable is due to the growth of contractual payment commitments relative to both money holdings and specified money flows. In terms of standard symbols, the PT of Fisher's $MV = PT$ should be broken down into components; that is

$$MV = \sum_{ij} P_{ij} T_{ij}$$

where i is the index for payment type and j is the index for classes of economic units. The argument is that over long-swing expansions the ratio's

$$\frac{P_{\alpha j} T_{\alpha j}}{P_{\beta j} T_{\beta j}}$$

change in a systematic fashion which tends to make the financial system less stable; in the language to be introduced α will represent balance-sheet payments and β represents income payments.

Money is a means of payment. For each class of economic units, we can distinguish three classes of payment: income, balance-sheet, and portfolio payments. The classification of payment types and sectors is of course a construct imposed upon the world. As is true of any classification system there are observations which do not fall clearly into one or another of the cells and adjustments are necessary as the format is applied.

Of course each payment has two sides: a payment and a receipt; and a transaction need not be the same type to both sides.

The simplest way to begin examining the various types of payments is to look at the balance sheet of an economic unit and the commitments to make payments as stated in the liabilities. At any moment of time each economic unit has a balance sheet; the liabilities in the balance sheet finance a "position" as stated by the assets. Each liability carries with it a dated, demand, or contingent commitment to make payments.

Each asset, in the case of tangible assets, various collections of assets, generates receipts; in addition if necessary the economic unit is able to sell assets to acquire cash.

The labels dated, demand and contingent balance-sheet payments help explain the content of each class of balance-sheet payment. Dated payments act to constrain behavior; units will operate so as to have sufficient cash on hand at the designated dates to fulfill the commitments. Demand balance-sheet payments are of special importance for depository financial intermediaries, although various other units do emit demand or well-nigh demand liabilities. Units issuing demand liabilities must have a guaranteed refinancing source if they are to be viable under pressure. The government and central bank financial organizations have taken on contingent liabilities which do extend what amounts to guaranteed refinancing for many classes of financial intermediaries; although private endorsements and insurance contracts also are contingent liabilities. Some of the contingent liabilities are demographic in character, such as social security and pension fund liabilities; others are related to the behavior of the economy, such as acceptances, endorsements, and mortgage insurance.

The production of income involves both intermediate and final "income payments." Obviously, as interest payments due to debts are included among balance-sheet payments, the final income payments do not include all the items that enter into "income" as conventionally measured. Dividends on common stock are the result of current income production, and hence it can be argued that they should be included among income payments; however, as common stock is an asset in household and other balance sheets it may be best to include dividends as a special type of "contingent" balance-sheet payment in evaluating the changing structure of payments over time.

Portfolio payments occur when assets, real or financial, are traded. The "portfolio" aspects of trading in existing assets is obvious. However, in the creation and extinction of certain classes of assets the transactions can be a portfolio transaction for one and an income or balance-sheet transaction for the other party to the transaction.

For example, the withdrawal of a deposit from a savings and loan association is a balance-sheet payment by the savings and loan association and a portfolio receipt by the depositor. The payments made in the production of a capital asset are income receipts to the producing agents and portfolio payments by the firm or household that will own the real capital.

As a long-wave expansion progresses the relative weight of the different types of payments change: balance-sheet and portfolio payments rise relative to income, especially final income, payments. For the income producing sectors, income receipts are the major source of funds for meeting payments due to liabilities. A rising balance-sheet payments-income receipts ratio for these sectors indicates that a given fall of income will force a larger proportion of units to try to obtain funds from other than their normal sources. These other sources are the sale of assets or alternatively "forced borrowing." That is, a "forced" portfolio transaction will need to take place as a result of a shortfall of income.

Portfolio sales will yield funds only if there are buyers (or, alternatively, lenders). If the order books are not thick relative to offers to sell, asset prices will fall sharply. Capital losses and a decrease in the protection offered debt owners by asset values will take place. Even units that were not initially affected will want more cash and risk free assets to protect themselves against becoming forced borrowers or sellers. Obviously a single unit's financial distress does not always lead to a financial panic; only if the initial financial situation is such that an income shortfall will affect many units and if asset prices are vulnerable to sharp decreases will this possibility exist.

Of particular importance for the development of a financial panic is the ability of financial institutions to meet these commitments and to continue acquiring assets. Financial distress for both bank or nonbank financial intermediaries affects both the ability of many units to make payments and the markets for assets. Hence "distress" for financial intermediaries seems to be necessary if a financial panic is to develop.

One element in the development of an "unstable" financial system is the rise in balance-sheet payments relative to final gross income for the income producing units. This will be measured by the ratio of debts to income for these units. A financial panic develops when a substantial number of units resort to portfolio sales to acquire cash, because the normal source of cash, income receipts, has not generated the expected amount. In particular, a financial panic can develop if financial intermediaries are forced to sell assets to acquire cash.

C. *Asset Prices.* During a period in which only short and shallow depressions occur, the economy will grow rapidly. As such a period increases in length, the market value of those assets that benefit from growth will rise to reflect not only the achieved growth but also expected growth. In addition, the value of protected private liabilities, such as bonds, mortgages, and deposits, will rise as the price of the underlying equity or real asset increases.

There is no "correct" price for a future income stream. The market price of an asset depends upon the time-path the income it yields is expected to follow as well as the certainty with which these expectations are held. As is well known, given that the capitalization rate for an

       AMERICAN ECONOMIC ASSOCIATION

unchanging stream of earnings in a given risk class is

$$\frac{1}{r} \ (r < 1),$$

the capitalization rate for a given stream of earnings in the same risk class that is expected to grow at g percent per year is

$$\frac{1}{r - g} \ (g < r).$$

As growth expectations take over, during a long-swing expansion, the capitalization rate for assets that are expected to benefit from the growth in income will rise from

$$\frac{1}{r} \ \text{to} \ \frac{1}{r - g} \ \text{times (current) income.}$$

The movement of asset values from

$$\frac{1}{r} \ \text{to} \ \frac{1}{r - g} \ \text{times income}$$

will of course generate capital gains to holders of the asset, especially while the numerator is increasing at g percent per year. The "equilibrium" rate of growth of the price of these assets is g percent per year. However, while the expectations that growth will take place are being reflected in asset values, the price will grow at a rate faster than the equilibrium rate.

A purely speculative secondary run up of asset prices can occur as prices begin to reflect capital gains that occurred when the capitalization rate was increasing. This speculative secondary wave is inherently unstable, for once the rate of growth of asset prices slows down, the equilibrium capitalization rate, given growth expectations, of $1/r-g$ becomes the determinant of asset values. The triggering event that breaks the secondary speculation wave can be a relatively slight shortfall of the rate of growth of income below the expected g percent per year.[4]

The implications of change in the capitalization rates and the secondary speculative rise in asset prices are of special importance for an

---

[4] It is worth noting that if the tax laws give a favored treatment to capital gains as against income, an annual income of $\$1.00 + \frac{g}{r-g}$ (\$1.00 dividend, $\frac{g}{r-g}$ rise in market price) with a capitalization rate of $\frac{1}{r-g}$ is worth more to the stockholder than an income of \$1.00 with a capitalization rate of $1/r$ even though both yield r percent per year on the asset price. That is, assets that generate a part of their returns in capital gains should have a smaller measured rate of return than assets which generate all of their returns in fully taxable income. This also argues for a rapid rate of increase in equity prices as growth expectations become generalized.

economy in which corporations are the dominant form of business organization and the ownership of corporate stock is widespread. The market price of real estate assets is also affected by growth expectations, and speculative waves in real estate prices occur.

The impact of speculative movements in real asset or common stock prices depends upon whether or not the inflated asset prices are fed back into the financial system as security for debts. The low margin stock market of the 1920's did feed assets whose prices reflected speculative factors into the balance sheets of financial institutions and nonfinancial corporations. The high margin stock market of the postwar period tends to minimize this feedback of common stock prices into the financial system, although the feedback from real estate prices and commodity transactions into financial institutions still takes place.[5]

D. *Ultimate Liquidity*. An economy's stock of ultimate liquidity consists of those assets whose nominal value is essentially fixed and which are not the liabilities of any private unit within the economy. The ultimate liquid assets carry no default risk and as they are essentially fixed in market value, they are always available to meet payment commitments. No private unit is constrained by payment commitments embodied in these assets.

In the United States the ultimate liquid assets consist of the gold stock, various types of treasury currency, and the public debt outside government trust funds. The inclusion of the government debt implies that if necessary support operations by the central bank will occur. A large part of the stock of ultimate liquidity is held by the monetary system. The extent to which the assets of the monetary system consist of ultimate liquid assets is a qualitative characteristic of the money supply. A growth of the money supply that reflects the growth of ultimately liquid assets owned by the monetary system has quite different implications for the behavior of the economy than a growth of the money supply that is due to the acquisition of private debts by the monetary system.

The ratio of the values of ultimately liquid assets and total financial assets in the economy is a measure of the extent to which financial positions are impervious to financial losses; the higher the ratio of ultimately liquid assets the more stable the financial system. In addition, the ratio of the value of ultimately liquid assets to income measures the extent to which a shortfall of income and its concomitant effect on asset prices will not result in a default of payment commitments.

Over a long-swing expansion the two major components of ultimate liquidity—the government debt and the gold supply—grow more

[5] Note that if the banking system grows less rapidly than income and the value of financial assets, and if nonfinancial business tends to decrease its dependence upon bank loans, a given proportion of stock purchases on margin can become a rising proportion of bank assets that reflect price sensitive assets.

slowly than income and other assets. As a result, the relative size of the stock of ultimate liquidity decreases, which tends to reduce the stability of the financial system. Of course, what happens to the size of the government debt is the result of policy decisions; therefore the decline in the relative size of the stock of ultimate liquidity need not take place over the long swing.

E. *Recapitulation.* A financial panic occurs when a not unusual decline in income or run of defaults on financial contracts occurs in a "favorable" environment. The favorable environment consists of (1) a high ratio of balance-sheet payments to income receipts for major classes of units, (2) equity and real estate asset values based upon growth expectations that reflect not alone the real growth potential of the economy but also the capital gains that occur as these assets are revalued to reflect growth expectations, and (3) a low ratio of ultimate liquidity to other financial assets and income. During a long-wave expansion each of these elements of the financial environment changes in such a manner as to increase the probability of a panic taking place; balance-sheet payments increase relative to income receipts, asset prices are bid up, and income and other financial assets grow faster than ultimate liquidity. Hence a financial panic is not something that just happens; it is an outcome of the very cyclical phase it brings to an end.

TABLE 1

RATES OF GROWTH OF FINANCIAL ASSETS AND LIABILITIES 1922–29, 1948–57 AND 1957–62

	GROWTH 29/22	RATES 57/48	%/YR. 62/57
A. GNP current prices...........................	5.2	6.1	4.5
B. Disposable personal income..................	5.0	5.6	4.4
C. Consumers and nonprofit sector: current receipts after deductions............................		5.5	4.5
D. Corporate nonfinancial business: gross profits after taxes.................................	4.5	4.3	7.9
E. Market value of stocks listed in N.Y. Stock Exchange...................................	19.0	12.6	
F. Common stock: consumer and nonprofit organization......................................		11.7	10.2
G. Internally held federal debt..................	−4.3	0.22	1.85
H. Ultimate liquidity	−3.2	.15	1.50
I. Demand deposits net and currency...........	2.9	2.3	1.54
J. Time deposits at commercial banks...........	7.8	4.5	11.4
K. Total: demand+time deposits...............	4.8	3.5	3.7
L. Household and nonprofit sector ratio of total liabilities to income..........................	7.2	8.4	4.3
M. Corporate nonfinancial business ratio of total liabilities to income.........................	0.3	3.8	−1.3

SOURCES: In general 1922–29 data are from R. W. Goldsmith, *A Study of Saving in the United States* (Princeton Univ. Press, 1955).

The 1948–62 data are from *Flow of Funds/Savings Accounts Supplement No. 5,* Board of Governors, Federal Reserve System, and various issues of the *Fed. Res. Bul.*

III. *Conclusions*

The evidence presented in the attached table indicates that during 1922–29 and 1948–57 financial changes took place that were destabilizing. In particular, both the household liabilities-income ratio and common stock prices increased rapidly and ultimate liquidity either declined or grew very slowly.

The economy grew at a somewhat slower rate in 1957–62 than in 1922–29 or 1948–57. During this period of somewhat slower growth, on the whole the financial structure continued to evolve in such a way as to decrease its stability, albeit at a slower rate than in either 1922–29 or 1948–57. Household debts continued to grow relative to income, common stock prices continued to rise rapidly, and the stock of ultimate liquidity grew at a much lower rate than other financial instruments and income. The one really stabilizing change since 1957 has been the decline in the ratio of corporate nonfinancial business liabilities to income.

This paper contains no answer to the questions as to whether or not a financial panic followed by a deep depression can now occur or whether a long-wave contraction can take place in the absence of a financial panic. The barriers to a financial panic erected in the aftermath of the great crash have not been tested; all we can assert is that during the period of slower growth since 1957 the destabilizing financial changes have continued at a slower rate. Neither an unwinding of the financial changes of 1948–57 nor a convergence to a steady, equal rate of growth for the various dimensions of the financial system has taken place.

Name Index